℘ Introduction

Into the Future We Go

Managers are the engines of our organizations, the critical link that connects the strategic intentions of leadership and the daily performance of teams. Being in the middle is not easy, and especially not today. *Change, complexity, global, networks, four generations, hyper-competition, agility*, and *engagement* are all terms that hint at the challenges and opportunities that modern managers face.

When ASTD Press asked me to sign on as editor for this *Management Development Handbook*, I eagerly jumped at the chance and then pondered—with double martini in hand—the approach I could take to make this book insanely helpful to managers and management trainers. There are other fine management compendiums out there, and more will surely be published. "How," I asked myself, "do I want this book to stand out?" The answer lies in the above paragraph and the phrase *modern managers*. The vision for this book has been to bring together dozens of great management thinkers and practitioners—people active in their fields *today* and people who are innovating *today*. I took on the role of curator—one who seeks out and brings together the greatest treasures. Modern managers face unprecedented challenges, and we need to look under many different rocks to find relevant guidance, perspective, and inspiration. This book explores management through the lenses of many different disciplines, mindsets, and opinions.

I have to give the folks at ASTD Press a lot of credit for supporting this vision because it was not the safest route. This book addresses topics you would expect and many that you might not. You will surely recognize several contributing authors but will likely not have heard of most. Their work is emerging in popularity and coming from the fringes of what might be considered managerial sciences. I love this aspect of the handbook!

This book offers many voices and stories, and I have made no attempt to ask contributors to structure their chapters with a consistent structure or treatment. There are longer chapters and several very short pieces. Some of the chapters are written in the first person and told as a story, while others offer an academic review of the latest research. Some of the chapters use graphics and pictures; others do not. Many of the contributors are also bloggers, and their conversational style shines through in their pieces—things like shorter paragraphs and an informal flow. Some of the chapters are excerpts from larger works, and many were written specifically for this book. When contributors asked me for the guidelines for the book, I told them that I wanted their work to be written in their most natural style and voice and that the chapter should express the ideas and recommendations that they felt would be most helpful to today's managers. I have not grouped the chapters by style or in any particular order except within the following four sections:

- Section I: Fundamental Ideas for Managers
- Section II: Managers as Culture Builders
- Section III: The Goal: Team Members Who Do Their Best Work Together
- Section IV: Management Is a Social Act

In Section I, you will learn about several fundamental concepts that will help you do your job. These meta topics and themes include complexity, energy, power, service orientation, irreverence, learning, and the brain physiology/performance connection. The contributors in this section will arm you with important and helpful belief sets and actions that will help you in all aspects of your work.

Section II focuses on the manager's role in creating and transforming organizational culture. Topics in this part of the book will enable you to create better workplaces that catalyze your hopes and intentions. Get ready to learn more about how to create workplace cultures where love, authenticity, openness, quality, community, happiness, and recognition flourish.

The title of Section III, "The Goal: Team Members Who Do Their Best Work Together," is an homage to Eli Goldratt's classic book, *The Goal*. In it, the essential question of "What is the goal?" is asked and answered. For management, the bottom-line goal is to help one or more teams of people do their best work in the service of organizational intentions. Managers, first and foremost, should enable team success. This section will help you achieve this goal by improving partnership, managing performance, building great teams, enhancing accountability, helping team members grow, launching and running effective projects, and engaging your team.

Section IV investigates how managers use conveyance to build performance and success. Here you will learn how to utilize the social context of work to create more inspiring, engaging, and productive workplaces. We will apply this social lens to how you manage information, use technology for learning and collaboration, and tap into your team's diversity and unique talents.

I hope this book invigorates and informs your managerial practice and that you enjoy getting to know more about each topic and our contributing authors. I also hope that you will continue to follow their work and seek out other emerging thinkers and doers. In the reference section at the end of the book, you will find a listing of their blogs, books, videos, and websites so that you can learn more about the topics that most interest you.

I have been a management author, trainer, and consultant for over 25 years. Even so, I would hesitate to call myself an expert (scholar, or learner, is more like it). There is no "been there, done that" when it comes to the new management acumen. We must all learn from and nudge each other to stay relevant, happy, and successful. Management is one of the hardest jobs out there—and it is both a burden and a privilege to be given the responsibility to shepherd talent for a living. I would love to hear your thoughts about this book and your managerial innovations.

Lisa Haneberg
www.lisahaneberg.com
lhaneberg@gmail.com

❧ Section I

Fundamental Ideas
for Managers

"The route to profit was an oblique one."

—John Kay

 **Chapter 1**

Complexity and Perseverance

Margaret Wheatley, EdD

Editor's Note

I asked Meg Wheatley if I could share the following three short pieces with you because I felt they helped kick off this book with a compelling context from which great management arises. Many of you might know of Meg's work from her now classic bestselling book, Leadership and the New Science. *Being a manager is a messy thing because the human condition is complex and unpredictable. And yet, small actions can make a big difference when they come from our intent to serve, and when they are applied again and again.*

It's Your Turn

Throughout human existence, there have always been people willing to step forward to struggle valiantly in the hope that they might reverse the downward course of events. Some succeeded, some did not. As we face our own time, it's good to remember that we're only the most recent humans who have struggled to change things.

Getting engaged in changing things is quite straightforward. If we have an idea, or want to resolve an injustice or stop a tragedy, we step forward to serve. Instead of being overwhelmed and withdrawing, we act.

No grand actions are required; we just need to begin speaking up about what we care about. We don't need to spend a lot of time planning or getting senior leaders involved; we don't have to wait for official support. We just need to get started—for whatever issue or person we care about.

When we fail, which of course we often will, we don't have to feel discouraged. Instead we can look into our mistakes and failures for the valuable learnings they contain. And we can be open to opportunities and help that present themselves, even when they're different from what we thought we needed. We can follow the energy of "Yes!" rather than accepting defeat or getting stuck in a plan.

This is how the world always changes—everyday people not waiting for someone else to fix things or come to their rescue, but simply stepping forward, working together, figuring out how to make things better.

Now it is your turn.

Leadership in the Age of Complexity: From Hero to Host
(With Debbie Frieze)

For too long, too many of us have been entranced by heroes. Perhaps it's our desire to be saved, to not have to do the hard work, to rely on someone else to figure things out. Constantly we are barraged by politicians presenting themselves as heroes, the ones who will fix everything and make our problems go away. It's a seductive image, an enticing promise. And we keep believing it. Somewhere there's someone who will make it all better. Somewhere, there's someone who's visionary, inspiring, brilliant, trustworthy, and we'll all happily follow him or her. Somewhere...

Well, it is time for all the heroes to go home, as the poet William Stafford wrote. It is time for us to give up these hopes and expectations that only breed dependency and passivity, and that do not give us solutions to the challenges we face. It is time to stop waiting for someone to save us. It is time to face the truth of our situation—that we're all in this together, that we all have a voice—and figure out how to mobilize the hearts and minds of everyone in our workplaces and communities.

Why do we continue to hope for heroes? It seems we assume certain things:

- Leaders have the answers. They know what to do.
- People do what they're told. They just have to be given good plans and instructions.

4

■ High risk requires high control. As situations grow more complex and challenging, power needs to shift to the top (with the leaders who know what to do).

These beliefs give rise to the models of command and control revered in organizations and governments worldwide. Those at the bottom of the hierarchy submit to the greater vision and expertise of those above. Leaders promise to get us out of this mess; we willingly surrender individual autonomy in exchange for security.

The only predictable consequence of leaders' attempts to wrest control of a complex, even chaotic situation, is that they create more chaos. They go into isolation with just a few key advisors, and attempt to find a simple solution (quickly) to a complex problem. And people pressure them to do just that. Everyone wants the problem to disappear; cries of "Fix it!" arise from the public. Leaders scramble to look like they've taken charge and have everything in hand.

But the causes of today's problems are complex and interconnected. There are no simple answers, and no one individual can possibly know what to do. We seem unable to acknowledge these complex realities. Instead, when the leader fails to resolve the crisis, we fire him or her, and immediately begin searching for the next (more perfect) one. We don't question our expectations of leaders; we don't question our desire for heroes.

The Illusion of Control

Heroic leadership rests on the illusion that someone can be in control. Yet we live in a world of complex systems whose very existence means they are inherently uncontrollable. No one is in charge of our food systems. No one is in charge of our schools. No one is in charge of the environment. No one is in charge of national security. No one is in charge! These systems are emergent phenomena—the result of thousands of small, local actions that converged to create powerful systems with properties that may bear little or no resemblance to the smaller actions that gave rise to them. These are the systems that now dominate our lives; they cannot be changed by working backwards, focusing on only a few simple causes. And certainly they cannot be changed by the boldest visions of our most heroic leaders.

If we want to be able to get these complex systems to work better, we need to abandon our reliance on the leader-as-hero and invite in the leader-as-host. We need to support those leaders who know that problems are complex, who know that in order to understand the full complexity of any issue, all parts of the system need to be invited in to participate and contribute. We, as followers, need to give our leaders time, patience, and forgiveness; and we need to be willing to step up and contribute.

These leaders-as-hosts are candid enough to admit when they don't know what to do; they realize that it's sheer foolishness to rely only on them for answers. But they also know they can trust in other people's creativity and commitment to get the work done. They know that other people, no matter where they are in the organizational hierarchy, can be as motivated, diligent, and creative as the leader, given the right invitation.

The Journey From Hero to Host

Leaders who journey from hero to host have seen past the negative dynamics of politics and opposition that hierarchy breeds, they've ignored the organizational charts and role descriptions that confine people's potential. Instead, they've become curious. Who is in this organization or community? What skills and capacities might they offer if they were invited into the work as full contributors? What do they know, and what insights do they have that might lead to a solution to this problem?

Leaders-as-hosts know that people willingly support those things they've played a part in creating—that you can't expect people to buy in to plans and projects developed elsewhere. Leaders-as-hosts invest in meaningful conversations among people from many parts of the system, and see that as the most productive way to engender new insights and possibilities for action. They trust that people are willing to contribute, and that most people yearn to find meaning and possibility in their lives and work. And these leaders know that hosting others is the only way to get complex, intractable problems solved.

Leaders-as-hosts don't just benevolently let go and trust that people will do good work on their own. Leaders have a great many things to attend to, but these are quite different from the work of heroes. Hosting leaders must:

- provide conditions and good group processes for people to work together
- provide resources of time, the scarcest commodity of all
- insist that people and the system learn from experience, frequently
- offer unequivocal support—people know the leader is there for them
- keep the bureaucracy at bay, creating oases (or bunkers) where people are less encumbered by senseless demands for reports and administrivia
- play defense with other leaders who want to take back control, who are critical that people have been given too much freedom
- reflect back to people on a regular basis how they're doing, what they're accomplishing, how far they've journeyed
- work with people to develop relevant measures of progress to make their achievements visible

■ value conviviality and esprit de corps—not false "rah-rah" activities, but the spirit that arises in any group that accomplishes difficult work together.

Challenges From Superiors

It's important to note how leaders journeying from hero to host use their positional power. They have to work all levels of the hierarchy; most often, it's easier to gain support and respect from the people they lead than it is to gain it from their superiors. Most senior leaders of large hierarchies believe in their inherent superiority, as proven by the position they've attained. They don't believe that everyday people are as creative or self-motivated as are they. When participation is suggested as the means to gather insights and ideas from staff on a complex problem, senior leaders often will block such activities. They justify their opposition by stating that people would use this opportunity to take advantage of the organization; or that they would suggest ideas that have no bearing to the organization's mission; or that people would feel overly confident and overstep their roles. In truth, many senior leaders view engaging the whole system as a threat to their own power and control. They consistently choose for control, and the resultant chaos, rather than invite people in to solve difficult and complex problems.

Leaders who do know the value of full engagement, who do trust those they lead, have to constantly defend their staff from senior leaders who insist on more controls and more bureaucracy to curtail their activities, even when those very activities are producing excellent results. Strange to say, but too many senior leaders choose control over effectiveness; they're willing to risk creating more chaos by continuing their take-charge, command-and-control leadership.

Re-engaging People

Those who've been held back in confining roles, who've been buried in the hierarchy, will eventually blossom and develop in the company of a hosting leader. Yet, it takes time for employees to believe that this boss is different, that this leader actually wants them to contribute. It can take 12 to 18 months for people's perceptions to change, when they come from systems where people have been silenced into submission by autocratic leadership. These days, most people take a wait-and-see attitude, no longer interested in participating because past invitations weren't sincere, or didn't engage them in meaningful work. The leader needs to prove him- or herself by continually insisting that work cannot be accomplished, nor problems solved, without the participation of everyone. If the message is sincere and consistent, people gradually return to life; even people who have given up on the job, who are just waiting until retirement, can come alive in the presence of a leader who encourages them and creates opportunities for them to contribute.

Leaders-as-hosts need to be skilled conveners. They realize that their organization or community is rich in resources, and that the easiest way to discover these is to bring diverse people together in conversations that matter. People who didn't like each other, people who discounted and ignored each other, people who felt invisible, neglected, left out—these are the people who can emerge from their boxes and labels to become interesting, engaged colleagues and citizens.

Hosting meaningful conversations isn't about getting people to like each other or feel good. It's about creating the means for problems to get solved, for teams to function well, for people to become energetic activists. Hosting leaders create substantive change by relying on everyone's creativity, commitment, and generosity. They learn from firsthand experience that these qualities are present in just about everyone and in every organization. They extend sincere invitations, ask good questions, and have the courage to support risk-taking and experimentation.

Are You a Hero?

Many of us can get caught up acting like heroes, not from power drives, but from our good intentions and desires to help. Are you acting as a hero? Here's how to know. You're acting as a hero when you believe that if you just work harder, you'll fix things; that if you just get smarter or learn a new technique, you'll be able to solve problems for others. You're acting as a hero if you take on more and more projects and causes and have less time for relationships. You're playing the hero if you believe that you can save the situation, the person, and the world.

Our heroic impulses most often are born from the best of intentions. We want to help, we want to solve, we want to fix. Yet this is the illusion of specialness, that we're the only ones who can offer help, service, or skills. If we don't do it, nobody will. This hero's path has only one guaranteed destination—we end up feeling lonely, exhausted, and unappreciated.

It is time for all us heroes to go home because, if we do, we'll notice that we're not alone. We're surrounded by people just like us. They too want to contribute, they too have ideas, they want to be useful to others and solve their own problems.

Truth be told, they never wanted heroes to rescue them anyway.

Edge Walking

People who persevere walk the undulating edge between hope and fear, success and failure, praise and blame, love and anger.

This difficult path often feels razor sharp and dangerous, and it is. Scientists call it the edge of chaos. It's the border created by the meeting of two opposite states. Neither state is desirable. In fact each must be avoided, no matter how enticing or familiar it appears. Possibility only lives on the edge.

Security is not what creates life safety, safe havens, guarantees of security—none of these give life its capacities. Newness, creativity, imagination—these live on the edge. So does presence.

Presence is the only way to walk the edge of chaos. We have to be as nimble and awake as a high-wire artist, sensitive to the slightest shift of wind, circumstances, emotions. We may find this high-wire exhausting at first, but there comes a time when we rejoice in our skillfulness. We learn to know this edge, to keep our balance, and even dance a bit at incalculable heights.

Walking on the edge never stops being dangerous. At any moment, when we're tired, overwhelmed, fed-up, sick, we can forget where we are and get ourselves in trouble. We can lapse into despair or anger. Or we can get so caught up in our own enthusiasm and passion that we lose any sense of perspective or timing, alienate friends, and crash in an exhausted mess.

The edge is where life happens. But let's notice where we are and not lose our balance.

About the Author

Margaret Wheatley, EdD, has been a bestselling author, consultant, and speaker since 1973. She taught graduate students at Cambridge College and Brigham Young University and is co-founder and President emerita of The Berkana Institute. Her website is www.margaretwheatley.com. See the recommended resources section for a partial list of her books.

"It's Your Turn" and "Edge Walking" are excerpted from *Perseverance*, by Margaret Wheatley, Berrett-Koehler, 2010. "Leadership in the Age of Complexity: From Hero to Host" by Margaret Wheatley with Debbie Frieze was originally published in *Resurgence Magazine*, Winter 2011. Parts of this article are excerpts from *Walk Out Walk On: A Learning Journey into Communities Daring to Live the Future Now* (Berrett-Koehler). Reprinted with permission.

Chapter 2

The Way We're Working Isn't Working: More and More, Less and Less

Tony Schwartz

Editor's Note

I was thrilled when Tony agreed to share this piece for this book because I think that energy management is critical to today's managers. I hear smart, hardworking professionals tell me how wrung out they feel. Tony's work is important, inspiring, and helpful. I hope it allows you to do your best by helping you understand how to produce and use energy, and live more balanced lives that can fuel your success. As you read this chapter, think about how you could help your team members engage in work and live more fully.

The way we're working isn't working. The defining ethic in the modern workplace is more, bigger, faster. More information than ever is available to us, and the speed of every transaction has increased exponentially, prompting a sense of permanent urgency and endless distraction. We have more customers and clients to please, more emails to answer, more phone calls to return, more tasks to juggle, more meetings to attend, more places to go, and more hours we feel we must work to avoid falling further behind.

The technologies that make instant communication possible anywhere and at any time speed up decision making, create efficiencies, and fuel a truly global marketplace. But too much of a good thing eventually becomes a bad thing. Left unmanaged and unregulated, these same technologies have the potential to overwhelm us. The relentless urgency that characterizes most corporate cultures undermines creativity, quality, engagement, thoughtful deliberation, and, ultimately, performance.

No matter how much value we produce today—whether it's measured in dollars or sales or goods or widgets—it's never enough. We run faster, stretch out our arms further, and stay at work longer and later. We're so busy trying to keep up that we stop noticing we're in a Sisyphean race we can never win.

All of this furious activity exacts a series of silent costs: less capacity for focused attention, less time for any given task, and less opportunity to think reflectively and long term. When we finally do get home at night, we have less energy for our families, less time to wind down and relax, and fewer hours to sleep. We return to work each morning feeling less rested, less than fully engaged, and less able to focus. It's a vicious cycle that feeds on itself. Even for those who still manage to perform at high levels, there is a cost in overall satisfaction and fulfillment. The ethic of "more, bigger, faster" generates value that is narrow, shallow, and short term. More and more, paradoxically, leads to less and less.

The consulting firm Towers Perrin's most recent global workforce study bears this out. Conducted in 2007–2008, before the worldwide recession, it looked at some 90,000 employees in 18 countries. Only 20 percent of them felt fully engaged, meaning that they go above and beyond what's required of them because they have a sense of purpose and passion about what they're doing. Forty percent were "enrolled," meaning capable but not fully committed, and 38 percent were disenchanted or disengaged.

All of that translated directly to the bottom line. The companies with the most engaged employees reported a 19 percent increase in operating income and a 28 percent growth in earnings per share. Those with the lowest levels of engagement had a 32 percent decline in operating income, and their earnings dropped more than 11 percent. In the companies with the most engaged employees, 90 percent of the employees had no plans to leave. In those with the least engaged, 50 percent were considering leaving. More than 100 studies have demonstrated some correlation between employee engagement and business performance.

Think for a moment about your own experience at work. How truly engaged are you? What's the cost to you of the way you're working? What's the impact on those you supervise and those you love? What will the accumulated toll be in 10 years if you're still making the same choices?

The way we're working isn't working in our own lives, for the people we lead and manage, and for the organizations in which we work. We're guided by a fatal assumption that the best way to get more done is to work longer and more continuously. But the more hours we work and the longer we go without real renewal, the more we begin to default, reflexively, into behaviors that reduce our own effectiveness—impatience, frustration, distraction, and disengagement—and take a pernicious toll on others.

The real issue is not the number of hours we sit behind a desk but the energy we bring to the work we do and the value we generate as a result. A growing body of research suggests that we're most productive when we move between periods of high focus and intermittent rest. Instead, we live in a gray zone, constantly juggling activities but rarely fully engaging in any of them—or fully disengaging from any of them. The consequence is that we settle for a pale version of the possible.

How can such a counterproductive way of working persist? The answer is grounded in a simple assumption, deeply embedded in organizational life and in our own belief systems. It's that human beings operate most productively in the same one-dimensional way computers do: continuously, at high speeds, for long periods of time, running multiple programs at the same time. Far too many of us have unwittingly bought into this myth, a kind of Stockholm syndrome, dutifully trying to mimic the machines we're meant to run, so they end up running us.

The limitation of even the highest-end computer is that it inexorably depreciates in value over time. Unlike computers, human beings have the potential to grow and develop, to increase our depth, complexity, and capacity over time. To make that possible, we must manage ourselves far more skillfully than we do now.

Our most basic survival need is to spend and renew our energy. We're hardwired to make waves—to be alert during the day and to sleep at night, and to work at high intensity for limited periods of time—but we lead increasingly linear lives. By putting in long, continuous hours, we expend too much mental and emotional energy without sufficient intermittent renewal. It's not just rejuvenation we sacrifice along the way, but also the unique benefits we can accrue during periods of rest and renewal, including creative breakthroughs, a broader perspective, the opportunity to think more reflectively and long term, and sufficient time to metabolize experiences. Conversely, by living mostly desk-bound sedentary lives, we expend too little physical energy and grow progressively weaker. Inactivity takes a toll not just on our bodies, but also on how we feel and how we think.

The Performance Pulse

In 1993, Anders Ericsson, who had long been a leading researcher in expert performance and a professor at Florida State University, conducted an extraordinary study designed to explore the power of deliberate practice among violinists. Over the years, numerous writers, including Malcolm Gladwell in his bestselling *Outliers,* have cited Ericsson's study for its evidence that intrinsic talent may be overvalued. As Gladwell puts it, "People at the very top don't just work harder, or even much harder than everyone else. They work much, much harder."

But that conclusion doesn't begin to capture the complexity of what Ericsson discovered. Along with two colleagues, he divided 30 young violinists at the Music Academy of Berlin into three separate groups, based on ratings from their professors. The "best" group consisted of those destined to eventually become professional soloists. The "good" violinists were those expected to have careers playing as part of orchestras. The third group, recruited from the music education division of the academy, was headed for careers as music teachers. All of them had begun playing violin around the age of eight.

Vast amounts of data were collected on each of the subjects, most notably by having them keep a diary of all their activities, hour by hour, over the course of an entire week. They were also asked to rate each activity on three measures, using a scale of 1 to 10. The first one was how important the activity was to improving their performance on the violin. The second was how difficult they found it to do. The third was how intrinsically enjoyable they found the activity.

The top two groups, both destined for professional careers, turned out to practice an average of 24 hours a week. The future music teachers, by contrast, put in just over nine hours, or about a third the amount of time as the top two groups. This difference was undeniably dramatic and does suggest how much practice matters. But equally fascinating was the relationship Ericsson found between intense practice and intermittent rest.

All of the 30 violinists agreed that "practice alone" had the biggest impact on improving their performance. Nearly all of them also agreed that practice was the most difficult activity in their lives and the least enjoyable. The top two groups, who practiced an average of 3.5 hours a day, typically did so in three separate sessions of no more than 90 minutes each, mostly in the mornings, when they were presumably most rested and least distracted. They took renewal breaks between each session. The lowest-rated group practiced an average of just 1.4 hours a day, with no fixed schedule, but often in the afternoons, suggesting that they were often procrastinating.

All three groups rated sleep as the second most important activity when it came to improving as violinists. On average, those in the top two groups slept 8.6 hours a day—nearly an hour longer than those in the music teacher group, who slept an average of 7.8 hours. By contrast, the average American gets just 6.5 hours of sleep a night. The top two groups also took considerably more daytime naps than did the lower-rated group—a total of nearly three hours a week compared to less than one hour a week for the music teachers.

Great performers, Ericsson's study suggests, work more intensely than most of us do but also recover more deeply. Solo practice undertaken with high concentration is especially exhausting. The best violinists figured out, intuitively, that they generated the highest value by working intensely, without interruption, for no more than 90 minutes at a time and no more than four hours a day. They also recognized that it was essential to take time, intermittently, to rest and refuel. In fields ranging from sports to chess, researchers have found that four hours a day is the maximum that the best performers practice. Ericsson himself concluded that this number might represent "a more general limit on the maximal amount of deliberate practice that can be sustained over extended time without exhaustion."

Because the number of hours we work is easy to measure, organizations often default to evaluating employees by the hours they put in at their desks, rather than by the focus they bring to their work or the value they produce. Many of us complain about long hours, but the reality is that it's less demanding to work at moderate intensity for extended periods of time than it is to work at the highest level of intensity for even shorter periods. If more of us were able to focus in the intense but time-limited ways that the best violinists do, the evidence suggests that great performance would be much more common than it is.

It's also true that if you're not actively working to get better at what you do, there's a good chance you're getting worse, no matter what the quality of your initial training may have been. As Geoffrey Colvin points out in his provocative book *Talent Is Overrated,* simply doing an activity for a long time is no guarantee that you'll do it well, much less get better at it. "In field after field," Colvin writes, "when it came to centrally important skills—stockbrokers recommending stocks, parole officers predicting recidivism, college admissions officials judging applicants—people with lots of experience were no better at their jobs than those with very little experience."

In a significant number of cases, people actually get worse at their jobs over time. "More experienced doctors," Colvin reports, "reliably score lower on tests of medical knowledge than do less experienced doctors; general physicians also become less skilled over time at diagnosing heart sounds and X-rays. Auditors become less skilled at certain types of evaluations." In some cases, diminished performance is simply the result of a failure to keep up with advances in a given field. But it's also because most of us tend to become fixed in our habits and practices, even when they're suboptimal.

Our Four Primary Needs

If sustainable great performance requires a rhythmic movement between activity and rest, it also depends on tapping multiple sources of energy. Plug a computer into a wall socket, and it's good to go. Human beings, on the other hand, meet four energy needs to operate at their best: physical, emotional, mental, and spiritual.

By moving rhythmically between activity and renewal in each of these four dimensions, we fulfill our corresponding needs: sustainability, security, self-expression, and significance. In the process, we build our capacity to generate more and more value over time.

The problem is that few of us intentionally address each of our key needs on a regular basis and organizations often ignore them altogether. When we fuel ourselves on a diet that lacks essential nutrients, it shouldn't be a surprise that we end up undernourished and unable to operate consistently at our best. "Value" is a word that carries multiple levels of meaning. The ultimate measure of our effectiveness is the value we create. The ultimate measure of our satisfaction is the value we feel. The ultimate measure of our character is the values we embody.

The primary value exchange between most employers and employees today is time for money. It's a thin, one-dimensional transaction. Each side tries to get as much of the other's resources as possible, but neither gets what it really wants. No amount of money employers pay for our time will ever be sufficient to meet all of our multidimensional needs. It's only when employers encourage and support us in meeting these needs that we can cultivate the energy, engagement, focus, creativity, and passion that fuel great performance.

For better and for worse, we've co-created the world in which we work. Our complicity begins, ironically, with how we treat ourselves. We tolerate extraordinary disconnects in our own lives, even in areas we plainly have the power to influence. We take too little responsibility for addressing our core needs, and we dissipate too much energy in blame, complaint, and finger pointing. We fail to take care of ourselves even though the consequence is that we end up undermining our health, happiness, and productivity.

We don't spend enough time—truly engaged time—with those we say we love most and who love us most, even though we feel guilty when we don't and we return to work more energized when we do.

We find ourselves getting frustrated, irritable, and anxious as the pressures rise, even though we instinctively recognize that negative emotions interfere with clear thinking and good decision making, and demoralize those we lead and manage.

We allow ourselves to be distracted by email and trivial tasks rather than focusing single-mindedly on our most high-leverage priorities and devoting sacrosanct time to thinking creatively, strategically, and long term.

We are so busy getting things done that we don't stop very often to consider what it is we really want or where we should invest our time and energy to achieve those goals.

Of course, we can't meet our needs and build our capacity in a vacuum. Most organizations enable our dysfunctional behaviors and even encourage them through policies, practices, reward systems, and cultural messages that serve to drain our energy and run down our value over time.

When the primary value exchange is time for money, people are replaceable. An increasing number of organizations pay lip service to the notion that "people are our greatest asset." Call up the phrase on Google, and you'll find more than a million listings. But even among companies that make the claim, the vast majority offload the care and feeding of employees to divisions known as "human resources," which are rarely accorded an equal place at the executive table. As a consequence, the needs of employees are marginalized and treated as perquisites provided through programs that focus on topics such as "leadership development," "work-life balance," "wellness," "flexibility," and "engagement."

In reality, these are largely code words for nonessential functions. They're funded when times are flush, but they're the first programs that are slashed when cost cutting begins. The vast majority of organizations fail to make the connection between the degree to which they meet their employees' needs and how effectively those employees perform.

The principles at the heart of this approach grow out of a rich body of research across disciplines ranging from nutrition to cognition; strength training to training strengths; emotional self-regulation to the role of the right hemisphere of the brain; extrinsic to intrinsic motivation.

These findings, generated by subject matter experts, remain mostly isolated from one another. Our mission has been to bring the evidence together underneath one umbrella to better understand how our varied choices influence one another.

Figure 2-1. The Renewal Quadrants

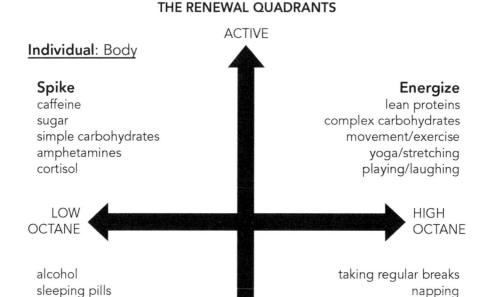

THE RENEWAL QUADRANTS

Individual: Body

ACTIVE

Spike
caffeine
sugar
simple carbohydrates
amphetamines
cortisol

Energize
lean proteins
complex carbohydrates
movement/exercise
yoga/stretching
playing/laughing

LOW OCTANE

HIGH OCTANE

alcohol
sleeping pills
overeating
television
painkillers
Numb

taking regular breaks
napping
meditating
sleeping
vacation
Chill

PASSIVE

We've also learned a great deal by studying great performers in various professions. In the corporate world, we've worked with senior executives at companies including Sony, Toyota, Novartis, Google, Ford, Ernst & Young, Grey Advertising, and Royal Dutch Shell. We've also worked with cardiovascular surgeons and ICU nurses at the Cleveland Clinic, police officers at the Los Angeles Police Department, and high school students in the Bronx. When we published an article about our work in *Harvard Business Review* in the fall of 2007, we received inquiries from companies and individuals in more than two dozen countries around the world including Singapore, Colombia, Russia, China, Korea, Germany, Austria, Italy, Thailand, Denmark, India, and Australia. Across disparate cultures and at all levels, people share both a visceral sense that the way they're working isn't working, and an intense desire for more satisfying, productive, and sustainable ways to work and live.

Beyond survival, our needs begin at the physical level with *sustainability*. Four factors are key: nutrition, fitness, sleep, and rest. They're all forms of renewal, either active or passive. Our physical capacity is foundational, because every other source of energy depends on it.

At the individual level, our key challenge is to create a healthy rhythmic movement between activity and rest. The left-hand quadrants in Figure 2-1 represent dysfunctional ways of generating and renewing energy. The optimal movement is between the upper-right and lower-right quadrants. Even then, too much of one at the expense of the other is suboptimal. Physically, most of us tend to fall on the side of not moving enough (lower left). By contrast, exercise (upper right) raises our heart rate and in so doing builds our physical capacity. It also provides a form of mental and emotional renewal, quieting the mind and calming the emotions. That's why exercise in the middle of a workday—especially after an intense period of work—can be such a powerful form of rejuvenation. On the other hand, too much exercise, too continuously, is called "overtraining" and can lead to breakdown and burnout.

The best violinists in the Ericsson study renewed themselves physically not just by sleeping more hours than their less accomplished fellow students, but also by taking more afternoon naps. Eating more energy-rich foods, more frequently—at least every three hours—is a means of stabilizing blood sugar. Many of us attempt to run on too little food for too long and then overeat to compensate. Eating too little deprives us of a critical source of energy we need to operate at our best, and eating too much pushes us into a state of lethargy.

At the organizational level, we work with leaders to build policies, practices, and cultural expectations that support employees in a more rhythmic way of working. When we introduced our work to the top officers at the Los Angeles Police Department, it rapidly became clear that sleep deprivation and exhaustion were defining issues for many members of Chief William Bratton's leadership team. Until we addressed this basic problem, nothing else we suggested was getting much traction.

At the conclusion of our work, Bratton and his team agreed on a series of nine policy changes that included limiting off-hours nighttime calls to commanding officers, in order to increase the quality and quantity of their sleep; changing the schedules for key meetings to ensure that they were held at times when the energy levels of participants were likely to be highest; and creating a series of new policies aimed at giving the commanding officers more opportunities to renew themselves during the workday. "What's happened is that our people come to work feeling more rested," Bratton told us a year after our intervention. "They were more able to focus, think clearly, and remain calm in the face of the crises that are part of our everyday work."

Figure 2-2. The Emotional Quadrants

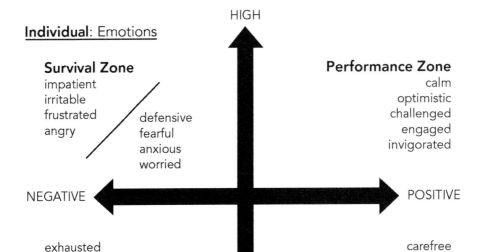

THE EMOTIONAL QUADRANTS

Our core need at the emotional level is for *security*, the sense of well-being that depends, in significant part, on the experience of being accepted and valued. How we feel profoundly influences how we perform. Feeling devalued pushes us into the Survival Zone—the upper-left quadrant shown in Figure 2-2—which increases our fear, distracts our attention, drains our energy, and diminishes the value we're capable of creating. The optimal rhythmic movement in this dimension is between the positive energy we feel when we're operating at our best—the Performance Zone—and the Renewal Zone, where emotional recovery occurs. The more we renew ourselves emotionally, the better we feel about ourselves and the more resilient we are in the face of life's challenges and stresses.

Before we began working with heart surgeons and ICU nurses at the Cleveland Clinic, several of our Energy Project team members spent 24 hours shadowing three shifts of nurses on a cardiac intensive care unit. During that time, we asked each of the nurses we encountered to describe their primary dissatisfaction with their jobs. They were unanimous in their response: lack of appreciation from the surgeons.

"We're the ones who keep their patients alive day in and day out, but the docs don't talk to us or seek out our opinion," one nurse told us, echoing many others. "They treat us like handmaidens. It's demeaning and frustrating." Later, we had the opportunity to ask the same question to more than a half-dozen surgeons on the same unit. They, too, were nearly unanimous in their response: lack of appreciation from hospital administrators.

Perhaps no human need is more neglected in the workplace than to feel valued. Noticing what's wrong and what's not working in our lives is a hardwired survival instinct. Expressing appreciation requires more conscious intention, but feeling appreciated is as important to us as food. The need to be valued begins at birth and never goes away. Failure to thrive is a syndrome in which newborns don't gain sufficient weight to develop normally. One key cause, research suggests, is the absence of touch, stimulation, and care from the primary caregiver. Without love and attention, babies become depressed and withdrawn. Very quickly, they lose the motivation to eat and to interact with others. They also begin to develop cognitive deficits, become more prone to infections, and, in extreme cases, even die. They literally become flatliners.

Most of us obviously have better coping mechanisms, but the deep need for connection and warm regard persists through our lives and influences our performance to a remarkable degree. The single most important factor in whether or not employees choose to stay in a job, Gallup has found, is the quality of their relationship with their direct superiors. Gallup has uncovered 12 key factors that produce high engagement, productivity, and retention among employees. Fully half of them are connected to the issue of feeling valued—including receiving regular recognition or praise for doing good work, having a supervisor or someone at work who "cares about me as a person," "having a best friend at work," and having someone "who encourages my development."

Happily, it turns out that we have far more influence over how we feel, regardless of what is going on around us, than we ordinarily exercise. Our first challenge is to become more aware of how we're feeling at any given moment. The more we can observe our feelings, the more we can choose how to respond to them. The second challenge is learning to intentionally and regularly renew the positive emotions that best serve high performance.

Our hardwired response to perceived threat drains us of positive energy. The bigger our reservoir of value and well-being, the less emotionally vulnerable we are to the challenges

Figure 2-3. The Focus Quadrants

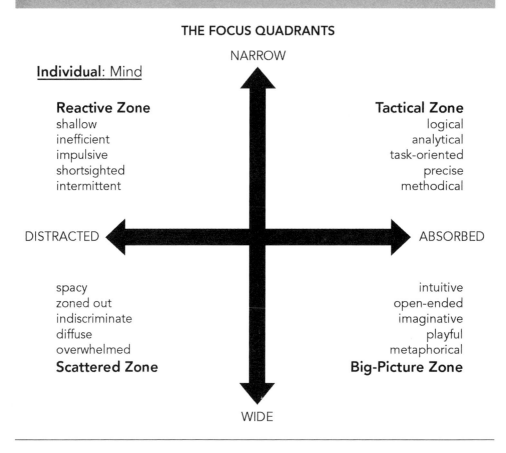

THE FOCUS QUADRANTS

we encounter every day. Resilience, the ability to recover quickly from an emotional setback, depends less on what occurs in any given circumstance than on the story we tell ourselves about what's happened to us. Although we're hardwired to be alert to danger and threat, we can also systematically train ourselves to be more aware of what's worth appreciating in our lives and to actively seek out people and activities that make us feel better about ourselves. Consciously cultivating a more realistically optimistic perspective refuels our emotional reservoir.

Our core need at the mental level is *self-expression,* the freedom to put our unique skills and talents to effective use in the world. Self-expression is fueled by our capacity to control the placement of our attention and to focus on one thing at a time. The optimal movement in this dimension is between deductive, analytic thinking, aimed at accomplishing a specific task—the Tactical Zone—and wider, more open focus which prompts creative and strategic thinking—the Big-Picture Zone (see Figure 2-3).

We live in a world of infinite distractions and endless demands. Many of us juggle several tasks at a time and struggle to focus on any one of them for very long. Lack of absorbed focus takes a toll on the depth and quality of whatever we do, and it's also an inefficient way to work, extending the time it takes to finish any given task.

At the individual level, the work of self-expression begins with recognizing that our minds have minds of their own. To tame them, we must systematically build our capacity for focus. The more control we have of our attention, the freer we are to make purposeful choices about where to put it and for how long. That's what the best violinists in Ericsson's study accomplished by setting aside uninterrupted periods of time in which to do their most challenging work. In the process, they not only developed their musical skills but also their capacity for absorbed focus. Eventually, they discovered that 90 minutes was the longest period of time for which they could sustain the highest level of attention.

From an early age, we're taught a form of tactical attention that we use to solve problems logically and deductively and to work step-by-step toward a desired outcome. To do so, we depend largely on the left hemisphere of our brain, where language resides. In order to think more creatively, imaginatively, and strategically, we need to cultivate a more intuitive, metaphorical attention that calls preeminently on the right hemisphere of the brain. It's only by learning to move freely and flexibly between right and left hemisphere mode—the upper-right and lower-right quadrants—that we can access the whole brain and achieve the highest and richest level of thinking.

The parallel challenge for leaders and organizations is to create work environments that free and encourage people to focus in absorbed ways without constant interruptions. One obvious way is to encourage more frequent renewal. At Ernst & Young, we conducted two pilot programs in which groups of employees were given the opportunity to regularly renew themselves in the middle of their busiest tax season. In large firms like E&Y, young accountants are typically expected to work 12- to 14-hour days in the highest-demand months between January and April, six and seven days a week. It's often debilitating and demoralizing.

We taught teams of E&Y accountants to work instead in more focused, efficient ways for 90 minutes at a time and then take breaks. We also encouraged them to renew intermittently throughout the day. Many of them began taking off an hour in the afternoons to work out at a nearby gym, an unthinkable option before we launched the pilot. When they returned

Figure 2-4. The Spiritual Quadrants

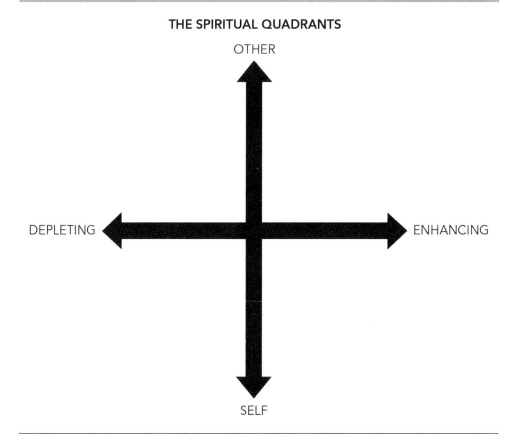

THE SPIRITUAL QUADRANTS

to work at 4 or 5 p.m.—a time at which their productivity typically began to diminish dramatically—they consistently reported feeling reenergized and better able to focus. Because they were able to get more work accomplished in the later afternoon, they were often able to leave work earlier in the evening. The result was more time to relax at home and more time to sleep, which allowed them to return to work the next day more energized and better able to fully engage.

Encouraging employees to set aside sacrosanct time to think creatively, strategically, and long term is even more countercultural in most organizations, which are characteristically focused on immediate results and urgent deadlines. Google is a company that specifically encourages more creative thinking. Its engineers have long been permitted to invest up to 20 percent of their time in projects of their own choosing, based on whatever interests them. Even so, many feel such urgent pressure from their everyday responsibilities that they struggle to get around to their own projects.

The need for *significance* at work is a manifestation of our inborn hunger for meaning in our lives. We call this spiritual energy, and it is fueled by deeply held values and a clear sense of purpose that transcend our self-interest and which we embody in our everyday behaviors. The optimal movement in this dimension is between nurturing our awareness of what we stand for, in the lower-right quadrant of Figure 2-4, and expressing those values through our actions, in the upper-right quadrant. Values are aspirations, and they come to life only through our behaviors.

Meaning and significance may seem like luxuries, but they're a unique source of energy that ignites passion, focus, and perseverance. Tapping spiritual energy begins with defining what we stand for amid all the forces that press on us. At his sentencing for the crimes he committed, the Watergate co-conspirator Jeb Stuart Magruder told the judge, "Somewhere between my ambition and my ideals, I lost my moral compass."

Deeply held values help us to avoid being whipsawed by whatever winds happen to be blowing around us. Values provide an internal source of direction for our behaviors. Unlike Magruder, most of us don't cross the line into breaking the law, but we're all confronted with opportunities to make expedient choices and to rationalize them after the fact. The antidote is taking the time to reflect not so much on what we want right now but what will make us feel best about ourselves over time—not just on our self-interest but also on how to add value to the greater good.

Unlike the other three quadrants, the spiritual quadrants contain no descriptive adjectives. That's because the qualities that fuel spiritual energy are more subjective than those in the other three quadrants.

Purpose is the external expression of what we stand for. The majority of people we meet lack a strong sense of purpose in their jobs, beyond taking home a paycheck and building their careers. Many of us are so busy trying to serve clients and customers—to simply do our jobs—that we don't spend much time or energy thinking about what we really want or how our choices affect others.

While selfishness makes us smaller and takes a toll on others, the costs of selflessness can be equally depleting. That's especially true for nurses, teachers, social workers, and others who work in the helping professions. Serving others can become so preoccupying that it occurs at expense to our own well-being and eventually to those we're committed to serving. "Compassion fatigue" is characterized by symptoms such as depression, inability to focus, decreased effectiveness, burnout, and breakdown. For people who spend their lives giving to others, the challenge is to equally value their own needs—to renew themselves both for their own sake and so they can serve others more effectively.

The intrinsic mission of service organizations such as hospitals, nonprofits, and schools can powerfully fuel people's need for meaning and purpose. But what about the vast majority of companies that don't so obviously manufacture products or offer services that clearly contribute to the greater good? Leaders of such companies can still build cultures that give people the opportunity to live their values and to feel purposeful at work.

Take Zappos.com, which sells shoes and other clothing. Not long ago, I spent a day visiting the Zappos headquarters, which are located in a bland industrial park in a suburb of Las Vegas. The vast majority of its employees are customer service representatives paid between $12 and $18 an hour, but many find their jobs very satisfying. Zappos inspires employees not only by treating them exceptionally well and by giving them an opportunity to express themselves as individuals, but also by generating a shared mission around providing an extraordinary level of service to customers.

In most call centers, employees are evaluated partly by how quickly they can get onto and off of calls with customers. These employees typically work from a tight script. At Zappos, agents are encouraged to stay on the phone in order to genuinely connect with customers and to build a relationship that is more likely to endure. This approach not only serves customers well but also makes employees proud to work at Zappos. Employees find significance less from the products they sell than from the relationships they nurture.

Meeting People's Core Needs

"How can we get more out of our people?" leaders regularly ask us. We suggest they pose a different question: "How can I more intentionally invest in meeting the multidimensional needs of my employees so they're freed, fueled, and inspired to bring the best of themselves to work every day?" As this book gets published, the perilous state of the economy has exacerbated people's fears everywhere. We live in a vastly more complex world that is changing at warp speed. The systems that worked in the past won't in the future.

To build competitive advantage, organizations must help employees to cultivate qualities that have never before been critical—among them authenticity, empathy, self-awareness, constant creativity, an internal sense of purpose, and, perhaps above all, resilience in the face of relentless change. And whatever our employers do, we serve ourselves well to cultivate these same qualities in order to be more effective and more satisfied, both on the job and off.

For Further Reading

Colvin, Geoffrey. (2008). *Talent Is Overrated.* New York: Penguin Books.
Gladwell, Malcolm. (2008). *Outliers.* New York: Little, Brown and Company.

About the Author

Tony Schwartz is the president and CEO of The Energy Project, a company that helps individuals and organizations perform better and more sustainably. Tony spent the first part of his career working as a journalist and then authored several bestselling books including, *Trump: The Art of the Deal, The Power of Full Engagement,* and *The Way We're Working Isn't Working.* His latest book is called *Be Excellent at Anything: The Four Keys to Transforming the Way We Work and Live.* Check out Tony's website and blog at www. tonyschwartz.com.

"The Way We're Working Isn't Working" is excerpted from the book of the same title (Free Press, 2010). You can take the Tony's Energy Audit by logging on to www.theenergyproject .com/resources. Reprinted with permission.

Irreverence as a Managerial Tool: What Managers Can Learn From Tina Fey, Martin Luther, and Bob Dylan

Michael Kroth, PhD

··· **Editor's Note** ···

In this original chapter, Michael Kroth invites us to peek into his work and explore the use of irreverence as a managerial tool. Many years ago I heard management guru Tom Peters say that if we did not do something that could potentially get us fired at least once per week, we were not doing our jobs. Irreverence is the mojo fuel all managers need to make a difference. I love the suggestions that Michael shares here and admire the honest and informal approach he has taken to describe his model. It is an important work in progress. In other words, you read it here first!

> *"Irreverence is the champion of liberty and its only sure defense."*
> —Mark Twain, author and humorist
>
> *"I hope it will not be irreverent in me to say, that if it be probable that God would reveal his will to others, on a point so connected with my duty, it might be supposed he would reveal it directly to me."*
> —Abraham Lincoln, 16th president of the United States

> *"Religion. It's given people hope in a world torn apart by religion."*
>
> —Jon Stewart, host of *The Daily Show*

I rreverence has gotten a bad rap.

Put yourself in Bob Dylan's shoes on July 25, 1965. He was about to "abandon" his folk roots and head toward rock. Was he thinking, "Will I step on the stage and then step off into oblivion?" That night, at the Newport Folk Festival, he was booed by a hostile crowd for playing the first live "plugged-in" electric guitar set of his career. Never one to bow to orthodoxy, Dylan had initially become famous in the early 1960s, influencing society and the social movement of the time by writing and performing protest songs. But he didn't stop moving in new directions after the Newport Folk Festival. In 1967, for example, he released what was arguably the first important country-rock record. He kindled new genres of music. His own tunes of the time, perhaps considered blasphemous by either his existing fans or the country's political leadership when he introduced them, became classics. Like many artists—musicians, painters, choreographers, writers—who started by challenging or even flouting convention, Dylan's work became the tried and true.

The threat of musical ignominy would have seemed a very small risk indeed to someone like Martin Luther, whose very life and freedom were at stake (pun intended) when he took on the Catholic Church and the Pope by writing his now famous *Ninety-Five Theses* that confronted, among other things, the church's practice of selling indulgences. Indulgences were used at the time by the church to raise money, and Luther objected to what he considered the sale of salvation. For centuries, heretics had been treated poorly (torture, like burning at the stake, from folks like Torquemada of the Spanish Inquisition top the list), so challenging the authority of the church was no small decision. Imagine the thoughts that would be racing through your mind if you were Luther on the day you were summoned to Rome by Pope Leo. It must have been a good deal more frightening than worrying about whether a crowd of folk music lovers would boo you.

Eventually, Luther was excommunicated and branded an outlaw. He continued activities that from the Catholic Church's perspective were irreverent, translating the Bible from Latin to German (which the average person could read), and continuing to challenge the authority of the Pope. The Protestant church and, more specifically, the Lutheran church were spawned by his efforts. Spiritual leaders throughout history who have challenged the existing beliefs and authority of the times have done so at their own peril, and yet the result through history of their irreverent and sacrificial acts has been the founding of new religions traditions.

Tina Fey changed the course of the 2008 elections. At least it's been said that her *Saturday Night Live (SNL)* impersonation of Sarah Palin and its result—many in the nation laughing at the vice presidential candidate—influenced the drop in support for Palin and presidential candidate John McCain. Fey's influence is debatable, of course, but what seems evident is the role that irreverent satirists like Jon Stewart, Stephen Colbert, and Fey play in today's public dialogue (assuming the argumentative nature of our political and pundit discourse can be considered adult discussion).

Though often humorous, using wit to make its point, satire is social criticism, and its tools include poking fun, irony, exaggeration, double entendre, and parody; its purpose is to shame people or society into improvement. Earliest examples come from ancient Egypt, with more modern satirists including *Gulliver's Travels* author Jonathan Swift (*A Modest Proposal*, which used satire to bring attention to the poor), Joseph Heller (*Catch-22*, to the military and bureaucracy), Mark Twain (*Adventures of Huckleberry Finn*, to southern society and racism), and shows like Chaplin's *The Great Dictator* (Hitler) and Peter Sellers's *Dr. Strangelove* (the Cold War). Most people are familiar with current satirical TV shows like *The Colbert Report*, *The Daily Show*, *South Park*, and *The Simpsons*. Although satirizing your boss or organization publicly is probably not a good career or leadership move, satire has played and continues to play an important role in impertinently raising important issues.

Betty Ford has been described as having had outspoken irreverence. As a person who spoke bluntly and with candor, her "unvarnished self-reflection literally saved thousands of lives." She might never have been elected herself—irreverence doesn't lend itself to ideology— but she openly addressed issues that others wouldn't, and consequently became a hero to many in her own right.

Geoffrey West, president of the Santa Fe Institute (SFI), one of the premier, truly multidisciplinary research centers, wrote that scientists at SFI "work with a seemingly contradictory combination of bold irreverence and humble respect for the rules that govern science, systems, and academia." That blend, he says, is especially important given the important problems of climate change, terrorism, pandemics, and violence, and other urgent problems facing the world today.

Closer to the business of this chapter is the role irreverence plays in business success. Consider Guy Kawasaki's book, *Reality Check—The Irreverent Guide to Outsmarting, Outmanaging, and Outmarketing Your Competition*. Or consider Richard Branson, who has been described as an unlikely stew of irreverence, flamboyance, and elegance, and whose company branding has been perceived as irreverent. Some companies, like Groupon, revel in the idea of being irreverent. Founder Andrew Mason has kept an irreverent quality from the start, going so far as to joke around about fire dancing classes and gorilla suits in Groupon's IPO offering.

The editor of this handbook, the insightful Lisa Haneberg, wrote a weblog post in 2006, asking managers to "cultivate productive irreverence." She said managers could (and should) nurture this idea by role modeling it and by asking for it. She somewhat playfully (or is it irreverently?) calls someone who is productively irreverent a "prodIR." (It "sounds like prodder," she says. How fitting for the irreverent!) Irreverence can be lots of fun, she states, and a prodIR is occasionally a troublemaker. Breakthroughs can occur by practicing irreverence.

And yet irreverence is not universally embraced. People perceived as irreverent can be "burned at the stake" either literally or figuratively. (Is there a Torquemada in your organization who enforces doctrine?) Dictionary definitions of irreverence seem mostly negative. They include descriptions such as lacking proper respect or seriousness, disrespect for a person or thing held sacred or worthy of honor, being aweless, showing no respect or reverence (e.g., for holy things, or people and things generally considered important), and having a lack of veneration. The synonyms given include words like *blasphemous, impious, profane, sacrilegious, impertinence, mockery, derision, cheekiness, evil, immorality, iniquity,* and *desecration*. Those descriptors don't normally hit the "top 10" list of desired managerial qualities, do they? Irreverent people often get dubbed as troublemakers or as wicked, immoral, or impudent.

But let me suggest some other words or phrases that we might associate with irreverence. How about critical thinkers, skeptics, doubters, questioners, scientists, assumption testers, strategic thinkers, and reflectors? How about *playful*? Consider the potential results when irreverent people are listened to, like declaring when the emperor has no clothes; asking if everyone really wants to be heading toward Abilene; questioning a company's requirement for everyone to come to a central location, when its biggest competitor lets its employees work remotely; or questioning the validity of such information like another country possessing weapons of mass destruction. It is the aligning strength of strong cultures that can also be their great weakness because they often reject those who raise questions or try to do things differently.

> "God is greater and more generous than the best of those who profess to know and serve him. This is the radical nonconformity with the conventional wisdom that Jesus both proclaimed and exemplified, and, alas, it cost him his life."
>
> —Peter Gomes, author of *The Scandalous Gospel of Jesus*

> *"Unity, not uniformity, must be our aim. We attain unity only through variety. Differences must be integrated, not annihilated, or absorbed."*
>
> —Mary Parker Follett, pioneer in organizational theory and behavior

This Chapter Is Different

Many of the chapters in this book, and most books that you will read about leadership and management, will give you answers. They will share truths, or steps, or simple methodologies "that work." In many ways, that's a good thing because we all seek uncomplicated answers to problems we face.

This chapter, however, is different. I don't have answers; I have questions and proposals. I don't have truths; rather I suggest that you question truths. I don't recommend tried-and-true solutions; instead I complicate things. The model I offer is a starting point for my thinking, and hopefully yours, about irreverence. My research is just beginning, and I want to invite you into the discussion.

I don't know if there are any truths in life. I expect there are, but because we are humans with imperfect knowledge I don't think we can ever truly know what those truths are. Too many times in history we thought we had the answers figured out (that the sun revolves around the earth, for example, or perhaps that the most productive work conditions require all workers to be in the same location from 8 a.m. to 5 p.m. Monday through Friday), and we didn't. Uncounted numbers of people have converted from one religious belief that they thought to be truth to something else they now believe is truth. And although it appears that what works over time validates the practice, all it takes is one invention (like the printing press), one new product (like an iPad), or one business practice (Deming's quality improvement) to radically overturn how people had thought and operated for years, decades, and even centuries.

In many ways, my thinking hasn't evolved enough. When we wrote *Transforming Work: The Five Keys to Achieving Trust, Commitment, and Passion in the Workplace* in 2001, Patricia Boverie and I said, "Wise people have deep sets of understandings about the world that they have developed by questioning them, by trying to understand them from multiple perspectives, and by listening to them being tested by others." We went on to say, "Beware [of] anyone claiming to know 'the answer' or 'the truth.' Listen and learn most from people who qualify their own knowledge by providing other perspectives" (p. 123). I still think there is much to contemplate about this perspective.

> *"A wide diffusion of doubt and irreverence thus leads often to unexpected results. The irreverence of the Renaissance was a prelude to the new fanaticism of Reformation and Counter-Reformation. The Frenchmen of the enlightenment who debunked the church and the crown and preached reason and tolerance related a burst of revolutionary and nationalist fanaticism which has not abated yet."*
>
> —Eric Hoffer, author of *The True Believer*
>
> *"Whenever you find yourself on the side of the majority, it's time to pause and reflect."*
>
> —Mark Twain, author and humorist

This is what I think about irreverence today and why it is an important quality for managers to embrace. My views will doubtless change over time as I learn more about it. First, I think irreverent people are often courageous. It takes guts to challenge conventional thinking, whether the one you are confronting is the Pope, the audience at a folk music festival, or your boss who has "always done it this way."

Irreverence—asking questions and challenging the way we do things—is always an option. It takes courage to exhibit it because the penalty if others are intolerant of dissent (or even of questions) can range from mild rebuke to getting yourself fired.

That brings me to the second point about irreverence. People who make a real difference are usually politically, socially, and culturally aware. It's one thing to fall on your sword for no purpose. It's another to know when the time is right to set yourself on fire, as Thich Quang Duc did, which led to the toppling of the 1963 South Vietnamese regime. Most of us are not willing to undergo self-immolation for something minor, but we might be willing to challenge environmentally harmful or abusive business practices that go unconsidered, even at the cost of future promotion or even employment. Again, it is the savvy irreverent who considers timing, political readiness, and openness to change before risking everything.

Third, truly irreverent people challenge other people's way of doing things while at the same time being able to challenge their own. Now that's a trick most of us have a hard time doing. If we feel strongly enough that something is important, then we tend to put our blinders on as we advocate for it. If we believe passionately in something, then we risk becoming closed-minded, intractable ideologues, who reject irreverence within our own belief system. We become the folk ideologues who booed Dylan for trying something new. We become the Catholic Church, founded on Christian principles, which tortured those who questioned it. We become the leader who started with great new ideas but now can't stand to try something new. That's kind of sad, don't you think? *Merriam-Webster* defines an ideologue as an impractical idealist, an often blindly partisan advocate or adherent of a particular ideology. Thinking that there's a better way to do things and asking questions can evolve into an unquestioning acceptance of one approach to the exclusion of other ones. At that point we have closed our minds to the irreverent who question us, and we become as limited as those we've criticized. So the trick is to advocate for something while at the same time always knowing that there is likely to be something even better than what you are proposing.

Irreverence for Leaders and for Managers

If we revere the way things are, or "the company way," or what the boss says is true, then we will never doubt conventional wisdom. I don't think that leaders and managers are generally different people—we all have some so-called leadership strengths and some managerial ones; it's all a matter of definition. But it's helpful to compare the two sets of skills in terms of irreverence. Leaders are expected, for example, to be visionary, innovative, and perhaps unconventional from time to time, and to take some risks. Managers also must have the courage to question conventional wisdom. Just because a process works, the irreverent question is: What would make it better? Just because the Deming Method or the Black Belt or the Red Hat or the Baldridge or any other process or methodology adopted by the company as sacrosanct is in place doesn't mean that it's the only or even the best way to approach a problem, right?

Another attribute is that leaders take the long-term view and managers a shorter view. Both time perspectives benefit from a sense of irreverence. In one, the long-term strategic assumptions about the future of the organization should be challenged—that's part of any good strategic planning. (Those who missed challenging the assumption that real estate will never go down in value can attest to that.) But in the shorter frame, the more proximate assumptions of "how we do things around here" should be challenged just as regularly. Short-term irreverence may be even more practical than long-term irreverence. The sacred cows of our workplace—workplace practices, policies, and organizational structures—are all fair game for the irreverent manager. The first rule of the irreverent: If something seems off limits, challenge it as soon as you are able.

The first rule of the irreverent[1]:
If something seems off limits, challenge it as soon as you are able.

---

[1] I'm sure there are second, third, and fourth rules; I just haven't figured them out yet.

I'm looking at my leadership textbook right now, and I see that managers accept the status quo and that leaders challenge it. I beg to differ. I think, as has been pointed out already, that managers have lots of opportunities to challenge not only the status quo but also any accepted knowledge and "sacred cows." I think the managerial attributes around efficiency, procedures, control, administration, and maintenance all lend themselves to irreverence. Challenging processes to make them more efficient; striving for continuous improvement; moving to more elegant procedures; assessing the tension between control, overcontrol, and enablement; and so forth are all fair game for the irreverent manager.

The Company Way

One of my favorite musicals is *How to Succeed in Business Without Really Trying*, which is in revival on Broadway as I write this. J. Pierpont Finch is our star. He is ambitious and ready to try anything to get ahead. Along the way he runs into other managers who have developed a fear of taking chances and trying—even thinking—anything different. One of the most telling numbers is called the "Company Way." The number starts as a discussion between Finch and Twimble, the head of the mail room. The lyrics start this way:

Twimble: When I joined this firm
As a brash young man,
Well, I said to myself,
"Now, brash young man,
Don't get any ideas."
Well, I stuck to that,
And I haven't had one in years.
Finch: You play it safe.
Twimble: I play it the company way;
Wherever the company puts me
There I stay.
Finch: But what is your point of view?
Twimble: I have no point of view.
Finch: Supposing the company thinks...
Twimble: I think so too.

The song revolves around a pledge to conformity to the company way, with the accompanying hope that the company will not dump the employees if they toe the line. Finch's irreverence—joie de vivre, ideas, risk taking, opportunism—and a bit of luck eventually land him at the top of the firm, as he bounds over everyone else. But what we find here, and in many other places, is that conformity is often valued and reinforced in organizational culture and irreverence is often bred out of even the most impetuous newcomers.

"All great truths begin as blasphemies."

—George Bernard Shaw,
playwright and co-founder of the London School of Economics

"I'm not a fan of facts. You see, the facts can change, but my opinion will never change, no matter what are the facts."

—Stephen Colbert, host of *The Colbert Report*

"It was a bad time in architecture. They just didn't have any talent. All they had were rules. Even for knives and forks they created rules. Picasso would never have accepted rules. The house is like a machine? No! The mechanical is ugly. The rule is the worst thing. You just want to break it."

–Oscar Niemeyer, recipient of the Pritzker Architecture Prize,
called the most prestigious award in architecture

The Model

Definitions of Irreverence

I have been tossing out definitions and quotes about irreverence from dictionaries and other people, but for the purposes of this discussion irreverence is defined as an act of *challenging current beliefs or practices.*

Challenging includes questioning and also trying. We might challenge authority or a dominant way of doing things, but we might also challenge our own way of thinking. We might challenge current practice by proposing or doing something different. Challenging is more active than (but does include) questioning, because irreverent managers often go beyond asking and actually *do something.*

Definitions of Reverence

Reverence is having a deep belief in something, which could be religious or spiritual, philosophical or political, but for us it relates to the theory and practice of management.

Quadrants

The model proposed doesn't have a name yet (how's that for different?), and it is based upon these two definitions. Its purpose is to help us to understand how reverence and irreverence interact and, more practically, how that interaction might help us to be more effective managers. One variable is irreverence, and the other is reverence, resulting in the four quadrants described here (also see Figure 3-1).

I. Low Challenging and Low Beliefs—The Quadrant of the Unengaged

In this quadrant, people aren't committed to any particular way of doing things, and they don't seek better ways either. They "go with the flow" and accept less than the best. They have settled. Managers here follow "the company way" and do what they think they must do to survive. They might have some ideas for improvement, but either their natural human propensity to improve has been acculturated out of them, or they just don't care about anything except getting along.

II. Low Challenging and High Beliefs—The Quadrant of Believing

People in this group have strong beliefs. They may have come by these beliefs by ascribing to a management guru or practice, by finding something that really works for them, and then becoming excellent at doing it. Members of this group may be passionate about what they believe. They may be surprised by something that contradicts those beliefs or by a new or different way of thinking about a problem or possible solution. While strong beliefs are very important, the danger is that they may become so strongly entrenched that creative thinking or new ways of leading, operating, or looking at their organizations may not be considered.

III. High Challenging and Low Beliefs—The Quadrant of the Uncommitted

How does it feel to have all sorts of questions but no answers? What happens when people don't trust anyone or any practice enough to take a stand? This group of managers may be wishy-washy, skeptical, or perhaps even cynical. They ask a lot of questions, but nothing really satisfies them. Maybe they've been burned before or don't have enough confidence to say, "I'm in!" If a new practice, procedure, or management philosophy is proposed, they'll question it endlessly, or they'll try one thing or another, without committing to an approach. These folks are very irreverent—they don't believe in much and they question everything.

IV. High Challenging and High Beliefs—The Quadrant of the Wise

In this quadrant are people with deep beliefs, who regularly test those beliefs. Note that this quadrant involves an iterative process of reverence (developing depth of belief) and irreverence (challenging beliefs and practices), which leads to wisdom. Managers here may have built a strong body of practice that works, but they are never satisfied that they have "the answer." Truth is always subject to updating based on new, perhaps quite diverse, information or perspectives. Here is where depth of belief meets strength of challenge to become depth of understanding. This is also the quadrant of transformational learning and epiphany.

Managers here are strategic thinkers who have a strong game plan based on significant experience and information but who also have their antennae out for what might be changing that might affect that plan. They are likely to have deep beliefs about what motivates employees but aren't locked into simplistic motivational systems. They have a desire for solutions derived from updated research, experimentation, and experience over time. They try out ideas to see what might work and adjust their worldview according to what happens.

Figure 3-1. The Kroth Model

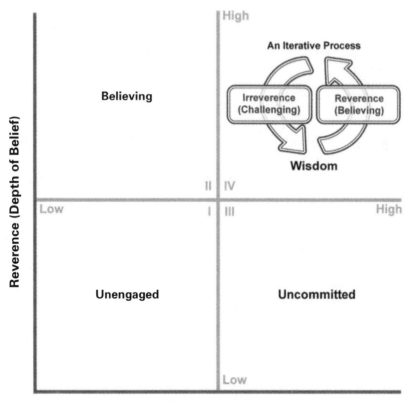

They aren't afraid of opposing or different views, but welcome them. They have a strong propensity for action—their commitment is strong—but they are open to learning something new.

I've played around quite a bit with these two variables and quadrants and propose them here for your consideration. You may have variations, see something that is lacking, or find they don't fit your worldview. Hopefully the model is provocative enough to initiate some thinking or ideas. You may also want to put this in the trash can, and that would be OK too, except that all the other chapters in the book have great material you don't want to waste!

Ideas for Practice

Clearly, this model has a desired quadrant—IV. Here are a few ideas to move managers and employees toward the quadrant of wisdom. Culture by its nature tends to reject difference—different views, different assumptions, different goals, different beliefs, and different people. Even a culture that extols difference rejects those that would promote conformity. A strong, positive, productive, healthy culture is a good thing, but its Achilles' heel occurs when the exploration about how to do things better ceases because things are already going so well.

Some things to consider to keep that iterative reverence-irreverence cycle going:

- Practice taking the opposite position of what you believe to be true. Honestly try it out with other people.
- Unearth your assumptions. Your assumptions (cars will never transport more people than horses; computers can't get any smaller; the earth is flat) dictate your actions and worldviews, and they often are invisible—you just take for granted that they are true. We all have incomplete and inaccurate assumptions to either greater or lesser degrees, sometimes to our sorrow.
- Think of three alternative approaches to what you are doing now. So what if what you are doing is working? You might be able to do a lot better.
- Immerse yourself in a completely different model, process, or culture. This of course is one of the best ways to open up your mind—if you will let it be open— to possibilities you never would otherwise consider.
- Scenario planning is another version of the "three approaches" strategy. It's just more formal and can involve more people.
- Take on different roles and perspectives. So you have a naysayer in the group, a troublemaker. Maybe she or he is your Bob Dylan, and you just don't want to hear about it. Try sitting in that person's shoes, or sit him or her down and really explore

why "the sky is falling," or consider that the Red Sea is opening up and you just don't see it. All of which leads to…

- Invite doubters into the room. Yes, you want folks to align themselves to what you've decided, but you should always be open to different practices and approaches, or even to hearing that the sky is indeed falling and you'd better do something about it pretty darn quick.

- Adopt a provisional, working beliefs approach. Part of the reason we fear testing our assumptions is that we think that if they are proven false we'll have nothing to hang on to, that everything we've done in the past was a waste of our time or life. A way to mitigate that is to have a continuously inquisitive mind.

- Hang out with different kinds of people than you normally do, including artists, theologians, ranchers, car wash attendants, and whomever. You'll learn a lot, and it will enrich your life.

- Satirize yourself. Yep, pretend you are Tina Fey, Jon Stewart, or Mark Twain and poke holes in your own pomposity, self-importance, or hubris. Laugh at yourself. Or, like court jesters of yesteryear, ask someone to make a little fun of you, your management style, or your organization. Be sure, like kings did for jesters, not to blame the person giving you a bit of a roast. Thank him or her for helping you laugh at yourself and to see some blind spots, even if it does hurt just a little.

- Finally, practice reverence. Rituals, traditions, deep reading, and discussions about your own management beliefs and projects are all good things. Consider how you can understand and learn more thoroughly the theory, thought leaders, research, experiments, and practices that you follow. What don't you understand about your performance management system that would make it even more effective? You communicate in a certain, effective way. What could you do as a manager to understand and practice communication with employees, vendors, and customers better?

This notion of irreverence is something I hope you'll consider, and especially how it can interact with reverence. I would value hearing from you and about your ideas for improving this model, about examples of irreverence that have made a positive difference, and in particular about people who have interesting stories of irreverence—in all fields—that have improved our world.

"I've had a perfectly wonderful evening. But this wasn't it."

—Groucho Marx, American comedian and film star

About the Author

Michael Kroth, PhD, is an associate professor at the University of Idaho in adult/ organizational learning and leadership and is a recipient of the university's Hoffman Award for Excellence in Teaching. He has written or co-authored four books including *Transforming Work: The Five Keys to Achieving Trust, Commitment, and Passion in the Workplace; The Manager as Motivator; Career Development Basics;* and *Managing the Mobile Workforce: Leading, Building, and Sustaining Virtual Teams.* His website and blog can be found here: www.michaelkroth.com and http://managingthemobileworkforce.com/ blog/.

The Five Universal Themes in Business

Todd Sattersten

Editor's Note

Todd Sattersten is likely one of the most well-read professionals I know. He knows business books and has helped cull the essence of what each can offer in terms of inspiration and practical tools. In this short essay, he shares the most prominent themes that emerge when looking across the most popular and well-respected business books. For managers, this is the micro "CliffsNotes" version of how to be successful.

W hat happens when you spend 18 months reading the best in business literature? In our case, two things happened—one expected, the other quite unexpected. The expected was the creation of a list of the 100 best business books of all time, which led to a book by the same name that was published in 2009. The unexpected came as we uncovered a number of meta-themes the books share that exist beyond any predictable grouping by subject matter. For example, Michael Useem's *The Leadership Moment* has surprising connections with as Taiichi Ohno's *Toyota Production System* and Gary Klein's *The Power of Intuition.*

Ultimately, we found five persistent meta-themes across our selection of the 100 best business books. Each meta-theme appears horizontally across traditional publishing categories, bridging such divisions as sales, management, narrative, and finance. Each meta-theme also scales in a vertical sense, applying to individuals, teams, and organizations equally.

So profound are these meta-themes, we argue, that these five universal insights act as the foundation for a leader dealing with any aspect of business, whether starting a new job or developing the next year's corporate strategy.

- **Clarity of Purpose:** Purpose provides direction and brings clarity to all work. For the individual in pursuit of purpose, author Po Bronson asks the ultimate question in his book, *What Should I Do With My Life?* Organizations struggle with the same kind of question when they craft their mission statements and massage their marketing slogans.

- **Wisdom in Decision Making:** The process of making decisions is often overly deliberate or completely unconscious. In both cases, we base our decisions on past experience and judge our successes only on the outcomes. In *Influence,* Robert Cialdini alerts us to how we use unconscious routine to make even the smallest decision, while in *The Power of Intuition,* Gary Klein provides a map to some of that scripting and shows how we can improve our gut instinct.

- **Bias for Action:** Tom Peters and Bob Waterman point out in *In Search of Excellence* that a quality of excellent companies is "the bias for action." This assertion that action trumps all appears in many great books, so what keeps us from taking action? Author David Allen *(Getting Things Done)* would say a person's focus is misplaced on time and priority, rather than action. Authors Jeffery Pfeffer and Bob Sutton *(The Knowing-Doing Gap)* would say organizations suffer from a gap between knowing and doing.

- **Openness to Change:** Understanding change is essential because change affects individuals and organizations constantly. Sales is about change. Marketing is about change. Corporate strategy is about change. Lou Gerstner says it was changing IBM's entitlement culture that was his biggest challenge. In *The First 90 Days,* new job guru Michael Watkins describes the waves of change that new managers must create. In *Crossing the Chasm,* Geoffrey Moore shows how products are adopted and what different constituents need to accept change.

- **Giving and Getting Feedback:** Imagine throwing a baseball in a dark room. You would miss seeing the trajectory the ball took or where it landed. Our success depends on feedback. Did we make the right choice? Did the action have the intended effect? Are things changing? Daniel Goleman *(Emotional Intelligence)* says self-reflection is a form of feedback and an essential piece of emotional intelligence. Engineering professor Henry Petroski, author of *To Engineer Is Human,* says failure is a critical part of learning. And in *Secrets of Closing the Sale*, Zig Ziglar says listening is the most important part of selling.

These five meta-themes are not only important on an individual level, but they also overlap and reinforce one another. For instance, Peter Drucker said in *The Effective Executive* that decisions are not truly made until someone is doing something different than he or she was the day before. And it is clear that feedback determines the success one has with any and all of the other meta-themes.

The five meta-themes feed into each other as well. Clarity of purpose provides wisdom in decision making, which informs action, which creates change, while feedback makes everything work better. They also resonate with the stages of the "hero's journey" made famous by mythology scholar Joseph Campbell. The archetypal heroes of myth and popular culture walked more or less the same path as Jack Welch.

It's painfully obvious that companies continually fail to absorb these simple lessons. The question is, what will it take for us to internalize the insights won by our heroes?

For Further Reading

Allen, David. (2001). *Getting Things Done.* New York: The Penguin Group.

Bronson, Po. (2002). *What Should I Do With My Life?* New York: Ballantine Books.

Cialdini, Robert. (1984). *Influence: The Psychology of Persuasion.* New York: William Morrow.

Drucker, Peter. (1967, 2002). *The Effective Executive.* New York: HarperCollins.

Goleman, Daniel. (1995). *Emotional Intelligence.* New York: Bantam Books.

Klein, Gary. (2003). *The Power of Intuition.* New York: Doubleday.

Moore, Geoffrey. (1991, 2002). *Crossing the Chasm.* New York: HarperCollins.

Ohno, Taiichi. (1988). *Toyota Production System.* New York: Doubleday.

Peters, Tom and Bob Waterman. (1982). *In Search of Excellence.* New York: Harper & Row.

Petroski, Henry. (1982). *To Engineer Is Human.* New York: Random House.

Pfeffer, Jeffery and Bob Sutton. (2000). *The Knowing-Doing Gap.* Boston: Harvard Business School Publishing.

Useem, Michael. (1998). *The Leadership Moment.* New York: Three Rivers Press.

Watkins, Michael. (2003). *The First 90 Days.* Boston: Harvard Business School Publishing.

Ziglar, Zig. (1984, 2003). *Secrets of Closing the Sale.* Grand Rapids, MI: Baker Publishing Group.

About the Author

Todd Sattersten is the founder of BizBookLab, a company that studies business books and the business of books. He is the co-author of *The 100 Best Business Books of All Time* and past president of business bookseller 800-CEO-READ. Todd's website can be found at www.toddsattersten.com.

Chapter 5

Positively Using Your Power

Sharlyn Lauby

---------------------------------- **Editor's Note** ----------------------------------

I have been a reader of Sharlyn Lauby's blog, called the HR Bartender, for years. We HR types have radar for what's getting in the way of a manager's success. I love Sharlyn's informal style and honest discussion of her topics. Recently, she wrote a great piece on power, and I was thrilled when she agreed to expand it here in this chapter. Many managers fail to use—and in fact misuse—power every day. We have more power than we think, and sometimes we use it in ways that drive people away from us. Highly successful managers, however, understand the dynamics of power at work and use the types of power that bring people together toward a common cause. Reading this chapter, and Sally Hoghead's chapter (section 4, chapter 32) together would make for a good primer on influence.

What is workplace power? Well, there's a quote by former Prime Minister of the United Kingdom Margaret Thatcher that says, "Power is like being a lady…if you have to tell people you are, you aren't." The study of power is fascinating because it's a moving target. Dictionary.com defines power as "a person or thing that possesses or exercises authority or influence." So in essence, when we talk about the use of power, we're talking about our ability to get something or make something happen.

Now, don't be modest and think to yourself, "I don't have any power." Everyone has power. And, that's not a bad thing. The issue becomes what kind of power a person has and how someone uses that power. This is what makes the topic of power both interesting and incredibly challenging. Power is one of those things that, as individuals, we aren't always comfortable admitting that we have.

In this chapter, we will explore the different kinds of power in the workplace. As you will see, there are lots of different ways power can manifest itself. And for that reason, it's important to realize that power exists in everyone. It's also possible that you have different kinds of power with different groups or situations.

The Seven Kinds of Power

There are seven different power bases we may use in influencing the behavior of others. They are as follows: coercive, connection, expert, informative, legitimate, referent, and reward power.

Coercive power is associated with people who are in a position to punish others. People fear the consequences of not doing was has been asked of them. Often when we think of individuals who are on the proverbial "power trip," we think of coercive power. There are some advantages to coercive power. For example, situations where there's a crisis or danger might call for someone to exert his or her influence in a forceful way for the safety of the team. So when there's a potentially harmful condition, coercive power might be exactly what's needed.

The number of emergency situations that justify the use of coercive power is probably limited. It's important to remember that there's a price to using coercive power. If used at inappropriate times or too often, it could prompt a backlash from employees. None of us likes to be forced into doing things. And if someone feels pressured into doing something, it could create resentment or distrust.

Connection power is based upon who you know. The person with connection power knows and has the ear of other powerful people within the organization. As a consequence of that connection, the leader is seen as being able to reward or punish appropriate or inappropriate behavior. Imagine the administrative assistant to the chief executive officer. Part of the administrative assistant's role is to manage the number of requests made to the chief executive. If a person wanted to see the CEO, it might be helpful to know the administrative assistant.

Or think of the times when you get a call from a stranger who says, "I got your name and number from [insert name of your best friend here]." If my best friend thinks I should connect with this person, I pay attention. Connection power is talked about frequently in the context of social media—not only in terms of how many connections a person has but also in terms of whether or not his or her connections have value.

Expert power comes from a person's expertise (duh!). This is commonly a person with an acclaimed skill or accomplishment. Leaders who are high in expert power are able to influence others because of their acknowledged skill or experience in a particular area or subject. Keep in mind the term *expert* doesn't have to mean Albert Einstein or a Nobel Prize winner. For example, I know a person who used to book speakers for big conferences. Whenever I have a question about speaking at conferences, I call her. She's my expert, my Albert Einstein, my Nobel winner. She has expertise and knowledge I don't have.

Think of the employee in your office who is the "go-to" person for certain types of problems or issues. It could be his or her knowledge of certain software programs, ability to source critical supplies, or mastery of project management.

Information power is based on information not previously available to others. Leaders who are high in information power can influence others because they possess or have access to information others see as valuable or important. I'm totally convinced this is where the "knowledge is power" cliché comes from. It references people who withhold information to become more powerful or influential.

But in today's world, information is everywhere. In fact, some would argue there's information overload. So access to information isn't the obstacle it once was. It's finding the information you need. *Curation* is the term being used to describe finding the right information at the right moment. Knowing what information is necessary, how to gather it, and, most importantly, the proper way to interpret it is an essential skill in today's workplace. People who can curate information will be in demand. Having information that is not available to others is a form of power. And now, an additional form of that power comes from the ability to find information the moment it's necessary.

Legitimate power comes from the position a person holds. This is related to a person's title and job responsibilities. You might also hear this referred to as positional power. Simply put, managers have more power than supervisors, directors more than managers, and vice presidents more than all of them. A former boss of mine once told me, "Once you become a director, you never go back." His comment referred to the power of the position and how you would always be viewed at that level. And as much as we might not like to admit it, on some level it's true.

People who are well-liked and respected can have referent power. There are people we know, regardless of their position, who are able to ask for things and get them because they are popular and well-liked. They have strong interpersonal skills and use them to build teams. It's important to understand who these people are in the organization. I've seen employees get very upset because a popular employee was disciplined—even if it was obvious that the employee did something wrong. That individual's likability within the organization was very powerful.

Reward power is based upon a person's ability to bestow rewards. Those rewards might come in the form of job assignments, schedules, pay, or benefits. One example is the manager who makes the schedule and can give an employee a holiday off. Another is the purchasing supervisor who gets sample products and gives them away to co-workers. These are examples of individuals who have the ability to bestow gifts. Part of the dynamic has to be that people want the gift that can be bestowed. I know a person who would give out Snuggies®— those hoodie/blanket things—to friends and colleagues. He had access to tons of them. If you wanted a Snuggie, he could get you one. Well, I live in South Florida. I need a Snuggie like a hole in my head. So what might be a great reward to someone in North Dakota doesn't have the same value to me. It's only powerful if the reward is valued.

Understanding What Kinds of Power You Have

To help you identify your "power zone," take a moment and think about how you try to influence action from others. You could use the power descriptions above as a pseudo self-assessment. Listed below are seven statements that describe reasons why others may respond positively to your attempts to influence their behavior. Use the following scale to describe the extent to which each of the seven statements is characteristic of your influence attempts.

1 = This statement is not at all characteristic of my attempts to influence others; it rarely is true of me.

2 = This statement is only sometimes characteristic of my attempts to influence others; it is only occasionally true of me.

3 = This statement is characteristic of my attempts to influence others; it is often true of me.

4 = This statement is very characteristic of my attempts to influence others; it is very often true of me.

5 = This statement is quite characteristic of my attempts to influence others; it is almost always true of me.

Again, use this scale to describe the extent to which each of the following seven statements is characteristic of the reasons why others respond positively to your attempts to influence their behavior.

- I can punish those who do not do what I ask.
- I am connected to powerful others in the organization.
- I have expertise in that particular area or subject.
- I have information that others need or see of value.
- I am, after all, the boss.
- I am personally liked or respected as a person by others.
- I can reward those who do what I ask.

Now you can chart your responses. Circle your reply associated with each type of power.

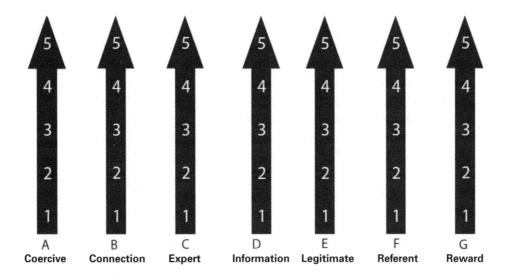

A	B	C	D	E	F	G
Coercive	Connection	Expert	Information	Legitimate	Referent	Reward

This self-declaration gives you perspective on the types of power you use the most, and the ones you are most comfortable with. It also highlights the types of power you use very little or not at all. Ask yourself the following questions:

- Am I comfortable with the types of power I'm using?
- Do I feel I'm getting the outcomes I want by using these types of power?
- Are there types of power I would like to use more often?

The answer to those questions will tell you if you need to develop some sort of action plan to refine your current types of power or maybe to work on developing power in areas that are important to you.

Developing an Action Plan

It frustrates me to no end when someone talks about a topic, and in the last couple of sentences says something to the effect of "… and I challenge each of you to leave this session and create your own personal action plan to … " Frankly, the speaker should tell us how to create the action plan. So I just told you to develop your power action plan, but let me go off on a tangent and tell you my favorite way to develop a plan. I'm a big fan of SMART plans and find it to be a very flexible way to deal with setting goals and creating plans.

I didn't always feel this way about SMART plans. I once worked for a company where, every time something went wrong, our president wanted a SMART plan explaining how we were going to fix it. Sad to say, we developed a lot of SMART plans. I thought it was some sort of punishment. It wasn't until a class in night school that I realized SMART plans have been around for many years and weren't some dreamt-up form of torture from senior leadership. So, back to SMART plans. SMART is an acronym:

- **Specific:** This is a statement of exactly what you would like to accomplish. Think of it as the who, what, where, when, which, and why of the goal.
- **Measurable:** The answer to this section should tell you how success is measured.
- **Achievable (or Attainable):** Outline the steps it will take to complete the goal.
- **Relevant or Realistic (some versions use Responsible):** There are two different ways to look at this: first, the goal must be important to you (i.e., relevant or realistic). Alternately, are there other people you need to help you reach this goal?
- **Time-bound (some versions use Trackable):** Identify the time frame to achieve the goal.

So as you're putting together your power action plan, you can use the SMART acronym. Here's an example:

- **S:** Let's say your goal is to develop more expert power. You feel that you're smart about the company's product or service and have a lot to contribute, but people don't look at you as the "go-to" person for answers.
- **M:** You'll know that you've achieved expert power when the company asks you to start participating in sales meetings with prospective clients to answer questions about how the product or service works.
- **A:** You're going to start writing short articles for the company blog about the product so everyone can see how much you know about the product or service.
- **R:** You'll need support from your boss (so you can take time to write the articles) and support from the marketing department (to post articles on the company blog).
- **T:** You estimate that it will take about six months for others to begin noticing your articles.

SMART plans force us to ask all the questions we need in order to develop a complete, well-thought-out plan.

Using Workplace Power

Now that we've developed our action plan, let's get back to using power at work. The two biggest mistakes I see with people using power both revolve around the way it's used. Either people try to use power they don't have, or they use the wrong kind of power to achieve results. Here are a few examples of how a subtle change in power can affect a situation:

- **Scenario 1:** A manager notices an employee in another department is not wearing his name tag. The manager tells the employee he needs to put on his name tag. The employee ignores these requests because he doesn't report to this manager. *This could be a situation where the manager has no positional power but thinks he or she does.*
- **Scenario 2:** A manager notices an employee in another department is not wearing her name tag. After work, the manager and employee play on the company softball team together. The team wins its game and goes out for pizza afterward. The next day, the manager sees the employee and reminds her to wear her name tag. The employee says, "That's cool," and puts the name tag on. *In this case, it's possible the employee likes the manager because they play on the company softball team together. So, responding to the manager's referent power, the employee complied with the request.*
- **Scenario 3:** A manager finishes interviewing an employee for an internal transfer. At the end of the interview, the manager reminds the employee to put his name tag on. The employee gets his name tag out right away. *And in this version, the manager has reward power. The employee hopes to transfer to this manager's department.*

So even with a simple request like "Put your name tag on," it's all in the power of the person delivering the message.

When a person abuses or misuses his or her power, it's immediately recognized. Trust and confidence in the person is damaged. Not having trust in the people around you can create dysfunctional teams. People have to trust each other for teams to be truly effective.

But when we think about trust, the question arises: Do we give our trust to others unconditionally or have others earn our trust? Trust is a pretty big thing—like love, respect, and admiration—and I don't know that we give those unconditionally. People have to earn them by their actions and by their words. And, once you earn them, if they're taken for granted or abused, they might be taken away—as in losing a person's respect. Sometimes I wonder if this is what really happens: When we meet people it's not that we give them our unconditional trust…but we also don't distrust them. There's a difference. Maybe there's a "trust limbo" where we all reside until a person decides to unconditionally trust us or to distrust us.

In spending time thinking about trust, what really resonates with me is the speed for which you can lose both a person's trust and the probability of regaining it. You can lose a person's trust in an instant, without warning and sometimes without even doing anything. There are people who have been labeled untrustworthy simply because someone else said so.

Once a person has the label of being untrustworthy, it's very difficult, if not virtually impossible, to regain that trust. Put this back into the context of power. If a person has power and uses it responsibly, he or she earns the right to continue using it. However, if that power isn't used appropriately, then the person loses the ability to use it. He or she might try to use power, but no one listens.

It's one of the reasons I believe power is so important. We can't kid ourselves into thinking we don't have it or that we're not using it. We must be open about the existence of power. When we do, it removes barriers and continues to build upon the trust that exists in our working relationships.

Bestowed Power and Earned Power

We've talked about earning trust and the impact it can have on power. It's important to know that some kinds of power are bestowed upon us. They're usually based upon our position or title. Or they may be granted to us in terms of who we have access to in the company, or what actions we are able to authorize (based upon our position). For example, as a human resources director, I could authorize payroll to cut a manual check for an employee. That was something I had the power to do based upon my title within the company.

That being said, even with bestowed power, if you abuse it, people will make things difficult for you. Bestowed power is not a license for a proverbial power trip.

Earned forms of power are related to who we are as an individual. Or what we know in terms of expertise and information. It's less about title and position and more about what we know. For example, I attended a focus group on HR and social media. It's related not to my job as a training consultant, but to my expertise as an HR professional who is also a blogger. During those meetings I was able to have a voice (aka power) toward suggesting changes for a new social networking community being developed.

Ultimately, we need to realize the importance of having both bestowed power and earned power. This isn't an either/or situation. And the more we can use earned and bestowed power together, the better it is for us and the people we're dealing with.

To effectively blend bestowed and earned power, there are four things that must take place.

- **Authenticity:** Simply put, be who you are. We can tell when someone is fake or phony, and others can spot it if we aren't being authentic as well.
- **Knowledge:** The world is constantly changing, and we have to be willing to change with it. This means opening ourselves up to lifelong learning and constantly increasing our knowledge.
- **Credibility:** Others have to know if we are individuals of our word. If we say we're going to do something, we must do it or renegotiate our commitment. And if we say we believe in something, then we need to demonstrate it in our actions.
- **Trust:** If we are authentic, knowledgeable, and credible, others will trust what we say and what we do. Having the trust of others is a precious gift that should never be abused.

Now that we know we have power and the key elements to developing positive power, it's time to put our power to use. Knowing the best time to use your power is essential. When faced with a situation, ask yourself the following two questions:

- What action do I want to take or would I like to see happen?
- Do I have the power to make it happen?

If the answer to both questions is yes, then it's a good use of the power that you've either earned or been given. Remember the components of trust, authenticity, and knowledge as you use power to influence an outcome.

If you can't honestly answer yes to these questions, then ask yourself if there's a way to align with a person who does have the power you need to make it happen. It's possible you need to connect with a person who has the power necessary to make something happen. You might need to ask for permission to exert power.

For instance, let's say you've been asked to chair a committee at work. Some of the tasks assigned to the committee are not in your usual decision-making authority. It's possible you will need to ask for permission to carry out the tasks given to you. This shouldn't be a big deal, but it does need to be discussed. Part of authority is not only being given the responsibility to do something but the power to get it done.

In Closing

Dismissing the presence and impact of workplace power is naïve. Power is not a bad thing. It's essential in business to get things done. What's troublesome about power is when people use it improperly and at the wrong times. You can avoid the negative traps of power by being conscious of how power is formed, maintained, and leveraged. Being an effective manager includes being able to manage power positively in the workplace.

References and Resources

French, J.R.P., Jr., and B. Raven. (1959). The Bases of Social Power. In *Studies in Social Power*, ed. Dorwin Cartwright. Ann Arbor: The University of Michigan, Institute for Social Research.

Greene, Robert. (1998). *The 48 Laws of Power*. New York: Viking Books.

Hersey, P., K.H. Blanchard, and W.E. Natemeyer. (1979). *Group and Organization Studies*. Volume 4, Issue 4. Englewood Cliffs, NJ: Prentice Hall.

Hersey, P., and K. Blanchard. (1982). *Management of Organizational Behavior* (4th ed.). Upper Saddle River, NJ: Prentice Hall.

Lauby, S. (2008). *HR Bartender*, a blog created to provide a friendly place to talk about work. www.hrbartender.com.

Raven, B.H., and A.W. Kruglanski. (1970). Conflict and Power. In *The Structure of Conflict*. New York: Academic Press.

About the Author

Sharlyn Lauby, SPHR, CPLP, is the president of the Internal Talent Management Group and an HR pro with more than 20 years of professional experience. She is the creator of the popular business blog called the HR Bartender, recognized as one of the Top 50 Business Blogs by Business Pundit, a Top 25 Talent Management blog by Fistful of Talent, and one of the Top 50 HR Blogs to Watch by EvanCarmichael.com. Sharlyn was named one of the Top 25 HR Digital Influencers in 2009, and has been quoted by ABC News, AOL Finance, the *Chicago Tribune*, and the *Miami Herald*. You can find Sharlyn's website and blog at www.hrbartender.com.

Chapter 6

New Evidence of Servant Leadership's Efficacy as a Managerial Approach

Bret Simmons, PhD

.... **Editor's Note** ....

Bret is an amazing thinker and writer, and I am thrilled that he agreed to share a synopsis of the recent research findings on servant leadership with you. I have seen managers curl their noses when hearing the term "servant leadership" like it is a nasty-tasting cod-liver-oil remedy. It's good for you, but who wants it? Here's the thing. Nearly every organization I work with is talking about accountability and results and engagement. If you want more of these outcomes, then managing in a way that serves your employees' needs is good business and a mighty tasty way to get the work done. I think you will find this chapter from Bret compelling, convincing, and useful.

Servant leadership is a follower-centric rather than leader-centric philosophy that results in leader behaviors focused on follower development rather than leader glorification. "Servant leaders, by definition, place the needs of their subordinates before their own needs and center their efforts on helping subordinates grow to reach their maximum potential and achieve optimal organizational and career success" (Liden et al., 2008, p. 163).

Servant leaders see themselves as a resource, not *the* source or oracle from which all organizational knowledge, wisdom, and direction must emanate.

I've found that servant leadership is a misunderstood and much maligned concept. Many have the impression that this group-oriented approach to leadership that emphasizes being resourceful, sharing power, and building a sense of shared purpose and teamwork is wishy-washy. The idea of a leader shifting the focus of attention and power from himself to the people he's been given the privilege to lead is not what many people have in mind when they think of leadership. People have a hard time understanding how servant leadership might work, mostly because they have rarely personally experienced leadership practiced this way.

Until recently, the research evidence to support servant leadership has not been very strong. This chapter will present recent and convincing evidence for the efficacy of servant leadership. This new research from three separate studies suggests that servant leadership affects important outcomes like trust, citizenship behavior, a positive service climate, and team performance.

The first study involved 191 financial service teams and 999 total participants suggested that servant leadership significantly affects trust in the leader and ultimately team performance (Schaubroeck, Lam, & Peng, 2011). This study looked at how both transformational leadership and servant leadership worked together to first affect two different kinds of trust. Transformational leadership is characterized by having a compelling agenda of high performance and change and providing clear structure to help team members pursue the agenda. Transformational leadership was found to affect *cognition-based trust,* which is trust based on the belief that the leader is competent, responsible, reliable, and dependable. Servant leadership was found to predict *affect-based trust,* which is trust based on an emotional bond to the leader because people believe the leader genuinely cares and is concerned about their welfare.

Cognition-based trust then predicted *team potency,* which is the belief that team members can achieve their objectives and realize the shared vision. Affect-based trust predicted *team psychological safety,* which is a shared belief that the team is a safe place for individual risk taking. The authors state: "High team psychological safety can improve team members' engagement at work because it means that members believe they can participate openly and actively without fear of suffering adverse personal consequences, such as being derogated for their ideas and observations and the manner by which they express them" (Schaubroeck et al., 2011, p. 2).

While both were shown to significantly affect team performance, the size of the effect of team psychological safety was almost double the size of the effect of team potency. This is important to note because it was servant leadership that produced an affect-based trust in followers, and that type of trust in the leader allowed teams to reach the highest levels of performance. The authors conclude: "Engaging in the behaviors associated with servant leadership and transformational leadership is important for a leader to cultivate and maintain team members' confidence in his or her agenda and competencies as a leader (cognition-based trust) and to gain their faith that he or she will act in a manner that supports both their individual well-being and that of the team (affect-based trust)" (Schaubroeck et al., 2011, p. 8).

The second study of 570 employees and 80 upper-level managers representing 95 separate teams examined servant leadership, team potency, and team performance (Hu & Liden, 2011). *Team potency*, defined as shared confidence in the team's general capabilities, was rated by team members with a seven-item scale (e.g., "The team I work with has above-average ability"). *Team performance* was rated by upper-level managers answering questions about both performance (e.g., "Rate the overall level of performance that you observe for this team") and citizenship behavior (e.g., "In general, the team members help others who have been absent").

This study examined how servant leadership affected the team goal setting process and its subsequent effect on team potency and performance. The authors specifically looked at both *goal clarity*—how well individual team members understand team goals and their own roles in working toward meeting the team goals—and *process clarity*—how well team members understand the procedures for accomplishing their roles as they work on team goals. Team members self-reported on servant leadership, goal clarity, and process clarity.

The findings were fascinating. Servant leadership was found to directly affect both team potency and team performance. And goal clarity and process clarity were shown to affect team potency; however, this relationship only worked in the presence of servant leadership. According to the authors: "Our results clearly demonstrated that goal and process clarity contribute the most to the emergence of team potency when accompanied by servant leaders, whose employee-centered focus is beneficial for facilitating team confidence and effective team behaviors. In contrast, the results showed that *in the absence of servant leadership, the impact of goal and process clarity on team potency was no longer positive or even became negative*" (Hu & Liden, 2011, p. 9).

If your organization depends on the performance of teams to deliver remarkable results, the members on those teams need to be able to look each other in the eye and clearly believe that they can get the job done (potency). If the team members don't clearly understand either the team goals or the procedures needed to accomplish the goals, it's folly to expect them to believe strongly in their collective ability to perform with distinction.

Setting the proper structure for remarkable team performance is necessary but not sufficient. Never forget that your team members not only need to believe in each other, but they also need to believe in you and your leadership. They need to know that you don't just care about the goals, but that you also care about each and every one of them as individuals.

If you lead a team, the evidence clearly suggests that you need to develop your servant leadership behaviors (e.g., behaving ethically, putting employees first, empowering, helping employees grow and succeed), and then train your team members to do the same.

Both of these studies measured servant leadership by asking employees in the study to respond to 28 statements about their manager. To get very specific about what servant leadership is, here are 14 of those 28 statements (Liden et al., 2008):

1. My manager cares about my personal well-being.
2. My manager can recognize when I'm down without asking me.
3. My manager is involved in community activities.
4. I am encouraged by my manager to volunteer in the community.
5. My manager is able to think effectively through complex problems.
6. My manager has a thorough understanding of our organization and its goals.
7. My manager encourages me to handle important work decisions on my own.
8. My manager gives me the freedom to handle difficult situations in the way I feel is best.
9. My manager is interested in making sure that I achieve my career goals.
10. My manager provides me with work experiences that enable me to develop new skills.
11. My manager seems to care more about my success than his/her own.
12. My manager puts my best interests ahead of his/her own.
13. My manager is always honest.
14. My manager would not compromise ethical principles in order to achieve success.

Do you work in an environment of servant leadership? If so, observe your leader carefully and try to learn and practice these behaviors yourself. If you don't work for a servant leader, you can still assume responsibility for trying to develop these behaviors on your own so that you will be able to practice them with your followers as you are given the privilege to lead.

A third study involving 815 employees and 123 supervisors found that servant leadership enhanced both the self-efficacy and the commitment to the supervisor of the individual employee (Walumbwa, Hartnel, & Oke, 2010). At the group level, servant leadership led to employees' perception that they were treated fairly (justice climate) and the shared perception that customer service was expected, supported, and rewarded (positive service climate). These individual and group effects combined to produce a significant impact on the organizational citizenship behavior of individual employees.

Employees who are good organizational citizens go above and beyond their formal job descriptions. If everyone in an organization only did what was required of them, the organization would be mediocre at best. Organizational excellence requires a critical mass of employees doing more than what is officially recognized and rewarded. The extant research has demonstrated organizational citizenship behavior is strongly associated with employee task performance, organizational productivity, and customer satisfaction.

Servant leaders are seen by their followers as both fair and supportive. This creates a positive climate at work where employees feel enabled to go above and beyond the call of duty to exceed the expectations of customers. This research strongly suggests that practicing servant leadership is one way to encourage this very important behavior from employees.

Taken together, these three recent studies provide very credible empirical support for the efficacy of servant leadership. If you decide to continue to ignore servant leadership, then you must also decide to ignore the evidence that suggests you should be doing the exact opposite. Evidence-based management cannot guarantee success, but it's far superior to anecdotes and hyperbole.

Servant leadership is a demanding approach to leadership. It focuses on both top- and bottom-line results by developing, enabling, and leveraging the organization's most valuable resource, its people. Becoming increasingly resourceful as a leader is a challenging objective in and of itself, not merely a means to an end. Help your people clearly understand what needs to be done and hold yourself accountable for developing them to the point where they are autonomous performers who only call on you and others when they need your help to obtain a resource they don't control or need to acquire a new skill to take their performance to the next level.

If your people don't trust you, there is no way they are going to be able to deliver the type of performance that will grow your business. You are *not* entitled to the trust of your people—you have to *earn* it by the way you behave toward them. Your people need to believe that you are competent *and* that you care. If you are not happy with how your team is perform-ing, before you blame any single team member, take a good look in the mirror and ensure your leadership is worthy of their trust.

References and Resources

Hu, J., and R.C. Liden. (2011). Antecedents of Team Potency and Team Effectiveness: An Examination of Goal and Process Clarity and Servant Leadership. *Journal of Applied Psychology, 96*(4), 851–862.

Liden, R.C., Wayne, S.J., Zhao, H., and D. Henderson. (2008). Servant Leadership: Development of a Multidimensional Measure and a Multi-level Assessment. *The Leadership Quarterly, 19*(2), 161–177.

Schaubroeck, J., Lam, S.S.K., and A.C. Peng. (2011). Cognition-based and Affect-based Trust as Mediators of Leader Behavior Influences on Team Performance. *Journal of Applied Psychology, 96*(4), 863–871.

Walumbwa, F.O., Hartnel, C.A., and A. Oke. (2010). Servant Leadership, Procedural Justice Climate, Service Climate, Employee Attitudes, and Organizational Citizenship Behavior: A Cross-level Investigation. *Journal of Applied Psychology, 95*(3), 517–529.

About the Author

Bret Simmons, PhD, is a management professor at the University of Nevada in Reno where he teaches undergraduate and MBA courses. Bret leads a training company called Sierra Management Research, Inc., and authors a blog called P.O.B., which stands for Positive Organizational Behavior. His research on employee attitudes, personality, perfor-mance, and health has been published in a number of peer-reviewed journals and books. Bret's website and blog can be found at www.bretlsimmons.com.

Chapter 7

Two Good Things About Cats and Eight More Perspectives for Results

Randy Boek

Editor's Note

Randy is one of those guys who can observe managers and leaders in action and see what they need to do to get to the next level of performance. He has been there, done that, and has gotten the shirt. In this chapter, Randy offers managers an honest look at ways they can continue to grow and makes the case for why we should. I love this chapter because it does a good job of answering, "What's it all about?"

Results through others—it is a simple concept of few words. It ought to be easier and more satisfying. Yet the inherent challenges cause both metaphorical and literal dogs to get kicked daily. Some call it leadership. Some call it management. It is a unique alchemy that moves seamlessly from one to the other at any point in time on any day. Some believe that at a granular level, leadership is about people and management about stuff (Bennis, 1994). To achieve results through others requires both. The term *leader* will be used herein as the catchall word to define the work of being the person in charge, the boss, the team leader, or the place where the buck stops for a specific group of people.

Leadership is the solution to what ails us, and we are seriously ailed in America at this point—largely due to leadership failure in both the private and public sectors. Amid a parade of hucksters and PR machine celebrity CEOs, we mentally sort the wheat from the chaff in determining credibility. Bernie Madoff, Dennis Koslowski, and Jeffrey Skilling go to prison. Richard Branson builds great companies with good people providing great service. Bill Gates and Steve Jobs build companies that change the world. Behind the scenes—and in no small part supporting and making possible the monumental success of great CEOs—is a legion of shop-floor to top-floor leaders who make it happen every day.

Getting business results through others can and should be easier and more satisfying. If leadership is the solution to what ails us, it should follow then that developing other leaders is a primary accountability of every leader regardless of level in the business. The ideal and reality are not always aligned, yet there is a great example where an ethic established in the first part of the 20th century created an enduring foundation at General Electric. Jack Welch built his success and celebrity CEO status on that foundation created by a great and largely unsung leader who preceded him.

Thomas Edison invented the light bulb, and from that Charles Coffin (1892–1912) invented General Electric. Inherent in that were two social innovations that established the foundation for Welch's success—research laboratories and systematic management development. According to leadership guru Jim Collins, calling GE "the house that Jack built" isn't quite accurate. In a *Fortune* article about the greatest CEOs of all time, he write, "In fact Welch was as much a product of GE as vice-versa" (Collins, 2003).

Commonly, people end up in a leadership role as a result of good performance in a technical or functional role. Produce persistently good sales numbers and you become the sales manager. Innovate, meet deadlines, and get along well with colleagues and you become the director of engineering. Do well on the production line and the tap on the shoulder moves you to production manager. In some cases these people work in an organization where there is a formal leadership training and development program that is consistent and well run.

GE Crotonville is the oldest corporate university in America and illustrates one of the most consistent corporate commitments to developing leaders (Knowledge@Wharton, 2010). The Disney Institute has taken the best practices used in developing internal leaders and made these training programs available around the world to other businesses. Nugget Market is a smaller privately held Northern California business with a creative approach to leadership development. These are unique exceptions, and a level of leadership learning and development that is well beyond the norm. "Toss them in the deep end and see if they can swim" is the more likely scenario for most leaders.

Perspectives for Success

The most effective leaders view the world differently than others. Perspective and beliefs drive behavior. What a leader believes about people, the leader's role, the business, accountability, relationships, the world, power, and position all provide filters that guide interactions and decisions. While position and title might presume a high level of awareness in this area, that is not necessarily the case.

The control freak micromanager who believes people are instruments of production and most are slackers is unlikely to adopt a "leader as coach" approach. Just to be clear, however, there is no sugarcoating here. Leading others is tough business. It is challenging. People disappoint. Objectives may be moving targets. Just when it feels like the next swing will be a home run, the 90-mile-per-hour inside curve ball knocks you to the ground. Like Sinatra said, "That's life."

While leading others is not as important a job as being a mom or dad, for the good of the business, there is no more important role. It is not easy, but it can be easier. It is not always satisfying, but in total it can and should be. Adopt these perspectives and you increase the likelihood.

Understand and Accept the Price of Admission

There are multiple components to this. What's good for the business takes priority over what is best for the individual or the team. Caution here in that there may be multiple views as to what is best for the business, some of which are driven by personal agenda. Best thinking of diverse minds is a good thing, but personal agendas are not necessarily so. A high-performing team can make personal agendas taboo.

Accepting accountability for getting results through others brings with it the accountability for getting good at doing so. The GE, Disney, or Nugget Market level of commitment to your development does not exist in most businesses. The best leaders understand and accept accountability for learning and applying the best and most effective leadership practices—whether or not the company provides or funds it. Regardless of what the business or leaders above do in this arena, the best leaders also coach and mentor the development of others. Remember, the leader's primary accountability is to leverage value and results through others. Accept that and it logically follows that learning something valuable and not passing it on minimizes leverage.

Human Beings, Who Must Produce, Are More Than Instruments of Production

Inherent in this perspective is the commitment to respect the dignity of those led. People will do stupid things, make bad decisions, and make mistakes. So will you. Learn from them and help others do so. In the rare situation when someone's behavior violates ethics and integrity, and demonstrates an unacceptable character flaw, get rid of him or her now. The team expects it. Do it in a way that respects the person's dignity, whether you think he or she has any or not.

Anyone who has worked with a highly competent and effective leader has grown as a result of the experience. "People are doing the best they can, they will do better when they know how" is an adage that has been around awhile in the realm of human development. A good addendum to that quote is that it is the leader's job to help them know how. The best leaders build better human beings, not just better employees. Consider adopting a personal value that everyone who works under your leadership will grow, improve, and be better as a result.

WIIFM Is Always in the Equation

Whether you are the CEO or a shop-floor supervisor, and whether your culture calls people employees, associates, or team members, no one really works for you except you. If you are really good at articulating an exciting vision and inspiring people to want to be a part of it, people will engage with you to help make it happen. Mother Teresa is not on your payroll. WIIFM ("What's in it for me?") is not selfishness, but it is—in reality—the way humans are wired. People engage with a leader to help achieve a vision because they get something out of it for themselves. That something is a different mix of tangibles and intangibles as unique as the individuals on the team. Increasing shareholder return is not where to start, when you're motivating people who are not shareholders. In these times of high unemployment some leaders deceive themselves into thinking, "My people are just happy to have a job." That mentality has a shelf life that is just about over, and the people in the business who sit on that shelf are not likely the best performers. Understand, the unemployment rate for educated professionals and skilled tradespeople hovers around 4.5–5 percent even in what we are still calling a bad economy. The golden rule in the employment relationship was long thought to be that the one with the gold makes the rules. That remains true, yet the best leaders understand that the agreement between employer and employee must be mutually beneficial, and the battle for talent rewrites the rules. Effective leaders, top floor to shop floor, are committed to helping others get what they want in exchange for the blood, sweat, and tears that go into helping the team and business get where it is going.

Your Team Is Not Homogenous yet Must Be in Alignment, Commitment, Focus, and Direction

The fashionable nature of the term *team* has outlived its usefulness. Pretty much every group of people working together in any organization is now referred to as a team. Few actually function as a high-performing team. Immediately shred every one of those lame posters that say, "There is no I in team." Don't dumb down individuality for the sake of team harmony. Give smart people a forum to disagree. Create clarity of mission and a level of trust that makes for productive disagreement so that innovation can emerge from conflict. Learn to lead through conflict to positive results.

There has been big change from the early industrial age Frederick Taylor model that people were instruments of production for a highly structured system and process designed by engineers and managers. Aspects of that model remain as a component of low-level highly repetitive production operations. While remnants of the model remain, high-performing companies have moved beyond.

Peter Drucker and Dr. Edwards Deming led a transition to a more human-centered and collaborative approach focused on accessing and using the best thinking of all people and accurate real-time data in the business to drive constant improvement. Drucker believed that "most of what we call management consists of making it more difficult for people to get their work done."

Daniel Pink is one of the current thought leaders on the topic. In his recent book, *Drive*, he cites a history of research that shows "there is a mismatch in what science knows and what business does to motivate people." From one of Pink's TED presentation slides: As long as the task involved only mechanical skill, bonuses worked as they would be expected: the higher the pay, the better the performance. But once the task called for "even rudimentary cognitive skill," a larger reward "led to poorer performance." Pink (2011) acknowledges fair compensation and benefits as a baseline yet concludes that there are three factors that motivate achievement when any level of cognitive skill is required:

- Autonomy: the urge to direct our own lives.
- Mastery: the desire to get better and better at something that matters.
- Purpose: the yearning to do what we do in service to something bigger than ourselves. Every team member is an individual. One size does not fit all.

Effective Leaders Give Trust

If you believe that trust is one of those "touchy-feely" things that live in the realm of stupid consultant tricks and "Kumbaya" around a campfire, let it go. Trust is a fundamental building block of any group of people effectively working together to achieve something of significance. With the people who are important to your success, trust must be the starting point—not some illusive locked door to which you hold the only key. Trustworthy people who somehow have to earn your trust first have to navigate the unknown territory of your personal baggage—something they can never fully accomplish. The "must earn my trust" mentality cuts both ways. Set your critical business relationships by presuming that others are adversaries rather than allies and you end up on both the giving and receiving ends of negativity. Energy spent trying to earn the boss's trust wastes time, money, and efficiency. When there is no trust on a team, the cost goes way beyond the workday and is greater than just dollars. Building and maintaining a high level of trust on your team is baseline accountability for high performance. That includes dealing with anyone who violates the team's trust.

Adopt the Two Good Things About Cats

The phrase "a cat has nine lives" came from observations of reality. Cats can fall from elevation, land on their feet, and walk away with self-confidence intact. Love them or not, these beasts own a unique combination of agility and resilience.

Things are the same, and then they are not. Last year the team was all under the same roof. The world changed, and then so did the work. Now the work team is geographically dispersed, and the members are an international melting pot comprising people who dress, speak, think, and believe differently. This is as exciting as it is challenging. Leading a product team with members dispersed around the world requires new skills, greater knowledge, and technology. Everything cannot be done virtually, so it also requires more time away from home and family.

We hear it and see it every day. The world is changing faster and in greater magnitude than ever. With those changes comes the fact that what we knew to be true yesterday may not be true tomorrow. These are realities over which we have no control. As a leader you not only have the responsibility that we all have to keep ourselves on the crest of the waves of change, but you also have the responsibility to anticipate emerging factors that require our teams to undo paradigms and related behaviors to succeed in new realities.

If behavior is driven by perspectives or beliefs, it follows that to stay on the crest of waves of change a persistent scrubbing of perspective is in order. Consider stereotypes like

"Generation _____ is lazy, selfish, noncommittal, etc., etc." From the *Wall Street Journal* to nightly news and documentaries, the differences between generations and how we need to change the way we manage as a result is to the point of being white noise. Good people doing great work exist across all generations. Effective leaders know their people as individuals and lead them as such. To do otherwise is lazy leadership. Judge people based on any sort of stereotype and bingo, you will find what you're looking for and in the process make it more difficult for good people to be successful.

"Multitasking is the solution to head count reduction." More with less is an endemic mantra, and in the down economy it went from bad to worse. It is time to stop pretending about head count reduction. The work of three people is not going to be done by one. The math doesn't work; one person still does the work of one. It may be composed of fractions of three, but remember giving 110 percent is hyperbole and getting 300 percent from one person is more than fantasy. Survival mode requires the leader who is caught in the middle to quickly get exceptional at prioritizing, eliminating, saying no, and being able to take a punch or more.

"It's up to me to put out the fire." This may seem expedient, and it can be in the short run. Leaders do it because it's exciting to be where the action is and it's rewarding to jump in, get a quick tangible result, and move on. Gratifying to the leader at the time, this approach is costly to the team. Jump in and make a decision when subordinates disagree and you take over their accountability. They are deprived of the opportunity to learn to make collaborative decisions. Facilitate them through logjams and they learn to do it themselves next time.

Effective leaders are good at anticipating change, adapting, and positioning themselves to succeed quickly and lead their teams to do the same. No matter how good you get at this, leading through changes that are good for the business yet bad for people you care about never gets easier.

The work relationship only works when it works to the mutual advantage of both parties. Not every change you must implement does so. Leadership presumes there are people to lead. It is essential to get clear on the life you want and how your company (and your role within it) is helping you get what you want. Is it helping you move you toward your personal objectives and live the life that is best for you and your family?

Ignore fearmongering and unemployment stats. There are more opportunities out there than you can imagine. You are a professional leader. Remember, leadership is the solution to what ails us, and plenty ails us. There is no job security. When the employment relationship is not overall mutually beneficial, have the courage to make a change, deliberately and on your own terms. There is career security, and it is based on reputation and connection. Build them as well outside of the business as you do within.

Those Who Hold Up a Mirror Have Their Greatest Value When You Don't Like What You See

Self-awareness is in short supply for too many leaders. In some situations self-awareness is inversely proportional to level in the business. Some believe that positional power makes it unnecessary.

It is ironic how bad behavior transcends generations in families. It also does so in management.

Absent any formal training and development, people learn to be managers and leaders based on experiences being managed and led. Some of it is good, valuable, and makes our lives as leaders easier and more satisfying. Other habits, styles, and behaviors are counter-productive and some downright wrong.

Strong self-awareness is a characteristic of the most effective leaders, top floor to shop floor. Take 15 minutes for a deliberate "look in the mirror."

While this two-step approach may seem trite for a serious leader with a business to run, you may well be surprised at the result from taking it seriously.

- Write down every management/leadership behavior that you have been on the receiving end of that was demotivating, disrespectful, abusive, or just wrong.
- Make a commitment to never do any of the things on your list to anyone else.

All bad leadership behavior brings with it justifications and rationalizations. They do not hold water. Lead, follow, or get out of the way. Thomas Paine said it a couple of hundred years ago. Business and military leaders have reused it persistently since. The conjunction is wrong. The accountability to lead is obvious. The need for a leader to follow is less obvious. Powerful leaders can stifle good discussion, idea generation, and decision making just by their presence and strongly held perspectives and opinions. The leader by title is not necessarily the best person to lead a specific discussion or decision-making process.

…or get out of the way. The direction is clear, and the team is aligned and moving forward. Competent team members are running their parts of the business. Don't be the bottleneck that slows things down. For expediency, effectiveness, and agility, most decisions need to be made without you. Trust your team to do so. Stop inserting yourself in the process and stop second-guessing the decisions made by your team. The quality of decisions made without you is a good meter of how well you have set the vision, aligned the team, and established the right parameters.

It is a good thing when your team functions well without you.

Most of us have heard of The Mirror Test. It was developed in 1970 by Gordon Gallup based on Charles Darwin's work with a mirror and apes at a zoo. The intent was to understand if an animal could recognize its reflection as an image of itself.

A high level of self-awareness is a characteristic of the best leaders. Arrogance and fear cloud the mirror.

Fall on Your Sword When You Must

Be a leader long enough, work in enough companies, and rise up to bigger levels of responsibility and sooner or later your courage and integrity will be tested. No moralizing here, just a suggestion that in the reality of business, good leaders do things they wish they hadn't.

Mistakes may or may not be undoable. Dishonesty and compromises of integrity probably are not. Relatively small things like deceiving customers, fudging numbers, and other little white lies, while indicative of low ethics and integrity, do not necessarily or directly harm anyone at the time. It's a big jump from there to insider trading, lying to the SEC, creating phony energy contracts and business entities, or building a Ponzi scheme. Yet the culture that develops under acceptable ethical compromises does not remain static.

Mistrust of corporate America is at an all-time high. The consequences of profound ethical lapses and criminal acts of few business leaders during the last decade have hurt many people and also hurt overall corporate credibility and the economy. Business schools have responded with new approaches and requirements specific to ethics in MBA programs. David A. Garvin, a professor of business administration, describes his Harvard course as "a way to give students a sense of the responsibilities that they will have to all these different stakeholder groups." With shareholders, they'll have to worry about fiduciary responsibilities. With customers, they'll have to consider "information asymmetries" (as Garvin explains it, "Under what circumstances do you need to disclose?"). With employees, students will be educated about treating them fairly. With the public at large, MBAs' responsibilities may be even greater—to deal with issues like child labor and freedom of speech (Epstein, 2010).

Harvard Business School's class of 2009 created an ethics pledge that was signed by 2,500 students.

There is a component of earning the right to lead others that is different and less visible than credentials, accomplishments, and a history of delivering solid business results. Being clear on personal closely held, non-negotiable values is part of earning the right to lead others. When there is not a fit between personal values and corporate values, there are only two choices. Change the values of the business—a tall order even for a CEO, and a monumental challenge yet not quite impossible for a lower-level leader. Work elsewhere now before you end up in a situation that forces the issue. Choose a third option of compromising personal values and it is unlikely that the outcome will be good. More money at too high a price is not ultimately good. For what will you fall on your sword? For John Belushi as Samurai Delicatessen, it was the shame of disappointing a customer (*SNL*, 1975).

Best of Intentions Don't Matter Much

Leadership action is what gets results. The right intentions are a starting point but are of little value absent consistent words and action in alignment with intentions. Tony Hayward of BP was in the media all day every day for weeks until he was deposed during the aftermath of British Petroleum's oil rig catastrophe. He was at the helm of every leader's nightmare. Eleven families who depended on his leadership had lost loved ones on his watch. He was the poster child for what may be the biggest environmental disaster of the century. He made commitments to fix it and compensate those who have lost as a result. He was doing the best that could be done in an impossible situation. Then he started talking.

From his perspective as CEO of a $239 billion business with 80,000 employees in 30 countries, the Gulf is indeed a big ocean, and the amount of oil leaking into it, given the volume of water in the gulf, was tiny. What he said was true. It did not, however, provide any empathy or level of confidence to the people in the Gulf and added to the damage already done to BP's reputation. People heard what was said and reacted before the actions of cleanup and compensation began.

Every day on teams and in day-to-day noncrisis activities of business, people do not hear the message that was intended to be sent, and there are negative consequences. What every leader must keep in top of mind is that communication is the responsibility of the sender. You must meet people where they are to bring them to where you are.

An innovative strategic plan is good intention. When key players are aligned, it gains power. When persistent tactical actions are taken to execute the intention of the strategy, momentum builds, and the actions that match intentions create leverage that moves the team and the business forward.

A leader's mantra might be "I know myself by my intentions, others know me by my actions."

References and Resources

Bennis, Warren. (1994). *On Becoming a Leader.* New York: Perseus Books Group.

Collins, Jim. (2003). The 10 Greatest CEOs of All Time: What These Extraordinary Leaders Can Teach Today's Troubled Executives. *Fortune.* Retrieved from http://money.cnn.com/magazines/fortune/fortune_archive/2003/07/21/346095/index.htm.

Epstein, Jennifer. (May 5, 2010). Economic Crisis Leads Business Schools to Meld Ethics into MBA. *USA Today.* http://www.usatoday.com/news/education/2010-05-05-ihe-mba-business_N.htm.

John Belushi's "Best of – Samurai Delicatessen." *SNL '75.* Retrieved from http://www.youtube.com/watch?v=OxZt4Kxj2cE&feature=related.

Knowledge@Wharton. (May 12, 2010). How Geo Builds Global Leaders: A Conversation with Chief Learning Officer Susan Peters. Retrieved from http://knowledge.wharton.upenn.edu/article.cfm?articleid=2488.

Pink, Daniel. (2011). *Drive: The Surprising Truth About What Motivates Us.* New York: Riverhead Books.

About the Author

Randy Boek is a professional outsider and president of Route 2 Result. He is known for seeing, saying, and doing what insiders can't or won't to improve leaders' effectiveness, results, and satisfaction. Randy is the author of a blog called Outside the Turn. You can find Randy's website at www.route2results.com.

⤜ **Chapter 8**

The Manager's Role in Creating a Learning Culture

Kevin Eikenberry

.... **Editor's Note** ....

Kevin is a guy to watch and read and follow. His instincts about management are spot on, and I love the simple but elegant way he writes about management excellence. In this chapter, Kevin helps us all get grounded and committed to creating a learning culture. Former GE CEO Jack Welch was famous for saying that his (and all leaders') job was to develop talent. Creating a culture where people grow is both a great privilege and a great responsibility for all managers.

The title of this chapter makes a couple of assumptions. Since good managers (and effective human beings) communicate better when they avoid assumptions, let me start by addressing those assumptions right up front. This chapter title assumes:

- you know what a learning culture is
- you know why building one would be a good and valuable thing.

Until you know those two things, talking about or thinking about your role in creating one makes very little sense. So let's start there, shall we?

Learning is an inherent part of being a human being. We all learn something every day. A quick look on Wikipedia tells us that learning is:

> Learning is acquiring new or modifying existing knowledge, behaviors, skills, values, or preferences and may involve synthesizing different types of information.

Let's dissect that definition a bit. *"Learning is acquiring new or modifying existing knowledge, behaviors, skills, values, or preferences."* All of this is true, and all of it relates to learning in the workplace. But when it comes to the workplace, not all learning is created equal, is it?

Values and preferences (sometimes lumped together by learning experts as "attitude") are important because until people are predisposed to or understand and believe in the importance of something, they are less likely to choose to learn more about it.

Knowledge is the basic building block of learning; it is what we most often think about when we think about learning and school (which is what most people think about first when they think about learning—more on that later), but knowledge alone seldom is what is needed at work, is it? What is needed is learning that relates to behaviors and skills. How can we get people to learn (and perform) new behaviors and skills? After all, even if we "believe in" and "know" something, isn't it behavior or action in the end that will make a difference in workplace performance?

Learning " ... may involve synthesizing different types of information." In the workplace, there is no "may" about it. To create the kind of learning that will make a difference for individuals and therefore an organization, we must synthesize and use different types of information from different sources, at different times, to create the kind of learning necessary to make a difference.

But let's get past a relatively academic definition of learning, shall we?

I often ask groups of people to think about their best learning experiences in life. I encourage them to think about any time they felt they learned valuable and important information or skills in a powerful and lasting way. I'd like you to do that too.

Think of such an experience now. It can be recent or long ago, it can be about personal or professional things, or it can be any experience—there are no wrong answers here.

And write it down here (participation will make this a more valuable learning experience for you—I'll wait—you have time).

My experience: _____

Now that you have identified a time, write down three things that made it such a good learning experience and so valuable to you (not the lesson or learning itself, but why or how learning it that way was so valuable and memorable). If you think of more, go for it!

_____

_____

_____

_____

_____

I (obviously) don't know what you wrote or thought about. Having done this exercise many times though, a number of important factors about effective learning show up over and over. An important short list includes:

- Learning is active. The best learning happens when the learner is actively involved in the process (as opposed to sitting and passively listening to a lecture).
- Learning is a process. Very few people identify a school or training situation as their best learning experience (but it is OK if you did). Why? Because while school or a training workshop can be the spark or an "aha," real learning happens over time—through practice and application, not in an instant. (Much more on this later, I promise.)
- Learning is emotional. Our most powerful learning experiences have an emotional component. They created joy or were borne from fear. They may have been painful or exciting experiences. Learning is a human endeavor, and people are emotional creatures—there must be space for emotion in learning (yes, even at work).
- Learning is self-directed. We learn best when we have a say in how we learn, what we learn, and when we learn. Giving people this voice and the ability to choose and create their learning makes it far more powerful.
- Learning is practical. Especially in the realm of workplace learning, but really in all cases, people must see relevance to them in what they are learning. The best learning helps people use what they have learned to make their life or their circumstances in some way better.

Learning is one of those "motherhood and apple pie" words. Everyone believes in learning. Have a conversation with a bunch of managers and talk about learning and all will nod their heads about the importance of it and talk about why it matters in their organization. Unfortunately, far too often that acknowledgement of importance is as far as it goes; the reality is that far too infrequently, intentional, strategic learning is going on inside of organizations.

I guess if that weren't the case, this chapter wouldn't be necessary, now would it?

Culture

Organizational culture is something we don't usually talk about, but we feel every day. A culture is defined by what is expected of people and what is valued in a given group or setting. It defines the norms of behavior and "how things are done" in an organization—whether that organization is a country, a community, a team, a business, or a family.

To be successful in any setting, it is important to understand the culture. This understanding allows us to navigate successfully through our day, be less stressed and frustrated, and instead be more confident and productive. Culture is important because it defines the boundaries of behavior and performance, which allow us to produce rather than discuss "how" to do everything. Culture becomes a shorthand way to get things done.

Cultures often develop from people's early experiences in an organization, and over time these experiences become the unspoken "rules of the road." This is natural and usually works fine, except that sometimes what naturally develops or evolves isn't exactly what we, as managers, might want those "rules" to be. While they may have worked in the past, now they no longer serve the organization very well.

Putting Them Together

Here is some simple math: Learning + Culture = Learning Culture.

As you can surmise from the previous section, there is a culture in your organization that tells people what to expect regarding training and development, the purpose and importance of it, how supportive managers are of those they lead, how much support people are given to grow into new roles, how often people are internally promoted and become successful in their new roles, and much more.

One effective way to gauge a culture is to listen to the stories that are told in the organization.

Specifically for this chapter, what kinds of things do people talk about regarding attending training, receiving coaching, the support and encouragement people get, and more? These stories, even (and maybe especially) the informal ones, will tell you a lot about your learning culture and literally "how things are done around here."

You and Your Learning Culture

Perhaps you are waiting for me to get to the point. Perhaps you are ready for a checklist or some specific things to do (don't worry, they are coming), but don't move on so quickly that you miss what you've already read—because I know what you might be thinking (because I've heard it a hundred times before).

You are thinking: Since these rules develop gradually and become deeply engrained, what do we do if we want to change them?

But what are you really thinking is, "Kevin, I get this—but I can't change culture—that is the C-Suite's job. After all, they are in charge of the organization—if something about the culture is holding the organization back, they should be responsible for fixing it."

This is a logical assessment, but woefully limited in application. In reality, the culture doesn't belong to a CEO or a senior manager. It belongs to everyone. And while there are cultural norms that spread across an entire organization, there are often differences within a department, a work group, or a geographical region.

Perhaps there are things in your organization's learning culture that you would like to change. If so, great—because you can influence it.

So if the culture belongs to everyone, what can you do to change it for the better?

What role can you play as a manager and as an individual?

High-Level Actions

Here are five specific actions you can take to start influencing your learning culture.

- **Have a clear picture of what you desire.** If, for example, you want to build an environment more conducive to people trying new things (in other words, learning), you need to be able to describe what you are looking for—not just think you will know it when you see it. Getting a clearer picture of what learning means in your situation is critical to you successfully adjusting the culture.

- **Understand the benefits of the change.** You need to see the benefits clearly so that you will stay motivated to change, but also because others won't change without understanding why. Define benefits organizationally and personally.
- **Communicate with others.** Once you have a clear picture of what and why, it is time to help others see your new picture. How can you expect them to help you change the culture through their actions, and buck the trend of "how things are done" if they don't see a better way?
- **Model the new behavior.** Want the culture to be different? It starts with you. Gandhi said, "We must be the changes we want to see in the world." These five steps form a specific plan that you can use to create the changes you want to see. But this fourth step is critical—you must embody and personify the new cultural norms yourself.
- **Begin to expect it of others.** Unfortunately, this won't be as easy as flipping a light switch. It will take some time for people to get onboard with a change even if they agree that it's a positive step. You start by encouraging them, supporting successful change, and recognizing progress.

You can do these things regardless of your organizational level. Start small (like with yourself). Then expand it to those immediately around you. If you are a shift supervisor, your actions won't affect the culture of your multinational employer overnight, but they can begin to positively change your immediate work environment. Regardless of your role, you can positively affect the culture in which you work, but only if you are willing to stand up and be accountable.

Don't shrug your shoulders; do roll up your sleeves. You are a co-owner of your organization's culture, and you can make a difference.

Learning vs. Training

All of this learning stuff seems well and good, but aren't we really talking about training here? I mean, isn't training the key cog in the learning machine in any organization?

I'm glad you asked.

Training is a specific, time-honored, and traditional way to create learning. Training (including seminars, conferences, workshops, and webinars) is an effective way to transfer knowledge. Training events are a critical part of your learning strategy and culture. And…

Remember your best learning experience earlier? It likely didn't happen in a traditional training setting. Why? Because training is an event and learning is a process. We learn (especially skills and behaviors) through practice and application, which rarely can be completed, or completed completely, in a training setting.

So learning is our goal as a manager, and training is just one of our tools. But since training is a very important tool, let's get tactical and talk about what you can do as a manager to improve the results and the return on your training investment.

How You Can Influence Training's Return-on-Investment

People often talk about increasing the return-on-investment for training, and generally, most people point to others to be responsible for that return, or measure that return. The reality is that there are three groups and one other factor that have significant impact on that rate of return, and they work together like the four legs on a chair. Like a chair, when any of them are weakened, the chair is less safe (or in our case, ROI is damaged), but if a leg is missing completely, watch out!

The Four Legs

Since discussing each of the four legs of training's ROI chair in detail goes far beyond the scope of this chapter, let's just identify them and talk about how they relate to you as a manager.

- **The trainer:** The trainer is responsible for what is delivered (and available to be learned), the environment, and the process for how it is delivered.
- **The learner:** The learner is responsible for being open to the learning, looking for ways to apply it, and taking action to apply the material.
- **The manager:** The manager is responsible for helping the learners see the value, holding learners accountable, and much more.
- **The culture and working environment:** The culture and working environment affects everyone's behavior, attitude, and performance in subtle and not-so-subtle ways.

While one of these people is you, as a manager you also have significant influence over the work environment as well, as we have already discussed.

The bottom line? When it comes to increasing the ROI of your training investment, stop blaming others and look in the mirror. Once you've realized that, what can you do?

Here are eight actions you can take that will have both an immediate and a long-term impact on the return on all your training investments.

- **Pick the right experience.** Know what the learning objectives of the workshop or learning event are—and match the workshop with the needs of the individual.

This may take some work for both you and the individual, and that time is worth it. Sending people "just because" or "because it sounds good" or even "because they asked" likely isn't enough. If you want intentional and strategic learning, make sure you are sending people to the right experience for the right reasons at the right time.

- **Talk to people before they go.** Discuss their goals (make sure they have goals for the learning experience) and let them know your expectations of application. Before this meeting is over, set up a time after the training to get back together to discuss it. This time spent up front helps them glean more from the experience and sends an important cultural message about how training and learning are viewed by you.

- **Meet with people after they return.** Have people share what they learned and what actions they plan to take. Find out what you can do to support their learning and application, and again, set up expectations for implementation.

- **Have the learner teach others.** Remember, too, that a great way to learn things is to teach them to others. This is a great way to solidify learning and take ownership of it. Having your employees share what they learned with you is great; but if there are people in the organization who could gain from what the others have learned, encourage a more formal sharing in a lunch-and-learn, webinar, question-and-answer session, or even a report sent to others.

- **Follow up.** Follow up on their learning and actions—hold them accountable. Be encouraging and supportive of their growth and application.

- **Monitor the work environment and culture.** Think about how people will be viewed and supported when they come back from any learning experience and try something new. If you aren't pleased with your observations, start influencing change today. In the interim, if you must, run interference for people or help them remove the barriers that will keep them from applying what they are learning.

- **Set overall expectations for application and growth.** This goes beyond a single person and a single training investment. As a manager, let people know that you expect them to learn from training and apply what they've learned. Let people know that mistakes and bobbles are OK if they are in the pursuit of improvement.

- **Support all learning and development.** As we have said, not all learning takes place in a workshop, and not all learning requires an investment of dollars. You increase your overall ROI when you encourage and support learning both formally and informally, all the time.

Oh, and one more idea (it's number nine if you are counting):

- **Be a learner yourself.** The most direct thing you can do, and the thing you have 100 percent control over, is to model the behavior of being a learner, and applying what you learn! This includes letting your team members know what you are trying to improve and asking for their feedback and support, being open about your mistakes, and consistently working to improve your behavior, skills, and performance. While all the other items are important, if you start here, you will be more powerful than you might think.

Please don't underestimate the power of this last point. In the end, culture change comes from actions, not words. When people see you as a learner—through attending training at times—but more than that, when they see you as curious, willing to try new things, willing to share a mistake, or talking about a book or article you read (or person you met), you are sending a very important message.

Some Final Thoughts

If you read back over or even just think about the arc of this chapter, you will notice we started out talking about learning and a learning culture, but seemed to end with practical things you can do as a manager to improve training results.

Didn't I say that training and learning are not the same thing, and that training is an event and learning is a process? Yes, I did (and I just reviewed those key ideas for you—an effective learning strategy itself). Now look at the last nine tips again. While the context of them is about "attending training," the sum total of the list is converting a training event into a learning process.

That statement is the biggest key to your role in creating a learning culture, in creating a place where people are productively learning and growing to become ever more valuable as employees. Your job is to create learning opportunities and provide for and support people in applying what they learn. When you do that, you will be fulfilling one of the most critical roles you can as a manager.

About the Author

Kevin Eikenberry is the leading expert in creating remarkable leaders, a bestselling author, speaker, trainer, consultant, and the Chief Potential Officer of The Kevin Eikenberry Group. You can learn more about the work of his team at http://KevinEikenberry.com. To receive an electronic copy of his *101 Ways to Unleash Your Remarkable Potential* go to http://kevineikenberry.com/uypw/index.asp.

Chapter 9

Managing Scenario Projects

Thomas Chermack, PhD

.... **Editor's Note** ....

I wanted to have a chapter in this book that explored scenario planning in a way that is useful to managers, because I think that today's business climate requires us all to get better at it. What is scenario planning? Here's how Tom Chermack describes it: "Scenario planning is a discipline for building alternative futures in which decisions can be played out for the purposes of changing thinking, improving decision making; fostering individual, team, and organizational learning; and improving performance. Scenario planning differs from strategic planning in that it gives up the assumption that the environment will stay the same." Managers are the engines for our organizations and need to manage scenario projects. Tom wrote the book on scenario planning and agreed to share a chapter of it here.

Introduction

The purpose of this chapter is to provide recommendations for helping you manage scenario projects. The skills and abilities required to make scenario projects work are diverse, and improve over time and experience. The nature of scenario work avoids specific procedures that are repeated in each project. However, scenario projects do lend themselves to frameworks (such as the phases presented in this book). ("Managing Scenario Projects" is an excerpt from the book *Scenario Planning in Organizations.*) In addition, there are several strategies I have learned from making my own mistakes, and from hearing about others. These insights from my own practice are followed by the presentation of 20 scenario pitfalls presented in the scenario planning literature (Schoemaker, 2005). These pitfalls are summarized and accompanying solutions are also provided. Therefore, this chapter is intended to serve as a guide, providing a few key leverage points for getting the most out of scenario projects.

Managing Scenario Projects

Scenario projects have many dimensions and need to be thoughtfully managed. Important strategies for managing scenario projects include:

- spending time on the problem, issue or question
- recognizing the importance of the team
- spending time on analysis
- defining important outcomes
- using internal and external forces in the scenario matrix
- putting your scenarios to use
- assessing your impact
- recognizing an evolving context.

These activities are suggested as important pieces of the scenario system, and when paid attention to, can help your scenario project stay on track, and deliver results. Each is described in detail.

Spend Time on the Problem, Question, or Issue

How the scenario project is framed influences everything. The initial problem, question, or issue must be referenced repeatedly throughout the project. The more specific you can be about the issue at the outset, the easier it is to consistently address that issue throughout. However, it is useful to keep in mind that initial scenarios are usually general "learning" scenarios that explore the external environment. So, if your organization is new to scenario planning, it is very useful to design a first set of scenarios focused on a general understanding of the external environment. Using these scenarios as context, you can then move into a second set of scenarios focused on a specific issue. This approach will allow thinking to sharpen on a specific issue and design a set of scenarios specifically to illuminate the problem. Because this second set of scenarios is highly focused, the project will be easier to assess, and is likely to have a more lasting impact on decision making.

If an organization is already using general level scenarios, a project team can jump directly into the "decision" scenarios. Thus, moving straight to the problem, question, or issue, and working directly on it.

The importance of spending time on the problem, question, or issue cannot be overstated. Having a specific issue creates boundaries for the project. Given the volatility, uncertainty, complexity, and ambiguity of the business environment, there will be difficulties enough in steering a project designed to "promote organizational learning." Such a general focus is not easily assessed. The more specific the focus of the scenario project can be, the more easily it can be assessed, and the pressure for specific assessment data can vary across organizations.

The importance of specifying a problem, question, or issue is intimately related to how decision makers view the utility of the project. Organizations using scenario planning as a one-time effort usually result in project failures. These failures are due to the generation of contextual learning scenarios that do not offer enough specifics for managers to exercise their judgment.

Recognize the Importance of the Team

The right team is critical to the success of any scenario project. Team members can provide valuable information about the history, context, issues, personalities, and politics. Therefore, teams must include members internal to the organization. Critical functions of the team include the administrative management of the project; keeping the initial problem, question, or issue central to the work done in the project; gathering relevant information; conducting research; and facilitating workshops. The team should also be multi-level, and cross-functional.

My own failure to recognize the importance of the team in an early scenario project is an example. I did not assign anyone as the project coordinator. As a result, workshops and meetings were poorly attended because there was nobody internal to the organization coordinating the various events and communicating the details of the projects among team members.

Another example from my own projects involved having someone assigned to the team who was looking to sabotage the project. While this does not happen often, organization politics can come into play. Team membership should be negotiated. The more committed, excited, and motivated the team members, the more likely the outcomes will meet and exceed the expectations of decision makers.

Spend Time on Analysis

Analysis activities allow the team to understand the problem, question, or issue in its context. Analysis activities should not be shortcut, or reduced to save project costs. This is a critical phase in the scenario system as it establishes what is known about the issue. Forecasts and trend reports can often be used as a substitute for thinking on the part of the user and therefore, the goal of analysis and the scenario Exploration Phase is to generate the team's own understanding and thinking about the problem, question, or issue.

Projects that reduce time and commitment to the Exploration Phase have little impact. This is because the workshops and subsequent phases are tailored to what is learned during analysis and scenario exploration. As is the case with any organization improvement activity, everything rests on this foundational work. I have seen projects in which little time is given to understanding the issue, and these projects have generally lacked the momentum for significant impact.

Define Important Outcomes

One key to making scenarios work is having an idea of what the expectations are. While these expectations can become a moving target, the more that is known about what decision makers hope to get out of the project, the more the project can be tailored to address those expectations. Some managers and executives are comfortable with ambiguity and vague outcomes like "continuous learning about the industry," but the vast majority will have specific desired outcomes in mind. Ask for them.

My own experience has told me that the type of organization matters as well. For example, scenario projects I have worked on with engineering firms have had specific, targeted outcomes. These projects have also required more effort to stimulate strategic thinking than working with design teams in technology driven industries. In other words, organization culture and personality can drive an orientation toward more specific or more ambiguous outcomes.

Using Internal and External Forces in the Scenario Matrix

The scenario matrix is built of two items high on "potential impact" and "uncertainty" from the brainstorming and ranking workshops. If these two items are external to the organization, the scenarios will by definition, be contextual scenarios or "learning" scenarios. One strategy that immediately brings the scenarios closer to the organization is to include one internal item, and one external item. This strategy automatically gives the scenarios a more familiar and relevant feel, and decision makers can see a critical uncertainty that they have some influence upon.

I have used this technique myself and found it useful in that it is observably easier for managers to see themselves inside the scenarios. Colleague Louis van der Merwe has also used this approach when there was a need to bring the scenarios closer to the organization, and there was not time for two separate rounds of scenario development (one external for macro scenarios, and one internal for a focused issue). This approach can be considered when time is short, but is not ideal, and should not be considered a substitute for two separate rounds of scenario development. Remember—people learn throughout the scenario system and the learning drives the development of strategic thinking.

Put Your Scenarios to Use

Perhaps the most common reason for disappointment in scenario projects is a lack of use. So many consulting companies now provide scenario planning interventions, yet few boast anything beyond developing scenarios for their client organizations. The development of scenarios can be highly creative and fun, but using them should be the most rewarding phase. The amount of time and effort spent on scenario development should be mirrored in scenario consideration.

This book provides a framework for using scenarios. Specific workshops have been described with guidance for making them work. Communicating and using the scenarios is the opportunity to begin an organization-wide strategic conversation. This conversation can be the catalyst for real change inside the organization. Do not let the delivery of three or four scenarios be the end of your project. You must use them to challenge thinking within and across the organization.

Assess Your Impact

Most scenario projects lack assessment or evaluation. How do decision makers know they are getting anything for their investment? Some claim to simply "know." Particularly in lean economic times (although equally important anytime), organization change interventions must have documentation of their delivered outcomes. This book has laid out a comprehensive approach to scenario project assessment. The proposed activities take time and resources. However, if carried out, these assessment techniques will make the case that scenario planning is easily worth every penny invested.

If you have experience with other assessment tools, use them. The purpose is to begin establishing evidence that scenario planning works. Scenario planning literature is full of claims about decision making, learning, and navigating the future, but little evidence is provided to support these claims. Most scenario planners could tell you stories of their successes or failures, which may constitute a form of evidence; however, few document these stories. These stories, while helpful, are not always compelling to financially driven executives. Scenario projects should include a cost-benefit analysis. Even if the figures it contains are estimates or forecasts, they should be included. The Scenario System presented in this book demands that you assess the projected financial benefits of the project at the outset. Following up at the conclusion of the project and beyond should be a simple exercise in collecting a few pieces of relevant data.

Recognize an Evolving Context

A very exciting aspect of scenario planning is the increasing variety of contexts in which it is being used. The Mont Fleur Scenarios (Kahane, 1992) were the first examples of using the scenario planning technique in a non-corporate context. The Mont Fleur Scenarios brought together a diverse group of business leaders, politicians, civil rights activists, artists, and others concerned with the future of South Africa. Their scenario efforts were aimed at building a community sharing a vision for a better South Africa. Adam Kahane was the primary facilitator and was previously the head of planning at Shell. Kahane has since focused his efforts more carefully in this area, moving on to scenarios for Colombia.

These projects (and particularly the Mont Fleur Scenarios) were a clear signal that scenarios could be useful beyond corporate planning. Part group decision-making process, part team building, part visioning, part analysis, among others, it is easy to see that the scenario system can apply in a variety of contexts. The world in general features the same characteristics (volatility, uncertainty, complexity, and ambiguity) as the business environment, and tools for thinking differently about the future can be applied to problems related to global climate change, health care, water supply, ecology, and other natural resources.

Additional Pitfalls (and Accompanying Solutions)

Twenty common pitfalls in scenario planning were described by Schoemaker (2005). In this section, the pitfalls along with corresponding solutions are presented. The 20 common pitfalls in scenario planning are divided into 10 process pitfalls and 10 content pitfalls. While there is some overlap with the strategies for managing scenario projects presented above, they will all be presented to keep the integrity of Schoemaker's list.

10 Process Pitfalls

The first 10 pitfalls are specifically related to managing the scenario project process (Schoemaker, 2005). These pitfalls are results of an inability to understand the nuances related to facilitating scenario projects, and the administrative side of directing, managing, and steering scenario projects.

Failure to ensure top leadership support. Any organization change intervention must have leadership support in order to be successful. Scenario planning is an executive-level activity, so if the executives aren't involved—forget it!

Not enough contribution from outside. The dangers of groupthink (too much homogeneity in the thinking) are ever present with scenario planning. Using outside sources—"remarkable people" or experts in a variety of disciplines—pays significant dividends (Wack, 1985). In my experience, each project should make use of a minimum of two external experts. The more participants involved in the project, the more external experts should be sought.

Lack of balance between line and staff people. A basic feature of scenario planning is that it must involve a cross-section of the organization. That includes levels and functions. If it doesn't, it's not scenario planning. Make sure each function in the organization is represented in the conversation.

Unrealistic expectations. This pitfall is avoided by clarifying expectations and documenting them in the scenario project proposal. Expectations should be clarified before any exploration or development work is begun.

Poorly defined roles. The scenario project proposal also demands the identification of team members and clarification of roles. The importance of this issue has been discussed thoroughly, but cannot be overstated.

Failure to keep on track. Again, the scenario project proposal demands the articulation of a strategic problem, issue, or question. Clearly defining this issue, and consistently coming back to it, is critical to success.

Too many scenarios. Do not use more than four scenarios. The system presented in this book is designed to produce four useful scenarios. Having more than four scenarios is overwhelming for decision makers and complicates the project.

Not enough time allowed. The scenario project proposal calls for an agreed upon timeline. If decision makers expect to complete a scenario project with two workshops in two weeks, explain the consequences and conditions required for thinking strategically. If they insist, an alternative is to suggest a different facilitator. It is important to be ready to remove yourself from projects that are set up to fail. Shortcutting with an unrealistic timeframe is a sure path to disappointing and low-utility outcomes.

Failure to link to existing processes. The scenario system presented connects scenario development to the organization through several workshops. Those workshops are specifically designed to link the scenario project to various existing processes inside the organization, including organization culture, structure, current strategies, human resources, design, and others.

Failure to link to our everyday world. Scenarios have to be relevant for the managers who will use them. Projects that fail to capture the things that managers are concerned with in their everyday decision making will have little impact. An effective way to overcome this pitfall is to use information gathered in the interviews and make sure it appears in the scenarios. The interview questions described in the scenario Exploration Phase are designed to draw out the things managers worry about in their roles as organizational leaders. If these items appear in the scenarios, relevance is increased that will catch the users' attention.

10 Content Pitfalls

The following 10 pitfalls are related to the content in the scenarios themselves (Schoemaker, 2005). Again, solutions are suggested based on the system provided in this book.

Failure to take the long view. Scenario projects should look ahead five, 10, or 20 years to stimulate creative thinking. The goal is to get participants into a space that is truly unknown to them. Targeting scenarios within a year or two is often too close to managers' mindsets, and their scenarios will often be extrapolations of their current thinking and their own understanding of trends.

Failure to take the wide view. Scenarios have to expand beyond your own industry. Given the complexity of today's business environment, it is difficult to see how an honest look at any issue would fail to link it to numerous other issues in a variety of industries. Thus, the Scenario Exploration Phase provides the tools for analyzing issues in their context, revealing their interdependencies.

Too much attention to trends. Trends are often used as a substitute for real thinking. Trends are not a viable shortcut to deep analysis and the development of real knowledge. Trends are a part of the scenario exploration phase, and should be considered. If allowed to dominate, however, trends can derail the development of understanding.

Too homogeneous a range of views. Again, using "remarkable people" or experts outside the organization from different industries can prevent this pitfall. Diversity of thinking is important, and one signal that views are too homogeneous is when meetings and workshops are completed quickly, with minimal dialogue or challenge. This can be an indicator of a very efficient team of people who work well together, but as the project leader, it may be a signal for you to bring in a different perspective.

Lack of internal logic. Scenarios are not compelling when they are not based on facts and research. This is why "scenario light" projects, based on concepts and ideas and without deep analysis, are so often useless.

Failure to look at deeper-level causes, failure to challenge mindsets, and failure to make the scenarios dynamic. These three scenario pitfalls are attributable to the fact that there are no methods or systems available for checking the utility of any given set of scenarios. This book presents a scenario quality checklist designed to promote deep analysis, optimize the likelihood of changing mindsets, and ensure dynamic, compelling scenario stories. Using a checklist like this, or developing your own, and asking for the input of the team to make sure these items are addressed will help you avoid these issues.

Irrelevance. Again, using information from interviews with managers will immediately bring the scenarios to their doorstep. Obviously, having people for whom the scenarios must be relevant involved in the process is critical.

Failure to create a real breakthrough. This pitfall signals an overarching problem with most scenario planning methods. What is a breakthrough? Existing methods don't push for a defined purpose, goals, or expected outcomes of the scenario project. So a breakthrough is a nebulous, undefined, and in most cases random event. True, there must be room in the scenario project for things unplanned to emerge (Mintzberg, Ahlstrand, & Lampel, 2005). However, breakthroughs can also be outcomes of deep, disciplined thinking about, and critical analysis of strategic issues. The system presented in this book is designed to optimize scenario projects toward articulated purposes, expected outcomes, and deep thinking.

Conclusion

Most of the pitfalls in scenario projects can be avoided by using the scenario system presented in this book. The Scenario Project Management Worksheet (Figure 9-1) is designed to make the scenario system immediately applicable, and help translate the concepts presented in this book to any organization. The worksheet is designed to help plan, structure, and manage the phases of performance-based scenario planning, and can be used as a guide throughout the project for avoiding the common problems in scenario projects that have been discussed.

Figure 9-1. Scenario Project Management Worksheet

Scenario Project Management Worksheet

This sheet is a general guide for planning and managing scenario projects and can be used as an organizational guide and project management checklist. There are a total of five phases to the performance-based scenario system.

Phase 1—Project Preparation Phase

Defined Problem, Question, or Issue: _____

Stated Purpose of the Project: _____

Project Scope and Timeline: _____

Roles and People Assigned:

    Project Leader: _____   Coordinator: _____

    Remarkable People: _____

    Team Members: _____

    Other: _____

Expected Outcomes of the Project: _____

Measurement Tools: _____

Phase 1—Project Preparation Phase Pitfall Management

Is top leadership participating in the project? _____

Are remarkable people recruited to participate in the project? _____

Is there balance between line and staff participants? _____

Is the timeline realistic given the expectations? _____

Does the project link to existing processes? _____

Will the project address fundamental issues in organization management? _____

Phase 2—Scenario Exploration Phase

A. External Analysis: (check those that apply)

    ☐ STEEP Forces

    ☐ Thinking Hats

    ☐ Trends and Forecasts

    ☐ Other: _____

B. Internal Analysis:

❏ Interviews (list interview participants):

_____

_____

_____

_____

_____

❏ Analyze the Business Idea

❏ Analyze the Theory of the Business

C. Analysis and Synthesis Tools Used:

❏ Questionnaires

❏ Observations

❏ Existing Data: _____

❏ Swanson's Performance Diagnosis Matrix

❏ Rummler and Brache's Nine Performance Variables

❏ Other Analysis and Synthesis Tools:

_____

_____

D. Analysis is thorough and demonstrates our own understanding of the problem or issue.

_____ Yes _____ No

Phase 2—Scenario Exploration Phase Pitfall Management

Scenarios extend 5, 10, 15, or 20 years into the future? _____

Other industries included in the analysis and scenarios? _____

Trends are included, but do not dominate? _____

Phase 3—Scenario Development Phase

A. Workshop Planning (Dates):

Brainstorming _____

Ranking by Impact _____

Ranking by Relative Uncertainty _____

B. Two Critical Uncertainties (High Impact + High Uncertainty) for the Scenario Matrix:

1 _____   2 _____

C. Draft Scenario Matrix:

D. Research Agenda (elements that require more data gathering and investigation):

_____
_____
_____
_____
_____
_____

E. Draft Scenario Titles / Themes / Possibilities:

_____ _____ _____
_____ _____ _____
_____ _____ _____
_____ _____ _____
_____ _____ _____
_____ _____ _____

F. Plots:

Suggestions:

____ Revolution

____ Cycles

____ Infinite Possibility

____ Lone Ranger

____ My Generation

Other:_____

G. Story Writing (name(s) of individual(s) to write each scenario):

1 _____ 2 _____

3 _____ 4 _____

H. Communication Strategy:

☐ Workbook ☐ Podcasts

☐ Website ☐ Presentations

☐ Video ☐ Workshops

☐ Activities: _____

☐ Other: _____

Phase 3—Scenario Development Phase Pitfall Management

Four scenarios (if other, check for novelty–avoid best/worst)? _____ _____

Scenarios have input from external experts? _____ _____

Scenarios are logical and well researched? _____ _____

Scenarios include deep analysis and are data driven? _____ _____

Phase 4—Scenario Implementation Phase

A. Workshop Planning for Using the Scenarios (dates):

Revisit the Initial Problem/Question _____

Theory of the Business _____

Business Idea _____

Analyze Current Strategies _____

Developing Signals _____

Experiential Exercise _____

B. Outcomes:
    Key Strategies Useful in All Scenarios:

    1 _____   2 _____

    3 _____   4 _____

    Signals:

    _____

    _____

    _____

    _____

Phase 4—Scenario Implementation Phase Pitfall Management

Scenarios are interesting and relevant for managers? _____

Scenarios can create a real breakthrough? _____

Phase 5—Project Assessment Phase

	Quantitative	Qualitative
Satisfaction Results		
Participant	Survey (10 items, strongly agree to strongly disagree)	Interview Questions:
Stakeholder	Survey (10 items, strongly agree to strongly disagree)	Interview Questions:
Learning Results		
Knowledge	Survey 1. _____ 2. _____ 3. _____ 4. _____ 5. _____ 6. _____	Interview Questions:
Expertise	Observations of behaviors where appropriate using the Scenario Expertise Audit (who will be observed?) 1. _____ 2. _____ 3. _____ 4. _____ 5. _____ 6. _____	Interview Questions:

Performance Results		
System	Estimates of system results based on the initial purpose of the project	Interview Questions:
Financial	Performance Value – Cost = Benefit Estimates of discontinuities avoided Estimates of profits due to strategic insights	Interview Questions:

This chapter has presented key issues in managing scenario projects. The guidance provided is largely a result of my own experience in designing, managing, and facilitating scenario projects. These issues were:

1. spending time on the problem, issue, or question
2. recognizing the importance of the team
3. spending time on analysis
4. defining important outcomes
5. using internal and external forces in the scenario matrix
6. putting your scenarios to use
7. assessing your impact
8. recognizing an evolving context.

This chapter has also presented the common pitfalls in scenario projects according to Schoemaker (2005). These pitfalls and accompanying solutions are intended to help you manage and facilitate your own scenario projects and avoid some of the more common issues that come up. Tips and advice for optimizing scenario projects are also suggested. Following this advice will help project facilitators avoid common traps and barriers to generating successful, strategically insightful scenario projects. Finally, this chapter has presented the Scenario Project Management Worksheet, which will help plan, structure, and facilitate a scenario project. This worksheet makes the concepts from this book immediately applicable in any organization.

References and Resources

Kahane, A. (1992). The Mont Fleur Scenarios: What Will South Africa Be Like in 2002? Available on the Global Business Network website, at www.gbn.com/SubjectDisplayServlet.srv?taxId=111.

Mintzberg, H., Ahlstrand, B.W., & Lampel, J. (2005). *Strategy Safari: A Guided Tour Through the Wilds of Strategic Management.* New York: Simon & Schuster.

Schoemaker, P.J.H. (2005). Navigating Uncertainty: From Scenarios to Flexible Options. In M.A. Hitt and R.D. Ireland (Eds.), *The Blackwell Encyclopedia of Management* (Vol. 3, pp. 190–193). Malden, MA: Blackwell.

Wack, P. (1985). Scenarios: Uncharted Waters Ahead. *Harvard Business Review, 63*(5), 73–89.

About the Author

Thomas J. Chermack is an assistant professor at the Colorado State University in the organizational performance and change program. Chermack's research focuses on the process and products of scenario planning (an alternative to traditional strategic planning). This unique approach to planning was born at Royal Dutch / Shell Oil and is largely credited with the ability to anticipate and navigate fundamental market changes and shifts. Tom is also the founder and managing partner of Chermack Scenarios, a scenario planning consultancy affiliated with the Centre for Innovative Leadership. He has authored over 50 research reports and a book called *Scenario Planning in Organizations.* You can find Tom's website at www.thomaschermack.com.

"Managing Scenario Projects" was excerpted from *Scenario Planning in Organizations,* published by Berrett-Koehler in 2011 and reprinted with permission.

✎ Chapter 10

A Note on Women and Power

Jeffrey Pfeffer, PhD

Editor's Note

This chapter is geared specifically toward female managers, and those who develop them. Jeffrey Pfeffer is an expert on the topic of power and organizational life. In this journal article reprint, Jeffrey shares the latest research regarding women and power. It is sobering, helpful, and important. I would encourage all my female readers (and the men who need to help develop female professionals) to read every page. Jeffrey's conclusions and recommendations are insightful and needed.

In 2003, Valery Craane, a stockbroker at Merrill Lynch, attended the company's annual shareholder meeting to confront its outgoing CEO, David Komansky, over the company's treatment of its female employees. Craane, who worked in the company with her daughter as a stockbroker, claimed that when brokers left the firm, the best clients were redistributed primarily to the men and that female brokers were disadvantaged in the allocation of new stock issues to offer their clients. Craane's complaints reflected the fact that Wall Street was and is a male bastion. In 1995, "95 percent of all vice presidents, 98 percent of sales managers, and 86 percent of brokers at Merrill were men." Komansky's response to Craane only raised her ire: "What we will not do is be blackmailed into paying an outrageous amount of money," he said. Merrill had already paid more than $100 million to settle discrimination and harassment claims filed in 1999.[1] Not much had changed since then. In 2004, Morgan Stanley paid $54 million to settle a discrimination lawsuit filed on behalf

---

[1] Patrick McGeehan, "What Merrill's Women Want," *The New York Times,* August 22, 2004.

of 340 women working in an investment banking division[2] and some years prior, there had been the infamous "boom-boom room" lawsuit against Smith Barney, the brokerage unit later part of Citigroup. That legal proceeding exposed hazing and physical abuse of female employees. In March 2010, three investment advisors working at Bank of America Merrill Lynch filed a lawsuit accusing the company of gender bias; in September 2010, three former employees sued Goldman Sachs arguing that the firm discriminates against its women employees;[3] and a month later, six current and former employees sued Citigroup, alleging discrimination in pay and promotion.[4]

Pay and promotion discrimination is neither a relic of the distant past nor confined to Wall Street. As briefly reviewed below, the data are clear: Women earn less than similarly qualified men, tend to work in occupations and job titles that pay less, and are underrepresented in senior management ranks, including CEO and board positions. Although the extent of gender-based career discrimination has declined somewhat over the past several decades,[5] its persistence raises fundamental questions as to why women are apparently disadvantaged in career tournaments inside organizations. One lens for gaining some insight into this question is to note that power and political skill are inextricably bound up with career success.[6] Consequently, one way of understanding women's underrepresentation in senior management ranks is to explore the relationship between gender and power dynamics.

An important question about attaining power is how the rules of the game differ, if they do, for men and women. A second question is that, if the rules are different or operate in ways that disadvantage women, what should or could women do to build a path to power? There is extensive research on women's attaining positions of power and also quite a bit of evidence that can help us understand the underlying mechanisms that partly explain why women are, on average, not as successful as similarly qualified men in getting to senior level positions or earning comparable salaries. This note reviews some of the most relevant data on these questions. The purpose of this note is to provide a brief summary of the existing social science theory and evidence that helps elucidate the interrelated issues of gender, power, and career success.

---

[2] Ibid.

[3] Peter Lattman, "Women Sue Goldman, Claiming Pay and Jobs Bias," *The New York Times,* September 15, 2010.

[4] Thomas Kaplan, "Women Accuse Citigroup of Gender Bias," *The New York Times,* October 13, 2010.

[5] Olivia A. O'Neill and Charles A. O'Reilly, "Careers as Tournaments: The Impact of Sex and Gendered Organizational Culture Preferences on MBAs' Income Attainment," *Journal of Organizational Behavior,* 31 (2010), 856–876.

[6] Jeffrey Pfeffer, *Power: Why Some People Have It—and Others Don't,* New York: Harper Business, 2010, Ch. 1, "It Takes More Than Performance."

The Facts About Women's Labor Market Experience

There are many theories and studies about men and women in the workforce, and the literature on the barriers women face is extensive. For purposes of understanding women's managerial careers in business, data collected by Catalyst are among the most relevant.[7] Catalyst is a leading nonprofit membership organization "working globally with businesses and the professions to build inclusive workplaces and expand opportunities for women in business."[8]

As one summary of the existing literature on gender and pay noted, "Numerous studies have concluded that women are discriminated against in the labor market: they receive lower wages than men with equal skills and attributes."[9] These results hold whether the data come from random samples of the entire labor force,[10] studies of specific firms and industries, particular occupations such as managers or college professors,[11] or alumni from specific elite colleges. Being female invariably has a negative effect on salary, with other factors such as education, years of work experience, and in some cases, measures of job performance (e.g., publication records in the case of academic salaries) statistically controlled. Many studies also find lower returns to schooling and years of labor force experience for women compared to men—in other words, there is a statistical interaction so that the positive slope relating salary to educational attainment and years of work experience is steeper for men than for women.[12]

Over time, research has expanded to consider the mechanisms that might account for differences in salaries between similarly-qualified men and women. One such mechanism is occupational sex segregation.[13] Women are disproportionately represented in certain occupations, professions, and industries which, for the most part, pay lower wages, even when occupational skills and other job attributes are taken into account.[14] The public policy manifestation of this finding of women's work being paid less is the discussion over "comparable

---

[7] Catalyst makes all of its reports available online and has done extensive research on women's representation in senior management and board positions over the years. See www.catalyst.org.

[8] Nancy M. Carter and Christine Silva, *Pipeline's Broken Promise,* New York: Catalyst, 2010, "About Catalyst."

[9] Yitchak Haberfeld, "Employment Discrimination: An Organizational Model," *Academy of Management Journal,* 35 (1992), 161–180.

[10] Beth A. Livingston, Timothy A. Judge, and Charlice Hurst, "Do Nice Guys—and Gals—Really Finish Last? The Joint Effects of Sex and Agreeableness on Income," paper presented at the 2011 Annual Meeting of the Academy of Management, San Antonio, Texas, August 15, 2011.

[11] Marianne A. Ferber, "Professors, Performance, and Rewards," *Industrial Relations,* 13 (1974), 69–77.

[12] See, for instance, Francine D. Blau and Marianne A. Ferber, "Discrimination: Empirical Evidence from the United States," *American Economic Review,* 77 (1987), 316–320.

[13] William T. Bielby and N. Baron, "A Woman's Place Is with Other Women: Sex Segregation within Organizations," in Barbara Reskin (ed.), *Sex Segregation in the Workplace: Trends, Explorations, Remedies,* 27–55. Washington, DC: National Academy Press.

[14] David Snyder and Paula M. Hudis, "Occupational Income and the Effects of Minority Competition and Segregation: A Reanalysis and Some New Evidence," *American Sociological Review,* 41 (1976), 209–234; Paula England and Dana Dunn, "Evaluating Work and Comparable Worth," *Annual Review of Sociology,* 14 (1988), 227–248.

worth"—the idea that there should not only be equal pay for people doing the same job (e.g., women holding the same position as men should receive comparable pay) but also there should be equal pay for jobs of equal economic value. Although this idea has gone nowhere in the United States, it is part of public policy in some other industrialized countries, such as Canada.

Of course, analyses at the level of occupations cannot explain why women managers earn less than male managers since both work in the same occupation. However, there is evidence for an effect of the proportion of women on salaries at the within-occupational level of analysis that provides useful insight. For instance, within the occupation of "doctor," medical specialties employing more women have lower average salaries than specialties with fewer women, and similar effects have been observed in the different subspecialties of law.[15] Academic disciplines that employ a higher proportion of women faculty members pay less, and this effect holds even after controlling for common predictors of salary and also labor market conditions.[16] There is both field and laboratory evidence showing that both men and women attribute less economic value to work done by women.[17] This devaluing of work because it is done by women extends even to the level of job titles. For instance, one study of senior-level jobs in higher education administration found an inverse relationship between the proportion of women occupying given job titles and the wages for those jobs. That research also found evidence of a tipping-point—a nonlinearity such that once a specific job title became identified as women's work, wages for both men and women doing that job decreased more rapidly.[18] The study was also able to explore causality; after controlling for wage rates in 1978, increases in the proportion of women occupying a given administrative job title negatively affected 1983 salaries, with many other explanatory variables statistically controlled. Another study of the wage rates paid in California civil service jobs—a context characterized by intense job analysis to set wage rates and many due process protections—nonetheless found that work done proportionately more by women and nonwhites was economically devalued.[19]

Another possible cause that has been adduced to explain the observed differences in earnings between men and women is that "women forego higher salaries in order to obtain other

[15] Kathleen E. Hull and Robert L. Nelson, "Assimilation, Choice, or Constraint? Testing Theories of Gender Differences in the Careers of Lawyers," *Social Forces,* 79 (2000), 229–264.

[16] Marcia L. Bellas, "Comparable Worth in Academia: The Effects on Faculty Salaries of the Sex Composition and Labor-Market Conditions of Academic Disciplines," *American Sociological Review,* 59 (1994), 807–821.

[17] Kay Deaux, "Sex and Gender," *Annual Review of Psychology,* 36 (1985), 49–81.

[18] Jeffrey Pfeffer and Alison Davis-Blake, "The Effect of the Proportion of Women on Salaries: The Case of College Administrators," *Administrative Science Quarterly,* 32 (1987), 1–24.

[19] James N. Baron and Andrew E. Newman, "For What It's Worth: Organizations, Occupations, and the Value of Work Done by Women and Nonwhites," *American Sociological Review,* 55 (1990), 155–175.

desirable job benefits"[20] such as flexibility or more pleasant working conditions, and that women do not value salary as highly as men do. Although some studies do find differences between men and women on how much they value various job characteristics including pay, many do not. Therefore, differences between the genders in preferences for job attributes or differences in the importance placed on salary do not appear promising as explanations for gender-based earnings differentials.

Men and Women Managers and Professionals in Business

Although these findings help account for why men and women earn different amounts, they obviously cannot completely explain why women and men with comparable educational backgrounds and similar levels of work experience, doing the same jobs (in terms of job titles) in the same companies face different career trajectories and outcomes. And men and women do have very different career outcomes in business, as data from the Catalyst surveys make clear.

One Catalyst report notes that although women constitute more than 45 percent of the U.S. workforce and more than 50 percent of people classified as holding managerial positions, "women represent just 3 percent of Fortune 500 CEOs, 15 percent of board directors at those companies, and less than 14 percent of corporate executives at top publicly traded companies around the world."[21] Moreover, although there has been some progress in recent decades in women advancing to more senior ranks in business, in recent years, the increase in the number of women reaching senior executive ranks has slowed considerably.

This plateauing of women's progress in business is one factor that stimulated Catalyst to undertake a major study of more than 4,000 women and men who graduated from full-time MBA programs at 26 leading institutions between 1996 and 2007. To be included in the survey, these individuals needed to be working full-time when the survey was conducted in 2007 and 2008. These were high potential people who were similar in many respects, and the differences in their career trajectories were telling. To summarize the Catalyst results:

- Even after statistically controlling for years of experience, industry, and global location, women were more likely to start their first job after the MBA at a lower organizational level than men.[22]
- "Men had higher starting salaries."[23]

---

[20] Teresa M. Heckert, Heather F. Droste, Patrick J. Adams, Christopher M. Griffin, Lisa L. Roberts, Michael A. Mueller, and Hope A. Wallis, "Gender Differences in Anticipated Salary: Role of Salary Estimates for Others, Job Characteristics, Career Paths, and Job Inputs," *Sex Roles*, 47 (2002), p. 140.
[21] Carter and Silva, op. cit, p. 1.
[22] Ibid., p. 3.
[23] Ibid.

- Regardless of starting salary, men had more rapid salary growth than did women after completing their MBA and entering the workforce.[24]
- Men were more likely to be at a higher managerial level than were women, even after controlling for years of experience, time since receiving the MBA, industry, and other possible explanatory factors. "More than half of women were at the entry or first level manager levels" and were more likely than men to be at those ranks.[25]
- Women were no more likely than men to take a nontraditional career path, defined in the Catalyst research as working in the nonprofit, government, or education sectors, being self-employed or working part-time before returning to work full-time, or dropping out of the labor force to care for children (only 3 percent of the women and 2 percent of the men said they had temporarily left the labor force to care for children).[26] However, women paid a higher penalty than did men for pursuing a nontraditional career—they advanced less rapidly than did men when they subsequently joined a "regular" company.[27]
- Not surprisingly, given the lower starting and current salary, the less rapid career advancement, and the higher proportion stuck at a first-level rank, women reported less career satisfaction than did men.[28]
- Other data show that although high-potential managerial women were even *more* likely to have organizational mentors than were men, for the most part women's mentors provided advice while men's mentors provided advocacy or sponsorship—substantive help in attaining higher level positions. As that study noted: "All mentoring is not created equal... interviews and surveys alike suggest that high-potential women are overmentored and undersponsored relative to their male peers... without sponsorship, women are not only less likely than men to be appointed to top roles but may also be more reluctant to go for them."[29]

The Catalyst data speak to the "pipeline" explanation for the underrepresentation of women in senior positions, which argues that the reason for the small numbers of women at the senior ranks is simply that it takes time for recent labor force entrants to move up and through career ladders to higher levels. Women's entry into the professions increased dramatically

---

[24] Ibid., p. 5.

[25] Ibid., p. 4.

[26] It is important to note that the Catalyst data cover only respondents working full-time at the time of the survey. Thus, the data do not speak to the proportion of women and men who had opted out of the labor force. The evidence shows that women are more likely than men to have opted out of the labor force, either working part-time, not working, or having temporarily interrupted their careers.

[27] Carter and Silva, op. cit., p. 7.

[28] Ibid., p. 8.

[29] Herminia Ibarra, Nancy M. Carter, and Christine Silva, "Why Men Still Get More Promotions than Women," *Harvard Business Review,* 88 (September, 2010), p. 82.

starting in the early 1970s, and increases in women's MBA enrollment occurred somewhat later than that, so one argument is that it is only now, as the many women who entered management reach their 40s, 50s, and 60s, that one might expect to see significant increases in women's presence in senior organizational ranks. The Catalyst data, and other data that show the same pattern, make the case that the problem is not just one of letting time take its course. Even for recent MBA graduates in the labor force who have graduated from leading business schools, women's salaries and career progress are worse than for comparable men. Nor is women's career disadvantage in business a phenomenon observed solely in the United States. In India, just 11 percent of chief executives are women.[30] In Britain, between 1974 and 1994 there was a 2.8 million decrease in the number of men in the labor force while the number of women increased 2 million, but between 1975 and 1984, the percent of women in senior management declined by some 3.5 percent.[31] A 2002 survey of 500 Australian MBA graduates found that the median female starting salary was just *half* that of their male counterparts.[32]

Some Possible Explanations for the Different Career Trajectories

Differences between men and women in family responsibilities and the effects of marital status and children on career outcomes help explain some of the gender-based differences in career outcomes. Although the Catalyst data are careful to control for parenthood, there is evidence from other research that marriage and having children have quite different effects on men's and women's careers. For instance, Martha Hill's research found that married men earned *more* than single men, whereas married women earned *less* than their single counterparts.[33] A study of more than 6,500 graduates from Harvard reported that "male earnings are strongly and positively related to the number of children in the family whereas female earnings are negatively related."[34]

Social psychologists Amy Cuddy and Susan Fiske asked 122 Princeton University undergraduates to rate "three fictitious consultants on traits reflecting warmth and competence," which are fundamental dimensions by which people are judged. They also asked the study

---

[30] Nilanjana S. Roy, "Ambitions Meet Reality in India," www.nytimes.com/2010/world/asia/15iht-letter15.html.

[31] Heli K. Lahtinen and Fiona M. Wilson, "Women and Power in Organizations," *Executive Development,* 7(1994), 16–25.

[32] Mara Olekalns and Carol T. Kulik, "Sugar 'n' Spice and All Things Nice: Gender and Strategy Choices in Negotiation," forthcoming in P. Murray, R. Kramar, and P. McGraw (Eds.), *Women at Work in Australia.*

[33] Martha S. Hill, "The Wage Effects of Marital Status and Children," *The Journal of Human Resources,* 14(4), 579–594.

[34] Goldin and Katz, op. cit., p. 367.

participants three questions assessing how likely they would be, as clients, to request on an engagement, recommend for continuing training and education, and recommend for promotion the people described in the profiles.[35] The results showed that "when working women become mothers, they trade perceived competence for perceived warmth ... working men don't make this trade; when they become fathers, they gain perceived warmth and maintain perceived competence ... people report less interest in hiring, promoting, and educating working moms relative to working dads and childless employees [e.g., women without children] ... competence ratings predict interest in hiring, promoting, and educating workers. Thus, working moms' gain in perceived warmth does not help them, but their loss in perceived competence does hurt them."[36]

It is not just that married women and men and men and women with children are perceived and evaluated differently. Because of the unequal distribution of household work and differences in labor force participation contingent on being married and having children, men and women have different resources for their careers. A survey conducted by the Center for Work Life Policy reported that 40 percent of the women felt that their husbands created more work around the home than they performed.[37] Sociologist Hanna Papanek wrote about the "two-person career," two people working on one career, and the institutional demands, particularly in middle-class occupations in the United States, that created a situation in which wives attained vicarious achievement through their husband's jobs.[38] Papanek argued that because people typically married others with similar educational attainment, a company hiring a highly-educated, married individual with a nonworking spouse often got more than one person's worth of labor for the price (salary) of the one employee.

Although Papanek's argument was originally proposed to account for the advantages that men with nonworking spouses seemed to enjoy over either single men or those with wives who worked, as women entered the workforce and moved up the managerial ranks, there were instances of husbands supporting their wives' careers and women being advantaged also when they can have a "two-person career." A senior executive at the large human resources consulting firm Hewitt (more recently Aon Hewitt, after the acquisition of Hewitt by insurance company Aon) told me that all of the most senior executive women had "househusbands." A senior woman leader at shoe company Nike related that in a meeting of

---

[35] Amy J. C. Cuddy and Susan T. Fiske, "When Professionals Become Mothers, Warmth Doesn't Cut the Ice," *Journal of Social Issues,* 60 (2004), 701–718. Quotes are from pp. 707–708.

[36] Ibid., p. 701.

[37] Cited by Sylvia Ann Hewlett and Carolyn Buck Luce, "Off-Ramps and On-Ramps: Keeping Talented Women on the Road to Success," *Harvard Business Review,* 83 (March, 2005), 43–54.

[38] Hanna Papanek, "Men, Women, and Work: Reflections on the Two-Person Career," *American Journal of Sociology,* 78 (1973), 852–872.

the top 100 women of the corporation, she saw few women who had traditional marriages. There was, for instance, a higher proportion of unmarried leaders or executives without children than there would be in a comparable group of men. A rising female executive with significantly expanding responsibilities at oil company BP who graduated from Stanford business school has a husband who stays at home and takes care of the children. As Dr. Frances Conley, the first tenured full professor of neurosurgery in the United States wrote in her autobiographical story of confronting sexism in academic medicine: "By the time of my tenure review in 1982, Phil [her husband] and I had decided, without any formal discussion about the pros and cons, that we would not have children … An untraditional family life [Phil, a Harvard MBA graduate, left his position at Raychem and built a career doing money management, mostly from home] was one of the trade-offs we informally accepted with each other so I could build an academic career, without need to compromise on the standard amount of time required."[39] The need to choose between marriage and a family versus a career is a more required trade-off for women than for men. Sylvia Hewlett's 2001 survey of women in business and the professions reported that 33 percent of high-achieving women (as measured by salary) and 42 percent of corporate women aged 41 to 55 were childless, and 40 percent of the high achievers and 43 percent of corporate women in that age group were unmarried. The comparable figures for men either unmarried or without children were substantially lower.[40] Between 2004 and 2009, there was a 28 percent increase in professional women with husbands who did not work.[41] Women corporate leaders in India were more likely to be never-married, divorced, or widowed than comparable women in either the United States or Europe.[42]

Another partial explanation for the wage and organizational position differences by gender that is relevant to both managerial and nonmanagerial careers is the fact "that women are more likely than men to interrupt their work careers for family reasons."[43] Women in India were more likely than men to temporarily leave the workforce to look after either children or elderly parents than were men—54.5 percent versus 15 percent.[44] In the United States, one study of 371 college students found that women expected to take 10 times as many months out of the workforce for child rearing than did men and also had lower anticipated working hours.[45] A follow-up study of Harvard student cohorts from around 1970, 1980, and 1990 found that on average, women had about 15 months of being nonemployed while the

---

[39] Frances K. Conley, *Walking Out on the Boys,* New York: Farrar, Straus and Giroux, 1998, p. 57.

[40] Sylvia Ann Hewlett, "Executive Women and the Myth of Having It All," *Harvard Business Review,* 80 (April, 2002), 66–73

[41] Sylvia Ann Hewlett, Laura Sherbin, and Diana Forster, "Off-Ramps and On-Ramps Revisited," *Harvard Business Review,* 88 (June 2010), 30.

[42] Roy, op. cit.

[43] James W. Albrecht, Per-Anders Edin, Marianne Sundstrom, and Susan B. Vroman, "Career Interruptions and Subsequent Earnings: A Reexamination Using Swedish Data," *The Journal of Human Resources,* 34, p. 294.

[44] Roy, op. cit.

[45] Heckert, et al., op. cit., 139–151.

comparable figure for men was approximately 4 months.[46] That same study also reported that the greatest earnings penalty for taking time off from employment was for people who had gone on from their Harvard undergraduate degree to also earn an MBA. This finding is consistent with other studies that show that taking time out of the labor force adversely affects subsequent career progress, an effect that is larger than just the fact of fewer years of work experience lost because of temporarily stopping out.[47] A study of more than 2,400 highly qualified women (those with an advanced or professional degree or an honors undergraduate degree) noted that women on average lose 18 percent of their earning power when they drop out of the labor force temporarily, and if they spent three or more years out of the workforce, the loss in earnings was almost 40 percent.[48]

Yet another reason for the differences in career outcomes is that women tend to work fewer hours than men, in part because they carry more family and household responsibilities. Earnings regressions that control for the number of hours worked typically find that this statistical control reduces, but does not completely eliminate, the effect of gender on earnings.[49] In a study of University of California, Berkeley, MBA graduates in the eight years following school reported a positive correlation between being male and hours worked and a positive relationship between work hours and income, with, in this study, hours worked completely mediating the effect of gender on earnings.[50] As one of the study's co-authors, Charles O'Reilly, commented, if one takes the idea of a career tournament seriously, over successive stages of these tournaments, differences in ability will be eliminated or substantially reduced for those who continue to move up. Therefore, at higher organizational levels, observed differentiation in success will become increasingly determined by effort. And from the employer's point of view, it is completely rational to select for those who are willing to provide more hours, given relatively small differences in talent.

One Consequence: Differential Rates of Dropping Out of the Workforce

Confronted with organizational environments that provide unequal rewards and other barriers to their advancement, and thus often experiencing less career satisfaction, women, particularly highly educated women who may have more choices and options, leave the workforce in higher proportions than do men. The study of almost 2,500 highly qualified women reported that 37 percent had left the workforce voluntarily at some point in their

---

[46] Goldin and Katz, op. cit., p. 365

[47] Ibid., 294–311.

[48] Hewlett and Luce, op. cit.

[49] See, for instance, Claudia Goldin and Lawrence F. Katz, "Transitions: Career and Family Life Cycles of the Educational Elite," *American Economic Review: Papers and Proceeds 2008,* 98 (2008), 363–369.

[50] O'Neill and O'Reilly, op. cit.

careers and for women who had children it was 43 percent.[51] Lisa Belkin's *New York Times* article on women dropping out contains the following illustrative statistics:

- ◾ "Of white men with MBAs, 95 percent are working full time, but for white women...that number drops to 67 percent."
- ◾ A survey of women from the Harvard Business School classes of 1981, 1985, and 1991 "found that only 38 percent were working full time."
- ◾ In other professions, between one-third and one-fourth of women trained in the profession are out of the workforce.[52]

Even women who have not dropped out of the labor force may drop out of their employing organization, founding their own nonprofit and for-profit entities as a way of avoiding environments in which they face disproportionate barriers, and also creating workplaces that provide more time use flexibility. The evidence suggests that particularly since the 1970s, which is when women's enrollment in various professional schools increased rapidly, this is precisely what many women have done. One study found a steady increase in self-employed women over the past three decades with self-employment for women increasing at a faster rate than self-employment for men. That study, analyzing time use data from 2003 to 2006, reported that self-employed women spent less time in work-related activities than did either self-employed men or women working for salary.[53] Although founding businesses and becoming self-employed provides a possibility for women to work in more benign environments where they face fewer career barriers and more flexibility in their working hours, it also removes them from the chance of taking over the management of large organizations that already exist.

Some Explanations for These Facts

There are numerous theoretical accounts that seek to explain these facts of women's disadvantage. The explanations are, of course, not mutually exclusive and many, maybe all, could be operating. What follows are some of the more prominent.

Stereotyping and Gender Role Theory

Gender roles are "socially constructed beliefs that describe how males and females are expected to behave" and disadvantage women because the characteristics of successful leaders are frequently described in masculine terms.[54] Social expectations and stereotypes affect women's attitudes and behaviors and how those in power perceive both men and women. In the evaluation of women leaders, for instance, one summary of the literature reported that

---

[51] Hewlett and Luce, op. cit.
[52] Lisa Belkin, "The Opt-Out Revolution," *The New York Times Magazine,* October 26, 2003.
[53] "Self-Employed Women and Time Use, February, 2009," http://www.extension.org/pages/Self-employed_women_and_time_use,_February_2009.
[54] O'Neill and O'Reilly, op. cit., p. 857.

although there was no evidence of a large bias against women leaders, there was evidence that when women in their leadership roles used more "male" behaviors (autocratic and directive), women were more devalued compared to male counterparts.[55] A more recent review article noted that the discrepancy between expectations for fulfilling the "female" role and the "leadership" role led to seeing women as less appropriate for leadership positions and for evaluating prescribed (often tough or directive) leadership behaviors less favorably when they were done by a woman.[56]

As for how these expectations affect women's attitudes and behaviors, in a *Harvard Business Review* article, psychiatrist Anna Fels asked if women lacked ambition.[57] Her answer was generally "yes" because, as she noted, even if women were ambitious, they were reluctant to admit it. For women, ambition "necessarily implied egotism, selfishness, self-aggrandizement" and other traits that were not considered feminine. If women hide their ambition and are not open about or even proud of being ambitious, after a while, attitudes will follow this verbal behavior and ambition will diminish.[58]

The fundamental problem is that the traits typically ascribed to women are not traits strongly associated with leadership. Catalyst found that both women and men held similar stereotypes about male and female traits and also held reasonably similar views of the traits of leaders.[59] Other research shows that characterizations of men and women managers have been remarkably stable over time, with men in general being described as more similar to successful managers than women in general.[60] In the 1970s, Merrill Lynch gave applicants a test that included the question, "What qualities in a woman do you consider most important?" "The choices were beauty, intelligence, dependency, independence, and 'affectionateness.'" Applicants received no points for picking intelligence or independence.[61]

Consequently, women advancing up the organizational hierarchy confront a double-bind. First, regardless of their actual qualities and behavior, they are, because they are women, more likely to have "feminine" traits ascribed to them, and since such traits are not those

---

[55] Alice H. Eagly, Monia G. Makhijani, and Bruce G. Klonsky, "Gender and the Evaluation of Leaders: A Meta-Analysis," *Psychological Bulletin,* 111 (1992), 3–22.

[56] Alice H. Eagly and Steven J. Karau, "Role Congruity Theory of Prejudice Toward Female Leaders," *Psychological Review,* 109 (2002), 573–598.

[57] Anna Fels, "Do Women Lack Ambition?" *Harvard Business Review,* 82 (April, 2004), 51.

[58] For a nice overview of the literature on choices and behaviors creating attitudes, see Daniel Ariely and Michael I. Norton, "How Actions Create—Not Just Reveal—Preferences," *Trends in Cognitive Sciences,* 12 (2008), 13–16.

[59] "Women 'Take Care,' Men 'Take Charge': Stereotyping of U.S. Business Leaders Exposed," New York: Catalyst, 2005.

[60] Madeline E. Heilman, Caryn J. Block, Richard F. Martell, and Michael C. Simon, "Has Anything Changed? Current Characterizations of Men, Women, and Managers," *Journal of Applied Psychology,* 74 (1989), 935–942.

[61] McGeehan, op. cit.

typically associated with leadership or with managerial success, there will be a subtle bias against women in the leader selection and, for that matter, the evaluation process. Second, to conform to social norms and expectations, women face pressures to actually exhibit these typically feminine traits and avoid masculine qualities, and thus display behaviors that are less associated with leadership. In fact, there is experimental evidence that women who succeed in "male" tasks are more disliked and derogated as a consequence of their very success—and recall that "leadership" and "management" are typically male tasks.[62] To conform to prescriptions about how they should be, women face pressures to actually be less successful and perform less competently. In conforming to social role expectations, women often act to confirm the stereotypes about women and thereby also make it less likely they will move as quickly up the organizational hierarchy.

Let's make this argument more concrete. The Bem Sex Role Inventory was developed at Stanford University in the 1970s to study gender stereotyping. Lists of many personality traits were given to both men and women who were asked to rank how *desirable* these traits were for men and women in America. Given cultural expectations, stereotypes, and social expectations, it was scarcely surprising that there was reasonable agreement among the raters as to what constituted "masculine" and "feminine" traits. Anna Fels provided the following list from this research literature. Masculine traits included "self-reliant, strong personality, forceful, independent, analytical, defends one's beliefs, athletic, assertive, has leadership abilities, willing to take risks, makes decisions easily, self-sufficient, dominant, willing to take a stand, aggressive, acts as a leader, individualistic, competitive, ambitious." The traits that defined femininity were: "yielding, loyal, cheerful, compassionate, shy, sympathetic, affectionate, sensitive to the needs of others, flatterable, understanding, eager to soothe hurt feelings, softspoken, warm, tender, gullible, childlike, does not use harsh language, loves children, and gentle."[63] Note that the list of male traits has two that explicitly include the term "leader."

Because the traits associated with leadership and masculinity overlap much more than the traits associated with femininity, women face a difficult, almost impossible dilemma. As articulated by Catalyst, "As 'atypical leaders,' women are often perceived as going against the norms of leadership or those of femininity. Caught between impossible choices, those who try to conform to traditional—i.e., masculine—leadership behaviors are damned if they do, damned if they don't."[64]

---

[62] Madeline E. Heilman, Aaron S. Wallen, Daniella Fuchs, and Melinda M. Tamkins, "Penalties for Success: Reactions to Women Who Succeed at Male Gender-Typed Tasks," *Journal of Applied Psychology*, 89 (2004), 416–427.

[63] Fels, op. cit., p. 56.

[64] "The Double-Bind Dilemma for Women in Leadership: Damned If You Do, Damned If You Don't," New York: Catalyst, 2007.

Socialization Into Different Values and Role and Behavior Expectations

The stereotyping argument is consistent with and logically follows from the fact that, at least traditionally, men and women have been socialized to occupy different roles and confront different expectations for appropriate behavior. This then leads to different career choices and preferences.

Recently, research explored why women are so underrepresented in careers in science, technology, engineering, and mathematics (so-called STEM careers). The study argued, and found evidence for, the proposition that women opted out of these careers because compared to some other alternatives, STEM careers were less likely to fulfill communal goals. Even after statistically controlling for previous experience and self-efficacy in science and mathematics, endorsing communal goals negatively predicted interest in STEM jobs.[65]

The point is that "social roles are critical to understanding people's reasons for pursuing... careers." Broader gender roles in a society influence the goals of individuals in that society, and "men have traditionally occupied leadership or breadwinner roles associated with a focus on agency or self-orientation, whereas women have traditionally fulfilled caretaking roles associated with communion or other-orientation." A meta-analysis of job attribute preferences "showed that the largest gender differences are women's greater preference for helping other people... and working with people."[66]

Although this particular study concerns people's career interests with a focus on math and science, the relevance to managerial and particularly leadership careers is clear. Women's choices, preferences, and values are constrained by the role expectations both they and their male counterparts learn. For instance, a longitudinal study of more than 10,000 1957 Wisconsin high school graduates found that women were more likely than men to be oriented toward communal relationships and also to be more agreeable.[67] The choices organizations make to fill leadership positions, and reactions to behavior, are also affected by gender-role expectations and stereotypes. Obviously, there are individuals who surmount these role expectations, and this line of argument cannot completely account for data showing that women with MBAs pursuing careers in the same industries and jobs as men do not do as well. But these data are consistent with the higher rate of women opting out of professional careers.

---

[65] Amanda B. Diekman, Elizabeth R. Brown, Amanda M. Johnston, and Emily K. Clark, "Seeking Congruity Between Goals and Roles: A New Look at Why Women Opt Out of Science, Technology, Engineering, and Mathematics Careers," *Psychological Science*, 21 (2010), 1051–1057.

[66] Ibid., p. 1052.

[67] Livingston, Judge, and Hurst, op. cit., p. 28.

Gender-Role Socialization Leads to Different Attitudes and Behaviors With Respect to Power

Because of different expectations for behavior in general as well as differences in socialization experiences, it is scarcely surprising that women relate differently to power and to political behaviors than do men, on average. A study of almost 500 college students and the same number of voters found that men were more social dominance-oriented than women, a difference that helped to explain gender-based variation in political attitudes.[68] An experimental study asking participants to rate the likelihood of their taking various actions in the case of an organizational dispute found that men were more likely to use coercion and women were more likely to use personal/dependent and negotiation strategies. That same study provided evidence that women "reported more negative attitudes toward having power than men." [69]

Men and women use different language and conversational practices that then affect their power in social interactions. "Women's language has been characterized as lacking forcefulness; women demonstrate politeness and uncertainty using, for example, tag questions (statements with a question on the end)."[70] Men use conversational devices that provide them more power in interactions, for instance, completing women's sentences and interrupting others, particularly women. Studies of conversations also show that men tend to give minimal responses to topics when those topics are initiated by women.[71]

Men and women approach salary negotiations—and negotiation more generally—somewhat differently. First, many studies have found that men have higher salary expectations than do women.[72] Even when presented with information about salaries, women persist in expecting lower salaries for themselves than do men. Of course, such lower expectations are consistent with what seems to occur in the work world, so one could argue that women are just being accurate. But lower salary expectations can create a self-fulfilling prophecy as women request lower starting salaries, are less likely to leave because of the lower salary given their diminished expectations, and may be less aggressive in their salary negotiations. Some research does show that negotiators who set higher targets do better than those who come in with lower aspirations.[73]

---

[68] F. Pratto, L. M. Stallworth, and J. Sidanius, "The Gender Gap: Differences in Political Attitudes and Social Dominance Orientation," *British Journal of Social Psychology,* 36 (1997), 49–68.

[69] Lynn R. Offermann and Pamela E. Schrier, "Social Influence Strategies: The Impact of Sex, Role, and Attitudes Toward Power," *Personality and Social Psychology Bulletin,* 11 (1985), 286–300; quote is on p. 295.

[70] Lahtinen and Wilson, op. cit.

[71] Ibid.

[72] Much of this research is summarized in Heckert, et al., op. cit., p. 140.

[73] C. Stevens, A. Bavetta, and M. Gist, "Gender Differences in the Acquisition of Salary Negotiation Skills: The Role of Goals, Self-Efficacy and Perceived Control," *Journal of Applied Psychology,* 78 (1993), 723–735.

But men and women do not differ just in their expectations as they enter salary negotiations. As one recent review noted, "Research suggests that, at every stage of the negotiation process, women make decisions that signal a more accommodating approach and consequently undermine their economic outcomes. This effect is amplified because the perception that women are 'soft' in their negotiating style invited their managers and peers to make less generous offers to them."[74] In negotiations, too, women face a dilemma. Research shows that "the stereotype of an effective negotiator is of someone who is rational, assertive, strong and dominant"—a male gender stereotype.[75] Thus, women who want to negotiate effectively have to act like men, but doing so often provokes dislike, derogation, and backlash. Once again, women confront a double-bind.

There is evidence to suggest that men and women differ in their competitiveness and their response to competition. In one experiment, an increase in the competitiveness of the environment resulted in performance increases for men but not for women. When men and women were paid by a piece rate—based on what they produced—there was no difference in their performance. But when the payoff structure was a tournament, in which payoffs depended not on absolute but on relative productivity—creating competitive interdependence—women did less well than men. And this effect was even stronger when women had to compete against men, indicating that this was a particularly difficult situation.[76] Another study of Israeli school children found that boys and girls ran a 40 meter race at about the same speed when running alone. But when the children had to compete in pairs, performance of the boys, but not the girls, increased significantly.[77]

A subsequent study argued and found that differences in women's and men's competitive behavior depended on the specific task. In presumably "male" tasks, men responded more to competition than did women, but in neutral tasks there was no difference in men's and women's response to competitive incentives and in "female" tasks, women reacted to competition more strongly than did men.[78] The argument is that women tend not to compete, particularly against men, in domains where they believe (correctly or incorrectly) that they won't do well. Given the gender-typing of leadership behavior, negotiation, and organizational competition for status, these recent studies suggest that yet another way in which women differ from men in power-oriented behavior is in their competitiveness and response to competition for hierarchical advancement.

---

[74] Olekalns and Kulik, op. cit., p. 4.

[75] Ibid., p. 12.

[76] Uri Gneezy, Muriel Niederle, and Aldo Rustichini, "Performance in Competitive Enviornments: Gender Differences," *Quarterly Journal of Economics,* 118 (2003), 1049–1074.

[77] Uri Gneezy and Aldo Rustichini, "Gender and Competition at a Young Age," *American Economic Review Papers and Proceedings,* 94 (2004), 377–381.

[78] Christina Gunther, Neslihan Arslan Edinci, Christiane Schwieren, and Martin Strobel, "Women Can't Jump?— An Experiment on Competitive Attitudes and Stereotype Threat," *Journal of Economic Behavior and Organization,* 75 (2010), 395–401.

Men and Women Face Different Reactions to the Same Behaviors

As already noted, even if women can overcome their socialization and the expectations that others hold for women to be likeable and "communal" and engage in more power-oriented, forceful behaviors, these actions can provoke different reactions from others compared to similar behavior by men. One model posits that there are widely shared social expectations for how people of different genders are expected to behave—men should not cry and women should not show anger for instance—and argues that violating these social expectations provokes negative reactions.[79]

Research has shown that displaying anger often results in perceptions of greater competence and gets the person who displays the anger more status. In particular, anger is a more "effective" emotion for obtaining power than either sadness or remorse.[80] Studies of bargaining show that anger results in better negotiated outcomes, in part because people are often conflict averse and want to avoid provoking an angry response and in part because displays of anger convey the limits of how much people are willing to compromise. Research by Aaron Sell has traced the evolutionary function of anger, noting that anger causes the target of the anger to place greater emphasis on the welfare of the person displaying the anger.[81]

But because displaying anger is inconsistent with expectations for women's behavior, some research suggests that the advantages of displaying anger accrue mostly or exclusively to men and that women suffer if they do the same thing. For instance, Victoria Brescoll and Eric Uhlmann found that while men who expressed anger in a professional context were accorded more status than men who displayed sadness, just as previous research had found, both men and women conferred less status on angry women than on angry men. Furthermore, regardless of the job level (CEO or trainee), women were accorded less status if they expressed anger than if they did not.[82]

Or consider another behavior, being agreeable. Although agreeable individuals are, not surprisingly, better liked by their peers, "empirical evidence suggests that agreeableness is negatively related to income and earnings."[83] However, using a number of different data

---

[79] L. A. Rudman and K. Fairchild, "Reactions to Counterstereotypic Behavior: The Role of Backlash in Cultural Stereotype Maintenance," *Journal of Personality and Social Psychology,* 87 (2004), 157–176.

[80] Larissa Z. Tiedens, "Anger and Advancement versus Sadness and Subjugation: The Effect of Negative Emotion Expressions on Social Status Conferral," *Journal of Personality and Social Psychology,* 80 (2001), 86–94.

[81] Aaron Sell, John Tooby, and Leda Cosmides, "Formidability and the Logic of Human Anger," *Proceedings of the National Academy of Science,* 106 (2009), 15073–15078.

[82] Victoria L. Brescoll and Eric Luis Uhlmann, "Can an Angry Woman Get Ahead? Status Conferral, Gender, and Expression of Emotions in the Workplace," *Psychological Science,* 19 (2008), 268–275.

[83] Livingston, et al., op. cit., p. 4.

sets and methods, Livingston, Judge, and Hurst found that the income penalty for being agreeable was larger for men than for women, and in most of their samples, the effect of agreeableness on income, or changes in income over time, was not statistically significant for women. Because "agreeable men disconfirm (and disagreeable men confirm) conventional gender roles" (while the reverse is true for women), it is not surprising that women do not attain as much of an income advantage as men from being disagreeable.[84]

This research and the logic on which it is based mean that women face constraints on their ability to exhibit behaviors that, when displayed by men, convey and confer power. In work environments, in competitive contexts, and in negotiation situations, some of the successful strategies available to men are less available to women because they violate expectations for how women should act.

The Reciprocal, Interdependent Effects of Choice and Social Constraint

Women's choices, including choices to be self-employed or drop out of the labor force completely, and which strategies they will use to acquire power, are affected by the environment and social structure they confront. How could these choices not be responsive to the social environment? At the same time, the decisions women make help reinforce and constitute the existing social structure.

To take a few examples, women are socialized into gender roles and to the extent they then conform to these social expectations, their (collective) behavior reinforces the appropriateness and legitimacy of this gender role socialization and the stereotypes about women. Women, even talented MBA women, facing careers that are less financially rewarding and satisfying than men, are (rationally) more likely to drop out, at least temporarily; this higher drop-out rate then becomes part of the justification organizations articulate for affording women different career opportunities. Women's lower salary expectations may contribute to their earning lower salaries. But salary expectations are based at least partly on the experienced world, so lower received salaries lead naturally to women having lower salary expectations, which in turn produce lower actual salaries. Women who do not use power behaviors such as being disagreeable, anger and self-promotion that are available to men are rewarded for conforming to social expectations for their behavior, but they are disadvantaged in their quest for power and the competition for status because they do not have access to the same ways of advancing as do men.

The point is that many if not most of the processes uncovered in the research described in this note tend to reinforce each other and perpetuate the present state of affairs. The

---

[84] Ibid., p. 3.

processes create cycles of behavior that are self-reinforcing, thereby diminishing the likelihood of change.

Conclusions and Recommendations

Acknowledging and even bemoaning the injustice of women's career disadvantage as detailed in this note will not, in itself, change anything. Many people believe in a just world hypothesis and therefore hope and even assume that things will get better because the world is essentially fair. But life is not always equitable and unfairness does not change just because it is unfair. Although some people argue that the "male" model of organizational leadership is weakening and the collaborative and relationship skills typically ascribed to women are becoming more important, there is little evidence that this is occurring outside the rhetoric of management books. People need to see circumstances as they are and navigate organizations as they exist, not as we might want them to be.

Both women and men face career trade-offs, particularly between work and family obligations. Many believe that a healthy society should make efforts to accommodate work-family conflict through policies such as family leave and flexible work practices. One should not have to choose between having a job and a personal life and family, whether one is man or a woman. The conflicting obligations of work and family seem to place a particular burden on women's careers, resulting in the higher tendency for women to leave the labor force. The United States trails most, if not all, other industrialized countries in mandating workplace flexibility and family-friendly policies. The United States is the only major industrialized country that does not require employers to provide paid vacations or paid sick leave. A 2008 study comparing the United States to 20 other industrialized economies found that "17 have statutes to help parents adjust working hours, 6 help with family care giving responsibilities for adults; 12 allow change in hours to facilitate lifelong learning; 11 support gradual retirement; and 5 countries have statutory arrangements open to all employees, irrespective of the reason for seeking different work arrangements."[85] Because the United States lags in family-friendly public policy, it is not surprising that "U.S. labor force participation for prime working age women ... is now lower than it is in 14 of the 20 high-income countries ... " and "labor force participation for college educated women in the United States is lower than in any of the other 20 countries."[86]

When the Family and Medical Leave Act came up for renewal in 2008—a law that provides the option for people to take *unpaid* leave to deal with family responsibilities such as children or elderly parents—virtually every major business organization, including the U.S. Chamber of Commerce, opposed the law's renewal. This fact made the idea of enhancing

---

[85] Ariane Hegewisch and Janet C. Gornick, *Statutory Routes to Workplace Flexibility in Cross-National Perspective,* Washington, DC: Institute for Women's Policy Research, 2008, p. vii.
[86] Ibid., p. 2.

the regulatory regime to lessen burdens on women—and men—who face family obligations seem far-fetched.

Women face obstacles men do not face in moving up organizational hierarchies. Opting out or refusing to play the power game will not change things nor will such choices ensure individual success. In a report on the career obstacles facing Asians in the United States, Sylvia Ann Hewlett provided some important insights and recommendations that apply, as she pointed out, to all disadvantaged groups. The report noted the importance of "executive presence" for advancement in the most senior ranks, with appearance, self-confidence, and poise being factors that contribute to executive presence. "Corporate culture in the United States places a high premium on assertiveness and individualistic thinking," while "self-effacement and modesty … is at direct odds with the realities of the contemporary workplace where assertiveness and directness are central."[87] Self-advocacy and self-assurance were seen as "essential leadership qualities in the American corporate environment."[88]

Therefore, it is not surprising that women who have succeeded have, for the most part, done so by being willing to break gender stereotypes and play the same game as the men. For instance, former Hewlett-Packard CEO Carly Fiorina noted, "I think women feel a special pressure to be pleasant and accommodating … That day [when, as a new sales manager, she was called 'our token bimbo' during a meeting] I decided that sometimes it's more important to be respected than liked."[89] Condoleezza Rice, former Stanford provost, secretary of state, and national security advisor to President George W. Bush, had a reputation as someone not to be crossed. While at Stanford, Rice cut the budget and opposed affirmative action and was not loved by many faculty and students. But, "Rice's credo, as she told one protégé, was that 'people may oppose you, but when they realize you can hurt them, they'll join your side.'"[90]

It is important to recognize that many of the studies that provide evidence that women suffer from violating behavioral norms to be nice and communal and not display anger rely on experimental paradigms where the participants making the judgments face no real consequences for their choices. In the typical study, people are asked who they would hire, the salary recommendations they would make, whether or not they think someone would be a good leader or other questions that ascertain how much status they would grant the (fictional) other. But in none of these studies do the participants have to get things done

---

[87] Sylvia Ann Hewlett and Ripa Rashid with Diana Forster and Claire Ho, *Asians in America: Unleashing the Potential of the "Model Minority,"* New York: Center for Work-Life Policy, 2011, pp. 21–22.

[88] Ibid., p. 23.

[89] Judy Lin, "Fiorina Learned Conservative Philosophy Early," http://www.mercurynews.com/fdcp? 1286477621723.

[90] Jacob Heilbrunn, "Consent and Advise," *New York Times Book Review,* January 20, 2008.

or otherwise seek allies and power for themselves—power coming in part through whom they decide to ally with and choose for jobs. Consequently, it is not surprising that like-ability, which comes from conforming to social norms and role expectations, has a large influence on the participants' judgments. It is possible that the results of many of the studies cited on the point of women benefiting from not displaying anger or other "counter-normative" behaviors would be quite different if people were choosing others to get something done for them, to help them in some internal decision-making task, or to be an ally in a political battle or negotiation. In those cases, people may be much more willing to select for strength and competence and therefore behaviors, including anger, being disagreeable, being a tough negotiator, and competitiveness, that seemingly signal those attributes instead of choosing women who exhibit more warmth.

Of course, women—and men—can learn to exhibit multiple emotions and display a variety of behaviors, either sequentially or even at the same time. After all, leaders often need to convey both empathy with the people they lead and also strength and high expectations at the same time. Women can be firm and even tough while also signaling that they place value on the relationship and are concerned about how others perceive them. Women—and men—can use humor as well as facial expressions and body language to mitigate what might be an otherwise harsh message. Nuria Chinchilla, a professor at IESE who has done research and advocacy for work-family conciliation, will often talk quite bluntly to corporate CEOs about their inaccurate ideas that the number of hours worked creates productivity or signals employee commitment, but she does so with a smile and a friendly demeanor. As she said, a tough message can be more readily accepted if it is presented in a friendly fashion. Placing behavior in context can also help—noting that taking a tough negotiating stance, for instance, reflects the importance of the issue. Laura Esserman, the director of the Carol Franc Buck Breast Care Center at the University of California, San Francisco, finds that people do not object as strenuously to her impatience and anger when she reminds them of the 45,000 women who die each year from breast cancer and the urgency of doing things to reduce this huge human toll.

In short, there are ways for both women and men to interact so as to convey competence and toughness as well as warmth. Former secretary of state and national security advisor Henry Kissinger was famous for his use of self-deprecating humor. But self-deprecation is something that should be done only when competence and power are already established. Powerful people often downplay their power and accomplishments as a way of softening their persona. Being skilled at displaying strength without provoking dislike and resistance means that people need to be sensitive at reading others and their effects on the audience. And the ability to put oneself in the other's place—one of the personal qualities that provides power—is also useful in this regard.

Women—and men—also need to understand and then develop, through practice, the personal qualities that provide power. Those qualities include ambition and drive, energy, focus, self-knowledge, confidence, empathy with others, and the capacity and willingness to tolerate and even engage in conflict. Men and women tend, on average, to have different strengths and weaknesses from the set of qualities on this list. As Fels has argued, women may lack ambition or at least admit that they are driven to succeed, and are often less willing to engage in conflict. Everyone is capable of developing in areas where they are not as strong, and if they seek power, should do so.

None of the behavioral subtlety or personal development essential to building power is necessarily easy to master, but if prevailing in the competition for power and status were effortless and simple, everyone could do it. Women and men face trade-offs if they want to achieve power. Climbing organizational hierarchies is tough work, and the competition gets more intense the closer to the top one is. Women do face obstacles that do not confront men to the same degree—a reasonable explanation as to why fewer women make it to the most senior positions. But there are women who have attained high-level positions in large companies and also in the nonprofit and political spheres as well. There is much to be learned from observing what they have done—which frequently entails not opting out, not complaining that life is not fair, and for the most part, outplaying the men at their own power games.

About the Author

Jeffrey Pfeffer is the Thomas D. Dee II Professor of Organizational Behavior at the Graduate School of Business at Stanford University, where he has taught since 1979. He is the author or co-author of 13 books including *The Human Equation: Building Profits by Putting People First, Managing With Power: Politics and Influence in Organizations, The Knowing-Doing Gap: How Smart Companies Turn Knowledge Into Action,* and *Power: Why Some People Have It—And Others Don't.* Jeffrey received his BS and MS degrees from Carnegie-Mellon University and his PhD from Stanford. Jeffrey's website can be found at www.jeffreypfeffer.com.

❧ Chapter 11

Brainpowered Tone Tools to Manage Excellence

Ellen Weber, PhD

Editor's Note

This is a chapter that you will want to review several times. Read it, go away and let it percolate, and then come back again. Ellen Weber is an expert in the field of practical brain research and how managers and leaders can apply it to build better workplaces. In other words, there are physiological brain triggers and functions that affect our ability to do great work, learn, and thrive for the long term. In this chapter, Ellen explores many of the ways our amazing brains act and react to help and hinder our success and tells us how we can utilize this knowledge to help our team members and ourselves perform. Fascinating stuff!

In today's challenging marketplace of ideas and practices, managers advance individual and organizational skills at all levels, as they seize new opportunities with brainpowered tone tools that enhance innovation for a new era.

It's remarkable how far study of the brain has come in the past two decades. The upshot? Managers could capitalize more on neuro-designed tone tactics to meet unique challenges that determine winners in the innovative era we've just entered. Tone affects talent's quality, and its skills forecast the proficiency pool that an organization can cultivate. Tone is the body language of communication. It's the smile of inclusion, or the snub of exclusion. It's both the warmth of a thanks and the chill of constant criticism. Tone fosters progress when managers facilitate talents in others, and shuts down brainpower when ego rules the communication. Good tone builds goodwill with those who disagree, and it also creates friction across differences. Tone risks novel ideas, or it eliminates communication that differs. Tone fuels wisdom from cultural, age, and gender differences, and it also extinguishes people's opposing views. Tone is the champion's communication in a healthy workplace, and it's the cynic or naysayer in a toxic workplace. Good tone helps people to look at problems with solutions in mind—while poor tone looks at problems and vents about the impossibilities. Some say that tone is the best predictor of an organization's innovation opportunities. Others say it powers up bottom-line possibilities. I say that just as tone drives excellence and cultivates talent, it can also work against managers. How so?

Tone Tools Create Goodwill in War Zones

Ever have a day when work became combat, and your workplace a war zone? When problems arise, the last place leaders look for solutions is within differences that caused battles in the first place. Consider the following example: Gary, a manufacturing manager, is typical of leaders we meet who see differences as a cause of the problem, and poor tone as a given. The inability to see the potential destruction caused by tone can actually prevent managers from finding the solutions. Does this happen where you work?

Gary's problem was with his union reps, and he spoke for many in his industry when he said that his company's constant problems were because union reps *"stick their noses into everything, and cause trouble for the entire company."* He went on, *"They make no effort to help with anything."* Even after Gary invited union reps to managerial meetings, he complained, *"They don't give an inch. Instead, they demand pay increases and easier working conditions—regardless of the poor economy."* Gary failed to recognize how tone on both sides had become an insurrmountable barrier to developing talents or forming a relationship between union and company managers. To his credit, Gary sought answers, and took several significant steps to remedy the tone troubles.

Using the survey below, Gary identified tone toxins he'd fostered in meetings that drove *union discontent.* After completing the tone survey, he admitted surprise to find that he too could be cynical at meetings. More importantly, Gary recognized several unused personal intelligences, which could strengthen his leadership to align shared values between union and industry.

Tone Survey to Develop Brainpowered Differences

1. *Do you foster diverse talents by learning from talented workers?* Yes _____ No _____
   If not, question, and wonder, with people who have a keen eye for diverse talents.

2. *Do you target progress by inviting input from diverse talents?* Yes _____ No _____
   If not, partner with others as equals to target improvements for innovation growth.

3. *Do personnel expect or cultivate quality differences?* Yes _____ No _____
   If not, ask about specific details to show you support people's unique interests.

4. *Do you jump at opportunities to share cutting-edge ideas?* Yes _____ No _____
   If not, encourage multiple perspectives throughout your entire organization.

5. *Do you use reviews to celebrate what people do well?* Yes _____ No _____
   If not, hold frequent "innovation celebrations" to support and showcase novelty.

6. *Does your organization address people as talented capital?* Yes _____ No _____
   If not, support and mimic staff who demonstrate good tone daily.

7. *Do you support diverse facilitators of innovative ideas?* Yes _____ No _____
   If not, listen more and partner more with leaders in different departments.

8. *Do you share knowledge and offer frequent innovation tips?* Yes _____ No _____
   If not, invite novel ideas in ways that reward staff and leaders to create exchanges.

9. *Do you promote social media to increase caring and curiosity?* Yes _____ No _____
   If not, appeal to IT experts to implement and engage innovative networks.

10. *Do you drive innovation, as new engines move vehicles forward?* Yes _____ No _____
    If not, fuel original talents weekly, those often missed by nondiverse organizations.

After two weeks of using improved tone, Gary admitted he was more comfortable sharing experiences that pointed respectfully to different angles of the conflicts he felt at work. But now he asks *What if…?* kinds of questions, rather than offer personal opinions when issues arise with the union reps.

Tone Turns Gunners Into Givers

Surprised at the brainpower behind tone tools, Gary also found thoughtful recommendations from the same reps who'd made his job miserable prior to his improved tone. Eventually, Gary invited several reps to his office to brainstorm insights that might inspire a more productive exchange at the next meeting. The tone that shut out diverse views in the past no longer caused workplace toxins. In fact, exchanges became *visably energizing*, in Gary's words, in keeping with serotonin's chemical impact to add focus for possibilities. Sometimes referred to as the miracle drug, serotonin levels were raised by Gary's tone choices, to transform toxic exchanges into communications filled with well-being.

By applying *serotonin*, the brain's *well-being chemical*, Gary generated strategies that engaged differences at work. Now Gary approached union leaders more as colleagues who'd collaborate solutions with him, before problems or misunderstandings dragged down discussions at meetings.

After receiving positive feedback and practical suggestions that came back from union reps, Gary also placed union concerns as a priority in the next union-rep meeting agenda. The result? Employees from several departments brainstormed winning solutions. Not only did this help the company to move forward, but Gary saw how cooperative union reps became— once their issues were addressed collaboratively with tone that fostered different views.

New practices from tools began to build goodwill in what had been union-industry war zones. When Gary focused on how *mirror neurons* work for or against leaders (see the fifth tool in the following list) he facilitated successful solutions from unexpected places—his former enemies, the union reps.

Before long, manufacturing industry leaders across several departments offered innovative suggestions for working closer with union reps. The same leaders who seemed to be most of the problem initially now became a key part of the shared solution.

25 Walkways Into Brainpowered Tone Tools

Gary plans to use these tools to combine the best of union and industry interests with mutual dividends. Can your groups benefit in ways that foster innovative growth?

1. Pass a "talking stick" at meetings to get positive ideas for new ventures. Replace fears, fueled by dangerous cortisol, with profitable adventures fueled by serotonin. Run highly interactive meetings to show confidence in others. Brainstorm innovative components so that all speak and feel heard. Avoid defaulting back to ruts by shifting up meeting facilitators. Then offer positive feedback on their facilitation strengths.
2. Join social media networks to discover new trends for workplace rejuvenation. Help your team to avoid relying on their basal ganglia's natural ruts for careless tone. Foster online results that engage serotonin, the miracle drug for workplace success.

3. Ask advice from novices at times, for mind-bending revelations can result from questions to people who differ. Growth comes to any organization where youthful interests lead novel ventures in shared directions at work.

4. Take risks to win cutting-edge advances, and the dopamine your brain requires to risk well and win tends to follow. Take failures in stride and reward excellence each time it surfaces, to keep risks alive and maintain dopamine levels for more edge-of-your-chair winning than whining.

5. Become the manager you'd like others to see in you. People will then copy your best, because brains come equipped with mirror neurons—an inner mechanism to mimic actions of people around you. Each time you act like a genius, your brain—and others'—builds new neuron pathways for similar actions.

6. Engage your right and left brain to solve problems and motivate whole brain solutions by including those who differ or disagree. Multiple intelligence tools can be gauged and engaged through a MITA growth survey, which is included in the next section.

7. Discuss problems and aim for solutions that engage curiosity for rejuvenated practices. Oppose even one habit that holds back innovation, and new solutions stand a chance.

8. Listen with your brain to discover what promotes or reduces listening at work. Listen for positive tone that helps people segue into doable solutions from different angles to resolve stubborn problems.

9. Focus on one growth area and move past former distractions, because the brain comes equipped with a neural bottleneck that thwarts multitasking, according to research.

10. Seek feedback and recognize the universal problem behind sinking morale and plummeting productivity. Seventy-five percent of employees claim to be disengaged at work. Poor tone destroys capabilities. Seek long-range benefits by jump-starting peace plans, where opposing views are welcomed, rather than settling for one side. Then track and share peaceful resolutions achieved.

11. Reward novelty by introducing and modeling one change weekly at work. Novelty ratchets up the collective IQ of any group and moves groups beyond gridlock or mere compromise.

12. Capitalize on gender and race differences by seeking benefits from male and female brains and by using unique insights from both. Lead in ways that fuse racial differences into mutual dividends, and support minorities as facilitators.

13. Chill with ethical people to show value-based brainpower that sustains growth for all. Not only does the moral brain shape culture—but workplace ethics also shape

brains. Contribute to a valued climate by supporting others' talent beyond personal plans for financial rewards without ethical results.

14. Hire older workers and expect agility because we now know how plasticity helps seniors to grow new brainpower daily—don't waste their wisdom.

15. Facilitate winning solutions for people who differ and discourage bullying. Increase peaceful solutions to see violence and conflict fade in favor of inclusion. Change one routine to create space for inspiration and growth. Improve your brain's executive skills by leading one shared solution weekly to prompt curiosity that sustains growth and squashes stagnation.

16. Tame the amygdala for tone's sake. Act calmly under pressure and your brain stores that reaction for the next flare-up, allowing you to come up with innovative alternatives in pressured settings. Research shows that the brain comes equipped with chemicals to tame the amygdala, and it starts with snipping that urge for kneejerk reactions.

17. Laugh at little things. Gain brain benefits from enzymes emitted with humor that respects all, laughs at self, and diminishes none.

18. Use people's names as you communicate. Add value and release chemicals for well-being through using people's names. Speak people's names in their presence, and research confirms you also spark their brain's sense of worth.

19. Remember more by outsourcing facts through creating lists, and using other memory devices such as sketching new ideas as you hear them. Or apply new facts to what you already do, and welcome novelty, which research now teaches will literally stretch your working memory.

20. Discourage cynical encounters. Model tone tools to open opportunities not available to critics who counter creativity with cynicism. Expect to find one growth possibility in unexpected setbacks. Engage cynics in the kinds of solutions that land you ventures like gifted pilots land jets on emergency runways.

21. Make mistakes into stepping-stones to success. Move past regrets that shut down brainpower by doing the opposite of what guilt does. Step past prior mistakes and build forward on lessons learned from the past.

22. Stretch working memory. Design with specialists to move past technical glitches into innovative results. Learn a technology communication skill such as sketching what you read; this will engage the brain's innate ability to use new mechanical tools, through new neuron pathways. Engage smart skills that combine hard and soft traditional aptitudes to form brainpowered leadership tools for whole brain ventures. For instance, integrate what's traditionally separated (such as different departments) by proposing innovative initiatives that originate from increased brainpower across multiple skills.

23. Reconfigure people as capital for higher ROI. Position people as capital at the center, and expect increased innovation ROI at the edges. Replace one limiting myth (such as the myth that more money makes for finer performance) with a new reality (such as improved talents will add more profits for all). Refuse to settle for living traditional myths that limit innovative progress.

24. Cross-pollinate brainpower between novices and experts to boost creativity in both. Move younger people into experienced pathways for growth, encouraging them to teach as they learn from experts. Integrate people, departments, career fields, and different developmental levels. Collaborate to fix broken systems by offering your talents boldly. Support diverse brains from many backgrounds to replace broken systems with high-performing tools.

25. Increase leadership IQ by doing one alternative act daily. Move leadership brainpower up a notch since we now know that IQ is not fixed. It is fluid and grows daily for those who act in the opposite direction of broken practices, rigid routines, and ruts.

Make one significant change weekly using these brainpowered tools, and watch workplace problems slip away—while you generate mind-bending resources rather than rely on mere methodological reasoning. Then hear and value success stories shared, to keep growth alive. It's really about how you'll equip yourself and others for innovative advantages, in spite of setbacks you'll likely encounter. Envision tone threats transformed into talent takeaways.

Talent-Building Tools Jump-Start High-Performing Minds

Talent is a lynchpin between tone tools and a manager's facilitation abilities to shape and lead new ventures. A leader's tone capability to draw from differences in ways that combine arts and sciences, for instance, adds innovative opportunities with cutting-edge advantages. Tone stokes talents much like spark plugs electrify your vehicle. They both ignite voltage, as Gary discovered in his encounters with union reps. Tone stokes innovative ventures best when new neuro discoveries get engaged in the process. How so?

Good tone releases chemicals at each *synapse*, which can intensify motivation to seek for solutions within talented circles. *Neurons* project extensions called *dendrite* brain cells—which connect and reconnect daily, based on talents used and developed. *Axons*, in contrast, relay information from the body back to the brain. In a rather complex *electrochemical* process, neurons communicate with each other in synapses that can stoke talent development in a variety of ways. These connections create chemicals called *neurotransmitters* that can spark an integration of the multiple intelligences discussed further in the next section, for instance.

You'll be glad to know that it's not imperative to memorize brain facts to manage well. Leave that to neurosurgeons. Still, it helps to recognize basic brain equipment and consider neuro discoveries that pony up your best leadership talents. In that regard, the next section links brainpowered tone and talent growth opportunities that managers use to raise IQ across entire organizations.

Tone to Trigger Multiple Intelligences

If you agree that every employee comes to work daily with multiple intelligences, you'll also likely admit that few managers wield tone well enough to ratchet up people's potential. Brainpowered tone unleashes eight distinctive intelligences as workplace tools, including:

- **language tools** that might design word games or generate verbal clarity for a project
- **intrapersonal tools** that might log personal steps toward innovative insights on a project
- **mathematical tools** that might track progress and share potential in numbers or statistics
- **musical tools** that might include a newly developed musical brand or marketing jingle
- **naturalistic tools** that might compare and contrast nature's impact on innovative designs
- **interpersonal tools** that might survey workers from all departments for wider array of input, to ratchet up technology skills for instance
- **spatial tools** that might design visuals to share and progress an innovation's progress
- **kinesthetic tools** that might build mock-up displays to inspire a shared prototype.

Have you ever belonged to an organization that became proficient in conventional knowledge, yet stagnated because managers bypassed genius talents in any of the above areas?

Does your organization *expect* more? Louis Pasteur expected answers from his theory of germs. Alexander Bell expected communication through telephones. The Wright brothers expected heavier-than-air flying machines to perform as if lighter-than-air. The Warner brothers expected talking to transform into acting, and The Beatles predicted new sounds from guitar music. Ellen Kullman expected new inventions DuPont had been missing for years.

Expect talented takeaways when tone fuses different innovative approaches. Blend insights from people talented in the arts and those skilled at sciences. Expect ideas from those who work analytically, more from their left brain, and input from those who see the big picture, a right-brain operation.

Age, gender, or cultural differences add mutual dividends, when multiple talents leverage across differences. Share opposing views on a controversial issue with good tone, and watch innovative talents pop up like corn kernels fly in a movie theater.

Invite staff to prioritize three top intelligences (see below) to enhance team efforts for an initiative, as a way to identify hidden and unused talent at your workplace. Nudge innovative ideas into inventions that draw from *multiple views*—using both sides of the brain—and multiple intelligences begin to surface in response. Or survey staff using the 40 identifying items below. Discover multiple intelligences that are easily honed into problem-solving tools, when good tone connects talent to growth of newly discovered capabilities.

To calculate your unique strengths, simply skim the list below quickly for 15 items that describe you best. Scribble the numbers on a paper for any items that describe you, for instance. Move quickly, without pausing to ponder any survey item. Rather than stop and think more about any statement, simply leave that item blank, and move on for best results.

Multiple Intelligence Tools Applied— MITA Growth Survey

1. Sitting still at work is hard since I do better when active. _____
2. Peers describe me as well organized on a daily basis. _____
3. Photography often says more, so I capture life in pictures. _____
4. Designing webpages comes easily. _____
5. Throwing or catching games win my interest. _____
6. I tend to design posters or charts to share project results. _____
7. To debate opposing views with clarity is my talent. _____
8. Background music helps me focus on difficult issues. _____
9. Stories often gain my interest. _____
10. Sketching or painting is easier for me than woodworking. _____
11. I often unpack details to help others understand new concepts. _____
12. I find multiple-choice tests easy and logical. _____
13. To support peers or friends, I'd likely join a march for a good cause. _____
14. I might play a musical instrument just to relax. _____
15. I maintain a personal journal to track progress. _____
16. For factual books, I tend to outline main ideas. _____

---

17. Metaphors work well for me, as a way to describe. _____
18. Often peers look to me to get along if stress strikes on team projects. _____
19. Whether working or relaxing, background music is great. _____
20. I tend to walk alone at times just to think or plan. _____
21. In novels, I tend to compare fiction with my own life. _____
22. With or without a map, I usually find destinations well. _____
23. Melodies replay in my mind after concerts. _____
24. Cooking freshly caught fish on a campfire can be fun. _____
25. I enjoy singing in a choir, even in a busy week. _____
26. Often I tell stories based on personal experience. _____
27. For me, patterns and big-picture ideas come from data. _____
28. Regardless of the season, I connect often to nature. _____
29. To brainstorm with other people builds my own ideas. _____
30. To help others complete a project brings delight. _____
31. Discovering solutions for numerical problems is fun. _____
32. I'd rather write a team press release than write one alone. _____
33. Often I participate in sports. _____
34. I'd jump to using gestures in a role play. _____
35. At times I identify my weaknesses as a way to grow. _____
36. New dance steps or moving to music adds enjoyment. _____
37. To observe animals' habits teaches me more about life. _____
38. Lessons easily come from lakes, creeks, rivers, or oceans. _____
39. I'd write an essay to enter a contest anytime. _____
40. At times I get up early just to enjoy a sunrise. _____

Answers from the above survey are matched with each intelligence listed below. Your strengths, and unique mix of intelligences, will become apparent in your scores.

- Verbal-Linguistic: 7, 9, 11, 17, 39
- Logical-Mathematical: 2, 12, 16, 27, 31
- Visual-Spatial: 3, 4, 6, 10, 22
- Musical: 8, 14, 19, 23, 25
- Bodily-Kinesthetic: 1, 5, 33, 34, 36
- Interpersonal: 13, 18, 29, 30, 32
- Intrapersonal: 15, 20, 21, 26, 35
- Naturalistic: 24, 28, 37, 38, 40

Retake the survey after a month or so to measure growth areas.

> ## To grow multiple intelligence tools in:
>
> 1. **Verbal-Linguistic:** tell stories, write essays, interview people, converse easily with peers.
> 2. **Logical-Mathematical:** solve problems, balance budget, create schedules, budget projects.
> 3. **Visual-Spatial:** paint, draw, design webpages, design workspace, make cards, create logos.
> 4. **Musical:** attend concerts, play instrument, hum melodies, sing with others, enjoy rhythms.
> 5. **Bodily-Kinesthetic:** engage in sports, enjoy movement, walk on tours, use body language.
> 6. **Interpersonal:** discuss in groups, do community projects, debate, join online chat rooms.
> 7. **Intrapersonal:** keep personal journal, read alone, study to answer personal questions.
> 8. **Naturalistic:** collect specimens, hunt, follow animal footprints, photograph landscapes.

Activate Risk's Neural Pathways

It takes risk to improve tone, and luckily the brain comes equipped to risk for managers who choose to lead differently. It's merely a matter of helping *neurons* and *dendrites* to spark new *synapses* for innovative change based on good tone.

Since a *neuron* is nothing more than a *nerve cell,* and your brain holds about 100 billion of these little critters, good tone marches them much more toward wins. Remember, synapses fuel growth from doing and leading things differently.

In Joseph Conrad's words: *The mind is capable of anything—because everything is in it, all the past as well as all the future.* Facilitators extend that kind of talent possibility further, by designing tone skills to build innovative solutions together.

When recession hits, or when challenges drain organizational momentum, few deny an urgent need for such innovative change. How will tone risk talent development where you work? Dr. Gregory Berns's bestselling book *Iconoclast: A Neuroscientist Reveals How to Think Differently* suggests that novelty offers elixirs to those who risk for advantage. Don't expect much support at first though. Remember, the past is imprinted in unaware brains of prominent voices.

"Slavery works," dominant voices demanded, while for centuries brilliant minority voices, with finer insight about equity, could have led a more prosperous way. Had they been

engaged earlier, they could have broken chains that still bind many today. Had they known that human brains build new neuron pathways from jaded acts into more of the same ruts, such inequity might have been less common in current organizations today. Simply put, one manager's tone can reshape the brain cell structure of entire groups.

Progressive organizations risk standing up to pressures against change. Well-known leader of innovation and risk, Parker Palmer (2011), refers to limitations that come with valuing one dominant voice only, when he suggests that people *seek deeper within self, and deeper within others.*

Mistakes become stepping-stones along risk's pools in brainpowered approaches. When financial challenges hit the MITA International Brain Center midway into the global recession, we turned to leaders who transformed defeat into success that raised their bottom line. In the midst of difficulties that sink many meritocracies in slim times, we mimicked practices from folks who found innovative solutions, in spite of tough times. In a live talk where MITA Vice President Dr. Robyn McMaster and I blogged internationally with world business leaders, I learned risk's value from iconoclasts like George Lucas. Lucas engineered *Star Wars,* after sidestepping Hollywood's rejection, and focused instead on creating some of the most brilliant creativity the big screen has seen to date.

Perhaps Bach-y-Rita's brilliant story that follows relates best to brainpowered tone as a life-changing turnaround tool for an entire health industry.

Tone Turned Bach-y-Rita's Risk Into Global Leader Title

Brains change daily, the father of *neuroplasticity,* Paul Bach-y-Rita, proved, as he converted life-changing defeat into mind-bending neuro discoveries. After his 65-year-old father's crippling stroke and despair after a month's therapy and little progress, medical experts suggested placing him in an institution as the only choice.

It's hard to see possibilities in their collective tone: *Brains cannot repair themselves*, every medical leader argued. *Nothing can help a stroke victim walk or talk again,* became their mantra. Rather than watch his father slip from respected professor at City College in New York, Paul brought his papa back to Mexico and focused on good tone and the talent that turns problems into possibilities. He leveraged the risks needed and simply taught his aging father to crawl again.

Onlookers ridiculed every risk taken, as mainstream medicine mocked. Using the wall to support his limp shoulder, Bach-y-Rita inched along clumsily for months, as he and his sons created marble games to play on the floor that required reach and movement. Cynics in medical schools warned that this was wasted time, and neighbors criticized the Bach-y-Rita family when their papa crawled outside, saying, "They are treating this old man like a dog." When progress began to show, Paul studied how the brain reorganized itself to take over damaged parts. The elderly Bach-y-Rita returned to teach at City College in New York, at age 68—three years after his stroke. Brainpowered tools improve difficult areas, reshape prosperity, and rewire a focus to win. Tools support action and ensure persistence on the other side of loss.

Paul Bach-y-Rita's life was shaped by what he described as *seeing with our brains and not our eyes,* as his papa's brain reorganized itself for new directions. Winning the highly respected title—*Father of Plasticity*—he went on to explain research behind key areas of plasticity, or the brain's ability to rewire and find solutions when cynics and naysayers shout words of doom and disaster. Brainpowered tools often extend beyond organizational solutions, and into designing prototypes. But what about cynics on the sidelines?

Awareness of Tone DNA in Cynics Avoids Talent Loss From All

Effective managers gain good tone buy-in by shaping practices *with,* and not *for,* their workforce. In spite of many mysteries that still occur in the quadrillion synapses within a human brain, wonderful benefits await skilled facilitators who use brainpowered tools to pre-empt or curtail cynicism.

People at every level in an organization will soon fully expect resources to follow, when reasonable expectations are met in energized circles that rid work settings of toxins that cynicism can add.

Brain facts below suggest how managers transform workplace toxins into tone tools. Diversity and talents need not be buried by bullies, cynics, or naysayers, if facilitators put into place one or two of the following brain-related strategies to engage curiosity. Most organizations either propel talents forward or tank them due to their awareness levels of the following brain operations:

- Amygdala for the cynic is that tiny sac of neurons that remains agitated most of the time, overheats easily, and triggers turmoil as an emotional pattern. Tools to tame your amygdala include creating a culture of gratitude by rewarding people who inspire and support others.
- Cortisol releases from cynics like falls at Niagara, as its potent chemical slams people into stress that shrinks human brains. Tactics to counter that cortisol surge

include facilitating a jointly created program to help workers identify and deal with stress.

- Neuron pathways for cynics create disagreeable expressions of gloom, and habitual synapses can reshape moods or jade perspectives into permanent problems over time. Since all today's actions shape tomorrow's mental wiring, encourage natural light and a healthy setting and stoke positive moods at work, for instance.

- Plasticity rewires the cynic's brain nightly for angry responses and deep-seated frustrations. Outwardly, poor tone cripples opportunities to prosper. Rewire against cynicism by doing its opposite, and teaching positive ways a brain changes itself based on risk-taking innovation, since every action you take today helps to reshape the brain as you sleep tonight.

- Dendrite brain cells connect negativity to negativity in cynics' minds, and this re-generates mental stagnation not seen in the curious. Practice one positive act and watch chemical and electrical activity reboot you mentally for more of the same.

- Basal ganglia, with its propensity to default back to ruts, stores and replays worst habits of cynics till others can cite their complaints by heart. Discuss and plan deliberate actions against racism, sexism, and other poisonous practices picked up and played routinely without much thought.

- Working memory sits unused and often remains mute for the cynic, who finds no need for mental equipment that prospers the curious or leaps into action for solution-bound minds. Focus on facts that build concrete solutions and working memory tools spring into action to solve complex problems out of bounds to the cynical mind.

- Brain chemicals refuel wretched moods in cynics, with decreased natural drugs for well-being, and increased hormones for negative behavior. Cynicism blocks sero-tonin, but tools presented in this chapter will strengthen this *molecule of happiness* and stir up chemicals that synapse for growth.

- Serotonin sinks lower in the mind of the cynic, leaving the brain without resources against anxiety, disquiet, anger, or conflict at work. Since each cynical act can lower a brain's natural serotonin supplies, increase serotonin through healthy foods, ex-ercise, and many behaviors that spike sincere satisfaction. (Check out Dr. Robyn McMaster's article at http://twurl.nl/eautmm to fuel your brain as you fill your plate.)

- Brainwaves of cynics rewire daily for more cynical performances. Organized by a hierarchy, electrical waves control how neurons communicate for better or for worse, and cynical forces can surge a brain's circuitry for negative outcomes.

Sadly, toxic tone quickly fills the vacuums when talents go ignored in any organization. Awareness helps here. Share the above list of toxins, and watch workplace tone tactics re-place harmful toxins in favor of leading innovative talents.

Lead Prosperity in Turbulent Times

Consider the missed genius in those who either cling to the past or regret what's here now.

Conventional approaches—that often include poor tone—won't blast your organization past gridlock or compromise. We know this from lack of punch needed to stretch and grow new job opportunities. We have a long way to go when it comes to tone toxins that stunt growth in less resilient workforces, while morale tanks. Loss and failure's no surprise when disconnect exists between what brains do well and tone managers neglect to use. It doesn't have to be that way.

10 Brain Facts Trigger Tone Tools

- Managers improve tone, increase talent, and transform training, based on how they do the following: Engage opposing views to use more *working memory* rather than remain in ruts. Otherwise you default to the *basal ganglia*—the mental storehouse that replays past tone habits.
- Access both *left and right brainpower,* to locate diverse pathways across isolated silos or departments. Combine hard and soft skills, for instance, or tame the *amygdala* to calm that seat of emotions when it heats during challenges.
- Run from stress and other workplace toxins, since stress literally shrinks brains and its *cortisol* chemicals crush progress. Laugh at the little things instead, and increase *serotonin,* the chemical for well-being, by using good tone.
- Question to stoke *multiple intelligence* responses in ways that increase curiosity. Gain innovative outcomes in *novel* ways to ratchet up workplace IQ for ongoing inventions.
- Cultivate *interpersonal intelligence* initiatives, especially in volatile markets, by meeting diverse customer needs through stoking more synergy between arts and sciences.
- Activate risk's neural pathways for new initiatives to spark the kind of *chemical and electrical circuitry* that gains well-being and higher productivity from all workers.
- "Mind guide"—or mutually mentor others—in ways that teach as you learn. Retain more by doing than by listening. Grow *brain cells* for mind guiding by teaching and learning in tandem.
- Facilitate improved individual and organizational DNA by creating more interactive meetings and developmental sessions where folks explore new ideas that offer the kind of hope triggered by the trapped Chilean miners, before being rescued in October 2010.
- Reflect with people rather than assess or critique their weaknesses in conventional ways. Acknowledge more success and trigger change with mutual dividends through the wonders of *neuroplasticity,* which reconfigures brains daily.

▨ Propose solutions for problems raised at work, and model brainpowered leadership rather than venting—which merely creates *neuron pathways* for more of the same.

Without doubt, organizational change can appear daunting at first. Those managers who lead even one neuro discovery from the list, though, already cracked open a window for rejuvenation and excellence in their organizations.

What if you simply stepped in the direction of one novel idea worth pursuing, as I did to design a brainpowered approach to managing excellence?

MITA Pillars for Excellence

To be honest, I wanted to lead excellence, far more than I wanted to design a model to make it happen. Had there been a model out there that valued people of all cultures, or that led excellent results for all, I'd have run with it—yes, even gladly forfeited a life's work to design the brainpowered leader approach featured in this chapter.

Had I located more managers who invited wonder, delighted in new discoveries, and supported people to live the scientific method for the sake of new discoveries, I'd have leapt for joy to lead with it. Instead, managers I met seemed settled in a maze of myths more about personal entitlement than about innovative greatness.

Had I found curious managers, for instance, who engaged and investigated new ideas, rather than talking as insular experts at meetings, MITA's brainpowered approach wouldn't have been necessary. To think I'd have saved 30 years of global travel to consult leaders in many countries and learn from diverse cultures. Rather than promote broken traditions or foster rigid routines, I spent a lifetime riding an advanced magic carpet over amazing wonders and woes of change around pillars of excellence, illustrated in Figure 11-1.

If mentoring had resembled reciprocal coaching more, I'd have embraced it. I'd not have bothered designing an approach for guiding excellence—which teaches and learns as it leads. Or if conventional managers had modeled the fact that IQs are more fluid than fixed, I'd have grown new capabilities with them in response. Just that one lived reality would have helped to find more of the leadership excellence I craved. Where was the manager who reached for the wider good or cultivated values and ethics at the helm?

I tossed around questions. For example, *could leadership shape mental and emotional health for people—promote more laughter and prevent unfair performance reviews?* I'd have contributed more to ratchet up workplace well-being. Instead I added another critical component to MITA's approach as a way to ensure access into the brain's heightened capabilities through laughter.

Increasingly, people lament failed leadership, as they observe political leaders unprepared to engage civility or without skills to learn from opposing views. Wasted possibilities of talents that could be managed, yet seemed ignored, compelled me to harness multiple intelligences into brainpowered tools for a finer future.

Had managers helped workers rewire more for peace that cultivates freedom, liberates humanity, and leaves folks primed for shared solutions—rather than settle for violence or war—I'd have jumped on board. Instead, holy cows of *critical thinking* promoted cynicism and truncated innovation, so I honed brainpowered tools. Determined that MITA approaches could lead adventure on the other side of cynicism, I regained hope alongside managers I admired.

Check out the ratio between what people and organizations might have been, and what they've become, and you'll likely agree that rejuvenated leader approaches are urgently needed. It was that reality check that launched MITA brainpowered tools with so much positive global response. It's also why the *MITA International Brain Center* continues to align workplace progress with dynamic neuro discoveries.

After years of working across many countries and cultures where *tone-related gridlocks* too often limit managers, MITA's five-pillar approach both cultivates and sustains tone just as it fosters innovative initiatives as the norm.

Brainpowered Tone Stokes Innovation

The five-pillar approach instructs that as managers, you should:

- **Question** possibilities with the kind of tone that engages opposing views, while at the same time building goodwill among those who disagree.
- **Target** improvements and collaborate solution possibilities from diverse angles that engage people's talents.
- **Expect** quality inventions by facilitating differences, encouraging growth, and engaging shared possibilities.
- **Move** multiple intelligences into well-shaped conduits that blend, use, and value people's unique strengths and different perspectives.
- **Reflect** on sustainable growth possibilities—in *brainpowered celebrations*—hosted across your entire organization to cross-pollinate ideas and track initiatives.

Each pillar finds roots in 17 learning and leading theories, is affected by relevant neuro discoveries, and applies to diverse cultural practices in several countries where it was implemented and designed.

Constructed to counter workplace toxins (see far right boxes in Figure 11-1), the model offers entry points for rewiring the brain in ways that promote innovative growth across differences.

Growth opportunities (illustrated in top boxes of Figure 11-1) result from implementing all five brainpowered pillars, while any one omitted (as illustrated in empty boxes) results in commonly encountered barriers to corporate innovation (represented in right column). It's time to support managers as cultivators of advanced potential in any organization. Have you seen it in action?

Imagine your workplace alive with innovative on-the-job problem-solving tactics. Feature motivated people who wield clever devices that affect the department's bottom line by opening new spigots to brainpower. Now you've looked straight through MITA's leadership lens. In reality, it's more dynamic than its manifesto (can be found at http://twurl.nl/exq3g3) and packed with more neuro-related punches that excellent leaders tout.

On MITA's most basic level, brainpowered tools simply equip managers to help drive winning productivity. Leaders like you drive its engines. Three specific problem areas, detailed in three following sections, urgently need to change before prosperity can surface.

Figure 11-1. MITA™ Leadership Growth Chart – 5 Pillars					
QUESTION Pillar 1	+ TARGET Pillar 2	+ EXPECT Pillar 3	+ MOVE Pillar 4	+ REFLECT Pillar 5	= GROWTH Pillars 1-5
	+ TARGET	+ EXPECT	+ MOVE	+ REFLECT	= PASSIVITY
QUESTION		+ EXPECT	+ MOVE	+ REFLECT	= CONFUSION
QUESTION	+ TARGET		+ MOVE	+ REFLECT	= SLOPPINESS
QUESTION	+ TARGET	+ EXPECT		+ REFLECT	= WASTE
QUESTION	+ TARGET	+ EXPECT	+ MOVE		= STAGNATION

In leadership courses at graduate levels, MITA leaders facilitate excellence as it shapes these three areas:

- **tone,** which builds goodwill, and reduces toxins among those who disagree
- **talent,** which converts hidden and unused cognitive capabilities into cutting edge workplace solutions across formerly isolated silos
- **training (or mind guiding),** which drives innovation for ongoing novel ventures. A closer look shows the pitfalls and the possibilities for all three.

How would MITA's brainpowered tools equip you to lead goodwill, unleash talent, and mutually engage others for a finer future with innovation as the norm?

Explore *What If* Possibilities

Awaken new intelligences or strengthen old talents by engaging original ideas through *what if…* possibilities. Invent and toss around genius insights, as Einstein did.

Most gifted managers, whom we work with globally, tend to develop childlike desire to blast open entry points with brainpowered tone tools that inspire innovation. At meetings, they add more zip to roundtables because people are encouraged to speak and feel heard. Across silos, they inspire shared language that leaves behind jargon in favor of meaningful communication. In learning circles they draw on multiple literacies that engage voices on many sides.

On projects they ask questions that may appear as stupid as Einstein's absurd ideas about riding a beam of light, and expect brilliant solutions that fit well into and find buy-in from a wider community. When met with diversity they ensure quality access for all by setting high standards and then encouraging alternative approaches. They model fair practices in business by guaranteeing ethics for all they engage.

When conflicts arise, facilitators seek kindness by modeling positive tone that builds goodwill among even those who disagree. Across genders they call upon insights and apply these in ways that equally represent perspectives from males and females. With fellow leaders they illustrate humility and resist arrogance in favor of visible innovation they lead and promote. In matters of change, skilled facilitators courageously avoid ruts to prosper growth and improvements for those they serve. Have you met them?

Far too few use tone tools as portals of discovery, though. Many managers tend to discuss inefficiencies or vent about organizational problems, such as tone that erodes workplace well-being. For example, researchers discovered glaring gaps in innovative skills required to lead well in the current era. The Center for Creative Leadership asked 2,220 leaders from 15 organizations in three countries what leadership skills appear inadequate to meet current and future demands. Experts surveyed found that missing was the leaders' ability to lead, plan, facilitate, inspire, communicate, persevere, and learn. Have you noticed how gifted leaders draw more from both sides of the brain to operate these skills, by creating space for genuine answers, and by building goodwill among those who may disagree on answers offered? To inspire questions is to begin the innovative process, to hear new and wider ideas about pressing problems.

When leaders ask questions, curiosity begins to carry expectations past dangerous cortisol chemicals that fuel frustrations in disengaged settings.

Poor tone may spread gloom faster than donuts disappear from Monday morning's staff room, *but curiosity generates mental refreshers and fosters new growth from unexpected places.*

Not All Questions Are Equal

There're no responses when I ask questions in training sessions, HVAC owner Mark said. *So nothing changes, nothing improves.* People who ask *what* if kinds of questions, on the other hand, hold people's attention until novelty becomes reality. To increase innovation IQ, question with two feet—or draw from both sides of the brain—and pre-empt poor tone at any session, before it springs.

Ask, for example: *How could this new technology program spark a winning innovative venture in your work week?* (One foot involves progress through new IT, and the other engages person in good tone possibilities.)

Or ask: *What can we do differently together when new technology problems surface?* Great questions increase buy-in, and model tone skills for civil discourse across differences.

When you question *what if,* synapses begin to convert brainpower into winning answers. The opposite is also true. Remember that first 17 days, when hope dimmed for the Chilean miners' rescue? They squabbled, and fostered deep despair. When they focused more on rescue opportunities through *what if* questions, miners collaborated solutions on a daily basis.

Ask advice from a novice, remembering that good ideas often seem stupid at first, as the great astronomers, Meso-Americans, found when they offered primitive ideas about the structure of the solar system. Consider their initial ideas about eclipses and planets revolving around the sun, and then ask yourself what a genius who values accurate predictions might do in a challenging situation you face. Then do just that. Research shows that brilliance is less tied to numerical scores of a fixed IQ than to visible multiple intelligences that are used and developed in ways that grow more intelligence, through confident breakthroughs that build on others' ideas.

Question a problem with solutions in mind, and engage curious leaders to make predictions about broken systems replaced with techniques that work. Innovative answers are often located on the other side of flawed systems—and they yield faster to those who question well. Ask compelling questions during a boring meeting, and target multiple responses by actively engaging diverse insights as plausible solutions. Ask people to contribute even off-the-wall ideas, including those that may fail, to facilitate skills from unique voices on your topic. Run a highly interactive meeting that engages all, and talent begins to surface in response.

Propose Solutions for Problems Raised at Work

Most leaders agree that *intelligent solutions are far more than facts accumulated and are highly flexible to be increased at work* (Kuszewski, 2011).

Armed with a sense of curiosity, brainpowered leaders stoke talented workers to invent mind-bending products or processes that will shape futures and sustain profitability in a new era. It's especially critical during hardships and anxieties recession brings.

When curiosity leads to new talent development, holistic brainpower follows. Good tone simply encourages invention from many minds, and empowers people to seek solutions that integrate soft and hard skills across both sides of the brain. When managers question possibilities, as opposed to value one way only, workers spot and capitalize on innovative opportunities. In that way, curiosity rids an organization of hindrances and opens windows to novel tone tools that holistic innovators crave. The prime requisite for facilitators is to apply the tone they wish others to see in themselves, so talents come together from different areas.

The most successful managers would likely agree with Albert Einstein, who claimed to have no particular talent but said that he was simply inquisitive. The brainpowered approach in this chapter uses diverse intelligences that rarely get engaged. Curiosity ushers in unique talents that most organizations crave—yet few develop tone to cultivate.

Seek *what if*…possibilities, and your workplace begins to develop new neuron pathways toward mental endowments that climb higher peaks.

How will your organization join talented managers, brainpowered tone in hand, to profit from innovative opportunities already on the horizon?

Good tone encourages diverse voices when facilitators affirm one another's ideas.

- Thank people for offering different views.
- Share personal experiences respectfully and invite the same from the group.
- Ask questions to engage others rather than offer your own opinions.
- Start with, *What's your solution to ...,* and engage left and right brainpower.
- Encourage unique ideas through *Where to from here ...* questions to inspire confidence in people on opposing sides of all issues raised.

References and Resources

Berns, G. (2008). *Iconoclast: A Neuroscientist Reveals How to Think Differently.* Boston: Harvard University Press.

Doidge, N. (2007). *The Brain That Changes Itself.* London: Penguin Group.

Gardner, H. (1999). *Intelligence Reframed: Multiple Intelligences for the 21st Century.* New York: Basic Books.

Koestenbaum, P. (2002). *Leadership: The Inner Side of Greatness.* San Francisco: Jossey-Bass.

Kuszewski, A. (2011). You Can Increase your Intelligence: 5 Ways to Maximize Your Cognitive Potential. *Scientific American.* Retrieved from http:/scientificamerican.com/blog/post.cfm?id=you-can-increase-your-intelligence-2011-0307&WT.mc_id=MND_20110414.

McMaster, R. (2011). Fuel Your Brain as You Fill Your Plate, Brain Based Biz Blog. Retrieved from http://twurl.nl/eautmm.

McMaster, R. (2011). Forbes, *Mind Makeover,* 12 Sparks for Heads-Up Creativity. Retrieved from http://www.forbes.com/sites/mindmakeover/2011/03/18/12-sparks-for-heads-up-creativity/

Palmer, P. (2011). *A Hidden Wholeness.* San Francisco: Jossey-Bass.

Weber, E. (2011). Forbes, *Mind Makeover,* Tools to Hear—Tone to Engage. Retrieved from http://www.forbes.com/sites/mindmakeover/2011/04/02/tools-to-hear-tone-to-engage/.

Weber, E. (2005). *MITA Strategies in the Classroom and Beyond.* Boston: Pearson Publishers.

Weber, E. (2010). The MITA Manifesto for Brainpowered Renewal—Brain Leaders and Learners Blog. Retrieved from http://www.brainleadersandlearners.com/change/mita-brain-manifesto/.

Weber, E. (2011). YouTube on MITA Brains to Learn and Lead. Retrieved from http://www.youtube.com/watch?v=QLWXRmRzXG0.

About the Author

Ellen Weber, PhD, is the director of innovative change at the *MITA International Brain Center,* a global leadership facilitator, and adjunct professor at The Bittner School of Business. She designed and teaches a brainpowered management course, Lead Innovation With the Brain in Mind, both online and in real time. Weber writes and speaks widely on innovative responses to leading innovation for diverse results, with the brain in mind, including on her blog called *Brain Leaders and Learners.* In addition to neuro research, Weber bases brainpowered practices on cultural proclivities. You can find Ellen's website here: www .mitaleadership.com.

Section II

Managers as Culture Builders

"I view my role more as trying to set up an environment where the personalities, creativity, and individuality of all the different employees come out and can shine."

—Tony Hsieh

Chapter 12

Who Says There's No Crying in Leadership?

Terry "Starbucker" St. Marie

Editor's Note

Terry St. Marie (aka "Starbucker") is a force of positive mojo, like a fire hydrant filled with chocolate. He oozes passion, energy, focus, and support—all important things we want from our managers. In this narrative chapter, Terry introduces us to his former manager and what he did to create an environment where Terry could flourish. In the end, we get the sense that Terry has done this for his team members, too.

We thought he was indestructible. Our leader, our inspiration, the man who entered every room with a smile on his face and a mischievous gleam in his eye, had just passed away after fighting a courageous battle with cancer. How were we going to deal with this? As senior vice president of operations, I was one of the primary connections between our CEO and all the field employees, so what I said and how I acted was going to have a big impact. So I approached my first visit to the field after his death with a great deal of trepidation. I had worked with this man for 16 years, and known him for 22. He had a style of leadership that I would classify as undeniably human, and personal.

I'll never forget how he found my resume in his stack of papers, and personally picked up the phone and called me, inviting me to come to his office in suburban New York. He picked me up from the airport himself, and then personally escorted me through a day of staff meetings, a lunch, and a memorable hour in his office. It was memorable not because of all the deep business discussion we had, but because of his incredible gift of making you feel at ease, and comfortable. That was his way of breaking down the walls of fear that typically could exist between the boss and the employee. I had absolutely no problem telling him my strengths and my weaknesses, about my family, about the high points and the low points of my life, and my high ambitions. I wanted to be a leader—something I had promised myself I'd doggedly pursue since I had hit my career bottom two years earlier.

He sensed this passion in me, but couldn't help but give me a dose of his mischief. At the end of our conversation I finally asked him about the job he had summoned me to New York to talk about, and he replied, "Job? Oh, I just wanted to see what you were up to. There aren't any jobs to talk about." There was a big pause, and then that smile. I got to know that smile a lot better over 16 years, and it was always a signal of something either very funny, memorable, useful, or prophetic. This time, it was all of those things. He mentioned that there just happened to be a staff manager position in the international division available (as if it had just occurred to him). Would I be interested?

It took all the discretion I could muster not to enthusiastically accept the position on the spot, without even knowing the salary or the responsibilities. That's the effect that man had on people. I eventually took the position, even though it was lower paying (and with less responsibility) than my last job, because I trusted him when he said that there would be opportunities to shine and advance. That's how our 16-year relationship began, and now that it had suddenly ended, as I got on the plane for my trip west to visit the field, that day in his office seemed like only yesterday, and as the plane took off I closed my eyes and let the emotions come to the surface.

It was good to have this kind of release, but I wondered, how should I handle this in front of everyone? Should I be the good soldier, stoic and measured, and keep the focus on the business at hand? Or should I be "just me"—the person my teammates would expect to be emotional at such a time? There was a lot of the "just me" in the past six and a half years—I finally got my chance to be the leader I wanted to be, and oh yes, I took advantage of it. The best part of it all was the freedom this boss gave us to express leadership in our own way, much like he did over his long career. And express it I did. In a lot of unique ways. I traveled to the field extensively. I had team meetings. I set a goal of at least meeting every one of the 1,100 employees in my department. I sang. I danced (strange, but true).

I also would hit emotional crescendos in a lot of my many speeches, almost getting to the point of tearing up, but never outright crying. I could get loud, I could get quiet. It was all out there for everyone to see.

Me, in all of my glory.

At first, the field staff didn't know what to make of it. They were so accustomed to buttoned-down executives, that is, if they ever saw them at all. Here was this guy, showing up, and not "acting" like an executive. He was putting himself out there, making himself vulnerable because of his lack of pretense or ego, and because he wore many of his emotions on his sleeve.

Yep, that was me. And it took a few years before we all got it figured out. There was a deep-seated distrust of "corporate management" that was cultivated and fanned by many years of neglect and false promises by previous owners.

I'll never forget the early conversations I had with some of the staff—all that frustration, all that unhappiness, all that anger. And for a while, it was directed at us. There were union drives and intense meetings, and some incremental progress, followed by setbacks. Yet, during this time, I could sense that there was going to be a break in the clouds, as long as I stayed true to myself and the style of leadership I was practicing—open, honest, passionate, caring, and emotional.

The break came one day as I spoke to a group in Colorado that was going to decide on whether or not they were going to join a union. We sat in a circle, the six of us, in the stock room, and we talked and talked and talked. I poured my heart out about the bond we wanted to form among all of our teammates, and that the only way to do that was to trust each other. "Trust us," I implored. "Trust me."

I told them we would take care of them. We would not lie to them. We would keep our promises. And if I was wrong, I'd personally come back, admit my error, and face the music. There I was, vulnerable again. I had just put myself way, way out there. At least I knew someone had my back on what I was promising. That man with the mischievous grin. He didn't always like my deeply personal approach—we had a few heated conversations over those 16 years—but in the end, he was always honest, encouraging, demanding (in a good way), and loyal.

The coolest thing was his knack of putting a positive spin on all but the most hopeless of situations, a trait that undoubtedly influenced my own "glass half-full" philosophy. That's why I could put myself on the line with the field staff—that's why I could put my passion, enthusiasm, and emotion to productive work. He trusted me. I trusted him. But now he was gone. And wouldn't you know it, the very first place I would visit after his death was one of those locations where I had to work the hardest to earn people's trust. These folks had suffered through a lot of poor management, and they had built a nearly impenetrable wall of corporate mistrust. But the thing that I liked about them was the fact that they were connected to each other—a team that had rallied around a common cause. Unfortunately, the "cause" was protecting themselves against "the man," aka the corporate office.

As you could imagine, my very first visit there was a little chilly. There wasn't much said—just a lot of listening and eye-rolling. You could just see it in their faces—"Here we go again."

But I kept coming back, and kept peeling the layers off that wall, once again by putting my feelings out there. Not long after my "Trust me" breakthrough in Colorado, I came back once again, and this time I knew exactly what I needed to do to completely break down the wall. I told them we would not only make their jobs better, but that we'd make them happy. Smiley face happy. I actually drew that on the whiteboard in the meeting room, right before I sang a little karaoke for them.

"Oh man, he's going crazy now," they must have thought. But I could sense that in that thought was more than a glimmer of "Hey, this guy's a real human, and I think I am ready to trust him."

Of course, I added some real goals and objectives to the mix—the things that would get them to happiness. I called them "the five things you need to know." Before long, every person in my department knew those five things, and why they were important. And, slowly but surely, the tide turned. It wasn't long before my visits there became like family reunions, where they could almost make my speeches for me (yes, I love the value of repetition), and the biggest question was the karaoke song I would attempt on that occasion. Through all of this I never changed my approach—if we had screwed up on some corporate initiative, I'd tell them, and apologize. If we had a victory to celebrate, we'd do it up right. My smiley faces only got bigger, and my passion and enthusiasm only got stronger. These folks had become a family to me, and now I needed to stand in front of them and talk about our late CEO and his legacy and address the "What happens now?" questions.

It was a long plane ride. I started thinking about all the things that man had done for me, the company, and all the other people who worked for it. I thought about his generosity, his bad jokes, and the way he would never let me off the hook when it came to continuous improvement. (I will not soon forget the time I was crowing about achieving a 95 percent success rate on a certain metric, and he turned to me and said, "Terry, I don't understand—why not 100 percent? Why can't you get 100 percent?) I didn't need to wonder how, over those 16 years, I was able to become a personal leader, one who cared for those he led, and who tried to lead with passion, integrity, and more than just a little bit of fun. It was because of him.

There was a time during those 16 years where we didn't own any businesses—and yet, he kept a team at his side, on his own dime, to see if we could find another magic bus to ride. He was determined to get the deal he wanted, and he used all the guile and charm he had to secure the last one, the business I was honored to be a part of for the last six and a half years. And when he got it, he made his desires clear—he wanted to build a company that cared for its customers and employees like no other, and provided the highest quality of service.

Those were my marching orders, and he trusted that I would execute them. And because I respected him so much, there was no way I was going to let him down. That's the thing about loyalty—it's a very powerful incentive. There's also a corresponding fear of failure, and in hindsight, that was a powerful motivator too—one that, in a strange way, allowed me to be "me."

How so? Because I just *had* to trust my instincts, rather than rely on someone else's definition of good leadership. My instincts told me to open up, to be vulnerable, to just *be there* for everyone, and they would trust me to do the right things for them. It worked, and we succeeded just as our CEO had hoped. But now, he wasn't there to enjoy that success.

I arrived at the airport and began my lengthy drive north, still trying to piece together the words I would say to the staff. I was working at this too hard, and I knew it. I never needed to prepare this much before. In fact, I loved to "wing it" for just about every speech I made out here, just because of the thrill of it, and the "realness" of it. It was yet another potential vulnerability, but it never really was a problem. As I neared my hotel, it finally dawned on me that I should approach this speech like any other—just speak from my heart. That made it much easier to get the rest I needed. It was going to be an interesting morning.

I arrived at the meeting place and found the atmosphere to be as welcoming as ever—these folks knew that I had lost one of my most important mentors, and they were very gracious and supportive. They all settled into their chairs, and when I began to speak, you could have heard a pin drop. "Boy," I thought to myself, "a big change from the first time I ever came here, when I could barely get anyone's attention."

I talked about the man we had just lost, but I really wanted to talk about his legacy—*us*. What we had accomplished. Why we accomplished it. And what it had done for us as a business, as a team, and as individuals. We were part of something bigger than ourselves—a company committed to service, to teamwork, and to being good corporate citizens. We worked hard because we cared about the results. We cared about each other. We just plain cared.

And why did we care? Because he did—boy did he ever. I remembered the time he sent a helicopter to the Grand Canyon, on his own dime, to rescue an employee's wife who needed immediate medical care. He didn't even hesitate when he heard about her situation. He just cared. That's when I cried. Right then and there. This time I couldn't stop it, and I wondered how I'd be received. I peered through my misty eyes and noticed that that there were many other people crying too. There were no awkward glances, or obvious discomfort. No, this was a big group cry and virtual hug. And it felt right. And while it was sad, it felt good. Who says there's no crying in leadership? Probably those who weren't fortunate enough to work for a guy like him.

This chapter is dedicated to the memory of Bill Bresnan, the founder of Bresnan Communications and one of the pioneers of the cable television industry, who passed away in November 2009.

About the Author

Terry "Starbucker" St. Marie is the managing partner of Inside-Out Thinking (IOT), a business development consulting group. He most recently completed a successful 23-year tenure as an executive in the cable television business. Terry also publishes a popular blog on business and leadership at www.TerryStarbucker.com, and is a co-founder of SOBCon, a biannual business conference and one of the best learning and development forums for owners of small and medium-sized businesses in the United States.

Chapter 13

The LPK Field Guide— An Inspiring Model for Communicating Expectations

LPK Design Team

Editor's Note

This is one of the most unusual chapters in this book because it contains portions of LPK's Field Guide for employees, and the story of how this extraordinary piece came to be. When I first saw the Field Guide, I recognized it as one of the most compelling expressions of how one company defines excellent work. To help their team members excel, managers must be able to articulate how they would define outstanding work—not just the "whats" but some of the "hows" and "whys." I hope you are as inspired and blown away by this example from LPK as I was, and I am very grateful that they allowed me to share this with you. Take note in the story that they took great care on both the design of the Field Guide and the launching of it. Hey managers—sometimes a little drama and positive theater is a good thing! A note on the layout of the field guide pages in this book: The original Field Guide is wider than it is tall—this book is taller than it is wide. What you will see is that we have included the pages that are left and right in the Field Guide and we set each page as an image on its own page in this book, centered within the page. When you open the book and are looking across the spread of two pages, you will be seeing it the same way as if you were opening the Field Guide itself.

Be yourself, not your client. It's not the easiest lesson to learn. But, when you get there, you'll find that not only might your client like the real you a whole lot better than the trying-too-hard-to-be-them you, you'll like yourself better, too.

We launched the LPK Field Guide in conjunction with a reboot of our corporate identity. At the heart of this undertaking was the crafting of a new organizational mindset brought to life by a new tone of voice, as well as a new logo, new colors, and new typography. We're a brand design agency, so this is the work we do for our clients day in and day out. We had just never done it for ourselves in such a comprehensive way.

In the weeks leading up to the launch of the Field Guide, employees were gradually turned on to the idea that change was coming. Invitations were sent to participate in new, people-focused corporate photography, and a countdown display in our street-side windows hinted that an event was imminent.

The LPK Field Guide was launched on day one, a symbolic moment that served as the culmination of the LPK identity reboot. At an 8:30 a.m. company meeting on a bright October Monday, our corporate status quo was challenged by a creative interloper, the spoken word artist Sekou Andrews, who announced to all in attendance:

> *There is a movement begun here / A shifting of tides*
> *Your workplace of yesterday has vanished before your eyes*
> *It matters not how it happened / matters only that you accept it*
> *That you recognize the power of a transformed perspective*

When Andrews's performance ended, the new logo was unveiled, and shortly thereafter, the meeting adjourned. As LPKers returned to their desks throughout our buildings, they found two gifts waiting for them: a box of brightly colored, redesigned, and customized business cards and a small booklet, the LPK Field Guide.

Within the Field Guide was a new message. Bringing together emerging ways of thinking from across our organization, it laid out our standards for "great"—what it looks like, how it sounds, and what it means. It set clear expectations for what each of us must do to achieve greatness, and its voice demonstrated a dramatic contrast to LPK's previous communication materials. Before, we sounded and felt more like our clients' voices and had even adopted their vocabulary. The Field Guide was presented in a first-person, creative-to-creative voice, making it clear that imitating client-speak was no longer our accepted way of thinking or talking. It reinforced our independence as an employee-owned design agency, and, most importantly, it reminded employees that their creative minds and voices are our organization's most valuable assets.

The LPK Field Guide is built around beliefs and values that are meaningful to our people, and it speaks honestly about design, creativity, and work. An inspiring purpose and aspirational vision are meant as true calls to action for everyone at LPK. The expectation is clear to all who read it that, as employee owners, each of us is accountable for the success of our business. If something is wrong, or even if we just don't like it, it's up to us to do something about it.

LPKers embraced the story they found in the Field Guide. Its statement that "creative is not a department" was a call to throw out preconceptions about traditional roles and relationships between all of the departments that make up our organization. It exemplified the courageous act of speaking up and emphasized accountability not just to the organization, but to each other and to ourselves.

The LPK Field Guide marked a symbolic moment in time for our organization. It was a chance for us to speak directly to our employees. It explains why we exist, how we act, what we value, and what we expect. It tells employees what they can expect from us and tells it in a simple, concrete, inspirational, and unexpected way. It acknowledges what, in the past, wasn't always said outright: "You are here for a reason."

The LPK reboot activities that culminated on day one provided real, distinct, and tangible opportunities for all employees to shift their mindsets and habits. It ushered in change to our organizational structure, marking the demise of the traditional department, setting the standards for a new employee performance development system, and launching "The Mechanics," LPK's approach to best practices and creative process. People began to see themselves as change agents and moved our organization forward with incredible speed.

Since it was launched, the Field Guide and its message have become fundamental to the voice of LPK. It's given to each new hire on their "day one." It distills the ideas that brought us through a time of transformation. Speaking up, expressing opinion, and taking chances are our responsibilities as co-owners of our agency. The LPK Field Guide is the road map to participation and success for every creative person at LPK.

About the Authors

LPK is a Cincinnati-based design and branding firm. You can find the company's website at www.lpk.com. "The LKP Field Guide—An Inspiring Model for Communicating Expectations" contains pages from the LPK Field Guide. Reprinted with permission.

Wheels Up

To achieve great things takes a great leap of faith and a fearless community to fuel you.

So here is what you can expect from the LPK culture: We will challenge you and expect you to deliver. We will get out of the way of the people who are getting stuff done. We will not provide answers, but we will be there to give inspiration, direction and support. We will give you the room to do your work your way, to chase the best ideas and to make our clients our raving fans.

Our culture is real and it is important. It's also a work-in-progress, and probably always will be. But trust us, in an often-dramatic, fairly cruel industry, we're one of the good ones.

Here's what makes our world go 'round:

Be resourceful.
And by that, we mean:
Reboot before calling IT.

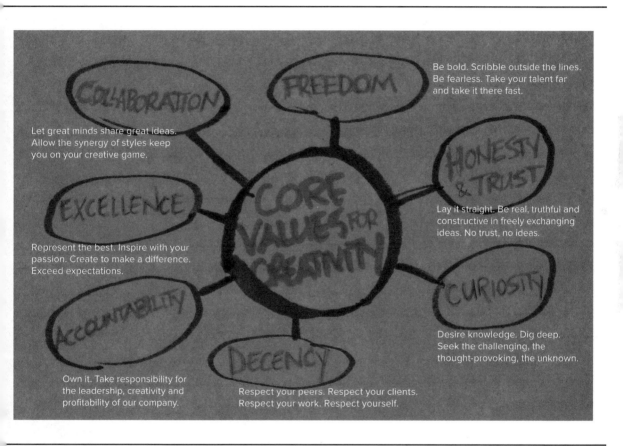

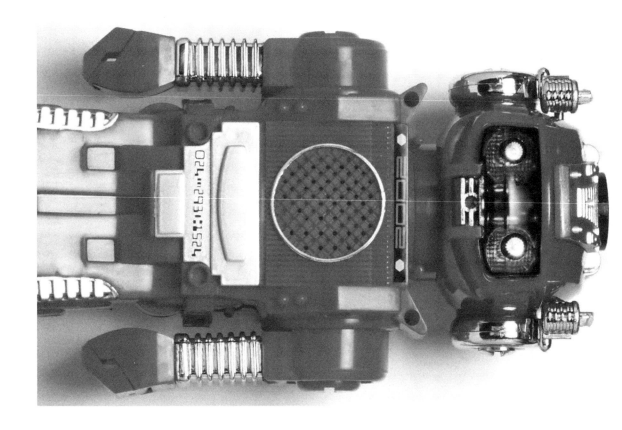

Destroy the Robots

Yes, we're all different. Blah blah blah. Not a news flash. But every culture has a way of walking and talking that's designed to navigate the day-to-day—a code of conduct. From the suits to the sneakers, here's how to act:

Be yourself, not the client. If you would prefer to work for one of our clients, that's understandable. You wouldn't be the first to go down that path. If that's the case, we'll wish you luck, tell you to enjoy the cafeteria food and only ask that you give us a call from the other side. But as long as you draw your paycheck from LPK, stay true to who you are—that person we hired in the first place. Stay creative and curious. Stay passionate but objective. Don't fall prey to the temptation to round off the edges, to use someone else's words, to tell 'em what they want to hear. Because if you look/sound/act like them, it won't take long before someone over there wonders why they've hired an agency who brings them nothing new, different or interesting.

Decide like your job depends on it. Cute words of advice, right? But in our case, they hold water. You are now an owner of this company. We all are. And as such, we are responsible for the future of the organization. So approach every situation as if it were a referendum on your future. Think things through. Be smart with money. Take some risks. Have a Plan B. Act quickly and responsibly. Return that call. Write that email. Find that perfect image. In the end, the decisions we make today will ensure our jobs for tomorrow.

Hell yeah, you work for an ESOP!
That chair over there?
Yours.
That pen?
Yours.
That seat at the company meeting?
Yours, too.
Feels good, doesn't it?

Less talk, more do. It was the great sage Yoda that famously said: "Do or do not...there is no try." Good advice in any galaxy—especially this one. Our industry is competitive. Right or wrong, people are keeping score. And it's the people who are doing stuff that are putting points on the board. Ultimately, no amount of emails, philosophical debates and Keynote decks can match an idea that is effectively executed and made real. Focus on what Design does best—making things.

Here are some tips:
- Make the most out of meetings and you can have fewer of them.
- Make a quick prototype or three.
- Make it happen.

Treat every day as a defining moment. Let us be clear—excellence is not some distant destination off in the horizon, years and years away. It starts at this very moment and continues to the next. String one little success with another, and pretty soon, they've added up into something big and meaningful. Who knew your work life should be so Zen?

Challenge and inspire. Your colleagues are counting on it. Goes double for clients.

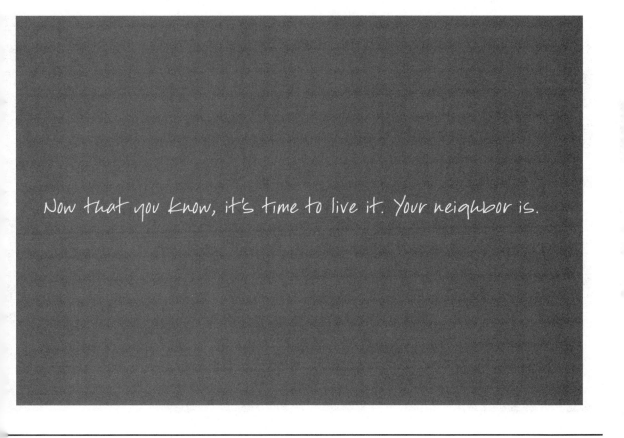

Now that you know, it's time to live it. Your neighbor is.

Creative is Not a Department

Once you grow to be more than three people, you have an "organization." That's just the way it is. An organization needs to have structure and departments, policies and binders. And that's fine, they help things run smoothly and allow us to focus on what's important—the work and our clients. But a quick word of advice: The more people ignore departmental boundaries, the better. The best idea is not yours or mine, but what is created when we mash the two together. We demand an idea be judged according to its merits, not its author. So if you are the one leading a team, stay objective and allow for the possibility (however miniscule) that someone else may have an idea better than yours. And if you are not leading the team, let the ideas flow and remind us why you have a desk in this place.

Research shows meetings run 35 percent shorter when everyone stands up. The studio table... Now your newest, bestest conference room.

Take That Hill

Theodore Roosevelt said, "Whenever you are asked if you can do a job, tell 'em, 'Certainly, I can!' Then get busy and find out how to do it." Sometimes clients ask for things that we've never done before. That can be frightening as hell or extremely exhilarating. Sometimes what they ask for is in our sweet spot. Either way, attack the work determined to smash expectations into tiny little pieces. Can't figure it out? Call a smart friend—there should be one sitting right next to you.

Outside These Walls

Value our clients. The good ones will enable our best work, tell their friends about us and happily pay the bill on time. The bad ones will weed themselves out.

Respect our vendors. They make us look good when we don't have the time, energy or expertise to do it ourselves.

Get along with our agency partners. This is just good business. Sure, they can be difficult. And sometimes they are just flat-out wrong. So deal with it in a constructive, positive way that will serve our ultimate master—the client's best interests.

1. Delivers Business Results:

2. Contributes to the Creative Culture:

3. Develops Skills:

Old Business Proverb: Measure What Matters

LPK's Performance Measures

> **Delivers Business Results:** Creates sustainable business benefits.
>
> **Contributes to the Creative Culture:** Inspires. Empowers. Collaborates.
>
> **Develops Skills:** Continually improves personal skill set.

LPK's Critical Skills

> **Leadership:** Envision a future state. Inspire and enable others to get there.
>
> **Priority Setting:** Right time + right energy + right things.
>
> **Opportunity Finding & Problem Solving:** Be open to new experiences. Find a way to fix problems.
>
> **Communication:** Get your point heard. Hear others as well.
>
> **Collaboration:** Be an additive force and pull your weight.
>
> **Functional Mastery:** Do a kick-ass job and deliver the goods.

Fuels to Avoid

> **Centralized control freakiness**
>
> **Passive-aggressive behavior**
>
> **Pecking behind the scenes**
>
> **Cynicism addiction**
>
> **Creative apartheid**

Eyebrow waves and head nods are only acceptable in the halls if your hands are completely full. We want more high-fives.

Chapter 14

Rethinking Your Organization as a Community—The Open Source Way

Chris Grams

Editor's Note

I heard management guru Gary Hamel assert that innovation happens on the fringe—in smaller, edgier places where individual ideas can have court and grow legs. This chapter from Chris Grams is an excellent example of how large organizations can transform with the right energy and focus. For managers, the challenge and opportunity is creating workplaces that foster fringe thinking and cultivate freedom and participation. Chris offers great examples from his days working at Red Hat—a company that took the open source idea and applied it to creating a better workplace.

Introduction

In October 1969, when experts at the U.S. Department of Defense Advanced Research Projects Agency (DARPA) connected the first two nodes of what is now called the Internet, they probably weren't considering the ramifications of their actions on the future of management. But in the past 20 years, the Internet has changed everything—about both our lives and our work.

For the most part, organizations have embraced the *technological* changes that have come with the Internet (or they have not, and have since disappeared). But fewer organizations have truly embraced or even begun to understand the *cultural* changes that the Internet has ushered in.

We may *live* in 2012, but given how many of our organizations are structured, we might just as well be *working* in 1912. What do I mean? Most of our organizations were built on top of a management framework that was designed at the beginning of the industrial age. It was revolutionary...in its time.

In his excellent book *The Future of Management*, Gary Hamel puts it this way: "Management's boisterous, inventive adolescence lies nearly a century behind us. In fact, most of the essential tools and techniques of modern management were invented by individuals born in the 19th century, not long after the end of the American Civil War.... Like the gasoline engine, our industrial-age management model is languishing out at the far end of the S-curve, and may be reaching the limits of its improvability."[1]

The traditional management practices that have guided organizations since the dawn of the industrial age are now being stretched to their breaking points by the shifts in society brought about by the Internet. Fundamentally, management and the Internet are at odds over one simple thing: Traditional management is designed for *control*. The Internet is designed for *freedom*.

That's why the principles used to manage assembly line workers in 1912 are often rejected in 2012 by a new generation of employees who have grown up enveloped in the freedom of the Internet. To them, the industrial age management model is an anachronism—a legacy system held onto by the old generation of leaders who are unwilling to give up control because they see freedom as a threat.

Against this backdrop, a new breed of organization has emerged. These organizations aren't bound by the shackles of traditional control-based management practices. Many of these organizations were born of the Internet era, often taking approaches to organizational culture and management that are centered on providing freedom rather than asserting control. These organizations have the advantage of being built from scratch in a new model, rather than having to overhaul a deeply entrenched organizational culture and set of management practices. Yet all organizations can learn from this new breed.

---

[1] From *The Future of Management* by Gary Hamel, p. 7.

The Open Source Revolution

Over the past decade, I had a firsthand view as one particular freedom-based organization emerged in the shadow of the Internet. From 1999 to 2010, I was part of the team that built the brand and culture of Red Hat, a company best known as the leader of the open source software movement. During this time, the company grew from 100 people in one small office in Durham, North Carolina, into a $1 billion worldwide software company successfully competing with some of the largest technology companies in the world.

Red Hat, founded in 1993, was truly a company born of and inspired by the Internet. Its employees were members of a worldwide community of people (often referred to as the open source software community) who freely shared source code with each other beyond the company walls in an attempt to collaboratively build a new computer operating system from scratch.

Open source software is fundamentally different from traditional software because the underlying source code is not owned and written by any one organization. Instead, many individuals, corporations, and even governments around the world work collaboratively, developing the software together. The resulting source code is "open"—meaning it is licensed in such a way that anyone can use it, improve it, or even develop their own products and services around it.

Why did open source community members find this sort of open collaboration valuable? Because by being open, they knew problems would only have to be solved once. They knew chances were good that someone else had already faced and overcome challenges similar to their own. When everyone shared, everyone benefitted from a huge reduction in duplicated effort. Innovation occurred faster.

The type of collaboration that drives an open source software project would not have been easy in a pre-Internet world. Many of the projects are distributed, with contributors never actually meeting each other face-to-face and often collaborating on projects from opposite sides of the world. Anyone with skills and desire can contribute to an open source project, and project leaders are chosen based on the quality of their contributions, not their seniority or connections.

The innovation spurred by this new development model has been spectacular. Today, much of the Internet itself is literally built on top of open source software. You may not be familiar with all of these tools—like the Apache web server, the Linux operating system, the Firefox web browser, WordPress blogging software, and the Drupal content management system—

but they are a part of the daily Internet experience of hundreds of millions of people using the Internet.

Because the people working on open source projects often don't work for the same organization and aren't always receiving financial compensation for their work, many traditional management practices used to organize, motivate, and reward employees just plain don't work on them. The open source world has had developed a very different set of rules and cultural norms in order to innovate rapidly in a cross-organizational community setting.

The Community-Based Organizational Model

At Red Hat, we didn't just use this community-based approach in our work with the open source community. We took many of the exact same principles we saw being used to create great software in the open source community and applied them to the organization itself. We began to rethink the organization itself as a community. This community-centered organizational model is not only the key to the success of Red Hat and the open source software movement, but also offers lessons for any organization looking for ways to thrive in a world defined by the culture of the Internet. In the following pages, I'd like to share some lessons I learned during my time at Red Hat illustrating how to build a community within an organization—the open source way.

Replace Control With Freedom

The open source software community began with a group of individuals who joined forces because they knew they could write better software together than on their own. These individuals were volunteers and had the freedom to work on whatever projects interested them, coming and going as they pleased.

In volunteer-based community settings, efforts to exert control are often poisonous. Volunteers will simply quit before being forced to do something they don't believe in or value. Yet in traditional organizational settings, control—over people, resources, and information—is a fundamental lever.

At Red Hat, *freedom* was the first of our four company values, and its effect was felt deeply within the organizational DNA. Many of our best technological innovations came courtesy of employees who joined a community effort not because they were told to do so by their manager, but instead because they personally saw great value or potential in the project. Many more great ideas came courtesy of memo-list, a companywide email list that everyone in the company was subscribed to and where anyone could suggest or challenge an idea—regardless of job title.

We systematically tried to replace control-based practices with freedom-based practices anywhere we could, putting employees in charge of their own destinies, allowing them the freedom to figure out the best path forward. We couldn't do this everywhere, of course, but when faced with a decision that required us to exert control or offer freedom, we chose the latter as often as possible.

By thinking of employees as volunteers in a community, rather than as workers to be controlled, you'll stand a better chance of keeping them engaged. When employees are forced to work on projects they don't believe in or value, they may not actually quit their jobs, but they will often quit in every other way—doing just enough to get by and keep their job safe, or in some cases even undermining the effort.

This is a fate worse than having them quit. They become organizational drones, complacent, indifferent, and dispassionate. They'll stop contributing ideas because they think no one cares. They'll stop giving full effort because they think it doesn't matter.

Replacing control with freedom is a great way to inspire your employees to become true volunteers, deeply engaged in achieving the organization's goals, rather than drones or mercenaries, who seek only safety and a regular paycheck.

Balance Freedom With Accountability

Red Hat was still a business, not a naïve communal utopia. We understood that offering uninhibited freedom by itself would not produce the results we were looking for. So we worked hard to ensure freedom was balanced by another Red Hat value: *accountability*.

We saw the balance between freedom and accountability occur naturally in the best open source community projects—filled with volunteers who not only worked on projects they cared about, but also held themselves (and each other) accountable for the progress they made.

At times, the management of the company demanded accountability from employees in return for the freedom it gave them. But, when we were at our best, accountability was not simply a management mandate. Instead, it was actually *the employees themselves* who would demand accountability from those around them. Much like in a productive volunteer community, the standards for good work were enforced not from the top down, but instead all around.

Collaboratively Discover Shared Purpose and Values

People join communities because they believe in what the community has set out to do or because they share a common set of principles or ideals with other community members. Yet many of our organizations do not have a clear purpose beyond simply sustaining themselves or making money. And if they do, it is not widely held or shared by employees.

To operate as a community, an organization must understand what bonds it together. A hollow mission statement and set of values printed on posters in the lobby of the headquarters is not enough. These ideals must be closely held, understood, and subscribed to by everyone within the organization. One great way to achieve this is to open up the process of creating the purpose and values for contributions from across the organization.

At Red Hat, the company values were collaboratively developed as part of a process that was open to input from all employees. Because the process of developing the values was open and collaborative, and many employees saw their beliefs and ideas reflected in the final product, the values were rapidly accepted as a core part of the Red Hat culture. A decade later, the same four values we uncovered as part of this initial process are still deeply held within the organization.

Red Hat used a similar process to develop the company mission. Ideas could come from anywhere, and they did. For example, one of the words in the final mission that had been particularly problematic for the team leading the effort was replaced thanks to a suggestion from a regular staff member responding to an online request for ideas.

Employees may accept a job, but they volunteer for a mission. Organizations envisioning themselves as communities must seek out and inspire the people who want to be part of something meaningful. One great way to ensure people are committed to the organization's purpose and live its values is to give them a key role in creating them.

Default to Open

The open source community is truly open in almost every sense of the word. Source code is shared in public repositories where anyone can access it, and all work occurs on public forums, websites, and mailing lists where anyone can see, comment, and contribute. Organizations that envision themselves as communities seek to ensure openness and transparency are the rule rather than the exception. They default to open: meaning, rather than keeping information, conversations, and decisions *private* by default, they are instead *public* by default. For example, the brand communications team at Red Hat shared a workspace where every employee, from the vice president to the intern, sat in an open area that allowed everyone to see and hear what others were working on. If someone needed to have a private conversation, we had rooms and offices with doors that employees could use.

But the key was that everyone was part of the open dialog by default. People had to make an active decision to be closed. Most traditional organizations operate exactly the opposite way; doors, information, and conversations are closed by default and only opened up by an active decision to do so. When an organization defaults to open, it creates the potential for the kind of sharing, collaboration, and interaction that adds enormous value and innovation. It also increases the transparency of decision making, which can be a key factor in keeping people engaged.

Let the Best Ideas Win

In most organizations, strategy is determined by those at the top, with the rest of the employees simply following orders. But the best open source projects operate as meritocracies, where the best ideas can come from anywhere, and often do. Sometimes people who have been working on a project for years and know it inside and out have the best ideas, while other times the ideas come from the fresh voices and talent that are new to the community.

Organizations operating as communities find ways to ensure the best ideas can bubble up from within the organization. The easiest way to do this is to make decision making as transparent and collaborative as possible. In the open source community, there is a saying: "Given enough eyeballs, all bugs are shallow." (In the software world a "bug" is a problem with the software code.) The same principle applies broadly to organizations—with enough people working together, any organizational "bug" can be fixed, and any innovative challenge can be tackled.

An organization operating as a community dispels the myth that the best ideas always come from the people at the top of the organizational pyramid. By creating a culture where good ideas can be heard and adopted, you'll not only be taking better advantage of the intelligence already found within the organization, but you'll likely be uncovering your future organizational leaders at the same time. Not to mention that you'll be inspiring people to contribute their ideas because they believe the organizational leadership is actually listening.

Release Early, Release Often

In traditional software projects, a new version of the software may be released only once every few years. But in an open source project, because the source code is open and visible to anyone who wants to see it, new improvements and innovations appear all the time. The principle of "release early, release often" guides most of these projects. The more quickly you can get your freshest ideas out there where others can see and improve on them, the more progress you'll make.

Yet most companies innovate behind closed doors, only releasing their strategy, plans, projects, or products when they are "ready." Organizations that transparently open up work for comment and improvement quickly cannot only expect to innovate faster, but they can often avoid large costly mistakes that could have been avoided if feedback and ideas were incorporated before the projects were "ready."

At Red Hat, we often opened up the decision-making process to scrutiny from the entire company via the memo-list email list. Memo-list might be used to gather ideas on how to address a competitive threat, or it could be a place to test a prototype and get feedback from employees, or it might even be a place to explain a decision that has already been made and get feedback from employees on how to make the next decision even more effective.

Organizations that want to operate like communities aren't afraid of getting feedback early. They "show their math" along the way so that employees have an opportunity to provide feedback, offer suggestions, and help improve things before the final project is revealed.

Share the Legends

Over time, every community develops a set of stories that help to articulate what is important to community members and why the community exists. Sometimes these stories are creation myths that help explain how the community first came together. Sometimes the stories are about events that put the community to the test, triumphs over adversity, or important victories or milestones. Most importantly, these stories often show the values of the community in action. They make it easy for new community members to understand what is important and figure out whether they'd like to be involved.

At Red Hat, we made sure to capture and share as many stories as we could. Some were truly legends, like co-founder Bob Young telling the three possible stories of how Red Hat got its name (his words: "There are three official versions, and *you* can pick").[2] Some, like the official Red Hat story, explored larger themes such as the company mission and the context behind it.[3] But we also captured everyday stories—the ones about employees living the values, progress we were making in the spirit of the mission, or examples of people from

---

[2] You can watch the video where Bob Young explains how Red Hat got its name on YouTube here: www.youtube.com/watch?v=SaxAOVsNl6c.

[3] Here is a blog post I wrote about the Red Hat story where you can watch the video and download the book: http://darkmattermatters.com/2009/07/29/sharing-your-brand-story-and-heres-ours.

outside the company who inspired us.[4] Some of these stories were captured on video, while others were written as mini-books, articles, or blog posts.

Organizations that capture and share stories and legends articulating their core purpose and values in action make it easy for new people to learn whether they'd like to "volunteer" for the effort. They also help reinforce the core purpose and values of the organization for those who already belong. These stories create heroes and role models. They inspire people to bring out the best in themselves and others around them.

Build an Architecture of Participation

The term *architecture of participation* was originally coined by Internet pioneer Tim O'Reilly in 2004. He used this phrase to describe the systems that must be in place to support participative efforts.[5]

An open, collaborative approach to organizational design won't work without putting in place systems and practices to support it. The core architecture of participation at the heart of the open source software movement is the Internet, and without it the kind of large-scale open collaboration necessary could never occur. Certainly, for collaboration to work, technology is important, and there are a number of great collaboration systems and tools now available that both improve organizational transparency and make it easier for employees to work together.

Yet, in my experience, most solely technology-based collaboration efforts in organizations today fail. Why? Many organizations fall into what I call the "tool trap." The tool trap is the belief that simply investing in the right collaboration software will make collaboration occur like magic within the organization. In many cases, planning time is spent almost entirely on deciding what is the right software tool to buy.

An effective architecture of participation for organizations attempting to operate as communities certainly has a technology component, but it also has an even more important *cultural* component. If the organization doesn't support, reward, and make it easy for collaboration and openness to thrive, they won't, no matter how good the technology architecture. Companies wanting to operate as communities will need to make not just technology changes, but also cultural and structural changes in order to build an effective architecture for participation.

---

[4] You can find many of these stories on the Red Hat website here: www.redhat.com/stories.

[5] Here is a link to Tim O'Reilly's original blog post titled, "The Architecture of Participation": http://oreilly .com/pub/a/oreilly/tim/articles/architecture_of_participation.html.

A Few Final Words

By their nature, organizations that were born during the industrial age were designed to be as effective as possible in an industrial world. By the same token, organizations born during the Internet age are designed to be as effective as possible in an Internet world.

But the organizations that have it toughest are those that were born during the industrial age (or built on an industrial age model), yet are trying to remain relevant today in a landscape where freedom is a more valuable management tool than control. Moving from control to freedom is one of the most difficult transitions an organization can make. This transition requires much more than simply a good strategy for change—it requires a *will* to change.

Those in charge of the organization—the very people who have the most to lose by giving up control—must make a decision that freedom is a strategic imperative. The competitive landscape is littered with the carcasses of formerly successful companies whose management team did not know how—or didn't have the will—to make the leap.

Even beyond the open source software world, the examples of successful freedom-based communities experiencing rapid growth and great success are plentiful. I wonder what the management teams of the biggest producers of encyclopedias would do differently if they could turn back the clock to a time before Wikipedia. Or what the newspapers might do if they could go back to an era before blogs and Craigslist.

The strategic decision to change a control-based culture into a freedom-based culture is not one that a management team should take lightly. But in order to compete with companies born in the age of the Internet, employing the children of the Internet, and built in the spirit of the Internet, *there may be few other options.*

About the Author

Chris Grams is the president and partner at New Kind. He builds sustainable brands, cultures, and communities in and around companies and organizations. He is the author of *The Ad-Free Brand: Secrets to Building Successful Brands in a Digital World* and is the community guide at Gary Hamel's *Management Innovation Exchange.* Chris blogs on brand, community, and culture at Dark Matter Matters, and on open source and the future of business at www.opensource.com. You can find Chris's website at www.newkind.com.

Chapter 15

From Quality to Excellence: Essential Strategies for Building a Quality-Oriented Culture

Tanmay Vora

······················· **Editor's Note** ·······················

If I wanted to know about how to create a quality culture, I would pick Tanmay Vora's brain over a virtual latte Skype call. Managers own quality but can only deliver on their responsibilities when they enable and support their team. In this chapter, Tanmay offers a detailed and compelling look at what it means to focus on quality in today's complex work environment. I love how he gets to the heart of the matter and dispels many unhelpful and narrow-minded views about what quality improvement efforts should look like.

Q uality is one of the top agenda items on most modern managers' lists because quality has a direct impact on the markets and profits. Companies remain concerned about how quality can be further improved to maintain customers' confidence, meet their requirements, increase productivity, and reduce cost/rework.

Quality is not just a competitive advantage anymore, but a strong platform on which speed, flexibility, and innovation can happen. To deliver quality is not just a part of a manager's

KRA (key result area), but it is also an obligation. Customers pay because they want quality. Team members work on a project because they want to do a great job. A manager's approach toward quality is always a key differentiator between a successful and unsuccessful initiative. *Managers have a direct impact on the quality of outcomes.*

Modern managers face three critical challenges:

- Most quality theories are built on industrial experiences, which are still necessary, but not sufficient in a knowledge-oriented world.
- The definition of quality is not completely clear. Different managers have differing and often subjective views about quality.
- Quality is not built on an assembly line anymore, but is built by people. In a project-oriented knowledge world, people-related challenges directly impact quality of outcomes.

The objective of this chapter is to put quality in perspective of modern management and outline essential strategies to build a quality-oriented culture in a knowledge world. For organizations, success can only be repeatable and sustainable when all managers relentlessly focus on building a culture where quality is not just expected, but also valued. As Crosby rightly said, *"The responsibility for quality lies 100 percent with management and the common language of the subject they transmit."*

Quality in Modern Management Context

To take this conversation forward, it is first important to understand what quality means in modern context. The first absolute rule of quality is that customers always expect a defect-free product. That is the starting point. "Good enough" quality is not enough. When schedule and cost take the front seat, managers tend to look for "good enough" quality. Absolute quality is a difficult target, but certainly a worthy one.

Every defect is a cost, and the way to reduce this cost and build quality is prevention. Too much attention is paid to correction, inspections, and testing. Prevention means you have to think about quality early and often. We have an old adage that is completely apt— "prevention is always better than cure."

In knowledge world, quality is not just "conformance to customer requirements"—quality is happiness. Happiness of people who develop and deliver, internal customers, business stakeholders, and external customers. A defect-free product that meets or exceeds expectations is a delight to have. Happy people deliver better quality and walk that much needed extra mile.

Achieving quality is a two-step process. First, you have to build remarkability into the design, strategy, process, and product features that exceed the expectations of customers (quality of design). Second, you have to comply with laid-out design and actually execute/produce according to the process (quality of execution). Excellence is always a product of quality of design and quality of execution.

Finally, quality is a moving target—each time a customer comes back to you, you need to deliver similar or better quality (of products, services, and experience), and you need to demonstrate improvement, care enough about the customer, stay on top of market trends, and keep changing the rules of the game (innovation). When you consistently focus on delivering value, your customers move higher up in the value pyramid to become advocates of your product or services.

Quality and Excellence—How Are They Related?

Quality is generally extrinsic. It is driven by external demands like customer requirements, process compliance, and best practices. Quality is more about meeting the requirements. Excellence is always intrinsic. It is our innate desire to go out of our way to deliver a superior experience, not because someone else demands it, but because *you* want it that way. Excellence is a "people game," and the one that pushes quality one step forward.

Quality is a route to excellence. People can do their best, walk that extra mile, and think of adding value once they are absolutely clear of how to do the basic things right. Processes give them a firm base on which they can build excellence. On the other hand, excellent people may fumble if they are not supported with the right set of guidelines on delivering quality.

Excellence has a lot to do with people's motivation to do a great job. It is their choice. Getting people to exercise their choice of delivering excellence is the number-one challenge for modern managers. It starts with getting the right people and building the right culture.

The Role of a Middle Manager

Here is a tweet from my first book titled #*QUALITYtweet:*

> #QUALITYtweet The first step of your process improvement journey is to know what really needs improvement.
>
> 31 seconds ago via TweetDeck

Strategies for growth and improvement that take a shape in corporate boardrooms are implemented on the floor by people at all levels. Middle managers translate these larger goals and vision into actionable tasks that teams execute. Middle management of your organization plays a pivotal role in mobilizing people to execute tasks in line with larger goals and values.

Most "quality improvement" literature focuses on *"commitment from the top."* That is the first step. I would also like to emphasize *"commitment from the middle management"* because the middle managers are a very important link between the top and rest of the organization.

The primary focus of the top management should be on nurturing the middle layer of management, for these managers can make a huge difference in organization's growth. They drive the culture, model the habits, and set a tone for people who execute. A strong middle management means a strong organization.

Typically, the role of middle managers in quality management is:

- to ensure that all actions, tasks, and behaviors are aligned to the broader vision and goals
- to build a strong customer-oriented culture by setting the right examples
- not just to manage people, but to truly lead them
- to have a strong business acumen to facilitate right decision making
- to be oriented to and driven by customer needs, hence building a customer-oriented culture
- to take accountability of culture building and not always look to the top for directions
- to mobilize people to drive quality
- to involve people at all levels in team in process improvement
- to ensure the right flow of information at all levels
- to manage employee behaviors and focus on team effort to deliver quality
- to define.

If you are a manager at any level, formally define and delegate the responsibility of process improvement to a group or an individual. If quality improvement isn't anybody's job, it is not surprising that it doesn't get done.

People look at their leaders as role models who are expected to be setting the right examples. Middle management behavior and attitude ultimately ends up shaping the overall organization culture. If you want to get a pulse of an organization, just observe how middle managers communicate and the content of communication. With positive communication and motivation, employees can be truly engaged to the mission of the project and hence the organization. Quality of communication and leadership with internal customers (people) is as important as that with external customers.

Managers tell stories that people believe in and adopt. Challenge for people at the top is to ensure that middle managers tell the right stories, which ultimately builds the right culture.

"Soft" Management Does Not Mean "Weak" Management

The best managers are confident and caring at the same time. The role of a manager is to help people achieve their goals, which involves a lot of caring, counseling, and two-way feedback sharing.

Recently, a seasoned project manager told me in a conversation,

> *The day I closely assessed my work as a manager, I realized that management is a huge responsibility, which gave me an inner confidence and elevated my self-esteem. I knew that I may fail, that I am vulnerable because my success depends on others. I came to understand that if someone raises a strong concern, disagrees, or openly expresses, it is not necessarily a sign of disrespect. If I seek opinions of my team members before deciding, it is strength. It will earn me tremendous loyalty and respect from my team.*

Confident managers know that caring is an essential part of being a manager. It is a combination of soft aspects (people, emotional intelligence, relationships, etc.) and hard aspects (plans, schedules, scope, cost, etc.). They know that being a "people-oriented" manager does not necessarily mean being a weak manager. To build a team where everyone counts, one has to cross that fine line between being a manager and being a leader.

Essential Strategies

If you are a manager at any level in your organization, here are a few essential strategies, pictured in Figure 15-1, that will help you in driving the mindset of your team toward quality and help them form the right habits to deliver quality and reduce the rework.

It Starts With "Focus on People" and Relationships

Great quality is always a result of good people working passionately toward the organizations' goals. People can be your strongest (or weakest) link that has strong influence in quality of

Figure 15-1. Quality Culture

your deliverable. As a manager if you don't give due consideration to the people aspect, process manuals and specifications can easily give you a false confidence that everything will go as per the process. People form the core of any project because they write specifications, understand, design, and develop your solutions.

Here is what I have realized: *organizations need good people to deliver quality*—process acts as a catalyst to drive the success and manage risks. *People are always the strongest or weakest link in success or failure of the projects.* One of the key challenges for managers and leaders is to build a "quality-aware" team where people know that quality is everybody's responsibility.

For example, having a set of production guidelines or inspection guidelines does not stop an individual from developing a bad product. The ability to develop a good product, associate it with business understanding, and find optimized ways of accomplishing things is an art—an intrinsic ability. Focus should be on people because they develop solutions with the help of a process (whether a formal or personal process).

Processes help you create the right management framework, manage risks, measure outcomes, and make the right decisions. *Processes act as a tool and help people perform better.* Knowing the priorities and business model, and having insight on what has really worked for you in the past, is crucial to see that processes drive growth and not become an overhead. The recipe for great quality is to have the right people following the right processes employing the right tools at the right time. *People are always the strongest or weakest link in success or failure of the modern-day initiatives.*

Quality of Relationships

In an increasingly service-oriented business environment, what you sell is not just a product but an experience. People may forget explicit details like specifications or price, but never forget the experience they had when they bought the product. Experience extended to end-customers largely depends on attitude, values, and behaviors of each individual who interacts with a customer. One of the most important challenges for a modern-day manager is to keep this group of people aligned to the organization's quality system and values.

Communication is the backbone of an organization's success in the marketplace. Effective internal and external communication within an organization ensures that:

- Your team members understand your value system.
- They understand what is expected out of them.
- They are motivated to walk an extra mile to deliver excellent service.
- Your customers know your value system.
- You build trust-based relationships with your people and customers with consistent communication.
- You manage expectations with your people and customers.

How can you motivate your teams to deliver excellent customer experiences through simple communication processes? Here are a few ideas to consider:

- **Train:** Training your internal team can be your biggest tool for clearly explaining the process of communication and how important it is for the business. Consistently train your people on value systems, leadership, quality management, effective communication, what works in customer management, what doesn't work, expectations of management, and cultural aspects of a client's location. Clients also need training on how best they can use your products. Companies organize client workshops to educate them about different aspects of a product/service. Train consistently to streamline communication.
- **Support:** Once your people are trained, you need to support them in doing the right things. Supporting can be a simple act of being there with your people when they talk to customers. Help them improve and share feedback on how are they doing. Some companies may see this activity as an "overhead," but it is an "investment" in your people.
- **Monitor:** Once you have confidence that your people will be able to do the right communication, monitor them. Take periodic feedback from them. Communicate consistently to ensure that they are motivated enough to continue doing it.

Delivering consistently superior experience to your customers (via quality of products and communication) results in a long-term relationship based on trust. In business, as in life, relationships are crucial. Quality of your relationships is as important as quality of your products, or perhaps even more important.

Set Expectations on Behaviors You Value

> *"You get more of the behavior you reward. You don't get what you hope for, ask for, wish for, or beg for. You get what you reward."*
>
> —Michael le Boeuf

As a manager or business leader, rewarding the behaviors you seek is a matter of constant choice. You can reward meeting the deadlines, or you can reward meeting the quality standards. You can reward by results, or you can reward by how those results were achieved. You can reward a person who talks a lot about work, or you can reward a person who lets his work speak. *A lot of what you build as a part of your organization's culture is a result of what you have rewarded over a period of time.*

Whether you are a project manager or a business leader, here are a few actions you can take to set the right expectations on behaviors you value:

- Identify your core values and behaviors that are important to your organization (e.g., customer orientation, respect for others, integrity, etc.).
- Constantly communicate the values and behaviors you expect from people. You can also set their KRAs accordingly to cover specific results and generic behavior
- Instantly validate and reinforce when you see the right behavior. Thank people, acknowledge that you took a note, give praise, or whatever. But do validate, because no action when someone behaves right often means that you don't appreciate or value it.
- Show people the way by counseling and giving constant feedback. You can use forums like kickoff meetings, retrospectives, one-on-ones, and even informal sessions to guide your team members. People always love to know what is exactly expected out of them.
- Strategically reward through appreciation, interim rewards, and performance appraisals. In performance appraisals, specifically mention the behaviors you have appreciated when reviewing overall performance. Share feedback.

You form a strategic reward system when you integrate performance (results) and behavior (how those results were achieved). The payoffs are huge because people are more aware and aligned to deliver better results. So the critical question is: Is your performance management system driving the right behaviors for the organization?

Empower and Support Improvements

At the core of progressive management is ability to support improvements. One of the biggest changes when an organization or team embarks upon a process improvement journey is the change in mindset. While the objectives change, business leaders tend to cling on to traditional management styles of "command and control." With "command and control," managers will control everything, and people will simply comply. Improvement may still happen, but long-term sustainable culture change may not!

Total quality management is all about empowering people to participate in the change. It calls for patience, extending help, and asking, listening, and communicating at all levels. Managers have to realize that they cannot change people's behavior unless they change theirs. If they believe in command-and-control style, the second-line leaders will never be able to practice "initiative-led" management style. You see, behaviors from the top trickle down through the organization and at some point become the culture.

Unlike factories, the dividing line between "people who think" and "people who do" has blurred. When dealing with improvement, everyone is equally strong and has equal potential to bring about a change. With empowerment, leaders just "unlock" that potential. That, to me, is the core of modern management—to empower people, enable them, believe that they are powerful, support them, and truly "unlock" their potential.

Working on organizational/team process improvement is a great way to practice these fundamentals of effective management and deliver "value" to business, people therein, and the customers.

Process Orientation and Systems View

As managers, the systems we shape end up shaping us. Traditional view of management is hierarchical (vertical), but work flows horizontally. Between teams. Between members of the teams. Between different departments. Work flows from one team member to the other. The intent, intensity, and diligence with which they execute that piece of work, and how well they are equipped to execute, largely determines quality of the outcomes. A lot of quality-related problems can be traced to gaps in this lateral movement of work.

As complexity of our work increases, it is very important to be able to see the patterns and interconnections of different activities. Having a process allows you to see the waste, identify patterns of nonperformance, pre-empt the failures, and improve.

Processes form the culture, since they directly impact the working habits of people. Processes also drive efficiency and help you meet the basic expectations of the customer. Sure, we live in a world where we need to "exceed" those expectations. But, how will you exceed the expectations unless you know how to meet them first? Process helps you build that platform where you and your team do not have to worry about the basic stuff.

Consider this story:

> Fuji Xerox was a joint venture between Fuji and Xerox. Fuji Xerox won the legendary Deming Prize for Total Quality Management even before Xerox, the parent company, got the Malcolm Baldridge Award for quality in the United States. The gentleman was explaining why process orientation is the key to building competitive success. Someone asked him vainly, "But Michelangelo followed no process?"
>
> Unflustered, the expert replied, "First, be Michelangelo."
> Everybody else, he said, must follow process.

Process Improvement

When you have a set of established processes that your team adheres to, here is the next challenge. At any given point, if your processes are not improving, they are stagnating. In a constantly changing business environment, static processes will soon become a barrier and take a toll on your efficiency.

As the saying goes, *"If you always do what you always did, you'll always get what you always got."* So, process improvement is not a destination, but a journey.

Simplify the Process

> #QUALITYtweet Want to add complexity?
> Get obsessed with a solution without
> focusing on the real problem.
>
> 42 seconds ago via TweetDeck

Albert Einstein believed that supreme goal of all theory is to make the irreducible basic elements as simple and as few as possible. He said, "Everything should be made as simple as possible, but no simpler." One of the critical elements of building a quality-oriented culture, and reducing overall waste in the process, is to ensure that processes are as simple as possible, but no simpler. Human nature is to make things complex, and it takes a lot of guts to simplify things.

Consider this story:

> One of the most memorable case studies on Japanese management was the case of the empty soapbox, which happened in one of Japan's biggest cosmetics companies. The company received a complaint that a consumer had bought a soapbox that was empty. Immediately the authorities isolated the problem to the assembly line, which transported all the packaged boxes of soap to the delivery department. For some reason, one soapbox went through the assembly line empty.
>
> Management asked its engineers to solve the problem. Post-haste, the engineers worked hard to devise an X-ray machine with high-resolution monitors manned by two people to watch all the soapboxes that passed through the line to make sure they were not empty. No doubt they worked hard and they worked fast, but they spent a whopping amount to do so. But when a rank-and-file employee in a small company was posed with the same problem, he did not get into complications of X-rays, and so on, but instead came out with another solution.
>
> He bought a strong industrial electric fan and pointed it at the assembly line. He switched the fan on, and as each soapbox passed the fan, it simply blew the empty boxes out of the line.
>
> Implementing complex review process or a complex work flow is relatively easy. Picking up an off-the-shelf best practice is easy too. Identifying the simplest solution that best solves the problem is difficult.

When you improve your processes constantly over a period of time, adding new steps to the process, it tends to get complex. Simplification of process requires you to think with a fresh perspective (and maybe a fresh set of people) and ask a simple question: What problem is this process intended to solve? The answer often reveals that there are much simpler ways of executing the work and solving the problem.

"First Time Right"

Building quality involves a cost. You spend efforts and energy on preventing the errors (prevention cost) and then checking your work (appraisal cost). These are positive costs, or rather investments that ensure that you get it right the first time.

The cost of rework when you or a customer identifies *a lot* of defects (internal/external failure costs) is huge and highly damaging too. It can have a direct impact on your business's bottom lines.

So how do you maximize your possibility of getting it right the first time when you deal with projects? Here are the three most important things I could think of:

- **Clarity:** In projects (or in any initiative), when you shoot in the dark, the bullet comes back to kill you. Most projects or initiatives fail because of lack of clarity. The project team needs to be clear of the purpose, the business need, the specific requirements of the customer, and other implicit expectations. Clarity also demands a clear visibility in process, setting up the right rituals, monitoring practices, and responsibilities of the project team. Clarity means openness in communication.
- **Discipline:** Execution demands discipline to do the right things consistently. The plan you established needs to be followed. When you decide to review early and often, you should. Discipline, in simplest terms, is your ability to fill the gap between what you know and what you actually do.
- **Constant Improvement:** You planned, you did, and then you also reviewed. Based on your experiences, you should be able to improve your processes. Change the tracks for better efficiency. Inculcate better habits. Fine tuning and alignment that happens in this phase not only helps you in this project, but also helps you in subsequent ones.

I do not undermine the need to make mistakes and learn from them. When we research or try to innovate, we essentially do that with the objective of learning. But what about applying our lessons well? We can always get that right the first time, only if we decide to!

Know What Needs to Be Improved

> #QUALITYtweet The first step of your process improvement journey is to know what really needs improvement.
>
> 31 seconds ago via TweetDeck

In modern-day sports, players and their coaches have sophisticated facilities to learn from recorded versions of the game with some great analytical tools. When reviewing these recorded versions with the team, an important job of a coach is to tell the player:

- What is going right? How can we consolidate that?
- What can be improved further? How will it help the game?
- What needs to change?

Management is no different. Improving as a team is all about optimizing your actions with a thoughtful consideration to critical aspects of business. You can do a lot of improvement in noncritical areas (and feel good about it). Just because you are improving something does not mean you are improving the right thing. The key to success of any improvement initiative is to pick the right areas. To get driven by operational nitty-gritty is one of the biggest mistakes most managers commit. Process improvement can become an important business enabler provided all improvement initiatives are business oriented.

Do a quick reality check by answering the following critical questions to gauge the return-on-investment of your process improvement initiative:

- If a particular area of operations is improved, will it have a direct impact on the customer's satisfaction level or experience? (Focus: External Value)
- Does the improvement in a particular area directly improve the productivity of team members and enable them to execute faster? (Focus: Productivity)
- Does improvement in a particular area directly have an impact on revenues and business? (Focus: Revenue)
- Does improvement in a particular area make it easier for people to generate qualitative outcomes and improved job satisfaction? (Focus: Internal Value)

How do you find out what "really" needs improvements? The answer is—by collaborating. You can never identify broader improvement areas by isolating yourself in a comfortable corner cabin. You have to actively collaborate with the following stakeholders:

- **Customers:** In a customer-centric process culture, feedback from customers is carefully assessed to identify the customer's expectations on what can be improved. Your customer can be your strongest ally in the improvement journey. Seek feedback.
- **Business development folks:** They are the ones who have maximum face time with customers. These could be project managers, account managers, or client relationship managers. They can give improvement areas that directly map with business.
- **Your team:** They are people on the floor who get things done. They are the best candidates to give suggestions on what can be improved operationally to deliver quality up front and improve productivity.

The famous 80:20 rule applies to process improvement initiative as well: 80 percent of improvement happens by focusing on continuous identification of 20 percent improvement areas. It helps to adopt a clinical approach in identifying the 20 percent—it does make a lot of difference.

Based on the findings, you can create a strategic plan for implementing the improvements in identified areas. A lot of organizations treat improvement as a project with a vision, a mission, a plan, and defined deliverables.

Reviews = Learning

We create, we review, and we make it better. Reviews are an integral part of product/service quality improvement. The core purpose of any review process is to "make things better" by re-examining the work product and find out anomalies or areas of improvements that the creator of the work product was not able to find.

Establishing a good review process in an organization requires management commitment and investment, but for returns that it generates, the effort is totally worth it. In the software world, a lot of emphasis is given to formal inspections, but they work best when a formal process marries with a set of commonsense rules. Here they go:

- **Reviewing early:** Reviews in the early phase of product development mean that findings are less costly to resolve. The later defects are found, the more expensive it gets to resolve those defects.
- **Staying positive:** The art of review is to report negative findings (problems) without losing the positive undertone of communication. Negative or destructive criticism will only make the process more burdensome. Stay positive and keep the process lightweight.
- **Keeping review records:** When a lot of time is spent on reviewing, it makes sense to track the findings to closure. Recording the findings helps you to effectively track the closure and trends.
- **Reviewing process, not the person:** Always question the process and not the person. Human beings are bound to make mistakes, which is why reviews are required. So accept that mistakes will happen. How can you have a more effective process so that these mistakes are not repeated? That is the critical question.
- **Training and more training:** Reviewers can make huge mistakes if they are not trained. If you don't invest in training your review teams, you cannot expect them to do it right, the first time.
- **Reviewing iteratively:** Review often. During the course of product building, product needs may change. New ideas may be implemented. Keep review process constant amidst all these changes. Discipline is the key.
- **Reviewing the process of reviewing:** Are we reviewing it right? Are we reviewing the right things? Periodically, assess the results and the benefits of having a review process. Assess how reviews helped improve product quality. In process

assessment, also identify if people are heavily relying on reviews. If that is the case, it is a bad sign.

Success of any process depends on 2 Es—efficient and enjoyable. The same holds true for your review processes. Review is a control mechanism, and hence the focus on getting it right the first time is still very important. A good review is just an internal quality gate that ensures that internal customers (reviewers) are happy with the final product. If your internal customers are happy, your external customers will be happy too!

Quality of Planning = Quality of Execution

When a project is executed, a plan is established. Work is broken down into smaller pieces, and a neat schedule is created. Team members are assigned, milestones are created, and the schedule is circulated to all concerned.

Then the execution begins with a great zeal. As the time passes, things like schedule slippage and effort variance show up. Everyone then tries find out why the schedule slipped. Different areas are evaluated, and a consolidated status report is created. But the core point is missed—and that is quality of the planning itself.

Constant and comprehensive planning is the secret of many successful projects because planning provides a direction to the team. It helps in setting precedence on what's important. It gives a message and tells a lot about what matters to you on the project.

Here are seven of the most important ideas to ensure that quality is built into your plan:

1. Quality of execution largely depends on quality of planning. Unfortunately, we invest very little effort in verifying the quality of the plan itself. (In the software development world, inaccurate estimates are a major cause of project failures.)

2. Planning and estimating, according to me, is not just about putting dates against tasks. Planning is about taking a comprehensive view of how work will be performed, how quality will be built, how challenges will be addressed, and how communication will flow.

3. Planning is never a one-time activity. Planning has to be done continuously, and plans have to stay fluid. If realignment in plans is not done periodically, you will never know if you are on the right track. Agility is the key to good planning.

4. Further, for longer projects and initiatives, you cannot plan the entire project together. Identify key milestones and create a plan for only the first few milestones. This helps you remain agile. A comprehensive plan for the whole project over a period of one year may look cool, but seldom works.

5. When plans are realigned, expectation management is the key. It is important to ensure that changes in plans are known to all.

6. Whenever possible, involve people in the planning process. This not only motivates them to think about their work, but also ensures a better buy-in of plans.

7. In projects, planning provides a direction and demonstrates your intent. If you want to get something done, plan it. For example, if you want a quality outcome, make sure you have adequately planned quality-related activities. Things that get planned get done.

In a way, these lessons also map with the fundamentals of agile planning. In my view, Agile is not just a software development methodology, agility is also a mindset.

So next time you plan your project or initiative, remember that quality of execution depends on quality of planning. If you don't plan for quality, you will never get quality.

That is probably why a wise man named William A. Foster said, "*Quality is never an accident; it is always the result of high intention, sincere effort, intelligent direction, and skillful execution; it represents the wise choice of many alternatives.*"

Balance Quality and Productivity

In F1 racing, one of the primary challenges for a driver is to keep a close eye on speed and direction. One wrong move at a high speed, and the car bumps with the edge of the track. "Speed" when combined with direction is termed as "velocity."

> #QUALITYtweet Tracking productivity without tracking quality of output is like tracking the speed of a train without validating direction.

One of the rules of management is "You can't manage what you don't measure." But an obsessive focus on metrics can prove harmful for organization's health because:

- You may be measuring things that do not directly relate to organization goals.
- You may only be measuring outcomes without focusing on qualitative aspects.
- You may be using measurement as a sole base for decision making without considering the variable/unknowing aspects of your business.

A lot of managers narrow their focus on hard-core metrics that reveal volume but not quality. Examples could be number of hours logged during a day (versus tasks achieved in those hours), number of modules completed in a day (versus quality of those modules), or number of cold calls made during the day (versus quality of research and depth of communication in each call). This list can go on, but you get the point. More, in this case, is not always better.

Metrics are important to evaluate process efficiency, but not sufficient. The quality system of an organization should have processes to assess both qualitative and quantitative aspects of work. How can this be achieved? Here are the three most important lessons:

- **Take a hybrid approach with a focus on good management:** Measuring productivity solely by units produced could be a great way to manage in manufacturing world. In the knowledge world, where the raw material for products or services is a human brain, taking a qualitative approach combined with commonsense metrics is a great way to ensure balance between quality and productivity. The key to higher productivity in a knowledge-based industry is "good management."
- **Think of quality as a part of process, rather than an afterthought:** Quality is not an afterthought. Quality has to be built through process by people. Process should have necessary activities defined at each stage of product development to ensure that a quality product is being built. These activities can then be measured and improved upon. Process also shapes up culture of an organization, and hence due care must be taken to ensure that the quality system does not form the wrong culture. Process has to take care of softer aspects of work including trust, commitment, and motivation levels of people.
- **Measure to help, not to destroy:** Metrics are like a compass that shows direction. To move forward, you have to walk the direction. Metrics can give you important trends, but these trends need to be analyzed and worked upon. A key challenge for any process manager is to ensure that metrics are used to evaluate process and not people. If you start using metrics as a base for rewards, you are not allowing people to make mistakes. When people don't make mistakes, they don't grow. As an organization, you don't grow either.

Process can be used to gain "speed" or to gain "velocity." You are the driver.

Effectively Managing Change

When you seek to improve your processes and influence habits of your team members, you will be the central force for implementing changes in the way you work. People change, not by "force" but by their "intent." With force, people may dispassionately comply with your processes, but for true involvement, their intent needs a direction. With this as a given, critical questions are:

- How do you make sure that you implement change by driving intent of people?
- How do you make sure that people are passionately involved in change?

The answer to these is "change leadership." Leading a change means undertaking the right initiatives, mobilizing resources, addressing soft aspects like motivation, overcoming hurdles, and aligning the teams to make it happen. How can change leadership drive the process improvement initiative? Here are a few pointers:

- **Accurately define what needs a change:** Apply the 80:20 rule to identify what needs improvement. It is easy to align people when they know that they are improving the right areas that have maximum business/operational impact.
- **Create a change timeline:** Humans work best when they work against a timeline. We often tend to get complacent when there are no deadlines. Reasonable pressure helps us become more creative. Create a timeline by when change will be implemented with a step-by-step action plan. This also creates a sense of urgency.
- **Engage people:** People tend to commit themselves to things they are involved in. Involve practitioners and managers in defining the change. They are the ones who will be impacted by the change. Engage them by explaining to them the larger context, vision, and business need. When they know the larger picture, they can align their actions accordingly. They also need to know the "What's in it for me?" part. How will they become more effective? How will this change help them improve their performance? They want to know this.
- **Review progress periodically:** If you don't monitor your people, you give them a reason to slow down. Have short and effective meetings (in a group or one-on-one) with people involved in change. Take stock. Understand people's problems. Help them do better. They get help, and you get the broader picture. If you hit some roadblocks, you still have chance to realign. Review early and often. This is also your opportunity to share progress and motivate people involved in the improvement initiative.
- **Lead:** Give them the context and set people free. Micromanagement on tasks can kill creativity and morale. Be there to help them, but let them do their work on their own. People learn the most when they try to do it themselves. They will make mistakes. Help them overcome and share the lessons learned. Set the right examples for them to follow.
- **Share rewards:** When you link participation with rewards, it will help you get voluntary participation from people. But after they have participated, it is only your leadership abilities that will keep them going. You will still have lot of people who will willingly participate.

Last but not least, people engage when they see continuity of effort. If your improvement initiative is temporary or ad hoc, people will not engage beyond the first cycle. When people see consistent results from a process improvement group, they willingly participate.

For any manager, improvement is a journey and not a destination. Who you travel with matters a lot. Choose the right people and inspire them into action. Your business will thank you for that!

Change Management: Five Mistakes You Should Avoid

Change is hard and painful and necessary for growth/survival. Process improvement is all about managing change—and in my view, change (and its respective benefits) does not happen when you:

- **Keep thinking big without starting small:** It is easy to get overwhelmed by the large goals you have set for improvement. But remember—the best way to eat an elephant is one piece at a time. Focus on big, but start small. Think about a few key things you can do now, that will take you one step nearer to your goal. You make things better not by thinking about it, but by doing something about it.
- **Focus solely on "enforce" rather than "enable" and "educate":** Changing habits and hence culture is a long-term thing. Unless there is enough buy-in for a change, it does not happen. The best way to implement change is to educate people, enable them, and hence empower them. Enforcement only results in dispassionate compliance.
- **Think too much about things you cannot change:** There are things you just can't do anything about. Worrying too much about them means losing focus on what is in your control. I remember a prayer that says, "God, grant me the serenity to accept the things I cannot change; the courage to change the things I can; and the wisdom to know the difference." Be wise!
- **Think change is all about processes:** It's not. Change is all about people and their habits. Processes are merely tools that guide them through the change process. Process acts as a compass, but people follow it. Lots of process consultants overly focus on compliance, standards, and processes. Focus on people instead, and processes will not only be adhered to, but also be improved upon by the same set of people.
- **Are a "sole warrior" in the improvement and change initiative:** If you are the only one who wants change in an organization, it doesn't happen. All improvement initiatives need sponsorship from the top. People observe people at the top and emulate behaviors. Setting the right examples and taking improvement initiatives seriously go a long way in building a constantly improving culture.

The Goal of Quality Culture Is Customer Orientation

A lot of companies have the phrase "delighting our customers" in their well-crafted mission statements and quality policies. I see "customer delight" as a cherry, with the cake being "solving customers' problems and meeting the expectations"—so when we say "cherry on top of the cake," the cake has to be right. Customers don't get delighted by cherries alone or by cherries on wrong cakes.

To be able to reach a state where you "delight" your customers, you have to first "know and meet" their basic expectations consistently. That is the core of your business—the reason why your customers come to you. Your products and services have to first meet the basic criteria of delivering the value that clients are seeking.

So when you think of delighting your customer, think of the basics first:

- Does your product/service meet the core expectation of the customer? Does it solve customers' problems? To what extent?
- Do you have a method to accurately identify customers' real/unique expectations? Their unique context?
- Do you have the right set of processes, people, and technologies that will help you deliver up to customers' expectations consistently?
- What is missing, and how can you scale up to ensure consistency of delivery? What are the gaps that need to be filled?

Once you have these basics right, your efforts and investment in delighting your customers through various innovative and inclusive programs will yield the right returns.

Acting on Customers' Feedback

Formal customer feedback is a proven tool for bringing about meaningful improvements in your business and offerings. Typical methods of collecting customer feedback include surveys, feedback forms, listening to the customer in a one-to-one meeting, or just watching customers use your products and services. But all improvement starts when you start "listening" to the voice of your customers and act upon it. It is easy to analyze customer feedback and create good-looking charts, but the key is to identify what feedback really means to you as a business.

Collecting customer feedback and not acting upon it is a huge waste—which also indicates that you collected the feedback to make the other party feel good about it. Smart customers will remember their feedback and take notice when you serve them next time. Mature organizations devise an integrated customer feedback program that includes both internal customers (people) and external ones. Having an internal customer feedback program ensures that you identify improvement areas from within. Here are a few ideas for you to ensure that your integrated customer feedback initiative delivers what it is intended to—meaningful business change:

- **Seek feedback on overall experience:** Most companies seek feedback limited to a product, service, or department. Ask the right questions to gauge the overall experience including communication, systems, ease of use, and pricing. With the right questions, customers will think broadly and give more constructive feedback.
- **Acknowledge the feedback and thank them:** Once customers share their feedback, acknowledge the receipt and do not forget to thank them. Make it personal. This is the starting point of post-feedback communication.
- **Reward:** A lot of companies offer discounts or freebies when customers share their feedback. This is a good way to ensure involvement and initiative. This works even better when seeking feedback from internal customers.
- **Keep them involved:** Share feedback with customers about their feedback and what you are doing about it. Most companies make a mistake of never going back to the customer after the first feedback cycle. If customers spare valuable time sharing the feedback, it is an obligation to inform them about your follow-up actions and status. In case of internal customers, you can also involve them in solution definition.
- **Treat your customer feedback program as a project:** This is very crucial to ensure that actions are followed through. After feedback is received, create a mini-project on improvement actions with defined deadlines and expected outcomes. Creating an action log helps maintain momentum and focus on improvement actions.
- **Ship results:** Show customers how their feedback has helped you improve your processes, delivery methods, and service offerings. Implement improvement actions on your customer projects and allow them to experience change.
- **Consider follow-up feedback:** Now that your customers have experienced improvements, consider follow-up feedback to ensure that they acknowledge your efforts and share their comments.

Customer feedback is never a one-way street—but a two-way lane that can allow your customers to become your partners in process improvement.

Core of Excellence—A Continuously Learning Team

Jack Welch said, "An organization's ability to learn, and translate that learning into action rapidly, is the greatest competitive advantage."

Continuous learning and its respective implementation to generate desired business outcomes are at the core of successful teams that deliver excellence.

Three Rituals for Constant Team Learning

When we work on large-scale projects, long-term assignments, or complex change initiatives, we decompose our work into smaller chunks that are more manageable. We create a set of smaller tasks that we perform according to a schedule to achieve milestones, and hence the objective.

It all begins with great planning, and then we narrow our focus to the tasks. All team members keep doing their part—and somewhere in this process, we lose the connection to the whole. People get so engrossed in tasks that they miss the big picture, and how their work contributes to the overall objective.

Have you seen situations where you meet all milestones and still do not meet the desired goal? Three rituals can help you overcome this:

- **Kickoff:** This project starts with a person who understands the "why" part of the work. Kickoff is an opportunity to share this learning with all team members. Unless everyone understands the purpose clearly, they will not have the capacity to contribute to the whole.
- **Reviews:** Reviews should be used as a ritual to align everyone to the goal. Most people report progress on tasks during the reviews. Let them also report on how their actions are helping the cause and what value are they adding. Review early, and review often.
- **Retrospectives:** This is the last piece that ensures that all the learning (as a team) gets consolidated, recorded, and implemented in the future assignments.

Learning organizations are made up of learning teams (and learning individuals), and these rituals ensure that teams raise their collective capacity to stay aligned to the broader goals of the work.

When this happens, teams start adding value, learning constantly, and improving relentlessly.

Establish Forums to Build a Quality-Oriented Culture

Total quality management (TQM) says that quality is everybody's job. Each individual's approach to work, understanding of quality, and personal standards of excellence are crucial for delivering quality. One of the biggest challenges for a lot of organizations today is to involve each and every team member in the quality game.

Most people in the organization can do a better job if they know:

- What are the key values and beliefs on quality/excellence in the organization?
- What key actions will help them to align themselves to those values and belief system?
- How will those actions add value to organization? How will it benefit them?

Constant communication (from top to bottom and vice versa) is the only way to answer these critical questions and keep people engaged in excellence. Here are a few forums you can establish and use to promote quality consciousness across the organization:

- Promote quality initiatives in all your monthly/weekly team meetings. Let people at all levels know that excellence in work is not optional. Use these meetings to give them a broad overview of strategies and purpose.
- Establish quality circles or improvement/quality focus groups and rotate people to give everyone a chance to participate.
- Deliver induction trainings to all new joiners and constantly train them thereafter. Train your managers on quality to build the right leadership ecosystem.
- Organize events like group discussions and brainstorming sessions to promote ideas and to share success stories, best practices, and project case studies.
- Spread awareness of your quality beliefs and systems by designing e-bulletins or newsletters. Record video messages on quality and upload them on your corporate intranet.
- Encourage discussions/participation by using internal blogs/wikis/forums.
- Set up a reward and recognition system to promote the right behaviors with respect to quality of products/services delivered to customers.

Quality improvement involves transformation, and these forums help in transforming culture for excellence in all spheres of an organization's activities. Moreover, they are excellent tools to answer the questions most people have.

TQM is not just a philosophy. It is a vehicle to drive excellence across the organization. Probably that is the reason why it is called "total" quality management.

About the Author

Tanmay Vora leads the corporate quality program at CIGNEX Datamatics Corporation—a global leader in open source system integration. He has 13 years of diverse experience in software development methodologies, quality management, software testing, and process improvement initiatives. Tanmay specializes in starting new initiatives within the organizations and forming new teams from scratch. He speaks and consults on quality management, leadership, and continual improvement. He is also the founder/host of QAspire Blog and the author of *#QUALITYtweet*. You can find his website here: www.qaspire.com.

Chapter 16

The Mesh: Access Over Ownership

Lisa Gansky

Editor's Note

I asked Lisa Gansky to share an essay for this book that would introduce managers to the concept of the Mesh. I had seen her talk on TED.com and was blown away by her ideas and the potential ramifications of them. As you read how Lisa describes the Mesh, think about how these broader trends ought to affect how you manage on a daily basis. Share this piece with your team and then ask, "How should our staff meeting change?" The discussion that ensues could be very interesting and helpful.

Among the most exciting side effects of the info-tech revolution that began in the mid-1990s has been the emergence of a powerful new business sector built on a foundation of resource-sharing and peer-to-peer transactions. Many of the most prominent brands—Google, Facebook, eBay, Etsy, Zipcar, Spotify, Zopa, Amazon, foursquare, and Groupon to name just a few—have blown away old ideas about the business-to-consumer and business-to-business supply chains, and enabled new kinds of commercial relationships that bypass traditional markets. As cobwebs have gathered on the classic ownership economy developed during the industrial revolution—in which big companies mass-produce goods for downstream retail distribution to individual owners—consumers and entrepreneurs alike are increasingly seeking alternative platforms for selling, sharing, exchanging, or rethinking and reusing goods, services, and talent via decentralized channels that did not become integrated in most regions of the world prior to 2000.

I have dubbed this vibrant web of people, goods, tools, governments, and business opportunities "the Mesh." It is a metaphor that emphasizes the interconnected and multidirectional nature of an economy in which antiquated distinctions between producers, retailers, and consumers have been tossed out the window. While the enterprises that are capitalizing on the Mesh, or "share," economy encompass a wide range of business categories and service models, they all strive to leverage data acquired via online social networks and other communication tools that introduce unprecedented efficiencies into the marketplace. They also serve to squeeze more value out of the energy and raw materials we consume. This is accomplished by driving up actual usage of existing assets and by recovering the value from what we have historically considered waste. In both instances, the long-term cost and environmental impact of our collective "assets" are effectively reduced. From a business perspective, the cost to developing products, managing teams, and bringing products to make is reduced, while the likelihood of successful adoption is improved. It is a winning combination and one that will shape the decades to come.

For today's business leaders, the strategic value of the Mesh extends not only to the design and implementation of consumer brands, but also to the fundamentals of how companies operate. Cloud computing provides a reliable and cost-effective alternative to owning and managing servers and software. The growing availability of shared workplace facilities and equipment allows companies to launch or expand without signing a lease or making long-term investments in highly specialized experts, durable goods, and infrastructure. It's now possible to tap into virtually any business service, human resource, or specialized skill set by connecting with other entrepreneurs through increasingly active networking platforms and on-demand talent pools. Whether we realize it or not, we're all operating on a significantly leveled playing field, and we must learn to view everyone else in the game as a potential partner, customer, supplier, or competitor.

Defining a business strategy for this highly decentralized and horizontal marketplace is not just about having a great idea and a sound financial model. The most successful ventures and brands will be those that effectively leverage the extraordinary marketing and operational efficiencies made possible by evolving information technologies and expanding peer-to-peer networks. The Mesh represents a fundamental shift in our relationship to the things in our households, communities, and businesses. It invites leaders at all kinds of enterprises—from kitchen table startups to the Fortune 500 corporations—to take a fresh look at the ways tightly networked communities are forming powerful markets in which access to goods and services triumphs over individual ownership.

With that in mind, here are six guiding principles for doing business—and thriving—in a Meshy world.

1. Mobile equals local and fresh. Get out of your chairs and on the streets, kids—the Internet has come to town. Literally. The IT revolution started with moving data around. Now mobile devices have spread the revolution to physical things—to the street. Making a reservation for a car, a bike, a home, or a meal from your phone connects you to the company via data. It may include information on your preferences, or how you compare to other people like you (to make juicier, more personalized, and compelling offers). And, through our daily activities, data are collected from sensors in the car, on the bike, at home, in the refrigerator, or at the cafe. Your social networks allow you to make better-informed choices of goods and services, as well as recommend the things you may want to explore. Mobile plus GPS changes everything. It allows others to meet you where you are—literally! It means you can get more of what you want exactly when you want it. It means convenient access to fresh goods and services. Convenient access means you don't have to own stuff to have a pulse on its whereabouts. You can share it, saving money and sparing hassles. For a company competing for its customers, it means that the relationship with its customers is a privileged one that must be won newly with each interaction. More simple, inexpensive, pervasive, and locally honed mobile tools makes sharing hard to resist. Advantage: Mesh.

2. Let's snuggle up. Barring some miracle in space, there's only one planet for us to inhabit. And by mid-century, roughly 3 billion more people will be joining in. It is expected that by 2050, 75 percent of the 9.3 billion people will inhabit the world's cities. With that math, it's not hard to predict that businesses that figure out more efficient ways to use the earth's resources will thrive. Also, urban areas will inevitably grow in density, which really favors the sharing economy. More people in the same physical area will necessitate fewer things per person. We will inevitably be trading fewer things for more rich experiences. For example, if you have more people in a neighborhood, it's easier to broaden the number of bikes, tools, local farmer's markets, or clothing swaps you can offer. You can also make your offers more convenient—more shared cars in the lot or on a nearby street. Density deepens community and, likewise, its Mesh of products and services. Owning a car outright, on the other hand, becomes a bigger and bigger expense and burden to maintain and park. Advantage: Mesh.

3. Hidden cost unveiled. If there's any good news about climate change, it's the amount of CO_2 that's unnecessarily puffed up in the air. We waste energy and water and other natural resources like, well, there's no tomorrow. Shared businesses are based on turning that waste into value. Think about the effort that airlines put into trying to get more passengers on any given plane, because many of the costs are the same whether they're flying one person or 200. Private cars, on the other hand, sit unused for an average of over 22 hours a day. By sharing them—as WhipCar in England is doing—you radically increase the efficiency of all the materials that go into making, running, and maintaining those cars. Plus the owners collect some ducats. Now combine car sharing with the power of coordination among bike-sharing services and public transit. Then add in better-designed, more efficient vehicles, with interchangeable and recyclable parts. That captured waste then adds up to huge savings—for the individual, the community, and the planet—and puts the ownership economy at a distinct disadvantage to one based on sharing. And as scarcity, increased demand, and regulations drive up the costs of sourcing new materials, the benefits of sharing-based models will only grow. Advantage: Mesh.

4. Now you see me. Now you don't. Buying stuff to own is usually a one-time transaction. A customer collects her purchase and marches out the front door, perhaps never to be seen again. Maybe, just maybe she, (but typically not) registers the product with your company. But share-based businesses and their customers must communicate every time the product or service is rented, leased, or borrowed, reviewed, and returned. Each point of contact becomes a better opportunity to get to know the customer, to wow the customer by presenting the brand, to cultivate trust, to refine the core offering, to extend your offering through partnerships, and to make new, personalized offers. Robust data sets come from the customers' choices, from product and usage information, and from the company's and customers' social networks—all of which serve to enrich offers and relationships. Add partners—a home share, a pop-up shop, and a bike share, say—and the quality of information, relationships, and offers shoots up again. Advantage: Mesh.

5. Make their day. Do it again tomorrow. Flip to the other side of the transaction. Mesh customers get superior products (because they're designed to last, not to be tossed). They get convenient service that is customized and timely, without the burden of buying, maintaining, insuring, storing, and disposing of more stuff. The more they participate, the better the offers get. More frequent communication also presents more opportunities for them to get (heck, demand) what they want. And all this at less overall cost. Advantage: Mesh.

6. There's more to life than money. When the bozos on Wall Street blew up the economy, it burst more than a housing bubble. As they lost their homes, jobs, and

savings, many people were forced to rethink what they truly care about. Maybe the collection of more stuff, bigger houses for storing it, and more debt wasn't all there was to life. Many established brands lost their luster. On the other hand, sharing-based businesses generally offer a greater feeling of connection and community. They are more trustworthy because they have to be. And they're better for the planet—a big and growing driver of consumer decisions, even as the recession deepened. Advantage—you guessed it—Mesh.

Today's business news is full of Mesh-related success stories. In the transportation sector, for example, Zipcar generated over $130 million in revenues in 2009 (674 percent since inception) and grew by more than 30 percent in just a year—one of the fastest company growth rates of the decade. WhipCar, a U.K.-based peer-to-peer car sharing firm, successfully added 1,000 vehicles to its network in six months, a milestone that took Zipcar six years to achieve a decade earlier. RelayRides and GetAround in the United States are joined by Buzzcar in France and Zazcar in Brazil, as peer-to-peer transport gains speed, and bike sharing has emerged as the fastest growing form of transportation in the world. It's only a matter of time before forward-thinking manufacturers begin to embed share-enabling technologies into every new car or bike that rolls off the assembly line.

Transportation is not the only rapidly changing business category that's grasping the benefits of Meshing. And the really good news is that we're still in the early days of this exciting economic revolution. The first flight of the Wright Flyer in 1903 was an important achievement, to be sure, but just think of how far flying machines have come since then. With thousands of companies already capitalizing on the power of shared resources and peer-to-peer transactions, the Mesh has clearly taken off, and even surpassed the Kitty Hawk stage of its development. But that is just the beginning. Like the airline business, the Mesh will undoubtedly evolve and grow in the coming years. The sooner we as business leaders engage, experiment, and learn, the more we have the opportunity to embrace the Mesh advantage. Welcome to this new era of connectedness. Engage. Learn. Share. Grow. Advantage: Mesh.

About the Author

Lisa Gansky is the author of *The Mesh: Why the Future of Business Is Sharing*, and the "instigator" behind the Mesh Directory (http://meshing.it). She often speaks on the topic of technology, social currency, and business platforms and models. You can find her website at www.lisagansky.com.

Chapter 17

Should Managers Care About Employee Happiness?

Michael Lee Stallard

Editor's Note

Michael has a masterful way of telling a developmental story, especially when exploring one of his favorite topics, a connection culture. It is useful and critical for managers at every level of the organization to understand the connections between their company's external and internal brand and the parts they play in creating everyday connection and meaning. The answer to the question in this chapter's title might be obvious—or maybe not—but the bottom-line impact of building employee well-being is clear, documented, and unambiguous. Now, we just need to start running our organizations with this knowledge in mind! Enjoy the ride.

Managers today suffer from time poverty. As global competition and the speed of innovation accelerate, demands on managers keep going up. On top of their already full "to-do" list, do they need to add "keep employees happy" to get workers to give their best efforts and align their behavior with organizational goals?

Surprisingly, the answer is both yes and no. The way to help managers cope with the demands of their jobs and boost employee discretionary effort is to create an environment where employees feel *connected* to their supervisor, to their colleagues at work, and to their organization.

To feel connected is to feel happy, but the term *happiness* doesn't do it justice. It's more accurate to say that connection brings about feelings of joy and contentment that inspire people to give their best efforts and align their behavior with organizational goals. Because of connection, employees are more productive and easier to manage. Ironically, by creating a culture of connection, the manager's overall workload is reduced as engaged employees do more and better work with less supervision.

I'm convinced that one of the most powerful and least understood aspects of business is how this feeling of connection provides a competitive advantage. Connection is the force that transforms a dog-eat-dog environment into a sled dog team that pulls together. Unless the people who are part of a business feel a sense of connection—a bond that promotes trust, cooperation, and esprit de corps—they will never reach their potential as individuals, nor will the organization.

Connection is such a powerful force that if you fail to cultivate it in your life, you will one day look back with regret. If, on the other hand, you are intentional about cultivating connection, you will experience the productivity, prosperity, and joy that come from having an abundance of connection in your life.

Discovering the Force of Connection

So what is connection anyway? At the firm I lead, E Pluribus Partners, we define connection as follows:

> *Connection: a bond based on shared identity, empathy, and understanding that moves self-centered individuals toward group-centered membership.*

When we interact with people, we generally feel that we connect with some and not with others. Phrases such as "we really connected" and "we just didn't connect" are common in our daily conversations. Connection describes something intangible we sense in relationships. When connection is present, we feel energy, empathy, and affirmation, and are more open. When it is absent, we experience neutral or even negative feelings. Although we know what it's like to feel connected on a personal level, few among us understand the effect connection has on us and on the organizations we work in.

Let me first explain the power of connection by sharing some observations and insights that emerged out of my personal experiences. I left Wall Street in May 2002 and began researching and writing the book *Fired Up or Burned Out* about some ideas and practices I had been developing to motivate people who work on the front lines of a business directly with customers. In addition to doing research in the fields of organizational behavior, psychology, sociology, history, political science, and systems theory, I did a great deal of reflecting about my own experiences in life. And to my surprise, many of the things I learned came from some of the least expected places.

In late 2002, my wife Katie was diagnosed with breast cancer. Fortunately, it was detected early, removed by surgery, and treated with radiation. During the course of Katie's treatments at our local hospital, we were comforted by the kindness and compassion that many of the healthcare workers showed us during this difficult time. We discovered that some of them were cancer survivors themselves. Because they had experienced cancer as patients, they knew what we were going through, and they went beyond the duties of their jobs to comfort and encourage us. The connection we felt with them boosted our spirits.

Over the course of 2003 I continued researching and writing about connection. In December, during Katie's quarterly checkup, some of the tests indicated that she might have ovarian cancer. The day of her surgery in early 2004 was one of the most sobering of my life. After Katie had been in the operating room for more than three hours, I knew it wasn't good, and I started having a hard time breathing. Shortly thereafter, Katie's surgeon came out and told me she did have ovarian cancer, and that it had spread some. I remember him telling me that he was sorry. That night, I went with Katie's mom and my daughters Sarah and Elizabeth—12 and 10 years of age at the time—to see Katie in the ICU. She looked pale and tired. Seeing her so weak and glassy-eyed scared the girls. Sarah backed up against a wall and began to faint. After an ICU nurse helped us revive her, we made our way out of the hospital. Walking through the empty hospital lobby, Elizabeth began to sob. I knelt down beside her, and Sarah and I wrapped our arms around her until Elizabeth regained her composure. At bedtime, the girls crawled into our bed. We prayed for God to watch over Katie, and the girls fell off to sleep. I'll never forget that night seeing them snuggled up together, asleep on their mom's pillow. I recall how utterly alone I felt, afraid of what the future might hold for our family. The thought of Katie not seeing the girls grow up and the girls losing such a wonderful, loving mother made me sad beyond anything I had ever felt.

During the first half of 2004, Katie had her initial six chemotherapy treatments. She took a break from chemo over the summer before starting a second round of treatments, this time high-dosage chemotherapy at Memorial Sloan-Kettering Cancer Center in New York City. Our experience at Sloan-Kettering really surprised me. Every time we approached the front doors of the 53rd Street entrance in midtown Manhattan, the exuberant doormen locked their eyes on us and greeted us with big, warm smiles as if we were friends coming to visit. The receptionist called everyone "honey." This is extremely unusual in New York City.

The security people and administrators were equally friendly. During our first office visit with Katie's oncologist, Dr. Martee Hensley, she spent an hour educating us and patiently answering our long list of questions.

By the end of the day, I had two distinct reactions. First, I knew that this team of doctors was one of the best teams to treat ovarian cancer in the world. I had done the research and I was confident of that. When you think about it, this is a very *rational* reaction. What surprised me was the second reaction I had, a reaction that was *emotional*. I knew they cared. I could feel it. And although the statistics for Katie's survival were sobering, Dr. Hensley and the people we met that day gave us hope and made us more optimistic that Katie could get through this.

One day during Katie's chemo treatment, I went to the gift shop to get something to drink and stumbled on a meeting in the adjacent lounge where Sloan-Kettering employees who worked at that location were discussing the results of an employee survey. I overheard them share that they loved working there because they loved their colleagues, their patients, and their cause, which is to provide what is stated on all their printed materials, "the best cancer care, anywhere." It was apparent that those healthcare professionals had formed a connection with one another and with their patients. During the time we spent at Sloan-Kettering, it struck me that there was more joy and esprit de corps in the atmosphere there than in 95 percent of the offices I had been in over my career. Who would have guessed that a place that treated cancer could have such a vibrant and positive atmosphere?

Today, I'm overjoyed to say, Katie is cancer free, and she feels great. Reflecting back on those days, I'm convinced that the connection we felt from the tremendous outpouring of care provided by healthcare workers, friends, and family helped Katie overcome cancer and protected our family's spirits. I recall reading an American Cancer Society publication that said one of the worst things for cancer patients is to feel alone. We rarely felt alone because we were constantly reminded that many, many people were pulling for us. We regularly had people stop by to visit. The visits weren't somber occasions, quite the contrary. We talked and laughed and enjoyed one another's company. Christian, Jewish, and Muslim friends told us they were praying for Katie and our family. Even our atheist friends said they were sending positive thoughts our way. All of this was very moving and encouraging to us—we knew that we weren't alone.

Having had such a good experience at Memorial Sloan-Kettering Cancer Center, we enthusiastically recommended it in 2005 to a friend of ours who was diagnosed with cancer. Because her cancer was not the type of cancer Katie had, our friend went to a different location at Sloan-Kettering for her initial consultation. Surprisingly, her experience was completely at odds with ours. After one visit where she felt alone and unwelcome, she never returned and instead decided to seek treatment elsewhere.

Reflecting on these experiences made me realize three things:

- First, connection is a powerful force that creates a positive bond between people based on both rational and emotional factors.
- Second, connection contributes to bringing out the best in people—it energizes them and makes them more trusting and resilient to face life's inevitable difficulties.
- Third, connection can vary tremendously across organizations depending upon local culture and leadership.

The Science of Connection

In recent years, neuroscientists have discovered that connection has a physiological effect on people. More specifically, it reduces the blood levels of the stress hormones epinephrine, norepinephrine, and cortisol. It increases the neurotransmitter dopamine, which enhances attention and pleasure, and serotonin, which reduces fear and worry. Connection also increases the levels of oxytocin and/or vasopressin that make us more trusting of others. And this is consistent with our personal experience. Connection provides a sense of well-being, reduces stress, and makes us more trusting.

Those discoveries about connection are also confirmed by the observations of psychiatrists. Manfred F. R. Kets de Vries, a professor at Insead, and Dr. Edward Hallowell, a practicing psychiatrist and former instructor of psychiatry at Harvard Medical School, have written that many of the business executives they encounter are deprived of connection with others, and they've observed that it makes them feel lonely, isolated, and confused at work. They also believe that people in organizations with a deficiency of connection become distrusting, disrespectful, and dissatisfied. They describe these cultures that lack connection as corrosive. To treat patients suffering from emotional isolation, they help them increase connection in their lives.

Other research establishes that connection improves mental and physical health throughout our lives as well. Consider the following:

- Babies who feel connected because they are held, stroked, and cuddled are mentally and physically healthier.

- Elementary school students who feel connected to their teachers perform better academically.
- Adolescents who feel connected at home and at school are more likely to be well-adjusted.
- Patients who feel connected recover faster.
- Adults who feel connected are more creative and better problem solvers.
- Adults who feel connected are less prone to depression and suicide.
- Seniors who feel connected live longer.

All of this evidence begs the question, What is it about connection that makes it so powerful? Without going too far into the psychology of connection, let me just summarize by saying simply that we are humans, not machines. We have emotions. We have hopes and dreams. We have a conscience. We have deeply felt human needs to be respected, to be recognized for our talents, to belong, to have autonomy or control over our work, to experience personal growth, and to do work that we feel is worthwhile in a way that we feel is ethical. When we work in an environment that recognizes these realities of our human nature, we thrive. We feel more energetic, more optimistic, and more fully alive. When we work in an environment that fails to recognize this, it is damaging to our mental and physical health.

And when you think about it, that makes sense. Let's consider how this plays out in the workplace. When we first meet people, we expect them to respect us. If they look down on us, if they are uncivil or condescending, we get upset. In time, as our colleagues get to know us, we expect them to appreciate or recognize us for our talents and contributions. That really makes us feel good. Later on, we begin to expect that we will be treated and thought of as an integral part of the community. Our connection to the group is further strengthened when we feel we have control over our work. Connection is diminished when we feel we are being micromanaged or overcontrolled by others. If we are overcontrolled, it sends the message that we are being treated like children or incompetents, and it's a sign that we are not trusted or respected. Connection is also enhanced when we experience personal growth. This is most likely to occur when our role, our work in the group, is a good fit with our skills, providing enough challenge to make us feel good when we rise to meet that challenge (but not so much challenge that we become totally stressed out). Finally, it motivates us to know our work is worthwhile in some way and to be around other people who share our belief that our work has meaning. To the extent that these universal human needs for respect, recognition, belonging, autonomy, personal growth, and meaning are met, we feel connected to the group. When they are not met, we feel less connected, or even disconnected.

The bottom line is that connection = flourishing and life, whereas disconnection = dysfunction and death.

Your Culture: Giving You Life or Killing You?

Lest you think I'm exaggerating, you should know that a recent 20-year study (1988–2008) by researchers at Tel Aviv University found that in workplaces where people reported less connection, there was a 240 percent higher mortality rate versus people in workplaces where they felt connected. Need I say more? People who are more connected with others fare better in life than those who are less connected. Connection, because it meets our human needs, makes people more trusting, more cooperative, more empathetic, more enthusiastic, more optimistic, more energetic, more creative, and better problem solvers. It creates the type of environment in which people want to help their colleagues. They are more open to share information that helps decision makers become better informed. The openness that emerges in a trusting and cooperative environment creates a robust marketplace of ideas that stimulates innovation.

Connection among people improves performance in an organization and creates a new source of competitive advantage. There has been extensive research that proves this. One measure of connection is Gallup's Q12 survey that asks questions such as whether people care about you at work, encourage your development, and seek and consider your opinion. In 2010, the Gallup Organization, working with the University of Iowa, published the results of a longitudinal study of 2,278 business units that established causation between employee engagement (i.e., connection) and business outcomes. Higher employee engagement leads to higher productivity, higher profitability, and higher customer satisfaction, as well as lower employee turnover and fewer accidents.

A 2004 study by the Corporate Executive Board was global in nature and included 50,000 employees. The study concluded that employees who felt connected were 20 percent more productive than the average employee. (That's an extra day of productivity each week!) The study also concluded that emotional factors were four times as effective as rational factors when it came to the amount of discretionary effort employees give in their work. This statistic surprises many managers—especially those who believe that people are capable of checking their emotions at the front door of their workplace.

I hope by now that you see and believe that fostering connection in the marketplace is a win-win for individuals and for organizations. It's too important for you to ignore.

How to Create a Connection Culture

For those of you who see the value of connection, I want to show you how you can bring it out in the workplace by creating a *connection culture*—a culture with the necessary elements to meet our human needs. The core elements of a connection culture that meet these human needs are vision, value, and voice.

Vision

The first element of a connection culture is vision, and it exists when everyone in an organization is motivated by the organization's mission, united by its values, and proud of its reputation.

When people share a purpose or set of beliefs they're proud of, it unites and motivates them. At Memorial Sloan-Kettering they are united and motivated by the aspiration stated in their tagline, "the best cancer care, anywhere," and the organization's reputation as one of the leading cancer centers in the world.

Another example of vision was Apple's "Think Different" advertising campaign. It was conceived following Steve Jobs's return to Apple in 1996 after a 12-year exile. As you may recall, Apple had booted Jobs and brought in an outsider to take Apple to the next level, which never happened. So the board of directors turned back to Steve Jobs for help. One of the first things Jobs did when he returned was to work with Apple's ad agency to create the "Think Different" ad campaign. It featured pictures of innovators in science, in philosophy, and in the arts, such as Albert Einstein, Mahatma Gandhi, the dancer/choreographer Martha Graham, the photographer Ansel Adams, the physicist Richard Feynman, and Pablo Picasso. The campaign communicated that Apple people were more than technologists; they were innovators and artists who gave others like themselves the tools to change the world. The result was that it created a powerful bond, a connection between Jobs, Apple employees, and Apple customers (who are, by the way, intensely loyal and evangelistic when it comes to spreading the gospel of Apple).

The late Dame Anita Roddick, founder of The Body Shop, also connected with people through the element of vision. She promoted all-natural cosmetic products that were environmentally friendly, didn't rely on animal testing, and were produced by companies in the developing world. For many years The Body Shop was growing by 50 percent a year, even through a recession.

Another one of my favorite examples of a brilliant leader who brought vision to a group of people goes back a few years. During World War II, President Franklin Delano Roosevelt traveled to Seattle, Washington, to meet with 18,000 aircraft workers at Boeing Corporation. FDR brought with him a young airplane pilot named Hewitt Wheless from Texas. The pilot had escaped death thanks to the resilience of the bullet-riddled B-17 plane he flew out of harm's way. His plane had been built at that very Boeing plant. Do you think seeing and hearing that young pilot thank them for saving his life connected them to a common cause? You bet it did. It transformed those welders and riveters into freedom fighters. From 1941 until 1945 American aircraft companies outproduced the Nazis three-to-one, building nearly 300,000 airplanes.

Value

The second element of a connection culture is that people are truly valued as human beings and not treated as human doings. My colleagues and I refer to this element in a culture simply as "value." It means that everyone in an organization understands the universal needs of people (that I wrote about earlier), appreciates the unique contribution of each person, and helps them achieve their potential.

Here are some examples of what value looks like in a culture. When David Neeleman was CEO of JetBlue, he met with 95 percent of new employees, showing them on day one that he valued them. He also set aside one day each week to travel on JetBlue flights where he served beverages and got down on his hands and knees to clean planes. This showed that he didn't devalue the work done by even the lowest-level employees at JetBlue. Nothing he asked them to do was beneath him. Throughout the course of the day the high-energy and outgoing Neeleman constantly connected with crew members and passengers. This showed that he valued people enough to take the time to connect with them. Neeleman knew that connection is important. In fact, he said that most airlines treat passengers like cattle, and that JetBlue was different because its employees made personal connections with their passengers. Do you suppose people want to work at a place like that? In 2002, when JetBlue had 2,000 crew member positions to fill, it received 130,000 applications. Do you think you could select a remarkably talented group of new employees from that applicant pool?

Another example is Jack Mitchell, the CEO of Mitchells/Richards/Marshs, a high-end clothing store with locations in Connecticut and Long Island. Mitchells/Richards/Marshs was the 2002 Menswear Retailer of the Year. Jack Mitchell describes his philosophy as "hugging" employees and customers by treating employees like family and customers like friends. He coaches employees to help them achieve their potential. When they are sick, he reaches out to them. He gives them autonomy. For example, when one older salesperson needed to take a short nap in the afternoons to get re-energized, Jack said that that made sense to him.

Value also includes protecting people from abuses such as incivility, sexual misconduct, or prejudice—actions that make people feel disconnected from their community because it failed to protect them. On a few rare occasions, Jack Mitchell has told customers to take their business elsewhere when they became verbally abusive to one of his employees.

Allan Loren, who led the turnaround of Dun and Bradstreet, showed people he valued them when he established a rule that no meeting would be scheduled on Mondays or Fridays if it required people to travel over the weekend. This shows that he cared enough to protect their personal time. Loren also valued employees enough to want to see them grow, so he matched everyone in the organization with a buddy who would give them continuous feedback about how they were doing in terms of their personal growth goals. Buddies were selected based on their strengths in those areas that a particular employee wanted to improve upon. Allan Loren also showed he valued people by having employee satisfaction surveys completed twice each year to see how people were doing.

Carl Sewell, CEO of Sewell Automotive in Dallas, one of the most successful automobile retailers nationwide, intentionally hires caring people and nurtures a caring culture that creates connection among employees and customers. His passion for hiring caring people intensified after he was treated for cancer at M.D. Anderson Cancer Center in Houston. Carl Sewell knows firsthand just how uplifting it is when we meet someone who really cares about us.

Voice

The third element of a connection culture is voice. The element of voice exists when everyone in an organization participates in an open, honest, and safe environment where people share their opinions in order to understand one another and seek the best ideas. When people's ideas and opinions are sought and considered, it helps meet the human needs for respect, recognition, and belonging. "Being in the loop," so to speak, makes people feel connected to their colleagues, just as being "out of the loop" makes people feel disconnected.

When A.G. Lafley was the CEO of Procter & Gamble, he was a master of using voice to boost performance. Lafley actively sought people's views. When he met with people, he told them what was honestly on his mind before asking them to share the issues they were thinking about. He encouraged them to "get the moose out of the closet" before they grow into bigger problems. When he first became CEO, Lafley conducted an employee survey to get their ideas, and he ended up implementing many of them. In his interactions with people, Lafley made it all about them rather than all about him, and the results he helped produce were stunning. At the time he took over as CEO, P&G was performing poorly, and morale was low. In his first 12 months, Lafley led an effort that resulted in a two and a half times increase in employee approval of P&G's leadership and a soaring profitability and stock price—so much so that P&G was able to acquire the Gillette Corporation.

A good way to remember the elements in a connection culture is to remember the following formula:

Vision + Value + Voice = Connection

When these elements of a connection culture are in place, it's a win–win for individuals and organizations.

The Character Connection

What kind of people make a connection culture happen? In our research we had an "aha moment" when we saw the clear link between certain character strengths and the elements in a connection culture. I was studying the field of positive psychology and the 24 character strengths that have been identified as being universal across cultures and religions. The positive psychologists believe these universal character strengths, viewed favorably by moral philosophers and religious thinkers throughout history, improve mental and physical health and favor the survival of civilizations. At E Pluribus Partners, we believe these character strengths improve the mental and physical health of people in organizations and favor the survival of organizations too. For example, when individuals possess the character strengths of humility/modesty, open-mindedness, curiosity, wisdom, love of learning, bravery, and integrity, the element of voice will be present in a culture.

The character>connection>thrive chain below (Figure 17-1) shows how all of this fits together. Starting from the left side of the diagram you can see that universal character strengths support the elements that create a connection culture. When a connection culture exists, the universal human needs are met that help individuals and organizations thrive.

Figure 17-1. The Character → Connection → Thrive Chain

THE CHARACTER ▶ CONNECTION ▶ THRIVE CHAIN

Universal Character Strengths in People	Create the Connection Culture	Which Meets Universal Human Needs	That Help People and Organizations Thrive	
			Individuals Thrive	**Organizations Thrive**
Purpose, hope, optimism, enthusiasm, appreciation of beauty and excellence	Inspiring Identity ("Vision")	Meaning Respect Recognition	Trust Cooperation Empathy	Employee Engagement Better Decisions
Kindness, love of people, fairness, forgiveness and mercy, social intelligence	Human Value ("Value")	Belonging Autonomy Personal Growth	Enthusiasm Optimism Energy	Innovation Productivity Profitability
Humility/modesty, open-mindedness, curiosity, wisdom, love of learning, bravery, integrity	Knowledge Flow ("Voice")		Creativity Superior Problem Solving	Customer Satisfaction Employee Retention Safety

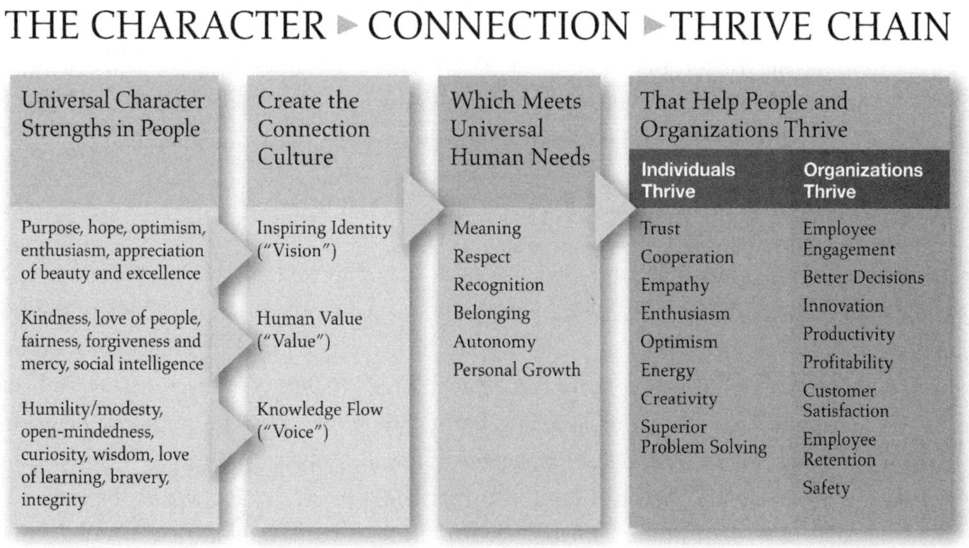

The bottom line is that we all need strength of character and connection to thrive at work and in life. There are literally hundreds of behaviors that boost connection, so the manager's challenge is to learn to understand connection, learn to understand the needs of the people he or she is responsible for leading, and develop a culture to meet that set of needs. Here are a few suggestions about how to get started:

- **Educate**: Everyone should understand what connection truly is and be motivated to continuously strive to increase it among the people with whom they live and work.
- **Vision**: Identify the vision that will unite and motivate everyone in your business. That vision may be becoming the best at what you do, bringing something new to the world, or conducting your business in a way that reflects your values. Charles Schwab's vision is to create "the most useful and ethical financial products in the world." Disney's vision is to "make people happy." E Pluribus Partners' vision is to "unlock corporate potential." To jump-start the process, get your most motivated people in a room and ask them when they have felt proud of the company. Listen to their stories and you'll likely find a vision to rally around.
- **Value**: Get to know the personal stories of the people you live and work alongside. Learn what has made them happy and what has disappointed them. Find out what their professional and personal hopes are for the future and then help them achieve those goals. As people get to know and help one another, value will increase, and connection will be strengthened.
- **Voice**: Like A.G. Lafley at Procter & Gamble, all leaders should regularly meet with groups of people to hear the issues on their minds, to get the "moose out of the closet" so they can deal with them, and hear people's ideas about opportunities and threats to their business. Leaders should look for good suggestions they can implement. You won't believe how much it will fire up people to see their ideas come to life. This brings voice to a culture and increases connection.

Great Leaders Connect

The wisest leaders are beginning to see the value of connection and community. I've written about several of them. Bono, of the rock band U2, makes the other members of U2 feel connected. He says they are a family. They split the economic profits equally. He is always praising his bandmates for their remarkable talents and strength of character. They've been there for one another through the difficult seasons of their respective lives. On one occasion, Bono received a death threat before a concert that said if he sang the song "Pride (in the name of love)" about the Revered Martin Luther King, Jr., the writer would "blow Bono's head off." The FBI told the band it believed the threat was "credible" and needed to be taken seriously. Bono, however, refused to be intimidated. While on stage, he closed his eyes as he sang "Pride." At the end of one verse, Bono opened his eyes and was stunned to find Adam Clayton, U2's bass player, literally standing in front of him to shield his friend from harm. When U2 was inducted into the Rock and Roll Hall of Fame, Bono thanked Adam for being willing to take a bullet for him. The audience laughed, but Bono wasn't kidding. Given the close connection among the members of U2 it should come as no surprise that they've been together all their adult lives, they've been awarded more Grammy Awards than any band in history, and just recently they set the record for the largest grossing tour, destroying the previous record held by the Rolling Stones.

A leader I know and have written about is the former chief of the U.S. Navy, CNO Admiral Vern Clark. He became the Navy's chief in 2000 when it wasn't meeting its re-enlistment goals for enlisted sailors. Admiral Clark and his leadership team went into action. One of my favorite things that Admiral Clark did was that he spoke to the master chiefs who are the leaders of enlisted sailors. He told them that when he was young and became a command-ing officer on his first ship, he was so green he didn't know the pointy end of the ship from the blunt end. Fortunately, Clark said, an experienced master chief on board named Chief Leedy mentored him and made Clark a better leader. Admiral Clark told the master chiefs he needed them to do for the young sailors under their command what Chief Leedy did for him. The chiefs didn't let "Old Vern," as they called him, down. Within 18 months first-term re-enlistment had risen from under 38 percent, the Navy's goal, to 56.7 percent. By the time the World Trade Center and Pentagon were attacked by terrorists on September 11, 2001 the Navy was fully staffed and performing at the top of its game. Within a matter of hours following the terrorist attacks that day, aircraft carriers, Aegis destroyers, and cruisers were in position to protect America's shores. This was due in part to the fact that naval leaders anticipated what had to be done and took action before they received orders. At the Pen-tagon in Washington, D.C., command and control of the Navy was quickly re-established, and planning for America's response began while the embers of the fire from the terrorist attack still smoldered a short distance away.

When my friend Frances Hesselbein, former CEO of the Girl Scouts of the USA, assumed the CEO position in 1976, the Girl Scouts' membership was falling, and the organization was in a state of serious decline. She put sound management practices in place and began developing a culture of connection. During her 24-year tenure, Girl Scout membership quadrupled to nearly 3.5 million, diversity more than tripled, and the organization was trans-formed into what Peter Drucker called "the best-managed organization around." Hesselbein accomplished the amazing turnaround with a paid staff of 6,000 and 730,000 volunteers. By the time she resigned from the Girl Scouts in 1990, the organization's future was bright.

Mrs. Hesselbein was paid the ultimate compliment by Drucker when he recruited her to be the head of the Drucker Foundation (renamed the Leader to Leader Institute).

At Southwest Airlines, the company learned that its performance at the gate improved when it maintained a 10-to-1 frontline employee-to-supervisor ratio because its supervisors could connect with, coach, and encourage those people. Many airlines have frontline employee-to-supervisor ratios as high as 40-to-1, making connection very difficult to maintain.

When Anne Mulcahy was named Xerox's CEO in May 2000, the firm was on the verge of bankruptcy, and its stock had dropped from $63.69 a share to $4.43. After bringing herself up to speed on the company's situation, she shocked Wall Street by announcing Xerox's business model was unsustainable. Her remark caused Xerox stock to drop 26 percent the following day. Thanks to Mulcahy's leadership that strengthened connection among the people at Xerox, employees rallied to support her, and together they restored the company to profitability and positioned it for future growth, leading observers like Xerox board member and former CEO of Time Warner Nick Nicholas to proclaim, "The story here is a minor miracle."

I've had the pleasure of visiting Pixar Animation Studios. While there I learned that Pixar's CEO, Ed Catmull, sees Pixar as an antidote to the disconnection that is the norm in the film production industry where independent contractors come together for a specific project and then disband upon the project's conclusion. In contrast to the independent contractor model, Pixar keeps the team together so that its members build connection among them. Connection occurs at Pixar when every employee, from the janitors to Catmull himself, has the opportunity to spend four hours each week in Pixar University classes with colleagues learning about the arts and animation and, most importantly, about each other. It's no coincidence that Pixar University's crest bears the Latin phrase "Alienus Non Dieutius," which translated means "Alone No Longer."

My heroes are the individuals who increase connection among the people around them, in their organizations and in society at large. Wherever you find great nations, companies, nonprofits, and sports teams, you will find these great men and women. George Washington, FDR, Reverend Martin Luther King, Jr., Mahatma Gandhi, Winston Churchill, Elizabeth Cady Stanton, Vaclav Havel, Nelson Mandela, John Wooden, Dean Smith, Coach K at Duke, and the leaders I mentioned above are but a few of the leaders who increased connection over the course of history.

It was connection that inspired us to name our firm E Pluribus Partners. E Pluribus is a nod to "E Pluribus Unum," the motto of the United States created by John Adams, Benjamin Franklin, and Thomas Jefferson. E Pluribus Unum is a Latin phrase that means "Out of Many, One."

Companies that sow the seeds of disconnection are doomed. Could there be a better example than Enron, a company whose leaders nurtured a dog-eat-dog environment, where the book *The Selfish Gene*[6] by Richard Dawkins was celebrated as a manifesto and traders boasted about their power to make grandmothers in California suffer from electricity rate increases and power outages? Leaders who nurture dog-eat-dog or even indifferent cultures may succeed for a while, but their success is built on feet of clay that will inevitably crumble. History is filled with examples of this recurring theme.

Connection is key. It unites the many into one where everyone wants to give their best efforts and sacrifice "the me for the we." Connection makes a difference in families, in workplaces, in schools, in volunteer organizations, in communities, and in nations. None of us, individually or collectively, can thrive for long without it.

About the Author

Michael Lee Stallard speaks, teaches workshops, and writes about leadership, employee engagement, productivity, and innovation. He is president of E Pluribus Partners, a leadership training and consulting firm, and primary author of *Fired Up or Burned Out: How to Reignite Your Team's Passion, Creativity and Productivity*. Michael contributes to leadership publications around the world and blogs at www.michaelleestallard.com.

This chapter was adapted from the book *Fired Up or Burned Out: How to Reignite Your Team's Passion, Creativity and Productivity* published by Thomas Nelson. Adapted with permission.

---

[6] Ironically, evolutionary biology that Dawkins's a book is based on supports helping others and developing connection in one's community, as opposed to being selfish, because helping and connecting convey a survival advantage.

Chapter 18

The Manager as Extreme Leader

Steve Farber and Steve Dealph

Editor's Note

I decided that I wanted Steve Farber to share his ideas about love, audacity, energy, and proof for managers from the moment I knew that I was going to be the editor of this book. The terms management *and* love *and* audacity *are not often shared in the same sentence, but they ought to be! Over the last 30 years I have observed the differences between managers for whom people want to work, and those from whom they would prefer fleeing. Steve Farber and Steve Dealph have articulated the most important distinctions in this chapter.*

Whether you're a new manager, or deciding to pursue your ongoing development as a manager, please understand that no one really expects you to just "manage" things. You may have been a great "doer" before, but that's no longer enough. Companies often make the mistake of promoting great "doers" and then expecting them to automatically become great managers of other "doers." But not only does the responsibility for other people require a new skill set; it takes a different mindset, too—particularly in these chaotic, extreme times.

This new skill set/mindset combination is something we call "Manager as Extreme Leader," and over the next few pages, we'll share four things you should do and think about to evolve into this new, life- and business-changing approach.

Recognize Fear

Fear is a fundamental and natural human emotion. A lot of management, leadership, and performance experts are exploring the concept of "emotion intelligence" and its impact on fear and both the positive and negative effect it has on us. In a positive light, fear is an emotional response that lets us know something or someone we value and care about is about to be compromised. It's a tool that can help us know if, when, and how to take risks.

But fear can also be a negative thing. We often allow fear to "control" us, and we let it keep us from doing what needs to be done or taking chances that need to be taken. We've all been there: that "deer in the headlights" feeling when we're so overwhelmed by fear that we freeze up, stopped dead in our tracks, only to find the situation getting worse and worse. As managers, we have to have the courage to move and act appropriately in these moments. Fear is also negative when we use it as a weapon or way to control others. Yes, fear has its place as a motivator. When you were a child and your parents told you the possible repercussions of not looking both ways when you cross the street, it was a useful thing.

The problem is that many managers overuse fear as a tool to get a desired behavior from an employee or, ostensibly, to squeeze more productivity out of a team. It often sounds something like this: "I'm your manager. Do this because I said so. Don't ask questions. Just do it!" (Implication? "Or else!") Often, it results in—at best—getting the minimum of what you ask for and nothing more. Further, it's not sustainable; you can only play that card so many times. And, finally, it has a terrible effect on employee engagement.

As a manager, it's important that you recognize that sense of fear when you encounter it. Don't be paralyzed by it; don't do nothing. Explore it! Ask yourself:

- Why am I experiencing this fear?
- What's at stake in this situation that's important to me?
- What are the consequences of dealing with this situation? What are the consequences of not dealing with it?

All too often we find ourselves in these situations, and the fear is created by whoever is yelling the loudest: the unhappy customer, the angry executive, or the frustrated co-worker. Each of these can create a fear of not acting quickly. But we have to be clear about what else is at stake.

So recognize fear, recognize the emotional feelings it creates in you (and all of us), and then use the recognition as a signal to slow down, take a deep breath, consider all that is important, and then make the appropriate decision as a leader.

One more point about fear … you're not the only one who fears it! When you find yourself responding to a client, colleague, customer, or supervisor who's berating you or demanding something from you, consider he or she is likely responding to fear. Your ability to recognize this in others—and help them overcome their fears—is a big part of being an extreme leader.

Don't Be a Poser!

What do we mean by "poser"? Think about it. In the context of leadership and management, posers are people who wear the team "leader" hat without throwing themselves whole-heartedly into the act of leading.

What does that look like? Well, it's those leaders who take credit for the work that gets done but who don't get their hands dirty doing it. It's those managers who expect you to do something "because I said so" but don't bother helping you understand the purpose of your work. Or maybe it's those managers who pit employees against each other to drive unhealthy competition, or maybe … well, you get the point. You're probably picturing a poser right now.

Think about the impact of that poser. Did he or she inspire you to do good work? Did you trust him or her? Maybe you even secretly fantasized about seeing this poser fail, even though it might hurt your business. Bottom line, posers are not the people we want to work for, and we often find it exhausting to do so.

Posers are often posers because they don't know how to be good leaders. Or because they are fearful (there's that word again) that if they do what should be done, they will lose something important to them. It's a bit like the "Emperor's New Clothes," in that they are often only fooling themselves and, sadly, they are often not even aware of it.

Reality check: You've probably identified others who have been posers in your life. Here's the tough question: When have you been a poser? We didn't ask *if* you have, because we've all been posers at some point in our lives. It happens when we find ourselves in a situation we haven't been in before, lack the experience or confidence to know exactly what to do, and, as a result, fall back on the one thing we have: power, title, authority, or something else.

Think about when you were a poser. Explore how you got there, how you acted, and how others reacted to you. If you are going to pursue real leadership, you run the risk of becoming a poser again. That's OK!

When you find yourself at that crossroads you can either a) opt to be the poser and constantly fear you will be discovered as a fraud, or b) recognize that you find yourself about to experience some significant growth. You may get a little banged up along the way, but you will come through it with respect, for yourself and from those whom you lead and interact. If you choose the latter, you're ready to pursue extreme leadership, and you're ready to take the radical leap.

Take the Radical LEAP

The manager as extreme leader takes a radical leap. It's what separates extreme leaders from posers. It's what makes them love their jobs and want to do more than is expected of them, and it's what makes their employees want to keep working for them and do more than is expected. And it's what makes customers and clients trust them and keep returning.

The cool thing is that it isn't brain surgery. If you're ready to keep fear from holding you back, and if you want to eschew the poser style of working, you'll find that the radical leap is easy to understand, and it's not that hard to do. Managers as extreme leaders cultivate **L**ove, generate **E**nergy, inspire **A**udacity, and provide **P**roof. Let's explore each element.

Cultivate Love

Love is the ultimate motivation of the manager as extreme leader: love of something or someone, love of a cause, love of principles, love of the people you work with and the customers you serve, love of a vision of what can be done when you collaborate with others.

Love? Really? Think of it this way: Odds are you're spending at least eight hours a day at your job and probably a lot more. That's a huge part of your waking life, and, simply put, life's too short—so why on earth shouldn't you love your work? And so should everyone you lead and work with.

Think about the best job that you ever had. Was it the best-paying job? Maybe, maybe not. More likely, you remember it because you loved what you were doing, whom you were doing it with, whom you were doing it for, and so on. You got excited going in to work, really missed your colleagues when you left at the end of the day, and went the "extra mile" for any of them.

That's what love feels like. And it's also what being an engaged employee feels like. Creating a work climate where employees do their best work and are extremely satisfied is the way the manager as extreme leader creates engaged employees.

It's become conventional wisdom that engaging our employees is the key to keeping them. More money is nice, and it is important, to an extent. But there will always be a job that pays more. What will keep employees doing their best work for you is engaging them in things that are important to them.

Dan Pink, author of *Drive*, tells us that the three key areas that motivate employees are autonomy (the desire to be self-directed), mastery (the urge to be better at what we do and to make a contribution), and purpose (the belief that what we do has transcendent value). Not only do our employees want these things, but we want them too. The manager as extreme leader cultivates opportunities for employees to love their work, love their teams, and love what they do. And that all starts with you and your capacity to cultivate love for your work.

It's not always easy. In fact, there are days when we are just not "feeling the love." And on those days we are probably not doing our best work, leading others well, or providing the best service for our customers and clients. When we find ourselves feeling "dread" about what lies before us, that's when we need to remind ourselves why we are doing what we are doing.

Ask yourself these questions:

- Why do I love this business, this company?
- Why do I love this project, this idea, this system, this procedure, this policy?
- Why do I love my customers/clients?
- Why do I love my team members and those I work with?

It's OK if the answers don't come to you right away. Often it's much easier to recognize why we *don't* love something than why we do. But we have to anchor ourselves when all the drama is pulling us in a million different directions and away from what is truly important.

In the process of trying to overcome fear, we have to find what is important, and what is loved. Instead of waiting for those fearful moments to discover what you really love, develop a practice of cultivating love now, so you'll have the clarity to act in moments of fear. As you explore these questions, be sure to say them aloud. Listen to what it sounds like and get comfortable saying it. Then, ask yourself this question, not with words but through your actions: How will I show that love in the way I work with, serve, and lead the people around me?

As you become clearer about what is important to you, you need to demonstrate it in your actions. What you say and what you do has to match; remember, posers only "say it," but leaders say it and do it. That's how we help others build trust in us and how we build confidence in ourselves to do more.

Generate Energy

The extreme leader is a generator, a powerful force for action, for progress, and an enthusiastic believer in people and their capacity to do the awesome. Do you know what energizes you? Make a list of your personal energizers and encourage others to do the same. (Want to bet autonomy, mastery, and/or purpose wind up on these lists in some form?)

What generates energy?

- love
- great ideas
- noble principles
- interesting work
- exciting challenges
- a compelling vision for the future.

Once you have clarity about what energizes you and others, ask yourself:

- What effect does my action have on the energy of the people around me?
- What goals can I set for my team and company today that will tap into the talents, skills, hopes, and aspirations of my people?
- What energy suckers—behaviors, policies, practices, and so on—are hindering our cause?

The cool part about generating energy is you don't have to do it all by yourself. The best way to generate energy is to engage others. Ask them what gets them energized. Ask them what the energy suckers are and how to minimize them. And then do everything in your power to eradicate those energy suckers on behalf of your team.

Inspire Audacity

We define audacity as "a bold and blatant disregard for normal constraints in order to change the world for the better." Fear keeps us from disregarding those normal constraints; love makes us overcome them.

The most common and insidious constraints are the ones that are imposed on us by others. Your organization's dominant logic, culture, or unwritten rules can semiconsciously drive your behavior, often at your own expense. Accepted responses like "That will never work here" or "We tried that once and it didn't work" may be common to your work environment. Or people may frequently tell you that you're being too idealistic. It's not that they're being malicious (not necessarily); they're likely coming from a sad, limited set of beliefs about what's possible. What they need is an extreme leader to help them see possibilities.

To inspire audacity, ask this: How are we going to change the world? Yes, world. If you don't think it's possible then it won't be. So be audacious, and think about the possibilities.

We know that changing the whole world is a challenge. In fact, many leaders fail at making positive change because they are so focused on the end result that they lack any understanding of what it looks like to get there. So, consider how to change the whole world and then think about how to get there and ask: How are we going to change the world of our company, our employees, customers, marketplace, and industry?

And, again, remember that posers talk it, while extreme leaders do it. So how are *you* going to change for the better? What are you going to do differently to change the world for those you love? Identify two to three things that will make a difference and then do them. Let others know you are making the change and enlist the support of others. You will be humbled by the support you receive, and you will inspire others to do the same.

Provide Proof

In the process of leading in an extreme way, you're going to be questioned, and you're going to be challenged—by yourself and others. You're probably going to fail in some of your efforts. In fact, you *need* to fail sometimes. If you don't, then you need to consider if you're being audacious enough or just playing it safe.

Questioning is a good thing. Others will want to know why you're managing differently. Tell them. They'll want to know how we're going to improve things. Show them. They'll want to know why we need to change something that wasn't really broken. Explain it to them. Provide proof.

Extreme leaders provide proof in three ways:

- They prove it to others.
- They prove it to themselves.
- They prove to others they are proving it to themselves.

In proving it to others, it comes back to not being a poser; it's not telling others to go out and do something without you being at the vanguard of the effort yourself. It's being the example for others. It's helping them see what can be, through your actions and through understanding what energizes them and leveraging that to help them see what can be.

Ask yourself these questions:

- What have I done today that shows my commitment to my colleagues and my customers?
- How have I changed the world, even a little bit, today? What measurable, tangible evidence can I provide?
- What will I do tomorrow to demonstrate the power of my conviction?

Proving it to ourselves is vital in extreme leadership. It's about building confidence to take purposeful risks, and then it's about reminding ourselves why we want and need to pursue the path after we've taken the leap. We have to remind ourselves about our purpose in the midst of all the chaos around us.

So how do you prove to *yourself* that you're really LEAPing into the manager as extreme leader life—that you're not just understanding it or desiring it, but really doing it? The answer brings us full-circle back to the element of fear.

In the right context, your experience of fear (or exhilaration, for that matter) is your internal "indicator, your proof, that you're moving in the right direction—that you really are leading, in other words. That scary/exhilarating experience is what we call the Oh Shoot! Moment or OS!M.

To put it bluntly: If you're using all the buzzwords and reading all the latest leadership books, and holding forth at every meeting on the latest management fads, but you're not experiencing that visceral churning in your gut, and you're not scaring yourself every day, and you're not feeling that moment as regularly as clockwork, then you are not doing anything significant—let alone changing the world—and you are certainly not leading anyone else.

Ask yourself the following questions:

- What are the OS!Ms in my past that resulted in my being where I am today? What lessons did I learn in those OS!Ms that I should continue to apply?
- What would I keep the same in spite of a particular failure? What would I change in spite of a particular success?
- What potential leadership opportunity is coming up that I can turn into my next OS!M? How will I do it?

Finally, we need to prove to others that we're proving it to ourselves. This is, if we do say so ourselves, the genius of the extreme leadership framework is engaging others in our own growth by letting them know we don't have all the answers and that we need their help in changing our team/business/world for the better.

To do this, try pursuing your OS!Ms in full, public view. Don't hide your risks. For many, this is a bit counterintuitive, but it's remarkably powerful—let others see you taking chances, stumbling along the way, and even screwing up royally. And if you're willing to share this very vulnerable, human experience, others will step up to support you and your efforts and begin to purse their own OS!Ms, too.

Ask yourself this: What do I need to do to improve as an extreme leader? Where am I screwing up? How can I get better?

You have to listen to the feedback you get—don't make excuses—and then act on it so others can see you making the effort.

Extreme leadership isn't a process; it's a framework. You'll find that each of its components—love, energy, audacity, and proof—support each other. Love permeates the framework; think of it as the glue that holds the rest of the frame together. When you're dreading some aspect of managing, cultivate love to shift your mindset, and you'll find that you are leading others differently as well. That love will energize you and others. That love will help you overcome the fears that stifle audacity. And love is our reason for providing proof.

The evolution from manager to manager as extreme leader is a very personal and enormously powerful journey, loaded with OS!Ms and packed with significant personal and collective achievement.

All you have to do is take that first LEAP.

About the Authors

Steve Farber is the president of Extreme Leadership, Inc. and the founder of The Extreme Leadership Institute—organizations devoted to changing the world through the cultivation of extreme leaders in business and education. A former vice president of The Tom Peters Company, Farber is the author of *Greater Than Yourself*, a *Wall Street Journal* and *USA Today* bestseller, and *The Radical Leap Re-Energized*, an expansion of his first book, *The Radical Leap*, which was named as one of the 100 Best Business Books of All Time. You can find his website at www.stevefarber.com.

Steve Dealph has worked in leadership development for over 20 years. He currently works in organization development for Warner Bros. Entertainment, Inc. in Los Angeles, and serves as practice leader for learning and development for The Extreme Leadership Institute.

Chapter 19

Winning With a Culture of Recognition

Eric Mosley and Derek Irvine

Editor's Note

This chapter offers a more strategic look at recognition and how managers can create a culture where employees feel that their work matters. Eric and Derek help link broader intentions, like values and goals, to daily managerial practices that build productive workplaces. I am thrilled to include this chapter because I think it will serve us well to understand the connections and interdependencies between values, culture, and recognition practices.

O rganizational culture is the most powerful force in business, and yet it is one of the most neglected (and misunderstood) attributes of any organization. Every organization has a culture, whether it is the culture the leadership wants or the one that has come to exist through inertia and management neglect. Businesses are societies, and society and culture are inseparable. In evaluating the culture of our clients' workplaces, the questions we ask are:

- Is your organization's culture deliberately managed or left to develop by accident?
- Is your culture aligned to and supportive of your company values?
- Does your culture contribute every day to your strategic goals or hinder them?
- And most importantly—can you prove your answers to these questions are correct?

Understanding your company's culture and shaping it deliberately, based on your values, is foundational to achieving your strategic objectives. Proactively managing company culture is critical to gaining competitive advantage. To say that corporate culture cannot be managed scientifically, with rigorous and authentic processes, is a myth with damaging consequences. An organization's culture can be learned, encouraged, ingrained, and applied to every business process, in many forms and across many different parts of the organization. Applied correctly, culture management through recognition is one of the most powerful, effective, and, most critically, positive ways to drive the success of your organization as measured by improvements in operating margins, income, and customer satisfaction.

Think of the hallmarks of your culture—your company values. These statements of desired behaviors and actions suggest and—when followed properly—reinforce your culture.

Executive Insight

"I really focus on the values and the standards of the organization. What are the expected behaviors? How do we want to treat each other? How do we want to act? What do we want to do about transparency? How can we have a safe environment where we really know what's going on?"

—Alan R. Mulally, President and Chief Executive Officer
of Ford Motor Company[1]

But how do you make your values real to every employee so they are meaningful in how employees approach their everyday tasks? Strategic recognition, implemented correctly, is the most powerful tool we know to manage, inspire, encourage, and measure demonstration of the values you have chosen for your organization.

What Is Organizational Culture?

An organization's culture is so much more than a slogan or poster. Culture is nothing less than the aggregate of tens of thousands of interactions every day. Leaders of great companies reinforce their values by rewarding and celebrating the behaviors that express those values. When a manager recognizes an employee's behavior, personally and sincerely, both feel proud, gratified, and happy. There's a human connection that transcends the immediate culture to create a shared bond. The power of this bond is stronger than you might think; indeed, it's the power that holds together great organizational cultures. Shared values, shared emotions, shared connections—these make organizations as much as they make civilizations.

---

[1] *New York Times,* Sept. 5, 2009 (http://www.nytimes.com/2009/09/06/business/06corner.html)

Creating a culture means choosing a limited number of values that define the company as surely as its products or logo, and then encouraging expression of those values in everyday behavior. No single set of values defines culture; greatness lies in authenticity. At Nike, for example, the culture includes keen competitive spirit. At Apple, designers will not put a power cord on a device that doesn't look incredible and is seamlessly aligned with the overall design of the product, because fabulous design is a top priority of the Apple culture. Some firms, like Ryanair and Walmart, thrive on driving down costs, while others, like BMW and Rolex, focus on premium-priced engineering. If you care more about driving cost out of the system, you belong at Ryanair or Walmart, not BMW or Rolex.

Furthermore, as any psychologist will tell you, positive reinforcement works better than negative reinforcement to foster a particular corporate culture. This is just as true for organizations as it is for individuals. Herb Kelleher, the legendary cofounder and chairman of Southwest Airlines, believed that "Culture is what you do when people aren't looking." It's the result of how employees behave when they step away from the power relationships in an organization and operate purely out of their own values. When those values are also shared with the organization, culture is nourished. Since culture is manifest in behaviors in ways that can be as dramatic as a once-in-a-career decision or as mundane as regular day-to-day behaviors, we have to ask, what guides those behaviors? What can managers do to establish and maintain their culture? Certainly they can lead by example and inspiration, but not everyone can imitate a great leader (even if they try). Management needs a tool that helps all employees learn for themselves how to "live the culture." Strategic recognition is that tool.

Strategic Recognition

Strategic recognition is the practice of integrating employee recognition initiatives with other management practices, taking recognition beyond the human resources silo and leveraging its power to shape behavior at all levels of the organization. (When we say power, we mean recognition's unique ability to help employees manage themselves, as opposed to just obeying directions from the "powers that be.") When individual recognition moments across the enterprise are recorded, analyzed, and understood, recognition becomes as potent a management tool as financial- or program-management practices.

Strategic recognition makes culture management possible. Strategic recognition is linked to strategic goals such as engagement, performance, retention, and culture change. But also, because you have those tools, you get to then use strategic recognition to manage the culture. In other words, you can emphasize a single company value that you feel doesn't have the traction you need to meet your strategic objectives.

Strategic recognition takes its place with the other "hard" management science practices. It has measurable processes. It is fully integrated into strategic planning and global resource management. It removes barriers to success. Self-sustaining, strategic recognition can enhance and define organizational culture, bring certain values to the surface, and drive a culture in which behaviors reflect organizational values and contribute to company success.

Research Insight

"For most companies, recognition is an underutilized asset, one that you can—and should—set on the right track. Your recognition programs telegraph what you value and what you want to happen; recognition is how your employees perceive what they are supposed to do. So if you're unsure of whether your message—or strategic plan, or shift in culture—is getting through, a well-run recognition program can tell you."

—Carol Pletcher, *The Conference Board Review* [2]

Strategic recognition aligns company culture to geographic, national, and even demographic cultures. The company's most important values are understood by everyone: young Europeans and older Asians, jocks in the financial planning department, hipster designers in marketing, and minivan-driving soccer parents in the call center. Strategic recognition becomes so much more than the relationship between manager and employee—it becomes the affirmation of belonging to the society we call a corporation. Its goal is not to continually add new incentives but to become a self-sustaining set of desired behaviors—to create an organizational culture.

How Recognition Works

The transformative power of rewarding behavior to drive values deep into an organization relies on clear and consistent communication at all levels and in every location of a company. No tool is more powerful for achieving this than strategic recognition. Managers may ask, "What's the point of recognition? Employees do their jobs and I pay them. Why should I do anything more?" To answer this question, we need to look at what drives workplace behavior and the extent to which managers can inspire increased engagement and thus greater performance.

Managers who rely on pay alone to get desired performance will meet some limited success. Employees who are just looking for the security of a paycheck will generally show up and perform the tasks in their job description. This is a recipe for mediocrity. In fact, this point of view demonstrates an obsolete view of management itself, for the manager

---

[2] *The Conference Board Review,* Fall 2009 (http://www.tcbreview.com/beyond-the-handshake.php)

must continually prompt, cajole, and direct behaviors. The usefulness of recognition to the manager lies in making the right behaviors and attitudes self-sustaining. To understand how recognition accomplishes this, consider the psychological effect of different rewards.

Employees think of a salary or hourly wage as the minimum contract between them and their employer. A business friend we know is fond of saying, "Whatever I pay someone, it won't be enough in six months. They'll get accustomed to the paycheck arriving (imagine their reaction if it didn't), but they'll stop relating it to the growing, ever-changing challenges of their jobs. Some other reward has to feel as fresh and immediate as today's big project."

The social architecture of every business bears complex interactions in which factors like power, prestige, friendship, affinity, hostility, prejudice (negative and positive), security, confidence, trust, and faith inspire action. In fact, it's not just the reality of these factors, but their perception, that matters a great deal to whether a person feels engaged in his or her work. Into this welter of emotions wades the manager, trying to inspire great performance and discourage mediocrity with a few tools. Compensation is a critical tool, but in most jobs it is the one the manager can affect least. In brief, a paycheck is the minimum requirement of the working relationship—no work, no pay.

Psychic Income

Human beings have a fundamental need for social acceptance, increased self-esteem, and self-realization. In a business setting, these needs can never be met by cash compensation, which organizational psychologist Fred Hertzberg found could only prevent people from being dissatisfied. Salary is what we call tangible income—vitally important, but related to material needs as well as status or power.

Study after study shows that nonmonetary rewards are the key to improved performance. These rewards, which we call psychic income, are cost-effective as well. They are more flexible, affordable, and immediate than salary. Psychic income is the provision of social acceptance, social esteem (leading to self-esteem), and self-actualization. Paid in the "currency" of recognition, psychic income is intangible but no less real than material income. Managers and executives pay out psychic income to employees with acts of respect, esteem, dignity, and high regard. They reduce psychic income with acts of disrespect, humiliation, disinterest, and low regard. The balance between these is the amount of psychic wealth accumulated at work.

Organizational psychologist Fred Hertzberg identified only one management tool—recognition—that could result in employee satisfaction because only recognition feeds psychic income needs. And you don't have to wait until payday to make a deposit.

Think of it this way: Financial management achieves organizational goals through accepted and predictable accounting practices. Sales management achieves organizational goals through accepted and predictable contract terms. Culture management achieves organizational goals through accepted and predictable application of values in the workplace.

The mediocre manager, contemplating paychecks going out every few weeks, likes to think that his or her employees should be grateful to have a job. Perhaps they are, but that attitude has culture management backward. In a well-run company, the organization and the individual manager acting on its behalf harness the power of appreciation not by receiving it, but by giving it to the employees. Let's look at the aspects of appreciation that make it essential to culture management:

- **Appreciation is motivating.** People like being thanked. It feels good, affirming their worth and value. How do they get more thanks? By repeating the behavior that wins thanks.
- **Appreciation is humanizing.** The ability to express appreciation is a key strength in a leader. Appreciation is an emotion that, in many cultures, lends power to someone else, in the expectation that they will receive it. Can you imagine having your thanks rejected? It makes the person saying "thank you" a little less exalted, a little more human.
- **Appreciation is specific.** "Thank you" is reacting to a specific act, achievement, or attitude that's recognized in the transaction. It also lends credence to the importance and value of that act.
- **Appreciation is empowering.** First, appreciation empowers by affirming the power of the individual to make a choice. (I don't have to earn your appreciation, but I choose to.) Second, because appreciation can be expressed by anyone in the hierarchy to anyone else in the hierarchy, it is a reward that potentially cuts across the class and culture lines of an organization.
- **Appreciation is powerful.** Spiritual leaders emphasize the importance of gratitude on the path to wholeness. National leaders thank soldiers for their service; mayors offer the thanks of a grateful public to first responders to emergency situations. And notice how often the most enlightened business leaders attribute their success openly and often to their employees.
- **Appreciation establishes a psychological contract between employees.** Complete that contract and you are assured more productive relations among workers. Break that contract and you are assured higher turnover, lower engagement, and a population of employees who deliver below their full potential.

Here are some tips for praising and appreciating employees successfully:

- Give specific praise that goes far beyond a generic "Great job!" to make recognition truly meaningful. With specific praise, you tell the recipients what they did, how that behavior/effort reflected the company values, and why it was important to the team/department/company or contributed to achieving strategic objectives.
- Praise actions that you want to see repeated. By giving employees such specific recognition, you clearly communicate what is important and encourage them to repeat those actions in the future. For employees to want to repeat such desired behaviors, however, you must....
- Make the praise and recognition authentic. Don't fall into the compliment sandwich trap by saying things like, "Great job on that task, but you forgot this one critical step. I know you'll get it next time, since you are so conscientious!" This is a confusing message to employees. Did they really do a good job if an important step was missed? Offer constructive criticism, which is also desired by employees, separately from praise for work well done.

Program Participation and Penetration

In recognition programs, broad participation is essential for success. A recognition program will not foster the desired culture, behaviors, and results if only 10 percent of employees receive an award once a year, because that's simply not enough penetration to raise awareness of the behaviors the company is trying to promote. Again, since the people are the culture, you're not going to change the culture by affecting one in 10 employees. In fact, if the recognition is only hitting 10 to 20 percent of the workforce, management has lost touch with the company. At the very least, the company is telling itself that it's not performing very well!

Our best practices, which have been substantiated by research conducted by the Stanford Graduate School of Business, have found that if the recognition program is promoted so that five percent of the workforce receives a recognition award each week, a critical mass will be achieved and the program will both maintain and promote itself. Top-performing companies ensure that 80 percent of the global workforce will be touched by the program each year, including peer-to-peer recognition—one of the most powerful methods for driving this level of penetration.

High participation levels get employees involved in promoting the cultural change among each other. Think of how eBay users have the star ratings for buyers and sellers to regulate each other for trustworthiness and customer service. The CEO of eBay doesn't decide whether a vendor is supporting the values of honesty, service, and transparency—the users do. In the same way, wide participation and peer-to-peer interactions through the recognition program support the values promoted by recognition. Exceptional employees are recognized by the group, and the group looks to them for informal guidance. Executive management needs only to structure the recognition program so that it reflects critical values (or a big global initiative), and the recognition program will provide incentive for behavior that supports it.

Research Insight

"The key to driving productivity gains is increasing engagement among core contributors, who represent 60 percent of the typical workforce. Highly engaged employees are already working at or near their peak but are often limited by their less engaged coworkers. Focusing on engaging core contributors can improve both groups' productivity."

—Watson Wyatt Worldwide, 2008/2009 WorkUSA Report[3]

Does Everyone Get an Award?

A common comment in reaction to recognition programs is, "Wait a minute. Not everyone is equally deserving. Not every contestant gets a trophy. If everyone gets an award, don't awards lose meaning?" That would be true if global strategic recognition were a zero-sum game, but this confuses the meaning of the recognition experience. The goal of strategic recognition is to reinforce certain values and behavior, not to make everyone feel good (the fact that it does make people feel good is a benefit, but not the goal).

Companies with high employee engagement generate better results and stockholder value. For a company like Procter & Gamble, that means tens of billions of dollars in additional shareholder value. Engagement won't improve by 15 percent (a percentage that correlates to a two percent improvement in operating margin, per Towers Perrin) if only 10 percent of the workforce is getting continuous feedback on its performance. Achieving a 90 percent participation rate in a recognition program will cause an increase in engagement in a significant percentage of the workforce. Delivering a 15 percent improvement suddenly looks possible.

In real life, when our clients get to 80 to 90 percent penetration with their recognition programs, a bell curve of award winners appears. The lowest-performing 10 percent of employees will get zero awards, as is appropriate. The middle 80 percent might get two or three awards a year. The top 10 percent will receive perhaps six awards a year.

---

[3] Watson Wyatt 2008/2009 Work USA report (http://www.watsonwyatt.com/news/press.asp?ID=20559)

The people who win 10 awards a year are a meritocracy, whatever their position in the company. They are receiving annual awards with an aggregate value of $1,000–$2,000. This is precisely the goal desired in a meritocracy. Top performers will be differentiated whatever their salary bands, whatever the budget for bonuses this year, because they lead your culture and the positive business results the culture is designed to deliver.

If penetration is high enough, the recognition program becomes self-marketing because the vast majority of employees are winning awards and giving awards. This is the ultimate goal: Employees know about the program, interact with it, redeem awards, and are reminded of the values being promoted by the company. The positive emotional impact from winning recognition ensures that employees are more likely to participate. High participation is inherently efficient. Otherwise, continuous program marketing is necessary, reminding employees it exists, getting them to participate—a death spiral that overtakes too many individual-recognition programs. (Look at it this way: If your benefits were structured so that only 10 percent of employees had them, would the other 90 percent think of benefits as part of their total rewards?)

The Role of Peer Recognition

Peer recognition is one tactic to encourage high recognition penetration rates. Recognition by peers is also a sign that the company's culture has spread from the elites to the majority. Colleagues at any level of an organization bond with their peers, associate with them, share their successes and their obstacles. To institute peer recognition is to empower coworkers to honor each other's achievements, which is a powerful and cohesive force. When peers recognize each other's contributions, they build trust. Silo walls fall and information flows more freely. Peer recognition feeds psychic income needs and boosts morale while also relieving managers of the pressure to stay close to everyone (peers often know one another's contributions better than the boss).

Because this is about professional recognition, not personal popularity, peer recognition, like other kinds, requires the discipline of management practice underlying it. This is another way in which a formal recognition program contributes to better managed departments. Who doesn't enjoy honoring a colleague? It's empowering and builds general good feeling. When most employees participate, the company acquires a precious asset: a company-wide culture of appreciation.

A Culture of Appreciation

Recognition cultivates a culture of appreciation among employees, management, and executive leadership. That culture merges into the existing company culture; it becomes part of the thousand acts a day that define employment. Since we're recommending exactly this, let's briefly consider what a long-term culture of appreciation, as opposed to single recognition moments, might mean for a business.

A culture of appreciation creates an expectation that, if an employee is doing the right thing, it will be noticed, honored, and appreciated (as well as compensated in tangible ways). This expectation motivates each person to consider what values-based behaviors will earn that psychic income, just as an expectation of promotion causes some to take risks, perform beyond their job description, or seek new skills. The culture of appreciation can be the uniting force across the inevitable "silos" and departmental cultures, for while highly valuable behavior in one group might not be valued in another, the fact that both are recognized as appropriate to their situation is universal.

For example, risk-taking might be appropriate in design or marketing, where creativity holds the key to great work, but it might be shunned in accounting, where predictability and precision are key. Appreciation can honor risk-taking in marketing, and risk protection in accounting—the fact that appreciation is given is the relevant point.

A culture of appreciation also aids the creation of a robust social architecture in which communication flows freely, consistently, constantly. Employees are universally encouraged to do their best—they are not just complimented, but acknowledged when their behavior is aligned to company values and delivers strategic objectives. In the global organization, the real differences among cultures are celebrated by a culture of appreciation, overcoming the alienation and miscommunication that is the hobgoblin of a multinational enterprise. It encourages trust and that almost mythical bonding that soldiers call "unit cohesion."

In summary, recognition uses a company's social architecture and a careful payout of psychic income to increase employee engagement and performance. That recognition should go beyond the moment between a manager and employee, beyond the single relationship of worker and boss. A culture of appreciation is self-sustaining and helps everyone live the values of the organization.

There is a much greater potential implementation of recognition, however, that brings all the acts of appreciation and motivation into the most rigorous practices of management, on a par with financial, legal, and operations management. That is strategic recognition.

Why "Strategic" Recognition?

Strategic recognition is all about delivering on your business goals. It helps employees understand the behavioral norms you have identified to achieve the desired business outcome—and it does this for every employee in your company, regardless of where they live and work. To understand the power of this concept, it's helpful to examine those two words separately.

Strategic suggests that if you do recognition right, you will care about this program beyond its boost to morale. A truly strategic program gives the CEO new insights into the behavioral norms and the culture driving the company. Appreciation will have a positive and measurable effect on productivity.[4] This means your system enables you to monitor, measure, and manage investments you're making in recognition, compared to discretionary spending that doesn't drive strategic outcomes.

Recognition in the strategic context means constant reinforcement of strategic values. For example, if quality is a corporate value, you must be able to give "quality" a rich meaning applicable to the way your employees behave every day. Recognition isn't just about delivering awards. The recognition system should help achieve critical strategic goals but shouldn't interfere with the very real human emotions that go along with recognizing and being recognized for positive behaviors.

In fact, we believe that old-fashioned recognition's emphasis on giving away a coffee mug with the company logo impinges on that positive moment by adding an object to an interaction. If the award is meaningful but the system is invisible, then the recognition moment becomes two people showing mutual respect, common values, and support. This is a much more human and intimate moment that may seem a little scary to some. What if, instead of focusing on the glass paperweight with the employee's name engraved on it, the moment was about real human appreciation? What if the focus was on the special wording in the recognition moment, and the material reward was chosen later by the employee? Managers would have to drop the organizational mask and show themselves as sincerely appreciative individuals! What would that do to the company's culture?

---

[4] "Productivity and Motivation," *Personnel Today,* July 1, 2008: "The unanimous finding of our survey was that appreciative colleagues have a positive effect on productivity: Two-thirds believed they were a lot more productive when given encouragement by their workmates."

The Five Tenets of Strategic Recognition

Five operating principles, or tenets, drive successful global strategic recognition throughout the organization. These tenets prevent the managerial and psychological "disconnects" that plague less effective programs.

Tenet 1: A Single, Clear Global Strategy

Global means universal, whether you work for a small organization or a multinational giant. A clear global strategy requires a clear outcome. Some examples of the outcomes that might be sought are increased customer satisfaction, increased employee engagement scores, more repeat business, higher net promoter scores (the metric created by loyalty expert Fred Reichheld), and a measurable increase in product quality or reduction in costs.

Research Insight

"A company's success depends on its people. But their collective power stems, in part, from an organization's ability to point them in the same direction and, importantly, in a direction that is aligned to the organization's business strategy. When an organization's leadership, workforce, and culture are aligned with its strategic priorities, people can be a major source of sustainable competitive advantage."

—Towers Watson[5]

Many clients have come to us with multiple, scattered, and even conflicting recognition programs, which leads to divisions within the company, confusion, and wasted money. A global strategy creates a single recognition brand and vocabulary. It creates clear visibility into budgets and can be audited. Executives in different divisions, locations, and markets can view uniform metrics that provide insight into program adoption, operation, and results.

You have to treat all employees equally. We have an expression across global companies, parity of esteem, which means that whether employees are in Ireland, Poland, Japan, or Argentina, they are all treated with the same regard. Equal treatment does not mean identical treatment, however. A clear global strategy includes recognizing the differences in languages and local cultures and assigning award values to align with the local standard of living. Rewards must be personally meaningful, culturally relevant, and equitable in the number of options and value of rewards from country to country.

---

[5] "Executing Strategy: Alignment Makes the Difference," Towers Perrin International Survey Research, June 2009.

If a company already has ad hoc recognition programs in place, the transition to a single strategy will be challenging. Some programs will have to be cancelled, and some people will be very attached to their ideas of recognition. To ensure consistency as well as manage the program, you have to integrate a single technology platform. You have to establish a return on investment in new technology across divisions (and factor in the savings of canceling the ad hoc programs and consolidating everyone on one platform).

Tenet 2: Executive Sponsorship With Defined Goals

Support from senior management is critical to success in any initiative, and this is especially needed in managing corporate culture. In market-leading companies, strategic initiatives are managed using process, metrics, incentives, and accountability, and senior executives monitor these. Success requires a rigorous methodology (such as Six Sigma's DMAIC[6]) and meaningful measurement. Managers must be held accountable for goals, including percentage of employees awarded, employee satisfaction and engagement scores, the match of award distribution to the bell curve, and the frequency of awards. Sponsorship and communication of the recognition program cannot be left to human resources staff; it must come from a group of unified top leaders—all of them.

The more exactly you can plan such details as award levels, the more precise your measurements of award activity and money spent will be. With a defined goal of 80 to 90 percent participation in the recognition program, your data will be actionable. With defined participation goals for division heads and managers, the cultural management of recognition can take hold.

Tenet 3: Aligned With Company Values and Strategic Objectives

As we discussed, when individual-recognition moments are consciously linked to company values and goals, employees understand how their actions directly affect the culture. They see how their behavior fits into the big picture. They gain both a sense of efficacy and a sense of accountability within the big picture.

For all this to work, you need to track the program in a far more rigorous and disciplined way than the usual recognition effort attempts. If you can count the number of times in a company that somebody thanks somebody else for going the extra mile on a value like quality, then you have an indication as to the amount of discretionary effort that's being expended in and around quality. Management science suggests you then add that all up and you accumulate this information. You put it together graphically in a histogram and you

---

[6] Define, Measure, Analyze, Improve, Control.

compare a quarter against a quarter, a country against a country, a division against a division. This can give you enormous insight into how your values are turning into behaviors and are displayed in discretionary effort across the company.

Monthly dashboards like a values distribution graph illustrate for managers the traction of each value, whether by region, division, or department. Targeted management intervention in places where values are ignored or misunderstood then becomes possible. The dashboards represent people's behavior, which as we've said is the reality check of a company's culture.

The visual impact of this graph (Figure 19-1) is especially helpful to managers who want to understand and cultivate culture. This example shows the percentage of awards in three divisions of a company, focusing on the reinforcement of four key values. The meaning of the metrics is found in each department's goals and makeup. Note that Division 2 is receiving many awards for respect and integrity, but few for innovation. Division 2 happens to be the accounting group, so this award profile is excellent (if this were the product development group, we'd have quite a different story).

Figure 19-1. Values Distribution Graph

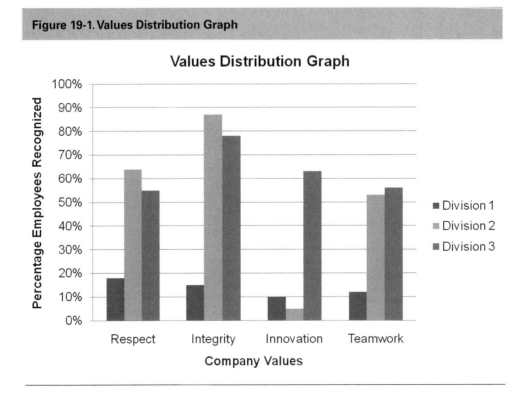

Division 3 is doing well across the board, with strong ties to each value. Division 1's performance is concerning. How is it that so little desired behavior is being recognized among all the company's most important values? Do the managers believe that 80 percent of the employees aren't aligned with the company's culture? Alerted by this graph, the division managers need to follow up and find the cause of the low numbers.

The values distribution graph can function as an early warning system for company culture, in the same way that certain business data indicate turns in a national economy. For example, if a company's research and development department shows a low score on the value of innovation, something's going wrong—it could be that the managers don't understand the program, but it could also be an early warning that the spirit of innovation has waned.

The early warning can be positive as well, such as finding a spirit of innovation in unexpected places, like customer service. Executives and managers who discover hidden strengths through a values distribution graph can capitalize on those strengths. If your customer service group is innovative, you might join that capability with sales and marketing efforts to increase customer satisfaction.

Tenet 4: Opportunity for All to Participate

All of the information gathered in the values distribution graph is made more accurate, and more actionable, by high penetration of the recognition program. Capture the data from a program with 80 to 90 percent participation and you'll have a deep, dynamic view of how the company culture is driving results. An elitist recognition program, with 5 to 10 percent penetration, is statistically unreliable (if only the top innovators get recognized for innovation, how can you know if innovation is on everyone's mind?).

When only a few elite members of the organization receive infrequent, high-value awards, it is impossible to affect the broader corporate culture. Giving many lower-value rewards to employees across the company, by contrast, results in a stronger impact on the company. Every recognition moment doubles as a marketing and communication moment, reinforcing company values in a positive employment experience. As more employees participate, the company gains greater voluntary alignment with shared values. As more participate, the data described in Tenet 3 above become richer, more detailed, and more accurately reflective of the entire company's attachment to particular values. As a side benefit, the presence of a broad-based recognition practice breaks down psychological barriers of class and rank, decreasing the chance of employee alienation from management.

Tenet 5: The Power of Individual Choice

The relevance of an award to an individual is more important than its material value, especially in a global program. When developing the roster of awards available, managers must consider the demographics of a worldwide workforce that might span four generations, all with different expectations and driving forces. Locally based choice ensures the award will always be culturally appropriate and to the recipient's taste while avoiding the varying cultural norms that simply cannot be known by every manager everywhere in the world. Allowing people to choose what is meaningful and personal to them increases the significance of the award. (Movie tickets aren't motivating for someone who doesn't like movies. A cupcake won't motivate someone on a diet. A designated parking space means nothing to someone who rides the bus.) Noncash rewards in the form of gift cards to local high-value venues take rewards beyond compensation to a socially acceptable trophy status everywhere in the world.

Realizing the Promise of Strategic Recognition

When we first start working with clients, we sometimes hear "but we've got several recognition programs," as if all recognition programs are alike. In our experience, this is not so much about the type of recognition "programs" you have implemented, this is about the type of recognition culture you are trying to create. A culture of recognition is much more deeply ingrained in the organization; it's the "way we do things around here." To illustrate how you can realize the promise of strategic recognition to create that recognition culture, we often describe a journey moving through the three stages of recognition beginning with a focus on individual recognition, then to enterprise recognition, and finally arriving at the culture management stage of strategic recognition.

Individual Recognition

Individual recognition is at the center of everything we write about in our book because it's where the connection happens between a manager and an employee. The manager notices extra effort or good performance and recognizes it with an award and a personal message connecting the behavior to a value that is part of the company culture. There are two connections: the association between behavior and values and the human connection between manager and employee. "Catch them doing the right thing" is the slogan for this kind of recognition. Proponents focus on the recognition moment—the positive interaction between manager and employee. They encourage managers to find many little ways to celebrate employee performance so that positive reinforcement becomes a habit.

We call this individual recognition because it is really a one-to-one connection. Most of us have seen managers who had a knack for recognizing and motivating their employees to become more enthusiastic about their jobs. On its surface, the chief appeal of individual recognition is its appearance of being easy and fun. People like to give and receive a pat on the back. (In fact, it's a sad comment on most corporate cultures that implementing individual recognition is an improvement on what was happening before.)

An unmanaged individual-recognition program works best in a small business, which is typically driven by the personality and leadership of the owner. Mallory's Appliance Repair, with 10 employees, is a small society in which Mallory can celebrate and recognize good work frequently. General Electric, with 320,000 employees, is a different story. The vast majority of employees is part of many layers of management or are thousands of miles removed from executives. Managers with diverse personalities, cultural expectations, and leadership abilities cannot be expected to behave in the same way or convey the same critical messages. An individual-recognition program that relies on creative and spontaneous impulse is out of place in the complex, data-dependent multinational corporation. Why? Because you can't possibly deliver this spontaneous behavior across thousands of individuals through hope, encouragement, or cajoling alone. Managers don't manage anything else on hope, so why recognition? In such a workplace, systems need to be in place to encourage the right behavior in the appropriate scale.

For a large organization to implement an individual recognition program in a sustainable way, it can't just depend on the enlightenment of every manager and his or her ability (or willingness) to find 1,000 ways to give trinkets to employees. Furthermore, a large organization risks complete chaos in its recognition efforts if it can't provide a scalable way for all managers to recognize their people.

Enterprise Recognition

Across the organization, enterprise recognition grew as "more of a good thing," and HR typically spread the good practices of individual recognition across the company. Program guidelines and structures were put in place. Relationships between managers and staff become richer and company goals were more widely discussed. Most important, recognition and appreciation began to be directly connected to company values and goals. Practiced across the entire company, even globally, enterprise recognition became more than "throwing a bone" to a good employee. Enterprise recognition flattened the moral hierarchy of the corporation by making values-based behavior everyone's job.

Enterprise recognition, while effective, is barely connected to the other management systems that govern the company. Enterprise recognition falls short of recognition's true potential because it is layered onto a culture in the same manner as a benefit program. It stays in the human resources silo—a positive step forward, to be sure, but not answerable like other disciplines to management practices of measurement against goals. That represents a significant missed opportunity, one that can be captured by the final evolution in recognition, which we call strategic recognition.

Strategic Recognition

Strategic recognition, in which the "soft" behaviors of recognition—which worked well at motivating employees—finally merge with the "hard" management practices of measurement, goal-setting, analysis, and strategic execution. The promise of strategic recognition is thus multilayered and multidimensional.

- For the employee, it teaches the connection between behavior and values; it increases morale and encourages engagement, loyalty, and attachment.
- For the manager, it compels thinking about which behaviors actually embody company values. This is new, for while it's easy to like certain behaviors, the manager must actually choose which employee actions deserve recognition. To manage is to choose. To manage is to get work done through others. It makes the manager more effective, more accountable, and more directed.
- For the executive, strategic recognition finally—finally!—makes a direct connection between encouraging certain values and knowing if and where those values are being lived by employees and managers. It brings the long-mysterious gifts of "people skills" and the proven need for "hard data" together, ending the false but enduring conflict between the "humanist" and "realist" schools of management.

Strategic recognition promises to help companies gain competitive advantage, foster employee engagement, improve performance, and increase profits. In a business world growing increasingly interdependent, with organizations growing less command-driven all the time, it is the supple and powerful new way to enrich and manage culture. Strategic recognition is more than a technique; it is a mission.

About the Authors

Eric Mosley is the CEO and co-founder of Globoforce, and **Derek Irvine** is the vice president of strategy and consulting at Globoforce. You can find their website at www .globoforce.com.

This chapter is excerpted from *Winning With a Culture of Recognition: Recognition Strategies at the World's Most Admired Companies* in which authors Eric Mosley and Derek Irvine also provide the detailed framework for planning, launching, and continuously improving a strategic recognition program designed to change company culture. Reprinted with permission.

The Goal: Team Members Who Do Their Best Work Together

"Never doubt that a small group of thoughtful, committed citizens can change the world. Indeed, it is the only thing that ever has."

—Margaret Mead

Chapter 20

Creating a Sharing Society

Rajesh Setty

Editor's Note

*Managers are tasked with helping their team members do their best
work, and this requires ongoing learning, collaboration, and sharing. Raj
Setty is one of the freshest thinkers I know, and this chapter on creating
a sharing society should be read and used by all managers. And it is the
perfect way to kick off this important section of the book.*

This is no secret. Organizations would be a lot more powerful if they had the right people on the bus and everyone on the bus cared about everyone else. A bonus requirement would be for everyone to share their best work to make everyone in the team better. Imagine an organization that was filled with extraordinary people who put the team before themselves and shared selflessly. Nirvana? Probably. Your organization may never reach that ideal situation, ever. But, don't give up yet. Just starting the journey toward such an ideal place will already make your organization a better place to work.

Let's start with the first stumbling block toward creating a sharing society in any organization. Here is the big dilemma for smart and ambitious employees: On one hand, they say the sum of parts is greater than the whole. On the other hand, they say that you need to distinguish yourself and stand out from the crowd. They say you put your team before yourself, and in the same breath, they say *you* are responsible for your own destiny. At the surface, it seems like a smart employee has two impossible choices to make—to care for his or her team at his or her own expense, or to care for himself or herself at the team's expense.

There are only 24 hours in a day for everyone, and decisions have to be made every day about how one invests his or her time and resources in these 24 hours. Unless the ambiguity is cleared up concerning how both the employee and the team will win together, actions of individuals will gravitate toward how they will benefit first; and only then they will think about how their team will benefit. The leader or the manager plays an important role in creating a culture where everyone knows that sharing is the only way to win—big—both for them and for the team. Ignoring the dilemma won't help much—one needs to acknowledge and attack it head on.

The Three Big Questions

You can make great progress on solving some questions as soon as you fully understand them. When it comes to creating a sharing society, we need to get to the bottom of why it is difficult to create a sharing society. Ideally we want the smart people in the team to be willing to share, willing to help, and able to communicate their ideas better. If we can get that going, we are almost there in terms of creating a sharing society. Let us address the following three questions to shed some more light on the problem at hand:

- Why don't many smart people share?
- Why don't many smart people help other people?
- Why do many smart people have trouble communicating their ideas?

So, let's get started: Why don't many smart people share? I am sure you have seen many smart people around you who are reluctant to share what they know. I have seen many of them up close. You might think the reasons for this are:

- They don't have time.
- They are selfish.
- They don't care.
- They don't have an incentive to do it.

I was perplexed on this too. I spent about six weeks talking to many of these smart people to understand what could be the reason. The results were very interesting. I have made some conclusions based on the findings from those conversations. Note: This is about smart people who are not sharing enough. So please don't generalize this about all smart people. In a nutshell: *Smart people want to give their best, and as they learn more, they find that they need to learn a lot more before they start sharing. So they learn some more, and they realize they need to learn even more. What they forget is that most of the expertise that they already have is either becoming "obvious" to them, or better yet, going into their "background thinking." Becoming obvious means that there is nothing special about it. Becoming their background thinking means that they don't even realize that it's knowledge. It becomes part of them. For example, think about alphabets and multiplication tables. It is in our background thinking, and we don't think about that as knowledge.*

Take a look at the following schematic (Figure 20-1). On the x-axis is time as they build their expertise. On the y-axis is the level of expertise.

Think about your own passionate topic on which you are an expert.

(A) You start at Level 1. Things are new and exciting, and since you are passionate you just realize how much you don't know, and there is a new level of hunger for the knowledge.

(B) You are in Level 2. You are at a new level of expertise. The earlier level (Level 1) seems obvious and common.

(C) You are in Level 3. You are again at a new level of expertise. The immediate previous level (Level 2) knowledge is now obvious and common. The levels below that (in this case Level 1) are in your background thinking. Remember that what's

Figure 20-1. Your Expertise Over Time

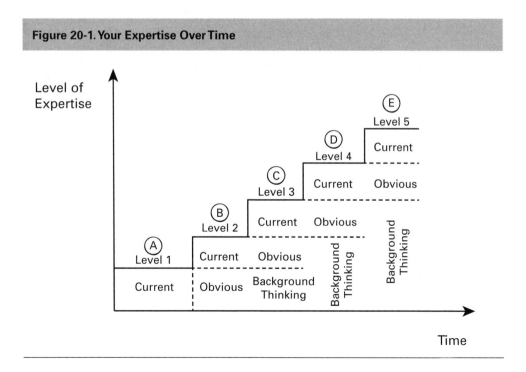

in your background thinking is almost invisible to you. You have that knowledge, but you don't think about it.

(D) You are in Level 4—a new level of expertise. Level 3 knowledge is obvious, and everything below that is in your "background thinking."

You can go on. You feel that you are not ready to share the knowledge at your current level, and there is no point in sharing what's obvious. And, what's in your "background thinking" has become part of you. So it's invisible, and there is no possibility of sharing that. So, what are you missing? Two important points to remember are:

- What is obvious to you is *not* obvious to many other people who are not at the same level of expertise; therefore, it is worth sharing with them.
- You must know what's in your "background thinking." It may be in your background thinking, but it's not in the background thinking of everyone else. Once you notice this, you can easily package this knowledge and share it.

Now, let's move on to the next question—why many smart people won't help other people. Most smart people are capable of helping other people. Some of them do, and some of them don't. People are happy with those people who help and often resent those who do not.

I have had many people share their frustration over not receiving a response to their request when they've consulted someone smart. They complain that it would have just taken "five minutes" for this expert to help them, but the expert "chose" not to help. You can attribute many reasons for this behavior. You could say:

- Those smart people are not the "helpful" type.
- They don't "care" much.
- They are too busy.
- They are "selfish."
- They don't have a "big heart."

I can go on and on about what the reasons might be. But let us take another look again. Here are a few things to consider:

- **Smart people are also human beings.** They cannot scale. On the same day, two social media stars Chris Brogan and Jason Falls opened their hearts and shared why it is difficult to continue to engage the way they were engaging. (See their blogs, Brogan's "Redrawing" and Falls's "Some Social Media Housekeeping Around the Explorer.")

- **It's not just "five minutes."** Smart people get hundreds of requests that individually take five minutes but collectively will take more than 24 hours in a day. Unfortunately they have their own lives to lead, and if they don't take care of themselves, they won't be there to take care of others.

- **One-on-one help requests put a dent on leverage.** Many smart people share a lot, and a large number of them are helpful on various social media platforms. Since they are spending a ton of time for "free" already, it may be tempting to think that they can simply give a "little bit more time" to you individually. Just remember that as they move to help one-on-one, smart people start losing leverage—unless you have proven to them that it is worth building a relationship with you.

- **Your request may have gotten just the attention it truly deserves.** One of the fundamental tenets of NLP (neuro-linguistic programming) is that *"the meaning of your communication is in its response."* If your request is worthy of being ignored, chances are that it will be. If it is a badly formed (or irrelevant or meaningless) pitch, you can be guaranteed that you won't get a response.

- **Dig your well before you are thirsty.** Sometimes you can get lucky, and you make a request and it gets fulfilled even if you have not built a relationship with the person. In most cases, that won't work. You have to build a relationship way before you make a request. If you take the famous banking metaphor, you have to make a deposit before you can make a withdrawal.

- **What is meaningful to you may not be meaningful to them.** In simple terms, the impact of fulfilling your request is not big enough compared to the alternative opportunities that these smart people have on their hand. Remember that they too only have 24 hours, and choices have to be made on where that time is invested. Your request might just have not made the cut.

Here is the point: If you blame smart people for not helping you, it won't help you much. You rarely can change how those people behaved, and you rarely can improve your chances of getting help from someone like them in the near future, simply because you don't improve by wishing that others change. You don't improve by focusing on others. You improve by focusing on what you can do to get better. There are (a minimum of) two things that you can do have a better chance of getting your requests fulfilled. Here they are:

- **Be an opportunity.** Unfortunately, if you are not an opportunity, you are probably an opportunity cost. Who is making the request is equally or probably more important than "what" the request is. The more you invest in yourself, the higher your chances are of "being an opportunity" for someone.

■ **Make the request more meaningful (to them).** Your request is definitely important to you. But can you spend a few minutes to make sure that fulfilling that request is meaningful to them? In the age of social media, it is not hard to figure out what is meaningful to them. In simple terms, it's called research. And yes, it takes time. And yes, it is worth spending that time before you go and make that request.

Now, let's address the last question—why many smart people have trouble communicating their ideas. All smart people are brilliant—in their heads. *Many* have a problem communicating that brilliance to others. Whether they are pitching something to their boss, getting a buy-in from their co-workers, or making a case for their product or service with their prospects, they lose the listeners halfway and frustrate themselves.

One explanation will be to say that people around them are not smart enough to "get" what they are saying. Unfortunately, in nine out of 10 cases, that explanation won't fly. However, if smart people start believing this, the confirmation bias will ensure that they will get enough proof to support their assessment. One reason to blame others for their communication problems is the convenience it provides. If they put the responsibility of understanding what they are saying to the listener, they can simply run away from their responsibility for communication. It is easier to complain than to take that responsibility. Rather than contemplating further, here are a few reasons for the communication breakdown:

■ **Smartness does not automatically make one a good communicator.** Smart people are smart in their field of work. That does not automatically provide a license to excel in communication. Yes, they can figure out a few things "on the go" about communication, but it's never the same as "investing" in learning how to communicate well. Communication is a skill. It simply involves two things—transmission and reception. A good communicator takes full responsibility for both these things.

■ **Many smart people forget to listen.** Why is it hard for many smart people to "listen well"? Because 1) they may be busy with their own thing—too many fun things going on to pay attention to what someone else is saying. In other words, they have no time to listen; or 2) what they are listening to may not be of immediate interest. But skipping the listening part would mean less knowledge of what's important to the person they are communicating with. This means they lost the opportunity to frame what they are telling in a way that the listener will find relevant.

■ **Many times they skip "obvious" details.** They have thought a great deal about their idea. It is crystal clear to them in their mind. When they start outlining the core elements of their idea, they skip a few of them—not intentionally, but why repeat some things that are "too obvious" and annoy the audience? They are passionate about their idea, and it is clearly demonstrated. In their mind, the "skipped elements" are so obvious that they don't even have it in their plan to include them in their communication. The listener on the other hand is seeing a "fill-in-the-blanks" puzzle. He can see the enthusiasm and passion. There is no question about that. But the idea seems like it's not been completely thought through. Now, the listener has a choice to request more details; but the listener is busy too, and it's convenient to not bother much or simply appreciate the idea and cite a couple of "obvious" roadblocks during the implementation phase and move on.

- **They use the weapon of communication destruction: jargon.** Recently someone I know pitched me an idea. In the first 90 seconds, he used four acronyms and at least two words that I thought were not part of the English language. I was busy decoding the puzzle instead of trying to understand the idea. By the time I figured it out by "Googling" a few terms, the person had moved on. The train had left the station. Jargon may provide shortcuts when discussing something with their cohorts, but outside of their circle, people may have no clue about what these "terms" mean.

- **Sometimes they forget about what else is required to execute the idea.** In the grand scheme, an idea is only a small part of the game. There is a lot more to executing an idea than presenting it. The listener (especially if he or she is the boss who needs to approve it) is thinking about "all the other things" that need to happen to make this idea a reality. When the listener does not see a well-thought-out execution plan, or does not believe that the person with the idea can come up with one, there is a good chance that the listener will dismiss the idea (also see the next point, related to this) and move on. Sometimes the best thing would be to make the idea somebody else's and give them full credit. That would require "letting go of the ego and credit," and it's not easy.

- **Sometimes they forget "timing."** They say nobody can stop an idea whose time has come. I don't know about that. But there will be many people who will be ready to stop an idea whose time has *not* come. They may have a brilliant idea, but if "timed wrong," it will go nowhere.

- **Their past history lacks "follow-through."** Last but not the least, their past history of "not following through" with their ideas haunts them. They may have presented a dozen ideas but didn't follow through with any of them for various reasons, including the most common one—"chasing the next idea that looks more promising than the previous one." With that kind of a past, the listener has "lost" them even before they begin narrating their idea. In the mind of the listener, this is "one of the many" ideas that will bite the dust in no time. So why bother listening?

What Can a Manager Do?

What a manager *cannot do* is to pontificate and ask for behavior changes to create a sharing culture. Remember that these are smart people he or she is leading, and they won't do anything that they don't believe in the first place. Here are five things to consider to get the sharing culture going.

Design Sharing as a Side Benefit

One of the reasons knowledge management systems fail is that the contributors who will make the knowledge in the system useful are busy, and the people who do contribute won't actually make the system more valuable. So, what happens? A knowledge management initiative starts with a big bang, and there is a ton of activity during the initial few months because of the seed content. There is also the fun of discovering in the initial stages. Then the reality hits, and people discover that it takes time and effort to contribute meaningfully to the knowledge management system. The contributions continue, but the quality drops as time progresses. Soon, the system as mediocre content fast overtakes quality content. Quality people desert the system quickly, thinking it's a waste of time, and once that happens it's downhill until its eventual death.

The solution? Design sharing to be a side effect of work. A few examples are given below to get you started on thinking in this direction.

- Get an intern who will become the curator of content. Ask the smartest of your employees to blind copy curator@yourcompany.com if they feel that something of value is being exchanged in the email—a presentation, a PDF document, a brilliant answer to a customer query, a competitive strategy, an insight on company products or business models—anything at all that is worth storing and reusing should be blind copied to the curator. It now becomes the job of the curator to somehow find the necessary help and resources to make it reusable.
- Create lunch-and-learn sessions and assign one or two people as note takers and one person as synthesizer. The note takers will take notes and forward to the synthesizer to curate and post to a repository. Ensure that note takers and synthesizers are rotating so that no one person has to do this job more than once a month.
- When a person reaches out for help via email or phone, the person who provides the help must require the person who receives the help to document what he or she learned and send it back to the helper with a blind copy to the curator for further processing.

- Have a "lessons learned" contest for the last quarter and ask people to submit entries and open up the entries for voting. Pick the best and move them to a knowledge repository.
- Create education webinars on topics of interest and get your people to run those webinars. Record the webinars and move them to the repository.

The above examples highlight a few tactics—some of them may be relevant to your situation, and some of them may not be. But you get the idea and approach.

Align Incentives Right

Any individual is doing one of two things—producing something meaningful or upgrading himself or herself to produce something meaningful. Teams are the same way—they are producing something meaningful, or they are upgrading themselves to produce something meaningful.

Incentives are typically reserved for results, and they should be. However, if teams are growing to produce meaningful results in the future, the organization will hit a dead end sooner than later. Think about redesigning incentives so that the system automatically encourages people to share, learn, and grow with equal vigor as compared to producing results.

People are generally not designed to see beyond short-term benefits of any activity, so they end up engaging in activities that yield short-term benefits. As a manager, it becomes your job to balance activities that will produce the right results both in the short-term and in the long-term.

Sharing Should Help Growing

Managers can rarely take people away from where they want to go. One reason a smart person has joined your team is because he or she thinks that working with you will help him or her to reach his or her personal goals.

Suppose one of your team members dreams of becoming an entrepreneur sometime in the future. You can design his or her sharing activities to contribute toward his or her personal goals. For instance, to become an entrepreneur the person would need to be a good communicator and a good presenter. Use that opportunity to give the person an opportunity to present the one or more topics to the group. The group benefits from the learning, and the person gets benefit by improving his or her presentation skills. Everyone wins.

If you can take the time to design sharing in such a manner that it will produce disproportional growth to the person who is sharing, smart people will jump at the opportunities to share in a heartbeat.

Upgrade the Dialogue

While the topic of this chapter is about creating a sharing society, you really want to design the system in such a way that the best members of your team share more than others. The quality of sharing is important. That brings another dilemma. The best team members are the ones that are also extremely busy in the team. We can't ask them to do more work. We solved a part of the problem in that regard by designing sharing as a side effect of their work. However, there is another part to the problem—what's in it for these very smart people to share beyond the incentives they get?

It is hard to get a good answer for this. So, one option is to upgrade the dialogue by regularly bringing in outside experts (even if it means that you need to pay them) to have conversations with your team members. They may present a topic or two, but the bigger goal is to bring them and get your team to experience having conversations with such people.

When smart people share, they are giving; when you upgrade the dialogue, they are getting too. External experts will benefit everyone, but most of the value from such conversations is captured by the smartest of the lot.

Teach People the Fundamentals of Leverage

Leverage won't provide people more time but it will allow them to get more out of their available time. If there is one gift you can give to your people, it will be the gift of leverage. Here is one quick way to increase leverage, for you or for any of your team members—find a second reason to do anything significant.

When you start any significant initiative all you need is one "good reason." Next time, change the game. Find another important reason to do whatever you are planning to do. Try to do this even if the first reason you have got is *really* good enough to engage in this initiative. Let me try to generalize this even further. Make this a fun exercise. Even for simple things that you do in your everyday life try to find a second reason to do it.

Finding a second, third, or fourth reason to do the same thing will not only stretch your creativity and imagination but will also show you how you can "leverage" yourself better.

There is one thing that is common to everyone on this earth—each person has only 24 hours in a day. However, we also know that different people get different levels of value out of those 24 hours. One common factor that high achievers have is that they can get higher leverage out of everything that they do. We can all get higher leverage only if we can think and act differently. Imagine the same eight hours of work that you put in every day producing multiple returns rather than one. Can this be done? Of course yes! Does it take a lot of discipline to do it? You bet!

Once you and your team increase your leverage, you will have more time to share and learn. Learning this will probably act as the biggest contributor to boost your capacity to create a sharing society.

About the Author

Rajesh Setty is an entrepreneur, author, and speaker based in Silicon Valley. He also creates and sells limited-edition prints at Sparktastic. You can find his website at www.rajeshsetty.com and follow him on Twitter at twitter.com/rajsetty.

 **Chapter 21**

Are SMART Goals Dumb?

Mark Murphy

·· **Editor's Note** ··

When I first read Mark Murphy's research on SMART goals being dumb, I was struck by two responses. First, I thought, "Of course, this feels correct." And second, I thought, "Wow, most people are inadvertently doing it wrong!" This is a great chapter and one that can instantly help you catalyze better team member performance and engagement.

Virtually every company sets goals for their employees, and what manager hasn't set a SMART goal (most commonly defined as Specific, Measurable, Achievable, Realistic, and Time-bound)? But right now, only 13 percent of employees believe that their current goals will help them maximize their full potential, and only 15 percent think that their goals will help them achieve great things, so there's obviously a big problem.

You may have been told that smart managers use SMART goals, but new research indicates that SMART goals are actually pretty dumb. Leadership IQ conducted a study of 4,182 workers from 397 organizations to see what kind of goal-setting processes actually help employees achieve great things. And what we learned is that SMART goals often act as impediments to, not enablers of, bold action, actually encouraging mediocre and poor performance.

As part of our study, we wanted to find out what aspects of goal setting really predict whether an employee will achieve great things. After all, the purpose of goals isn't to help people achieve mediocre results; goals are supposed to help us achieve extraordinary results. And we wanted to know, for example, do achievable and realistic goals drive people to great achievements, or does greatness come from having goals that are really difficult and that push us out of our comfort zone?

To answer these questions, we conducted a stepwise multiple regression analysis to discover what kinds of goals were most likely to drive people to achieve great things. Stepwise multiple regression is a statistical technique that predicts values of one variable (e.g., achieving greatness) on the basis of two or more other variables (e.g., whether goals are achievable or difficult).

This analysis revealed the top eight predictors of whether somebody's goals were going to help him or her achieve great things. In other words, if we want employees to say, "Wow, my goals this year are really going to help me achieve great things," there are eight characteristics that their goals should have.

Here are the top eight factors, in order of statistical importance:

1. I can vividly picture how great it will feel when I achieve my goals.
2. I will have to learn new skills to achieve my assigned goals for this year.
3. My goals are absolutely necessary to help this company.
4. I actively participated in creating my goals for this year.
5. I have access to the formal training I will need to accomplish my goals.
6. My goals for this year will push me out of my comfort zone.
7. My goals will enrich the lives of somebody besides me (customers, the community, etc.).
8. My goals are aligned with the organization's top priorities for this year.

Now, when you really think about what this analysis is saying, a few things should immediately jump out at you. First, issues related to SMART goals do not appear on this list. Whether goals were specific, measurable, achievable, realistic, or time bound had no unique predictive power in this analysis. In fact, when we conducted a separate correlation analysis, we found that the question about SMART goals (i.e., "We use SMART goals as our goal-setting process") had no meaningful correlation with employees achieving great things.

The second thing that probably hits you is that for people to achieve great things, their goals must require them to learn new skills and to leave their comfort zone. This is quite the opposite of what SMART goals tell us (goals should be achievable and realistic, etc.). "Hold on a minute," SMART goals seem to say. "Don't push beyond your resources, don't bite off more than you can chew, but play it safe and stay within your limitations."

And once again, using a correlation analysis, we found that the question about achievable goals (i.e., "My goals are achievable with my current skills and/or knowledge") had no meaningful correlation with achieving great things.

If we pause here for a minute, we've just learned that the typical goal-setting processes companies have been using for decades are *not* helping employees achieve great things. And, in fact, the type of goal setting we *should* be doing (assuming we actually want our employees to achieve great things) is pretty much the *opposite* of what organizations have been doing for the past few decades. If your people don't have to learn new skills, and they don't have to leave their comfort zone to achieve their goals, those goals probably won't drive them to achieve greatness.

Another insight from the regression analysis is that goals need to be much more than just words on a little form. For a goal to help people achieve great things, that goal has to leap off the page. It has to be so vividly described that people can feel how great it will be to achieve it. It has to sing to them, to touch the deepest recesses of their brain. When is the last time your goals did that?

And statistically, to achieve greatness, a goal also has to be bigger than the doers of that goal. We have to identify whose lives will be enriched by our goals. And those goals had better be absolutely necessary (and also aligned with our organization's top priorities), or they just aren't going to help employees achieve great things.

Right now, most employees are falling short of their goals. And our study shows that it's because the goals they are being given are too easy. It's time for an entirely new goal-setting process, one that meets the all the top criteria that most inspires employees to achieve great things. And toward that end, we created HARD goals: goals that are Heartfelt, Animated, Required, and Difficult. Here's a breakdown of how HARD goals work.

HARD Goals

HARD goals are for every manager who believes that people have more potential than they're presently using. Unlike SMART goals, HARD goals push employees beyond their current self-imposed restraints and help them discover where their limits, if any, really exist. You don't have to be a world leader to issue a HARD challenge, nor do you have to have thousands of followers. Every business plan, sales presentation, customer interaction, budget request, and financial approval provides an opportunity to push employees toward untold greatness.

But what are HARD goals? In a nutshell, for any goal to inspire greatness, it has to be:

- **Heartfelt:** Employees have to feel an emotional attachment to a goal; it has to scratch an existential itch.
- **Animated:** Goals need to be motivated by a vision, picture, or movie that plays over and over in your employees' minds.
- **Required:** Goals need to feel so urgently necessary that employees have no other choice but to start acting on that goal right here, right now.
- **Difficult:** Goals need to drag employees out of their comfort zone, activating their senses and attention.

These four factors likely ring true with your own experiences. Think for a moment about the most significant professional or personal accomplishment in your life. Maybe you invented the coolest product in your industry, doubled your company's revenue, got that big promotion, or even lost 30 pounds or ran a marathon. Whatever it was, I'd be willing to bet that the goal that drove that great achievement was incredibly challenging, deeply emotional, and highly visual. I'll bet it was a bit scary, pushing you out of your comfort zone and forcing you to learn new things. It was the kind of goal that flipped some internal switch that made your mind alive and buzzing with the thrill of it. And when you finally hit your big goal, you felt as fulfilled as you've ever been. And even now, months or perhaps years later, you still feel highly satisfied just thinking about the experience. And I'm not talking about some temporary high like you get from eating chocolate; I mean deep, life-altering, perspective-changing fulfillment. Let's dig a little deeper into each of these four components.

Heartfelt

The typical approach in most organizations is to create goals that are measurable. Employees are asked to translate goals into a simple number that's easily trackable—not get all warm and fuzzy about them. And that's exactly what's wrong with the way most managers train their workforces to set and achieve goals. Because whenever employees are asked to take goals they might "feel" good about or have an emotional connection to, and translate those into a simple number that analytically fits their spreadsheet, it can actually reduce motivation to achieve that goal by 50 percent.

Animated

A necessary part of making a goal compelling—so motivating, inspiring, and necessary that your employees will move heaven and earth to achieve it—is making the goal imaginable. This works thanks to a concept called "pictorial superiority effect," whereby if we can imagine a goal, see it, picture it, and so on, we're a lot more likely to process, understand, and embrace that goal. In fact, when we hear only information, our total recall is about 10 percent when tested 72 hours later. But, add a picture, and that number shoots up to 65 percent. Animating a goal creates a lasting visual image that helps sear that goal into your employees' brains. And that goes a long way to inspiring people to say: "I am going to sacrifice whatever it takes to achieve this goal."

Heartfelt and Animated Are Great Friends

While it might seem a little strange, or even too easy to be true, visualization activities (and that includes drawing pictures) really do significantly improve emotional attachment to a goal (and thus dramatically increase goal achievement).

I recently conducted an experiment with employees at a large healthcare company. I was training folks on goal setting, and while most of the course was work-related, the CEO asked me to show his team how to apply HARD goals to their personal lives (specifically, saving for retirement).

I began by asking everyone to take our HARD Goals Assessment to gauge the effectiveness of their current financial goals. Not surprisingly, they felt their financial goals were required and difficult, but they had low heartfelt and animated scores. Like too many folks these days, they struggled with feeling a strong emotional connection to, and visualizing, their financial goals.

So I asked everyone to draw a self-portrait of how they felt about the current state of their financial goals. There were a lot more stick figures than Picassos, but even the folks who claimed to have zero artistic ability were able to adequately animate their goals. For the most part, the drawings vividly depicted people who were frazzled, struggling to carry a large weight, or missing some important aspect of their lives. Then I asked everyone in the group to draw another self-portrait, this time showing how they would feel if they received $500,000 (tax free). This time the pictures showed people who were relieved, happy, and decidedly less stressed.

After our fun drawing exercise, the group again took the HARD Goals Assessment, and the scores went up significantly. The exercise of animating how their lives would look with the addition of $500,000 (an achievable number, we're not talking millions here) allowed people to envision themselves less worried, less anxious, happier, and more carefree. And that helped every person in the group to gain a greater emotional connection to his or her goals—the kind of heartfelt connection that HARD goals require.

But OK, I know what you are probably thinking right now. So we did an exercise and got some test scores to go up, but does that actually change anything in the real world? The answer to that is a big yes. Six months after this training, we emailed the participants and asked them to complete a brief survey about their progress toward their financial goals. Of the 147 managers who completed the survey, 141 of them said that they had made "significantly more progress" toward their financial goals in the six months following the training than they had in the six months prior to the training. With those kinds of results, I'd say we definitely had an impact.

When it comes to financial goals, whether personal or work-related, most people don't struggle as much with the required and difficult aspects as they do with the heartfelt and animated parts. The media certainly do a good job driving home the fact that saving for retirement is required and non-negotiable in this age of uncertain Social Security. And we know it's difficult because while almost two-thirds of workers say that they're saving for retirement, according to the Employee Benefit Research Institute's 2011 Retirement Confidence Survey, more than half of them have less than $25,000 banked.

It's a challenge to have an emotional attachment to something that is so far away, much less visualize it. Why pass on the new shoes that you can wear tomorrow, or the fancy dinner you can eat right now, in favor of an extra $100 toward a retirement that is 10 or 20 years in the future?

It's also tough to get excited about goals that are expressed purely in numerical terms. If someone says you have to save money, you usually don't think, "Why do I care about this?" or "Why am I emotionally attached to this?" It's just an abstract money goal—here's a number, and that's it. But people don't care about the numbers per se.

But by animating a goal through the drawing of a simple picture, the reasons behind why we do care about our goals (reasons that may not otherwise have come to light) suddenly become quite apparent. In creating an animated goal, people take the time to think about what saving that amount of money would mean for their lives—for example, more time with grandchildren, a few days a week on the golf course, sunny vacations with their spouse. And that takes the goal out of the practical and into the emotional. And as I've said, when we're emotionally connected to a goal, we become far more inspired to move heaven and earth to achieve it.

So how can you use that retirement experiment to your own benefit? First, estimate how much you'll actually need for retirement. Then imagine a retirement funded by that amount. What will you be doing in your retirement? What will having that money at your disposal mean for your life? Draw it out, in detail, including visual representations of your-self engaged in the experiences that kind of money could buy. Then hang it where you'll see it every day, like near your mirror, by your computer, or on the fridge. Jean Chatzky, my favorite TV financial guru and financial editor for the *Today* show, has written quite a bit about our experiment. She had the brilliant idea to make smaller versions of your drawing to keep in your wallet—including wrapping one around your credit card.

Finally, take the time to revisit your animated goal every couple months or so. Are you making progress? Has your vision changed? If so, make the necessary tweaks and keep re-energizing the emotional connection you have to your goal.

Required

Procrastination is the killer of many a goal, so you need to give every goal a deep sense of urgency. There are lots of ways to do this, but one of the easiest (and most successful) is a technique I call "cutting in half."

The first step is to take an objective long view of your HARD goal and approximate its end date. Some goals are more naturally time-bound than others, but as accurately as you can, estimate the timeframe by which the goal will be completed. To keep things simple for this example, I'm going to pretend that your HARD goal will take you a year to accomplish (but again, the "cutting-in-half" technique works with goals of any duration).

Now, cut that yearlong timeframe in half (six months in this example) and answer this question: What must be accomplished at the six-month mark to know we're on track to achieve the full HARD goal?

Now, cut that six-month timeframe in half (i.e., three months) and answer this question: What must we have accomplished at the three-month mark to know we're on track to achieve the six-month targets?

Of course, you know what's coming next. Cut that three-month timeframe in half and answer: What must we have accomplished at the six-week mark to know we're on track to achieve all of the three-month targets? When you've got it spelled out, do it again: What must we have accomplished at the three-week mark to know we're on track to achieve all of the six-week targets?

Once you've gotten to a timeframe that's under a month, do this exercise two more times. Ask: What must we have accomplished within this next week to know we're on track to achieve all of the three-week targets? And then ask: What must I have accomplished today to know that I'm on track to achieve all of my one-week targets?

The purpose of the "cutting-in-half" exercise is threefold: First, it shows you exactly where and how to start pursuing your HARD goal. Second, it monitors and keeps you on track to achieve your HARD goal (and intensify your efforts where necessary). And third, this exercise shows you that every single day needs to contain some activity in pursuit of your HARD goals.

Difficult

The idea that difficult goals lead to better performance seems counterintuitive, but there's decades of research to back it up. Difficult goals demand our attention and engage the brain. And with that extra neurological horsepower comes enhanced performance. But it's a challenge to create goals that perfectly hit the sweet spot of difficulty—that place where people feel right between "so hard I want to quit" and "so easy I can't be bothered to try."
Here's a quick way to test whether your goals are difficult enough to inspire optimal performance. Ask your employees to think about a recently set goal and determine whether or not the following three statements apply:

- I'm really going to have to learn new skills before I'll be able to accomplish this goal.
- This goal is pushing me outside my comfort zone; I'm not frozen with terror, but I'm definitely on "pins and needles" and wide awake for this goal.
- When I think about the biggest and most significant accomplishments throughout my life, this current goal is as difficult as those were.

If your employees can't answer yes to all three statements, the goal isn't difficult enough. Remember back at the start when I asked you to consider your own great accomplishments, and how those achievements demanded serious work, got your brain buzzing, and made you feel like you were perched on pins and needles? It was the challenge of that goal—not the reassurance that your goal would be a piece of cake—that inspired you to push past stubborn roadblocks. And it was the challenge that made you embrace (instead of dread) honing your knowledge and learning new skills.

OK, so setting difficult goals leads to better performance, but how difficult is difficult enough? One determinant of an adequately difficult goal is that it will demand the doer of that goal to have two to four major new learning experiences. This stretches the brain and excites the neurons so the brain is focused and anxious to achieve that goal. The ability to say, "This goal is a breeze, I don't need to learn anything to ace it," is a clear sign that goal is under set. Just as if more than four new things need to be learned, that goal is over set.

The best way to determine whether a goal is in the sweet spot of difficulty, or if it's under or over set, is to ask your employees how much a goal is requiring them to learn. The following two tests will give you the information you need to determine if a HARD goal is hard enough.

Test #1: Ask your employees what new skills (if any) they have to learn to achieve a goal. If they aren't learning all sorts of new skills, then the goal is probably not hard enough. Try making the goal 30 percent harder (more on this in a minute) and then evaluate again in three months (using this same test). Otherwise, if employees are learning a lot, move on to Test #2.

Test #2: Ask your employees at the outset of a goal if they know they can achieve that goal. HARD goals should be a bit scary and force us to question our abilities. That's part of what gets the brain amped up and excited about achieving the goal. If folks say they feel sure they can accomplish a goal before they even start, try making the goal 30 percent harder and then evaluate it again in three months (using this same test).

Adjusting a goal by 30 percent is usually enough to engage the brain. So if you find more difficulty is still needed—employees aren't learning two to four new things—then take the goal difficulty level up another 30 percent. If you are over setting your goals, start by sliding them back 30 percent and reassess the situation. Stick to the 30 percent rule because if you start arbitrarily tripling or quadrupling the difficulty of your goals, they will all too quickly go from difficult to impossible.

Everyone's sweet spot of difficulty may be at a different and unique level, but the experience of a perfectly set HARD goal is the same for everyone. The awareness of being outside the comfort zone—not so far that you are on a bed of nails, but not too comfortable either— that's the place where each of us is driven to achieve our absolute best.

Any Goal Can Be HARD

You can improve any goal and make it HARD. So the next time you're setting a goal, ask these four questions:

- Heartfelt: Why do you want to achieve this goal? Describe at least three reasons why this goal appeals to you.

- Animated: Think about where this goal will get you, and describe exactly what you're doing (what kind of work, who you're working with, what your days look like). To make this even better, put that description into a drawing.
- Required: What are the three to five most important skills you'll need to develop to achieve that goal? How will you develop those skills?
- Difficult: What do you need to have accomplished by the end of the next six months to keep you on track to achieving this goal? What about by the end of the next 90 days? Next 30 days? What's one thing you can accomplish today?

Conclusion

Virtually all managers set goals for their employees, but those goals just aren't working. The goal-setting methodologies that we've used for decades (like SMART goals and others) don't lead to employees achieving great things. If you want to set goals that inspire people to achieve great things, those goals have to be:

- Heartfelt: They exist to serve something bigger than ourselves.
- Animated: They're so vividly described and presented that to not reach them would leave us wanting.
- Required: They are as critical to our continued existence as breathing and water.
- Difficult: They're so hard they'll test every one of our limits.

Not only do effective goals drive greatness, but people also feel better about them. An additional finding from the Leadership IQ Goal-Setting Study revealed that employees who have HARD goals are significantly more engaged than employees who don't.

We asked survey respondents to answer the question "I recommend this organization to others as a great place for people to work" (our research indicates that this question is a very good proxy for an overall measure of engagement). We discovered that people who "strongly agreed" with the goals questions from the regression analysis had significantly higher scores on the "great place for people to work" question than those who "strongly disagreed." For example, we found that:

- People who answered "strongly agree" to the question "I can vividly picture how great it will feel when I achieve my goals" had 49 percent higher employee engagement than people who answered "strongly disagree."
- People who answered "strongly agree" to the question "I have access to any formal training that I will need to accomplish my goals" had 57 percent higher employee engagement than people who answered "strongly disagree."

- People who answered "strongly agree" to the question "My goals for this year will push me out of my comfort zone" had 29 percent higher employee engagement than people who answered "strongly disagree."
- People who answered "strongly agree" to the question "My goals are aligned with the organization's top priorities for this year" had 75 percent higher employee engagement than people who answered "strongly disagree."

Every manager on earth should want employees who happily come to work every day and who passionately devote 100 percent effort into making great things happen. When we set HARD goals for our employees, it leads them to achieve greatness, and that's an amazingly satisfying experience. HARD goals make people stronger, braver, and more confident to go after even bigger and better things—to set even harder goals. That's why successful people are always making news for achieving extraordinary success again and again. They've done it before, and they know they can do it again.

About the Author

Mark Murphy is the CEO of Leadership IQ (find his website at www.leadershipiq.com) and author of *HARD Goals: The Secret to Getting From Where You Are to Where You Want to Be* published by McGraw-Hill (2011).

Chapter 22

How Team Building Really Works

Steve Roesler

·· **Editor's Note** ··

You know how sometimes it is nice to hear someone call it "like it is"? Steve Roesler offers a candid and fresh perspective on team building in this chapter, and I know you will benefit from the "pow!" of his words and "umph!" of his recommended practices. Great managers know that it is not wise to leave the health of their teams to periodic external events that do not resemble the real workplace. Even so, Steve articulates this message in a way that will make you want to share this chapter with your peers and managers. Feel free to use this as ammunition to thwart efforts by well-intended but clueless internal or external consultants when they suggest team-building activities that make your eyeballs twitch. And feel free to use Steve's advice to build a better team.

We need team spirit (so I've set aside Thursday). Would you prefer a masked hijacking or a walk on burning coals?

Managers at a Swedish telecom company were apparently hard pressed for a memorable team-building exercise at their international sales conference a few years ago. They wanted something more than the standard fare: ropes courses, white-water rafting, and other extreme sports. So they naturally turned to hostage taking.

Really.

Unbeknownst to salespeople riding in a corporate bus headed to a conference session, the company had hired two men with masks and weapons to stage a hijacking. The exercise was reportedly designed to test the employees' demeanor under stress. However, the performance was cut short by a meddling passerby with a cell phone who called the authorities. "Definitely, this was very unfortunate," noted a corporate spokesperson. "The mistake was not giving notice to the police."

Really. That was the only mistake?

While most companies stick to torturing their workers by forcing them to hold hands and accomplish pointless tasks—preferably while blindfolded—others have gone to extremes. Unfortunately, these exciting games have put some team players on the disabled list. In England, for example, one insurance company sent 13 salespeople walking across a bed of hot coals on the advice of a management consultant. Guess what? Seven burned their feet, two badly enough to require hospitalization. The company says it has learned its lesson and now sticks to more conventional bonding exercises.

Note: Both of these items were courtesy of Time, Inc., and thus received plenty of coverage. I'm guessing that most of the team building actually took place inside of the organizations' respective PR departments.

What's Going On Out There?

Building business teams is about business results. The assumption is that if people can find ways to work more smoothly together, better results will follow. That's usually true, especially when reducing conflicts that involve lack of role clarity (who should really be doing what) and process (how things get handed off to whom, and when). Here's where it often begins to fall apart:

- The manager wants to "improve morale and collaboration." So she hires a consultant to "do something" that will boost morale and cooperation. The problem: Morale is usually a function of management and organizational policies and procedures. Collaboration is, in part, what a manager is paid to orchestrate.
- The manager may not understand the distinction between building effective work groups and having a "group event."

- The manager may not understand the array of "help" that's out there: Here are a few examples:
  - Genuine business team consultants who work closely to understand the immediate issues, interview the team members, and then work with the team leader on a design that will address what's really happening so that things will be different afterward if people choose to address them honestly. This requires an experienced consultant/facilitator, a leader who is also willing to look at his/her part in the team's performance, and a group of people who believe they can improve with some focused help.
  - "Event" consultants who do the rafting/paintball/trust walk sort of thing. Leaders need to understand—and be clear with their people—that an event is being staged with the hope that some lessons will be transferred back to the job. These can be effective if the specific activities are designed to be "processed" in the context of an on-the-job issue. The consultant also has to have done a real-life diagnostic and know how to direct an activity toward the "live" business issues.
  - Note: Absent the organizational expertise, these activities can still be fun if they are framed as just that. When everyone agrees beforehand that it could be good to blow off some steam together and swing from trees and mountains, it probably beats karaoke. If it's a big surprise and participation is required in activities that are uncomfortable at many levels, the best result might be a lawsuit settled out of court.
  - "Team therapists" who work their mojo. It's pretty amazing what is sold—and bought—as "team building." These types usually have their favorite intervention, jargon, and model of "being" that they bring into the workplace masquerading as team building. What I've learned from seeing these people appear on the scene is that they view the "group" as an entity with a "problem." They are the doctors. But there is often a twist with this crowd. They are often "doctors" who haven't performed a diagnosis, don't understand the business issues, and don't offer a cure. Instead, they opt for a reflective approach, tossing a verbal bone to the group every so often with the assurance that "you are the experts and architects of your own lives ... you can figure this out." Without context and a structured group task focused on real-life team performance, participants wonder where they are and how they got there.

There are times when you'll want to get some outside help. You might need a good diagnostician to help uncover issues, a solid meeting facilitator who can serve as a model for you to emulate, or a white-water expert to take your group out for a good time together.

Right now, I believe it's most important to focus on this important fact, described below.

Managers: Your Team Is Your Task

After 30-plus years in corporate life as a manager and consultant, I'm still baffled by the number of managers who view team building as an event separate from everyday work life and everyday management. This is akin to a mother and father perceiving their home as a place to watch TV, mow the lawn, kick the soccer ball, and cook meals. Then, once a quarter, the whole gang goes "off-site" to build relationships, divide up responsibilities for maintaining the house, discuss what's happening at school, and acknowledge any birthdays that have occurred.

Whether it's a work unit or a family unit, success depends on people working together to get "it" done. So the whole working-together thing is, well, huge. In an era where we deify leaders, none of them can get anywhere without everyone else. If you're one of those managers "in charge" of getting it done, here's a mantra that will serve you well: *Every team meeting is team building.*

It is. The dynamics are like dinner at home with the family. Every time you come together, the interactions lead to some degree of increased satisfaction and performance or a sense of disarray and dysfunction. The effectiveness of regularly scheduled meetings will impact the health and productivity of the group more than a "one-off" session (although if you need to get back on track, do it). So, it makes sense to become really effective at knowing when and how to pull people together and what to do when you're there. As I write this, there is a research report sitting on my desk nudging at me. It's a summary of a survey of 664,000 employees worldwide, representing every conceivable type of organization: corporate, nonprofit, government, and so on. One of the glaring conclusions is something I hope will be helpful. The employees surveyed, regardless of organizational level, stated that their immediate boss was the single most influential factor in their work lives. And they expected their manager to bring people together to collaborate on issues, questions, and decisions that impacted the team. Now, to take some of the pressure off, there is one more bit of information I think you'll find useful. The respondents also said they didn't expect the manager to come up with answers or to know everything. In fact, the employees said that what they wanted most was a manager who would ask great questions.

You can do that. And if you do it every time your gang is together, you'll be building a team.

Seven Things Your Team Is Looking For

Over the years I've noticed some overarching themes when it comes to identifying what employees are looking for as part of a team. Although each person will have some unique want or need, you'll be on solid ground if you start focusing on these:

1. **Clear sense of direction.** In an era of misunderstood "participative management" and daily change, people are hungry for direction and clarity. That's the only way a group can understand and rally around a shared sense of purpose.

   This is a management issue. If you are the manager, continually check your own clarity compass. If people are running in 10 different directions that means that you are, too. Focus.

2. **Talented colleagues.** I don't know how you operate, but my own commitment and performance is either lifted up or dragged down by the people around me. When I join a team I quickly check out two things:

   - Do we have depth and breadth of talent to accomplish what we want to do?
   - Are these the kind of people I want to do it with?
     Note: "I have found the enemy, and it is me." There are times when I'm the one that doesn't fit. When that happens, it's important to acknowledge it and either:
       - make a physical change and move elsewhere
       - make a personal change, if possible, and suck it up if the goal is important enough to me.

   What that means for you as a manager: When you see that someone is simply not a good fit for the group, help him or her find another place to be productive. It's just a fact of life that every so often someone won't "fit in." That's what culture is about, and if you have a cultural/interpersonal mismatch, it's not helping anyone. In fact, it may be draining everyone.

   Every survey I've read in the past 10 years reflects a desire on the part of employees to be around talented colleagues who will lift them up because the standards are naturally high. The next time you are in a position to bring someone new onboard, avoid the natural tendency to get the vacancy filled and move on. Think about the candidate's professional impact on the rest of the team.

3. **Clear and alluring responsibilities.** Who is supposed to be doing what, are they in their "talented" zone, and how do we make sure we pass the baton to each other at the right moment in the right way?

You get paid to manage "what" happens. "How" people go about collaborating will determine your team's success. Ed Koch, a former mayor of New York City, would constantly ask people, "How am I doing?" It became his tagline. It also gave him the information needed to recalibrate if things weren't going so well.

Every time your team is together, ask people, "How are we doing?" Then sit back until someone starts the conversation. For even greater effectiveness, take a look at your projects and, for each, ask people, "How are we doing with _____?"

4. **Procedures that work.** It's enticing to point fingers when something goes wrong. But the question to ask first is, Do we have a systematic approach that works for everything from designing effective meetings to manufacturing our product?

Good systems can allow talented people to use their talents. Bad systems cause award-winning landscape architects to spend their time fixing lawnmowers.

5. **Healthy interactions.** Back to the dinner table. People want to know they can have a dissenting point of view that gets heard and not stomped on. Likewise, when something really good happens, your people want some kind of acknowledgment or celebration to follow.

Über-note: I've experienced much less willingness among some managers to "spend valuable time" celebrating versus arguing opposing viewpoints. These managers feel that it's OK to debate, because "that's work." But it's not OK to celebrate because "they're already getting paid to do what they're supposed to do."

Maybe I travel in the wrong circles, but I can't begin to tell you how often I have to have a conversation with clients about the importance of acknowledgement, especially in front of one's colleagues. I can also tell you unequivocally that, over time, those managers who don't want to "waste time celebrating" have seen their upward mobility halted as a result of that attitude.

6. **Noticeable accountability and related rewards.** This is different from number five. You and I notice it when someone who doesn't do his or her fair share ends up

with the same goodies as everyone else at the end of the year. And if teamwork is so important, then it's important for team contribution to somehow be factored in to the organization's "reward" equation.

There's somewhat of a conundrum when it comes to team performance. On the one hand, things get done by people working together. On the other, each person has a well-defined role to play in that. If the manager doesn't pay attention to the individual accountabilities involved, the genuine performance issues can be lumped inappropriately under the banner of "we've got a team problem." The team problem is that individual not contributing.

7. **Good relationships outside of the team.** It's tough to get things done when IT hates the Customer Call Center or if another department is using a software program that's incompatible with yours. It's a really good idea to ask the diagnostic question, Where is the organization itself getting in the way of our success?

That gives you, the manager, one more thing to deal with when the meeting is over. But if you think about your managerial life, you already know that you spend as much time clearing obstacles for your team as you do other tasks. However, that's part of your role as a team member.

This list isn't exhaustive, but if you pay attention to all seven all the time, you will dramatically bump up your managerial game.

What to Look For in Teams

Most organizations value collaboration so highly that it's a critical component of the screening process when hiring and promoting. It would make sense, then, to learn as much as possible about the dynamics associated with groups. Some years ago, organizations spent a fair amount of time educating people on the fine points of group dynamics. The research was new and fascinating. New is good. Now that this body of work has been around for a while, it's no longer "what's happening." The human condition—and certainly the organizational mind—is always looking for what's new. The world of advertising slaps the word *new* on packaging and products for a very good reason: New is good. Old isn't bad—it just gets ignored.

There's no ignoring the importance of understanding groups. So here are some things to ponder when you are leading, or part of, a group or team.

1. Whenever one person leaves or one person enters a group, the dynamics change. Why? We learn how to function in our groups based on the roles people play, how they play them, and the balance of power and influence that results. Groups are about equilibrium.

2. That means that each time the group composition changes, it's a signal to sit down and talk. When a new member enters, the first two things that person thinks about are:
   - Why am I here? (Task/Role)
   - Who are you? (Getting to know more about the other members and vice versa)

3. If you skip this step, it will only be a matter of time before you notice that something is not quite right with the group. That's the indicator to stop, get together, and clarify number one as well as spend time doing number two).

4. When a reasonable amount of comfort and trust is established, you enable the group to be able to make decisions together. The question then is: How will we make decisions? Which ones are left to the group, which are the purview of the leader, and why?

5. Now you are in a place to implement and actually get the work of the group done. That means you need to agree on "how" things will happen. Note: "How" is important because implementation is the element of group work that allows individuals to use their talents and uniqueness. People lose interest when they don't feel as if they are uniquely part of the "how." It can be difficult for a manager to let someone handle a task in a totally different way than the manager would do it. Think about this: When you were doing hiring interviews, you made your choices based upon some unique contribution each person could make. Give people a chance to make it.

6. If you've attended to all of the steps so far, then solid performance should be the result.

If you find your group struggling, go back one step and see if you paid appropriate attention to the relevant issue. Keep going back until you take care of the business at that step and then start moving forward again.

Teams are a huge part of our lives. For managers in all types of organizations, the team is the foundation for their organizational success. It's just as important for a manager to know how to orchestrate and respond to group dynamics as it is to interpret the quarterly financials. Anything with such an impact on performance isn't a "soft" skill if it's directly linked to generating "hard" currency.

And remember: *Every meeting is a team-building meeting.*

About the Author

Steve Roesler is the principal and founder of the Steve Roesler Group and has been developing managers and leaders for over 30 years. He is the author of the blog, *All Things Workplace.* You can find his website at www.steveroesler.com.

Chapter 23

Get Rid of the Dotted Lines: Accountability and Authority in Managerial Relationships

Tom Foster

---------------------------------- **Editor's Note** ----------------------------------

Tom Foster has a wonderful way of describing real workplace challenges and the inadvertently ineffective ways we sometimes approach them. He uses stories, dialogue, and no-nonsense approaches that help managers grow. In this engaging chapter, Tom explores the topic of accountability and the various roles we play in team success. This is a particularly good chapter for those of you out there who are control freaks (or recovering control freaks like myself).

"You are not a manager so people can report to you," I chided. "You think your biggest question about management is who reports to you. That is not the critical question.

"For you, it is a question of control. For me, it is a question of output, production, getting the work done. For me, the question is, Which manager should be held accountable for the output of the team?"

Paula stopped. In mid-thought, she blurted, "But my direct reports, they report to me."

"That's a nice thought," I nodded. "And the truth is, your team members report to people all over the organization. One member of your team reports its daily unit production to accounting so they can tweak their forecasts. One of your engineers is responsible for a project segment in another department. You loaned one of your team leaders to the sales department for technical support in a rocky sales presentation. Your team reports to people all over the organization."

Paula's eyes were growing wider, so I stopped, but only for a moment. "Each member of your team reports to people all over the organization, but they can only have one manager, one manager that I can hold accountable for their output."

Paula was a new manager with the company. She arrived highly recommended, a resume of successful projects. On her team was one of our brilliant engineers. Super-smart, Duncan could solve problems faster than most engineers. Like he had a photographic memory, given a problem to solve, Duncan could see the solution, piecing together best practices that most people had forgotten. His motto: "Why start from scratch, when we have already solved this problem before?"

And Duncan was always late—not on solving problems, but arriving at meetings on time, turning in time sheets, stuff that drove Paula up a wall.

"I can pass him in the hallway," Paula complained, "and it's like I am not even there; he's in another world. I get no respect. I call a meeting, and he shows up late—sometimes not at all. I know he has been here for eight years, and I have been his manager for only three months, but, after all, he does report to me."

I smiled. Paula got the drift. "OK, he reports to people all over the organization, but I am his manager."

"And I hold you accountable for Duncan's output."

How Can You Hold Me Accountable?

"How can you hold me accountable? He doesn't respect me; he doesn't even acknowledge that I exist, except when he needs a new computer or piece of software to track some engineering process."

"Paula, why do you think we hired you? You are not an engineer, yet you are running an engineering department."

Paula had to stop complaining and think about the larger picture.

"You guys hired me, because of the last three projects I worked on at my old company. All three, each of them, took 18 to 24 months to complete. They were design-build, so we designed the project as we went along. In the middle, there were supplier problems, change orders, and subcontract disputes. All three projects came in on time and on budget."

"And, yet, running an engineering department, you are not an engineer?"

"If you had an engineer in my role, you would have elegant engineering solutions to complicated problems, but the project would be late and full of cost overruns," Paula explained.

"So, how did you finish on time and on budget?" I asked.

"Well, I had a great team, a team who respected me as their leader, who trusted me to make good decisions, decisions that balanced the engineering design with the constraints of the projects."

"And how did you gain that trust, earn that respect? Did you tell your engineers how to do their engineering work? Give them expert engineering advice?"

"Heavens, no. I'm not an engineer. You see, my engineers were really good at solving engineering and design problems, but they often ran up against a decision they didn't know how to make. Occasionally, they would run into an engineering problem that they didn't know how to solve."

"So, then you would tell them what to do?" I smiled.

"No, I am not an engineer, but I do know how to ask questions, and I can ask enough questions to help them discover the right answer."

What Is Work?

"Paula, what is work?" I pressed. "To one of your engineers, what is work?"

"Well, it's drawing and drafting, measuring, assembling all the pieces, on a computer into a final design." Paula raised her eyebrows, testing her response.

I nodded. She detected the trick in the question. "It's not drawing, drafting, measuring, and assembling, is it?" she asked.

"No, that's the output. That's what I hold you, as the manager, accountable for. Work is making decisions and solving problems. If work was drawing, drafting, measuring, and assembling, we would just get a robot to do it. But one thing a robot cannot do is make a decision or solve a problem."

It's All About the Work

"So, on those projects, last year, how did you gain the trust, earn the respect of the engineers on your team?"

No trick in this question. Paula was quick to answer. "Over time, I helped each engineer solve a problem or make a decision."

"You didn't tell them what to do?" I smiled.

"No," Paula replied.

"You are not a manager so people can report to you. You are a manager to bring value to the decision making and problem solving of each of your team members. And I hold you, as their manager, accountable for that output."

Back to Duncan

"When Duncan passes you in the hallway, without so much as noticing that you are there, do you think he is thinking about you, as his manager?"

"No, like I said, he exists in another world."

"When your engineer is in another world, what is he thinking about?"

Paula was smiling now. "I suppose he is trying to solve a problem or make a decision." Paula stopped to connect the dots. "So, if I want to gain Duncan's respect, all I have to do is bring value to his problem solving and decision making?"

"Do you bring value by telling him what to do, or giving him grief about showing up late to a meeting?"

"No, I do it by asking questions," Paula sighed. "I have been working with engineers for five years. I know this."

"And if you want Duncan to show up to a meeting, make sure the meeting brings value to some problem he is trying to solve or some decision he is trying to make. My guess, he will be on time."

Managers do not exist so people can report to them. Effective managers bring value to the problem solving and decision making of each member of their team. This managerial relationship is necessary, required, for an organization to complete work of any complexity.

Cross-Functional Relationships

Cross-functional relationships are, most often, defined on the organization chart by a dotted line. Dotted lines create ambiguity. Ambiguity kills accountability. Get rid of the dotted lines on your organization chart. They are killing you.

In cross-functional relationships, two managers work together, but neither is the manager of the other. Or, we have managers and team members from different teams working together—more dotted lines, even more ambiguity. This circumstance most often exists in project teams of short duration and where team members participate on more than one project at the same time.

Most organizations don't know how to define these relationships, so they are often left undefined, and that is where trouble starts. It looks like a personality conflict or a breakdown in communication, but it is a structural problem because the relationship is not properly defined.

This ambiguity gave birth to an even more dysfunctional arrangement called matrix organization. It looked like a spreadsheet and attempted to identify who the team member reported to, depending on the functional work at the moment.

If you want to make someone schizophrenic, assign them two managers. And if you would like to set someone free, give them three managers. No one will be able to hold them accountable for anything. Matrix organization was dotted lines on steroids, an attempt to clarify project accountability, which created more ambiguity.

The central question is not who the team member reports to. The central question is which manager can be held accountable for the direct output of the team member. This subtle shift in placing accountability makes a huge difference in organizational effectiveness.

It's Not That Complicated

The most coherent discussion comes from the research of Elliott Jaques, *Requisite Organization*. Remove the ambiguity by clearly identifying the accountabilities and authority in the cross-functional relationship. Jaques spent 50 years observing functional and dysfunctional organizations and arrived at these seven cross-functional roles. These are not managerial roles, but clearly identify, when two people are working together, who is accountable and who is the authority. These seven are:

- prescribing relationship
- audit relationship
- coordinating relationship
- monitoring relationship
- service-getting relationship
- advisory relationship
- collateral relationship.

On the face of it, defining these relationships, up front, resolves the dotted line, resolves the ambiguity, and creates accountability.

- Who can call whom into a meeting?
- Who can instruct whom to do something?
- In a disagreement, who decides?

Rather than use a dotted line, use a real line and define the accountability.

Prescribing Relationship

The role of the prescriber is often associated with the project leader and has broad authority to prescribe work to be completed within the scope of the project. It has the seductive trappings of a managerial relationship, but with distinct differences. The prescriber role is temporary; it usually only exists for the duration of the project. If there is a skill deficiency, rather than send the person for training, the prescriber will most often ask for a replacement project team member or an additional project team member.

"Gordon, I asked you to this meeting today, with Henry, to talk about your role as project leader for the Rising Sun Project that kicks off in three weeks. As the project leader, I know you are already deep in the planning phase and looking to get things started.

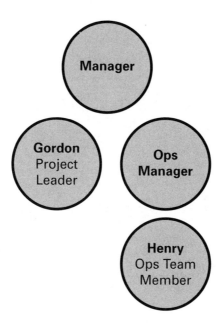

"To help you in the project, I have borrowed Henry, a team member from our operations group. Since the project is slated for completion in a three-month window, your project team is temporary, and Henry still has additional duties outside the scope of this project. I estimate that he will be able to devote approximately 80 percent of his time to you.

"As the project leader, you will be assigning tasks for Henry to work on. Because this is your project, you can assign, stop, delay, or reschedule any task associated with this project, and Henry will do his best to accommodate.

"Regarding the sequence or any process on this project, you have the authority to determine the order or method. If Henry has a question about any of his work, or disagrees with how it should be done, I expect you to sit down and explain the project guidelines. Give it your best shot, but if there is still disagreement, you win. You are the project leader, and ultimately, it is your accountability.

"Henry, we have assigned you to Rising Sun Project because of the good work you did on your last project. We think you will do well on this project, as well. We expect you to do your best, bringing your talents to the table. Because you have experience in this area, there may be a time when you disagree with a work instruction or sequence. This is Gordon's project, so I expect you to listen to his explanation and direction with an open mind. At the end of the day, his decisions stick.

"Henry, you also will remain responsible for some of your operational work. I expect you to devote approximately 20 percent of your time to those tasks. Your ops manager is still your manager, for those tasks and any scheduling conflicts. Your ops manager will keep Gordon informed on your scheduled priorities two weeks in advance. If Gordon needs more of your time for a specific task, he will talk with your ops manager to make arrangements.

"Gordon, if there are any difficulties with this assignment, please work it out with Henry's manager. Henry's manager is aware of the priorities in the Rising Sun Project and has agreed to this."

The prescriber is given broad authority in this relationship, but the prescriber is *not* the team member's manager. The prescriber is only assigning tasks within the authority of this project.

Should the project become permanent, or where the team becomes permanent, the cross-functional relationship may be reconsidered. If the prescriber has capability one stratum above the team member and the team member is working exclusively under the prescriber's direction on a full-time basis, the relationship may be redefined as a managerial relationship, rather than a cross-functional relationship.

Audit Relationship

The auditor in a cross-functional relationship rarely initiates task assignments, yet carries broad authority. Defining this authority, up front, removes ambiguity and clarifies accountability. You will often find auditors on projects where safety standards or other strict guidelines govern project parameters.

"Paul, as the project leader, you know this project has to conform to strict standards set, not only by our client, but also by state statute. I know you will be focused on getting this project completed on time and on budget, but all that can be derailed if we violate any of the project guidelines. I am assigning Steve to work with you in the role of auditor.

"Steve, I am assigning you to this project team in an audit role. You have a background in the technical standards required on this project. Here are your authorities.

"If you observe something that violates any of the standards, you are required to inform Paul so he can stop the activity. If Paul fails to stop the activity, you have the authority to stop the project on your own.

"Paul, if Steve says we need to stop the project, please understand, I am giving him the authority to do so. He will tell you first, but, if you don't take action, I expect him to. If there is a disagreement between the two of you about the standard, we are relying on Steve's technical background to make the judgment to stop or delay. Steve wins. Once the activity is stopped, we can sort out the next step.

"Steve, I expect that in the event of a disagreement, as the auditor, you will do your best to present the technical details to Paul and make your case for all the reasons why. You will have access to all the workflow data, including progress reports and any work instructions published by Paul.

"And, Steve, I expect to be fully informed of your observations and findings related to the standards we have to maintain on this project."

While the auditor typically does not assign tasks, there is full authority to delay or stop a project.

Monitoring Relationship

The monitoring relationship is similar to the audit relationship, except we remove two authorities. The auditor can delay or stop a project, and the monitor can delay, but cannot stop, a project.

If there is disagreement, the monitor can only report to the manager.

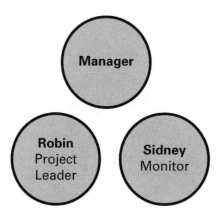

"Robin, we are finally going to start the Brickell Ave Project. As the project leader, you know there are some specific guidelines specified by the client that we have to follow in their design. I have assigned Sidney to monitor those guidelines as an extra pair of eyes for you. Please use Sidney in that capacity.

"Sidney, as the monitor on this project, it is your responsibility to examine the work as it is being completed to make sure the design guidelines from the client are being followed. If you see something that needs attention, Robin needs to know immediately. You have the authority to delay the work in that vicinity while you are talking to Robin, but Robin makes the decision on whether to proceed or not. If you believe that Robin has made a mistake and you are not able to convince her, Robin's decision sticks. In that case, I need to know, so I expect an email or a phone call, but Robin's decision sticks in the field until Robin and I can discuss the situation."

The monitor can delay, but cannot stop, a project.

Coordinating Relationship

We expect people to cooperate, and are often disappointed. The coordinating relationship clearly describes those expectations.

"Carmen, I have called you in today to meet with Frank. Both of you are project leaders on the Baltimore Project. Frank is in charge of operations on the project, and Carmen, you are in charge of marketing. Both of you were chosen because of your experience in difficult projects, and a lot is at stake. Timing is everything. There are some statutory guidelines we have to follow, which prevents us from normal marketing activities until the merger has been approved. But Frank, you have to get operations up and running in the background, so when the approval happens, we can move everything within 72 hours.

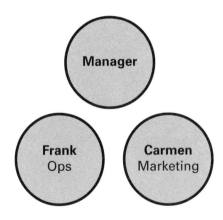

"This will require high levels of cooperation from each of your teams, and each of you will be using a pool of shared resources. I will be the last word, but I need the two of you to be in constant contact, meeting and coordinating this project without me. This is one of four projects on my plate right now. Both of you are pros; you have done this before. I am scheduled to be in this office every Tuesday, so if you need me face-to-face, that's it.

"You will *not* be giving each other things to do, you have your own tasks to complete, but one of you may need to delay the other for some reason. Either of you can call a coordinating meeting with the other, in the conference room, on the phone—it's up to you. If one of you calls a meeting, I expect the other to be responsive—no excuses. You will share each other's progress and agree on the best way to meet your teams' project goals. Where you have a decision that cannot be resolved, pull me in and I will make the decision. I am accountable to the client, and I need each of your to do your best."

Service Getting

The larger the company, the more likely there will be specialized services required, where the resource is in another department. A manager needs services or support from another department with another manager.

"Cheryl, we're meeting today about the XYZ Project. As you know, Phil is the project leader and needs accounting support to track the expense budget on this project. Christine is your manager, and we hold her accountable for the work you produce. Christine selected you because of your great work on the Phoenix Project last month. We need that same kind of work for the XYZ Project.

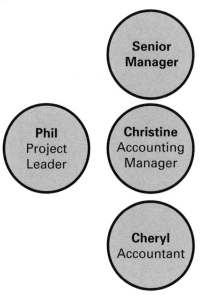

"Phil, as you work through this project, you will need expense budget tracking. Christine's accounting department has resources that can support your project needs. As the project leader, you will decide exactly what support you need from Christine's department, and Cheryl has been specifically assigned to your project. So, decide what you need and tell Cheryl.

"Cheryl, you have other task assignments, as well, so when Phil tells you he needs something, make sure he gives you a specific deadline or timeframe, so you can schedule the priority. If you have a scheduling conflict you cannot resolve, Christine, your manager, can help you make the appropriate decision.

"Christine, the XYZ Project is important to us, so if Phil is not getting the support he needs from your department, it is up to you to figure out how to get it done. Cheryl may need more help, or may have to work overtime. You know your resources and your own budgets, so we are counting on you to give Phil that support.

"And, Phil, if Cheryl is not giving the support needed, I expect you to work with Christine to make sure the project gets what it needs."

Specifically, Jaques defined the service getting cross-functional relationship:

- Phil has the authority to request a service (ask Cheryl to do something).
- If Phil's request is not met (falls short, misses deadline, requires more support), he has the authority to talk to Cheryl's manager.
- Cheryl's manager, Christine, is ultimately accountable for Cheryl's work output.

Advisory Relationship

The advisor has limited authority, yet can make or break a project. The only authority the advisor maintains is access to the project leader to explain. The explanation may be technical and based on past experience, research about the project, or sage wisdom.

"Thanks for coming to the meeting today on the ABC Project. Paul, Robert, both of you will be working on this project. Paul, you are the project leader. The outcome of this project will clearly be your accountability. You, as the manager, are accountable for the direct output of your team. This means that all problems that need to be solved and decisions to be made will be on your shoulders.

"Robert, you will be on this team in the role of an advisor. You will bring your technical expertise to the project. You will have access to Paul to explain the technical mechanics of what is happening inside the project.

"Paul, if Robert calls a meeting with you, you can be assured it will contain important data you will need to make some of your decisions.

"Robert, understand that your role will only be that of an advisor. All decisions, priorities, and the accountability for the project will be on Paul."

Having an advisor on a project can be extremely valuable. The role of the advisor is very clear, as is the role for the project leader—no dotted lines, not two people in charge of the same project, but clear accountability.

Collateral Relationship

Collateral cross-functional roles occur when team members, with the same manager, are working on the same project or the same operation. Each team member has his or her own goals and resources, but one may stumble onto problems or decisions where he needs the cooperation of another. Neither team member can direct the other to take any action, but both are required to listen to each other, to solve problems and make decisions.

"Denise, Allen, I called the two of you in, today, to talk about the operational workflow in the department. Our biggest customer has just placed a standing order that will eat 30 percent of our production capacity.

"Denise, you are in charge of production, and it is your accountability to meet that schedule. Because of this high demand, some of our smaller orders might get bumped so there may be some difficulty setting priorities.

"Allen, you are our lead salesperson, and those smaller orders that might get bumped are yours. I need the two of you to cooperate where there are conflicting priorities.

"Denise, I need you to post the production schedule on a rolling seven-day plan. Post that schedule in the sales room so Allen and the rest of the sales team can see it. Allen, I need you to check that schedule every morning, looking forward seven days to make sure your best customers are being taken care of. You know what's important. If it looks like a problem, talk to Denise and explain your circumstance. Make the decision the way I would make it.

"Denise, we can't let down our biggest customer, but Allen's customers pay their bills, too. You have the authority to schedule up to 20 hours of overtime per week to make sure all the production is getting done. If you feel you need more resources, see me.

"Allen, you can be as persuasive as you need to be, but you understand the priorities as well as Denise. Use your best judgment. In the end, if you cannot resolve a problem or make a decision, then find me, but only after the two of you have had a significant conversation."

It's Not a Communication Problem

When things in a company turn chaotic, the two most cited reasons are communication issues and personality problems. Yet, most of the chaos is created by the failure to define how people work together. What is the accountability, and what is the authority? If these elements have not been defined, the organization can have all the communication seminars it can afford, but will still experience the chaos.

Get the structure right, define the relationships, define the accountability, define the authority, and most issues related to management and motivation disappear.

About the Author

Tom Foster is a management and leadership expert, coach, and trainer. He authors the popular Management Skills Blog, and you can find his website at www.managementblog.org.

Chapter 24

Performance Management at Ground Level

Wally Bock

.... **Editor's Note** ....

I have been a fan of Wally Bock's blog for years, and I admire his ability to get to the crux of the matter and explain what state-of-the-art management looks like in action. This is extremely helpful because we often agree on the concept, only to splinter apart when it comes to defining and using managerial practices. Performance management is one of the most important responsibilities that managers have, and it is also one of the least well-understood managerial systems. In this chapter, Wally offers an excellent primer that will help you understand your role in managing team member performance and ways that you can reinforce great performance and address some of the more uncomfortable performance management situations.

The CEO has the 50,000-foot view. He or she can see all the way to a distant horizon. The corporate jet is plush and comfortable. Thanks to technology, the CEO can keep track of what's happening down at ground level, but it's hard for the CEO to reach individual workers with important messages.

No one understands this better than General Electric's CEO, Jeff Immelt. On any given day, some 300,000 people go to work at GE. Immelt can reach them with mass communications. He can come down from 50,000 feet and meet some of them face-to-face. What he can't do, what no CEO can do, is reach individual workers regularly, personally, and often. That's the job of the crew chiefs and supervisors and middle managers. That's your job. Jeff Immelt knows that better than most CEOs because of his life experience. Today, Jeff is the CEO of GE. His father worked for GE for 28 years, not as an executive, but on the line. In 2005, Fast Company interviewed Immelt. The interview includes the following exchange.

"When your dad had a bad boss, did he behave differently at home?"

"Yeah. He came home in a bad mood, uncertain about the future. And when he had a good boss, he was pumped. The frontline folks are critical to how the company does."

Your boss has more impact on your morale and productivity than anyone or anything else. And, you have that same impact on your team and your team members. That impact can be positive or negative. Career Realism recently carried an article titled "Retention Problem? Perhaps It's a Career Development Problem," which summed up the negative:

> *Research on why employees leave companies has been conducted for many years and the answers always come back the same—the number one reason employees leave a company is because of an issue with their direct manager.*

The positive side comes from that master of analysis, Google. In 2009, the company initiated an effort code-named "Project Oxygen" to identify what great bosses do so that the company could teach those things to other managers. The inspiration for the project came from something that many managers have noticed. Laszlo Bock (no relation), the top human resources person at Google, put it this way: "The starting point was that our best managers have teams that perform better, are retained better, are happier—they do everything better. So the biggest controllable factor that we could see was the quality of the manager, and how they sort of made things happen."

Ground level is where bosses like you drive results and morale. And the core of what you do is "performance management." Over a quarter-century ago, I did what Google did. I went looking for top-performing bosses, rated excellent by three key groups: peers, team members, and their own boss. Then I spent time with them to find out what they *did* differently to get those great results. Traits are wonderful. Characteristics are great. But if you want to become a great boss, if you want to do performance management well, you have to understand what great bosses do so that you can do it, too. Even though we're going to concentrate on those behaviors, we still need to discuss principles.

Five Principles

Principles are important because they can guide you when you're in unfamiliar territory. Use them to test your decisions and your choices. There are only five of them, but if you follow them consistently, you're on the way to creating a great working environment, one where productivity and morale are high.

Your job is to help the team and the team members succeed. It's not enough to make your numbers; how you make your numbers is important. Treat people fairly and honestly so you maintain the trust that helps you keep great workers and attract others to you.

Your job is to accomplish the mission today and make sure you can accomplish it tomorrow. Part of your job is helping your people grow and develop so they can handle tomorrow's challenges, whether they're working for you then or not. You're most likely to succeed if you help your people and your team build on their strengths and make their weaknesses irrelevant.

Dealing with the observable gives you the best chance of success. Pay attention to behavior and performance. Behavior is what a person says or does. Performance is the measurable result of work.

Use the behavior you control (your own) to influence the behavior and performance of others. The truth is you have no power because your team members always have a choice. They can do what you suggest or not. They can avoid what you suggest or not.

Apply the Damon Runyon Principle. Runyon was a newspaperman and a heck of a writer. As a newspaperman he covered any sport you could bet on and big news stories including FDR's inauguration. He wrote stories about the slightly shady but quite glamorous world of New York after dark. His characters all seemed to have memorable names like "Dave the Dude," "Harry the Horse," and "Good Time Charley." Two of his stories were turned into the musical *Guys and Dolls*.

You don't have to run out and read his work. Just memorize one quote and use it as a guide for how to do your job. Here's the quote: "The race may not always be to the swift, nor victory to the strong, but that's how you bet."

That's the conclusion of a horseplayer who's watched the horse that was going to win him money fall and break a leg after leading by six lengths. It's the view of a boxing writer who knows that the best fighter didn't win the match. It's also the conclusion of a gambler who just learned that a rich uncle left him enough to pay his debts.

Sometimes you'll do everything right and have things turn out wrong. Not every team member will respond to good management techniques. Even tried-and-true techniques don't work every time. But, other times you'll get lucky and win with a weak hand. Sometimes the lout that you were dreading firing will quit. If you're a boss, the lesson is that you'll come out OK in the long run if you play the odds and apply the principles. Keep the principles in mind and remember this: Great bosses are great because of what they say and what they do.

Preparing the Ground: Three Simple Things to Do

Great gardens don't happen by accident. When you see a glorious flower garden or a productive vegetable garden, you know that someone did the right things over and over and over. Great teams don't happen by accident, either. You job is to do the right things over and over, day after day, to create the environment where a great team can grow.

It all starts with preparing the ground. For a gardener, preparing the ground makes it more likely that plants will thrive. For you, preparing the ground means doing three simple things. They're not hard, and they're not big, but if you don't do them, it's very, very hard to do performance management well. When you do these things consistently, though, the odds for success go way, way up.

Touch base a lot. Make time for face time. Everything good starts from this. Face time increases trust and makes your presence a natural part of the workday, not a special event or a harbinger of bad news. Touching base a lot lets you catch problems when they're small, increases the opportunity to convey important messages, and allows you to learn more about the people on your team.

If you and your team members all work in the same space, contact should be a frequent and natural part of your day. But you need to make sure that you're touching base with everyone, not just the people you like or are comfortable with.

If you have a team with virtual workers, contact them frequently in ways that don't involve typing. That usually means phone contact, but it can mean a visit. If your team members are scattered around the globe, the challenge is to have meaningful time with people in far different time zones.

Have conversations. Conversations are the way you grow relationships. They are also the most important tool of your boss's trade. Some conversations will be exclusively about business, but most will be a mix of personal and business matters.

This is where you get to know your people, but to do that, you must listen. This is also where you have an opportunity to convey important messages. Take every contact and conversation as an opportunity to move things forward.

Create and deliver your elevator speech. Marketing people talk about their "elevator speech," a short statement of key marketing points. Most great bosses I've known have something similar. Here's one example from one great supervisor named Bud:

- Show up on time and ready to work.
- Pitch in to help us get the job done.
- Ask for help if you need it.

When Bud finished listing those three things, I asked him, "That's all?" He replied, "That's all I need."

Susan was another great supervisor. She didn't call it an elevator speech, but she told me, "I don't have many rules, but I enforce every one of them."

It turns out that you can run a whole company on just a few rules. Nucor is one of America's most profitable steel companies. They don't have a policy manual. There are just five rules for everyone in the company:

- Know the job.
- Ask questions and experiment.
- Share what you learn
- Do what it takes to be sure something goes wrong only once.
- Let us know how we can help.

Getting good at performance management isn't a matter of mastering complex theories or intricate strategies. It's pretty simple, really. Apply the five principles. Prepare the ground by doing three simple things over and over, day after day. Following the principles and doing the three important things to prepare the ground will set you up for good performance management, all through the cycle.

The Performance Management Cycle

Performance management has a rhythm, just like other processes in business and the rest of life. There's a rough order to the steps in the cycle, and you'll find that if you do the first ones well, the later steps will be easier. Start with some preparation. Analyze what needs to be done. Most jobs, and therefore most team members, will have a limited number of things that they need to do. There are usually no more than four of these. You should be able to describe the differences between unacceptable, acceptable, and excellent performance on each one.

Do this well and your team members will be able to judge their performance without you telling them. That's a great situation because it lets people improve their performance on their own. It also establishes a common understanding of what the job entails.

Caution. This is an easy concept to grasp, but it takes practice to do well. The good news is that you should get better with time. You will get better faster if you make this and setting clear expectations an area where you actively critique and modify what you do.

Evaluate your team members' behavior and their ability to do the work. Take behavior first. Determine how each person measures up to what you expect (see "elevator speech" above) in terms of basic standards—for example, whether they come in on time, pitch in to help others, and so on. People who do these things need less attention than those who choose not to.

Now evaluate each team member on each task. Determine what decisions you think team members should make, based on their ability. Those decisions will fall into three groups.

In some cases, you will make all the decisions about the work when you assign it and follow up closely afterward. This is what some people describe as "micromanagement." It's extremely time intensive and emotionally draining. It's only appropriate for tasks where the team member either doesn't know how to do the work or cannot be counted on to do it acceptably.

In many cases, you will allow team members to make decisions but consult with you before implementing. In my research, I found that this was the level of control that most bosses were comfortable with. In interviews, they said that they felt secure that mistakes would not be made. That sounds sensible, but there's a dark side.

Most of your team members would prefer to make their own decisions. If you keep control when they feel they're able to make those decisions, you put a damper on their morale and initiative.

The solution is fairly simple. Let them tell you what they propose. Offer any feedback you think is appropriate. Then let them try it their way. They will make some mistakes. That's what people do. But they will also learn. Remember that your job is helping the team *and the team members* succeed. This isn't difficult to understand, but because the emotion of fear may have its hooks in you, it's often hard to do. As incentive, remember that as your team members develop mastery, you can turn your attention to other things.

What you're working toward is a situation where a team member can make all the important decisions on a job. That's what most people mean by delegation. The more team members you have who can handle their work on their own, the more productive your team will be and, usually, the higher the morale will be.

Your team members will be developing their knowledge and skills, so your evaluation of what decisions they can make will be a moving target. Do a quick re-evaluation every month or so of where each team member stands on each task. That will make you more effective in your quest to help people grow and make it less likely that you will overcontrol.

Unless the work to be done changes, you will only have to analyze it once. Evaluating individual abilities and willingness should be regular. The stages of the performance management cycle that follow are things you should be doing every day.

Set clear and reasonable expectations. Most of us think we're better at giving direction than we really are. Giving direction or assigning work is a skill. You will get better at it if you critique yourself and keep striving to get better. You'll also be a more effective boss if you check for understanding when you give direction. Your expectations should be reasonable, too. Don't ask people to do the impossible. Encourage them to stretch, but don't set targets so high that failure is likely.

Follow up to make sure understanding turns into performance. This is where touching base a lot helps you. It's also where you benefit from the work you've done on understanding the tasks and describing what good performance looks like.

Look for things you can praise. Praise is the tool that gets people to try things or to put in extra effort. Praise things that merit praise, but consider effort and improvement, as well as achievement. Give your praise straight; don't qualify it with a little criticism or an attempt at humor. Give your praise right away; the closer to the behavior you're praising, the better. Adjust as needed. Smaller, more frequent adjustments are better than fewer, bigger adjustments. The time to deal with a performance issue is when you notice it.

Start by describing the behavior or performance you want to discuss. Be objective and describe; don't judge. The best way to do that is to describe without using adjectives.

Then tell your team member why it's important to discuss the behavior. The best way is to describe the result of the behavior or performance. Here's an example: "John, your report was due to me at 11 a.m. You're bringing it to me now, at noon. Because your report was late, I wasn't able to complete my report to the boss on time."

Then wait. Your team member should talk next. There are several things you may hear. You may hear a valid reason. You may hear an excuse. Most often, at least in my experience, the team member will agree with you and sometimes take action so the problem won't happen again.

Whatever you hear, it can be the starting point for a discussion. Most great bosses do most of their work informally. A participant in one of my programs said that they work "in the cracks in the system."

Repeat the process. We've just run through the basic performance management process. Use the principles and repeat both the basic behaviors that prepare the ground and the behaviors for specific parts of the cycle. You do them over and over and over. It's your job. It's also your job to deal with three special cases.

The Special Cases

What we've covered so far works with most people most of the time, but there are three special situations we need to address. We'll start with the problem employee. Problem employees are a special case. You won't get through your career without having at least one person on your team who simply can't or won't do the job and work well with the team. Those situations are intense and draining, but they are the exception.

Remember that. "Write it on a rock" as my friend Jim Blasingame would say, or use it as the copy for a tattoo. Most of the people who work for you want to do a good job and want to be part of a successful team. But some people can't or won't improve to minimum standards. Those are the people you need to work with intensely and where you need to document the issues and your discussions. Start by giving them notice: "Sarah, you've come in late three times this week. I'm going to watch your behavior, and I'll be documenting any more late arrivals. If that keeps up, you could be subject to discipline."

Why give notice? Shouldn't Sarah know that's she's come in late and that there are consequences? That's true, but there are two reasons why giving notice is a good option. First, you may learn something important.

Sarah could be coming late because she's had to change child care. You might choose options in a case like that which aren't on the path to discipline. Depending on the situation, you might want to give her some time (a week?) to master the new schedule or investigate teleworking as an option.

The other reason to give notice is emotional. Even if people "should" know things, they're likely to feel ambushed if you simply spring the discipline on them. With notice you avoid that and give your team member the opportunity to clean up his or her act without formal action.

Alas, even with notice some people can't or won't do what's required and expected. That brings us to the land of documentation. Documentation should be prompt, objective, and accurate. Times and dates should be part of it.

You'll usually have specific company procedures for this, and most follow the same general path. They make an attempt to gain compliance and, if that fails, there are progressive levels of discipline leading to termination. This is one of those times when HR can provide help and guidance.

Strivers are the people who want to move up. They're a special case, too. They're special because they really want to do well and are willing to work at it.

They're also special because there aren't many of them. Most of the people who work for you are likely to want to do a good job and develop mastery of what they do, but they don't want to make the time or attention commitment that excellence and upward mobility demand. That's OK.

The strivers will make up for it because they'll take everything you have to offer. You need to document your meetings and discussion with them because you may be asked to evaluate them for promotion or re-assignment and you want to have evidence handy.

You have two challenges with strivers. You want to find opportunities for them to grow and develop. And you must keep them realistic. That means discussing mistakes so they can learn from them. It often means reminding the strivers that they have to do their job as a team member as a precondition to whatever comes next. The annual performance review is a special case. The formal annual or semiannual event where everyone uses the same forms is a reality of life for most bosses. You have to do it. You have to do it when everyone else does it, following the same guidelines that everyone else follows.

I think that the annual performance review should be just that, a review. If there are surprises for you or your team member, it probably means that you didn't do a good job of performance management. If you have done a good job, the formal review offers an opportunity to discuss what comes next. There are usually two kinds of discussions.

Some people will not be performing up to standard. The discussion with them will center on what they need to change to meet minimum performance levels. The discussion with people who are performing at acceptable levels usually centers on what they want to try or how they want to grow in the year ahead.

Performance management doesn't have the glamour of the CEO's job. It's not one of the hot topics in the business press either. But if you do performance management well, you will make a difference. You'll create an environment where a great team can grow, produce results for your company, and make a difference in your team members' lives.

About the Author

Wally Bock has been studying the most effective bosses to learn what they do and then teaching those behaviors for more than 25 years. In that time he has trained hundreds of managers in a variety of industries. Wally is the author of *Performance Talk: The One-on-One Part of Leadership* and the *Working Supervisor's Support Kit*. He also writes the popular Three Star Leadership Blog (http://blog.threestarleadership.com).

Chapter 25

The First Secret of Improvisation—Yes! Space

Karen Hough

Editor's Note

I often suggest that managers become "yes" people—people who are positive forces in enabling things to happen—people who ooze positive energy and catalyze possibility. In this electrifying chapter, improv expert Karen Hough shares an improv technique that you will want to begin using tomorrow—or this afternoon. This is not some wishy-washy stuff, and Karen shares the research and examples that will demonstrate how creating a "Yes! Space" can reduce turnover and improve results.

*I*magine … *You are backstage at a theater, listening to the sound of an excited crowd taking their seats out front. As you stare at the empty stage, you suddenly realize that you have no script, no costume, no props. You look around at the shadowed faces of the other people backstage, and from their nervousness you realize that they also have no idea what's going to happen next. Suddenly, the lights dim in the house and go up onstage. It's your cue. You have to go out! You're pulled onstage by the motion of the people behind you. One of your troupe members steps up to the lip of the stage and says, "I need a one-word contribution." Someone in the back of the audience shouts, "Vegetables!" The audience laughs mildly and your troupe member accepts it. "Great! Vegetables is our subject!" He steps back. Then nothing else happens. The faces of the audience regard you and the silence feels crushing. You've got to do something! So, without a net, you step out and proclaim, "I feel like a rutabaga!" The crowd titters, but you don't know what to say next. Silence stretches out in front of you* *and you start to get warm around the armpits. Before you know it, a hand slaps you on the shoulder and one of your troupe says, "Yes, and you look like one, too!" The crowd laughs ...*

Does this sound like a nightmare? A movie script? A joke? Actually, it's what happens every night to an improvisational actor. Improvisation is an art form that demands that a troupe of performers walk onstage in front of an audience when they literally do not know what is going to happen next. The troupe onstage asks the audience to supply ideas for characters, a plotline, a style of music, a current event, anything. Taking that idea from the audience, the troupe starts to create a show, play, comedy scene, or game. The troupe members think entirely on their feet, making it up as they go along. They really never know, from moment to moment, what the other troupe members might say or do. They just have to go with it and make the performance work.

I've spoken to people who have watched improv and can barely believe it's real. "How do they do that?" they say, or "It's incredible that they can come up with all of that stuff on the fly. It must be a special talent!" or "There has to be a trick." The truth is, there are a few tricks. But these tricks are actually a solid set of guidelines that make it possible for improvisers to work wonders. They are simple, effective, and impressive. And you, too, can use those guidelines in your work and life to improve performance, collaborate radically, and build trust.

When we adopt the improviser's mindset and behaviors, we create trust every day, moment by moment, in the workplace. We will dive into the specific definitions, secrets, and behaviors of improvisation that I have seen applied in the workplace for over a decade.

We all improvise, every day. Every time we deal with an unexpected setback in the office or collaborate on a great project with our team, we are using behaviors grounded in improvisation. Wouldn't it be nice to know how to do it well, like the professionals? And while we're improvising, wouldn't it also be incredible if we could build a strong, effective, and supportive network of trust? To do so, we need to explore the key secrets of improvisation.

In the onstage scene described above, you and your fellow improvisers were a living example of the first secret of improvisation, Yes! Space. A troupe of improvisers can build a game, a scene, or an entire one-act play in the moment because they have agreed to say yes. The Yes! Space concept allows for endless possibility, and is very easy to accomplish. To fully understand what happens in Yes! Space, let's break it down into components:

- Say yes.
- Put the critic on hold.
- Make it public.

Say Yes

The very action of saying the word *yes* is critical to improvisation. It's also key to building a collaborative space where people believe they can take risks and be creative. Saying yes is an effective tool for both the improv stage and the workplace. Think about the vegetable scene onstage. As you remember, you were onstage, in the spotlight. There was no question that you had to act, even though there was no plan. You blurted out the first thing that came to you: "I feel like a rutabaga!" Then one of your troupe members joined you in the scene. She immediately agreed with you. She said, "Yes, and you look like one, too." The very first word your troupe member said was *yes*. You experienced Yes! Space. It's really that simple. Your contribution to the performance, being a rutabaga, was immediately accepted. No assessments, no lifted brow, no devil's advocate. Just "Yes!"

The power of that little word is amazing. By taking the action to say the word *yes* you have entered into positive possibilities. This power of yes is not a new concept, and it is not confined to improvisation. Many modern disciplines have explored the concept of positive power, and they all agree on the transformational power of positivity. Unfortunately, positivity runs counter to our natural propensity to be negative, and it takes work. For example, researchers have discovered that we actually are wired for negativity in our language and culture. Of 558 emotion words in English, 62 percent are negative. And when people are shown photos of bad or good occurrences, we spend a longer time viewing the bad ones.[1]

We have to work harder to learn to use Yes! Space. That might mean getting comfortable with a little discomfort. But the benefits are very much worth the work.

> *"yes is a world*
> *& in this world of*
> *yes live (skilfully curled)*
> *all worlds"*
>
> —from e.e. cummings, "love is a place"[2]

Getting to Yes is the Harvard Business School study and book on collaborative negotiation.[3] It changed the face of negotiations and opened a new space for both sides to find the best result in a negotiation. The work of these authors overturned the notion that negotiations must be confrontational, difficult events.

---

[1] Chip Heath and Dan Heath, *Switch: How to Change Things When Change Is Hard* (New York: Broadway Books, 2010).

[2] George J. Firmage, ed., *E. E. Cummings: Complete Poems, 1904–1962* (New York: Liveright Publishing, 1978), 443.

[3] Roger Fisher, William Ury, and Bruce Patton, *Getting to Yes: Negotiating Agreement without Giving In* (New York: Houghton Mifflin, 1991).

Dale Carnegie based his blockbuster *How to Win Friends and Influence People* on the concept that smiling and expressing a genuine curiosity for others can lead to personal success in life and more sales in business.[4] Consistently questioning and seeking to serve the other person's needs builds safe environments and relationships and makes sales. People prefer to give their money to people and organizations they trust.

Stephen Young, the author of *MicroMessaging*, discusses the great effect of microscopic positive behavioral changes.[5] Simply by nodding, making eye contact, or saying a person's name with respect, Young contends, you have the power to influence how others perceive that person. So the act of saying yes in your slightest inflections, and in a public way, can have a gigantic effect on another person's confidence and success.

The concept of appreciative inquiry contends that, rather than seeking to solve problems in a corporate environment, companies need to focus relentlessly on what they're doing right. That upon which you focus, grows. Under the power of the growth of the good stuff, the bad stuff will minimize. The combination of Yes! Space and appreciative inquiry had a great influence on one of the nation's top children's hospitals. In 2008, the hospital was undergoing major changes in both clinical and administrative functions. We created an improvisational engagement that enabled participants from all areas of the hospital to focus on their ultimate goal: better patient outcomes.

During times of great change in organizations, we often see consistently negative behaviors and competition. By embracing the improviser's mindset and behaviors of Yes! Space, this hospital staff was able to approach the change phase positively and collaboratively.

In the improvisational mindset, any contribution, no matter how ridiculous, is greeted with immediate agreement. As an improviser, I could trust that if I stepped out onstage and shouted, "I'm the queen of Sheba!" all of my troupe members would say, "Yes, you are!" and start treating me like the queen. By voicing the word *yes*, you are saying yes to possibility. Yes is not a literal commitment, as in "Yes, we will." It is a commitment to considering a possibility, as in "Yes, we could." This means that every idea or contribution is considered valid. No one sneers, shakes her head, or says no the moment an idea pops out of someone's mouth. The improviser's belief that every idea is valid also assumes that every person is valid. Simply because an idea has been contributed, improvisers believe it is imperative to acknowledge its existence and importance by saying yes to both the idea and the person.

---

[4] Dale Carnegie, *How to Win Friends and Influence People* (New York: Simon & Schuster, 1936).

[5] Stephen Young, *MicroMessaging: Why Great Leadership Is Beyond Words* (New York: McGraw-Hill, 2007).

Saying yes becomes a reflex for improvisers, and it can become a reflex for you. The particular idea offered may not be the one we pursue. We have simply agreed that it could be one we pursue and that we will explore it together. By agreeing to give it a chance to live and breathe, even for two minutes, we have said yes to its possibility.

Saying yes is imperative for improvisation because the performance would never go anywhere if we kept denying ideas. When I shout, "I'm the queen of Sheba," my troupe member could say, "No, that's not a good idea. Let's be mechanics instead. I know all about mechanics but I don't know anything about the queen of Sheba, and neither do you." After that, another troupe member could say, "Mechanics aren't funny. Let's sing a song instead." Can you imagine how dumb that would look onstage? Time would be wasted, the audience would be confused, and the troupe would not be working as a team, only as individuals out for themselves.

Yes! Space and saying yes means that we are going to get the performance rolling right away. Because there are no preconceived notions about what must happen, as there is in a scripted show, we can accept anything. And by accepting every possibility, at least for a while, the performance moves quickly and efficiently. What does the say yes reflex mean for everyday encounters?

Whenever I work with groups, the event organizers approach me afterward to discuss the high level of engagement: "So many people spoke up! We had people contributing who had never engaged in a training session before! How do you do it?" I say yes. That's how I do it. The first word out of my mouth, every time someone contributes, is *yes*. When that happens, the group learns that it's safe to share. They realize that they won't be criticized or ignored, and suddenly they want to start being a part of the conversation. When I ask open-ended questions, there often are moments of silence until some brave soul decides to fill the silence. When they are greeted with agreement, they feel validated, strong, and they contribute again. Then the people around them start to contribute and soon you have a room full of interacting people. Try it sometime. You'll be amazed at the exponential increase in engagement.

When we say yes, we're agreeing that others have the right to air their ideas, and we are saying yes to possibility. As the session progresses, we may debate the idea or change to another topic, but we can always agree that a person's contribution was worthwhile by saying yes in that moment. This can be particularly effective when people are struggling or need to share something difficult. By saying yes, we can create a place in which it is safe for everyone to share.

I remember a particular session when my ensemble was working with groups from an insurance company that included call center personnel, managers, and even board members. We had a tight time frame in which to teach a few concepts. One woman who had not spoken up during the entire session responded to our discussion of Yes! Space by saying that she felt ignored by her colleagues and that people never thanked her for her hard work. She was, by nature, a rather gruff person. I said, "Yes, and that must be hard for you. What more can you tell us about your feelings on this?" She shared that she loved her work and really wanted people to recognize her accomplishments. At that point, other members of the group chimed in and said they would agree to be her sounding board. One man even said, "Yes, I noticed your good work. I'm sorry I never commented on it." The conversation was cathartic and positive, and in a few minutes the woman asked me to continue with the exercise, for which she volunteered.

The point here is not so much her response as the response of the in-house trainer after the session. She thanked me for managing the event and then singled out that particular moment in the session. "I would have been so scared!" she said. "I would have just tried to steer the conversation back to the agenda and not comment on that uncomfortable situation. I would not have wanted to let her keep talking for fear it would become a big issue. I'm so glad you managed it!"

Saying yes does indeed create some risk, but it also creates resolution, as it did for the woman who needed to be heard.

Put the Critic on Hold

Imagine a critic. In my mind, I see a wizened pundit peering over his glasses with a sarcastic sneer. He knows so much more than me. I know he'll discount or even laugh at anything I say. And if he really hates an idea, he'll literally scream, "No!"

Put him on hold. Seriously. Punch the pause button on the video in your brain and stop him in his tracks. This is absolutely necessary to Yes! Space. Putting the critic on hold addresses how Yes! Space deals with something we want to reject. Saying no is a human defense mechanism. When we are faced with an idea or situation that makes us feel surprised or uncomfortable, it is safer to say no. That way, we will not need to stretch, change, or say or do anything that feels risky or scary. We are trained to be logical, rational, linear thinkers.

When I suggest that I am the queen of Sheba, you may first react with logic, reason, or even sarcasm. It is a ridiculous statement and it would be far safer to simply kill the idea than to take part in it. Putting the critic on hold is the loophole for the logical mind. It's another reflex that teaches your brain to say to itself, "That sounds utterly ridiculous and improbable. However, I am going to stop myself from using negative judgment right now. I'm going to allow my brain to agree that this idea is possible, if only for a little while." Knowing that evaluation and critique can happen later also allows the critic to relax. The critic in your brain can say, "OK, I really want to speak up now, but I'll lie low until this idea has been fully, positively vetted. Then I'll be better able to judge its merit."

Every time you see a movie featuring aliens, space travel, fictional creatures, or anything you know is not real, your brain puts the critic on hold. For those two hours in the movie theater, we agree to believe the impossible is real. If every time a weird, creative idea arose for a novelist or scriptwriter, his or her colleagues said, "That doesn't exist. Don't do it," we would have no *Star Wars*, no *Lord of the Rings*—no SpongeBob, for that matter.

Let's think about our discerning, professional minds. At school and at work, we're evaluated on how critically we can think. We like to ask questions such as "Where are the problems? How can we anticipate all the bad stuff?"

If you are handed a document to review, the first thing you look for is typos, bad grammar, loose content, and you send it back full of red ink and comments on what was wrong. If your significant other or child comes up with a crazy idea for the weekend that doesn't immediately appeal to you, you probably try to introduce doubt. And during meetings, if someone goes off the agenda with a new idea or suggestion, we inwardly seethe. When a new employee throws out a suggestion, it is often met with any number of the following responses:

"I don't know about that."

"We tried it two years ago and it tanked."

"Good idea. But it will never work."

When the critic moves into our relationships with people, we shut down contribution, ideas, trust, and Yes! Space. You may be thinking, "I'm a lawyer; I have to say no sometimes." Or "I'm a parent. For the safety of my children, I have to say no sometimes!" You're right. You do. This is where theory meets practical application. Yes! Space does work onstage, but even improvisers sometimes introduce no for the sake of comedy. If that scene with the vegetables had gone on for a while and then had become boring or was getting no reaction from the audience, believe me, a good improv troupe definitely would have switched gears. The troupe would give the idea space to grow, to be tested, but if it wasn't going to work, they'd realign for the sake of the show.

Sometimes, we just have to say no. One great way to begin getting used to Yes! Space is to learn to say no in the Yes! Space. My ensemble and I facilitate an activity about finding different ways to say no and involving another person in the solution. It opens new avenues for everything from effective negotiations to better client interactions. It teaches you to communicate in a way that brings people into collaboration rather than conflict. The key is to ask open-ended questions about what someone really wants and about their needs and motivations.

The next time you want to just say no, try to do it without using the words *no, but, if, however*, or any negative contraction such as *can't, won't, don't, shouldn't,* and so forth. It will be tough and frustrating at first. We often fall back on telling or demanding, relying on negative words. But if we first seek to understand, some surprising things can arise.

Question, question, question. Use phrases like "Help me understand" and "Tell me more about your ideas behind this." You may discover a middle ground to replace the no, and the person you're speaking with may realize that the best answer is no, without you ever having to say so.

I worked with a marketing manager at a large national bank who had been an improviser in college, and she related a funny story during our session. When she married, she told her husband all about the secrets of improv. However, he started holding her accountable to those principles. Whenever they had an argument, he would smile and say, "You're denying me! You're not saying yes!"

The whole group cracked up at her story, and we went on to talk about how saying yes does actually work in conflictive situations. Her husband was reminding her that, although they had different opinions, she had to remember to honor his, listen to his, and consider the possibility of accepting his. He understood that he might not get his way, but he was asking for the conflict to be positive in nature.

Putting the critic on hold is a way to quicken the pace of collaboration. Think about the vegetable scene again. You are onstage in front of an audience that is expecting a performance right now! You didn't know they would suggest vegetables, and it surprised you. You'd certainly rather pick a subject that you know more about or think might be easier to use as a comic foundation. You are feeling pretty uncomfortable already, but something has to happen. If you don't do something with your troupe now, the entire show, and all the money invested in the venue and rehearsals, lights and attendants, will go out the window. The audience will demand its money back, bad reviews will circulate about your lack of professionalism, and the theater could close. By not falling prey to the critic, you can get the show rolling immediately.

Putting the critic on hold is one of the toughest demands of Yes! Space. It requires adjusting and changing your mind, your opinion, and your actions. It can be difficult even for trained improvisers, because the unexpected can really surprise and throw a person off. I've been surprised many times onstage when a troupe member introduced something I didn't expect or like. But I know I have to adjust and keep the reality working onstage. Maybe I'm pantomiming digging a hole but my troupe member looks at my movements and interprets something else. She says, "Rowing a boat can be such good exercise." I want to feel mad that she misinterpreted my intentions; I want to take control of the scene. But in Yes! Space I've got to put my critic on hold. I've got to dump my idea and justify the fact that we are now in a boat.

In real-life situations, I've struggled with this part of Yes! Space. When someone tells me something I don't agree with, my improviser's reflex pushes me to say, "Yes!" But then I pause, because even though I've followed through on the first aspect of Yes! Space (saying yes), my brain needs time to adjust to the new reality and to put my critic on hold. I have to think to myself, "OK, I didn't expect that idea and I don't like it right off the bat. However, it is valid, and this person deserves the chance to air the idea with someone who will support it in a positive way." After I've quieted the screaming critic, I can keep moving forward. The critic will have her chance to speak later.

It's interesting to note that following through on these concepts is easier at work or onstage than at home. I've always believed that if you can put a management or interpersonal concept to the test at home, you can make it work anywhere. For instance, I once returned from conducting a workshop focused on Yes! Space when my daughter, Kate, who was four years old at the time, had a friend over. The kids were happily engaged in the basement and as I cooked dinner I noticed out of the corner of my eye that Kate was running up and down the stairs. First she changed into her bathing suit, and then she was carrying different toys down from her room. I heard laughing and felt confident that all was well. Then, about twenty minutes later, Kate's friend came up and announced, "Kate is pouring buckets of water into the playroom. Is that OK?" I ran down to discover about an inch and a half of standing water in our slightly sunken basement playroom. In my greatest moment of self-control ever, I put my critic on hold. The critic wanted to scream, "What are you doing?! You've ruined our basement and your toys! Get to your room right now! Time out!"

Instead, I tried to think about the lessons I had just been espousing and I said, "Kate, darling, can you help me understand why you poured water into your playroom?" And my little girl said, "Oh, Mommy, remember yesterday you said you were so tired of winter and missed the pool? See, I made a pool right here, and we can go swimming soon and you'll be happy!"

I'm so glad I didn't let the critic speak first. Granted, it was a terrible cleanup job, but Kate and I did it together and we both learned a few things that afternoon. I learned that understanding underlying motivations is key to building relationships, and she learned that water does not work everywhere.

Make It Public

The last and most powerful way to create Yes! Space is to make it public. By entering Yes! Space with at least one other person, the event becomes public. However, it also involves some risk, because it forces us to take action on our positive intentions. We may want to support others' actions or ideas, but until we publicly engage, we have not shared that power.

Yes! Space can be an individual activity. We can have immediate positive thoughts, say yes to occurrences and unexpected events in our lives, and put the critic on hold in the case of our own ideas and what we see and hear. However, Yes! Space in its truest improvisational sense is a team experience. We engage and risk together, and when we involve even one other person we make it public.

There's a very simple wrap-up game my ensemble plays in our workshops. We stand in a circle. One person turns to the person on his or her right. The two people make eye contact, raise their fists in the air, and shout "Yes!" simultaneously. Then the second person turns to the right, makes eye contact with a new person, and together they shout "Yes!" The yes goes all the way around the circle, speeding up and gaining volume as it goes. The people laugh and watch, anticipating the moment they'll join the yes circle as well. At the end, we all shout "Yes!" one last time together, facing the middle and watching one another. When I ask participants "Where is the Yes! Space in this game?" they move to the middle of the circle. The entire environment, the whole room and all of us in it, is part of the Yes! Space. We just created it. By paying it forward and giving the yes to each member of the group, we created organizational Yes! Space. We have made it completely public and involved everyone in the room.

This game is a metaphor for the energy and benefit of Yes! Space in an organization. When we make it public, we are not only sharing; we are also reflecting the positivity in ourselves. Making Yes! Space public supports the idea of a place where ideas are heard.

When people feel that they are heard, that their ideas are considered and vetted, they want to continue to contribute. Public yes is elemental in creating a trusting, positive, and innovative environment.

I once worked with the CEO of a biopharmaceutical research company. He shared with me that he sometimes hesitated to compliment his direct reports. "I don't want to be seen as playing favorites. I demand a lot from all of my direct reports, and I want to be fair." I talked to him about making it public and about the fact that support, when made public, actually benefits everyone. Keeping silent to be "fair" actually withholds important feedback that people need to hear. We worked on ways that he could mention and compliment exceptional effort whenever he saw it. We soon found that when behaviors were illuminated and commented upon by this important leader, everyone began to engage in more exceptional behaviors. There was a greater environment of trust and those direct reports, in turn, began to support their own reports more vocally.

The act of making it public also is the cornerstone of organizational transformation. There is no way that new concepts and behaviors can be repeated and their trust benefits reaped until there is visibility. Everyone needs to start doing and saying. After teams begin to publicly see each other saying yes and putting the critic on hold, they in turn will exhibit those behaviors. It's just so easy. Walk through these three steps the next time someone says, "I have a crazy idea," say yes, put the critic on hold, and make it public.

You'll be standing in Yes! Space.

How Yes! Space Applies to Business

In our example vegetable scene onstage, the improv troupe and the audience have decided that vegetables will be the topic for the show. Think about that. A roomful of people have decided that they are willing to watch a performance about vegetables. Vegetables! The most hated word in a four year-old's vocabulary. A subject for nutrition, not performance. Yet here we all are, saying yes to this crazy idea. In the interest of comedy, we are willing to suspend our penchant for results, logic, and reason. The question is: How is that important to our actual lives?

How would it feel to have the entire office shout "Yes!" after all of your suggestions? Probably unreal, like you're in a funny commercial. Or wry, like you're in the classic scene from *When Harry Met Sally*. Or maybe great? It might make you want to contribute again. It might make you feel like a creative, intelligent person.

My company has an exercise in which volunteers brainstorm about a crazy idea and the entire room responds by shouting "Yes!" after every idea, no matter how unusual. I've facilitated this exercise over 300 times and the volunteers always comment on how energized they felt, how smart they felt, how the flow of ideas sped up as the exercise progressed. The people in the audience always comment on how much they wanted to jump in with their ideas, how fun it was to watch and shout "Yes!" along with the volunteers. And in almost every session, an audience member will say, "At the beginning, I was so glad I didn't volunteer to stand up there. Yet, by the middle of the exercise, I was wishing I could play, too." As the exercise progresses, people want to contribute, they want to be part of the solution, they want to be a leader.

Doesn't that sound like an employee or colleague you'd like to have? Because the format of the game demands that all contributions be greeted with yes, volunteers can trust that they will not be criticized, no matter what happens. They enjoy all three aspects of Yes! Space: their team says yes to every idea, all critics are put on hold because no evaluation or critique is allowed, and the Yes! Space is made entirely public because the brainstorming and responses are done together. In the space of a simple improv game, Yes! Space and very high levels of trust are built.

Here's the tough part: For years, I've been conducting an informal survey after the yes game. In every group I facilitate, I ask the participants how many times in their professional career they've had someone support them as strongly as we did in this exercise. How many times has a manager or colleague smiled, slapped you on the back, or exclaimed, "Wow! That was a great idea! Yes!"? In over 300 sessions, with anywhere from 15 to 100 participants in the room, I've had exactly three people say they had experienced a strong yes at work.

Three people.

One of the three people was a woman who said a boss had been so thrilled by her idea that he hooted "Yahoo!" right outside her cubicle, then told everyone that she had thought of a great cost-saving initiative. She was so energized and thrilled by it that she realized she wanted to contribute even more to her team. She found herself arriving at work early and diving in with gusto for almost a month. It made her feel valued, smart.

If you are a leader or manager, it's time to assess the effect of your communication on the morale of your team. Count the number of times in the past week you have told peers, reports, or colleagues that their idea was extraordinary or their contribution valued. When do you say yes? Are you setting a public example of Yes! Space? Albert Schweitzer once said,

"Example is not the main thing in influencing others. It is the only thing." People learn and change by seeing others do. By saying yes to ideas and contributions, just long enough to enable them to breathe and live for a while, you take a break from the critic ruling your interactions, and your positive example creates safety, trust, and collaboration among your team. Unfortunately, according to my informal survey, Yes! Space is an exception rather than a rule. Everyone wants engaged employees who care, who give discretionary effort, and who go above and beyond. Lots of time and money is spent surveying and defining how engaged we and our associates are and how we might improve performance. Can it really be as simple as saying yes?

A 2001 paper from the Consortium for Research on Emotional Intelligence in Organizations found that for every 1 percent improvement in the service climate (a company in a good mood), there's a 2 percent increase in revenue.[6] This study, conducted by Benjamin Schneider at the University of Maryland, looked at banks, insurance companies, call centers, and hospitals. Can you believe that? By simply raising the mood, positive encouragement, and emotional stability of your team by 1 percent, you can increase your revenues by 2 percent.

So, if you took a little time to say yes, put the critic on hold, and make it public, what could that accomplish? It could make your associates feel heard and valuable. It could create a sense of stability, confidence, and well-being across the office environment. It could improve your bottom line. Could any of us do that tomorrow, or even today? The answer is yes! Another study, conducted by HealthStream Research, found that improving the relationship between managers and employees, and inserting positivity and recognition of achievement, reduced turnover at a major healthcare system from 32.5 percent to 12.7 percent in just three years.[7] Management started to say thank you (which is another way of saying yes to a contribution). They put their critics on hold and looked for the best in people rather than the worst. And they made it public by giving those people rewards and recognition for their achievements.

A Yes! Space Place

We work with one of the largest scientific organizations on the globe, and this organization is the first and only corporate setting where our yes game was received with complete understanding. As a matter of fact, in piloting a new training, the stakeholders told us that

---

[6] Daniel Goleman, Richard Boyatzis, and Annie McKee, *Primal Leadership: Learning to Lead with Emotional Intelligence* (Boston: Harvard Business School Publishing, 2002).

[7] Adrian Gostick and Chester Elton, *The Carrot Principle: How the Best Managers Use Recognition to Engage Their People, Retain Talent, and Accelerate Performance* (New York: Free Press, 2007).

saying yes, accepting new and crazy ideas, was an ingrained part of their culture. They were old pros at saying yes, putting the critic on hold, and making it public. Therefore, they wanted to delve into a different aspect of improv. When I asked about this part of their culture, I was told with a smile, "It's our mission to be great scientists and innovators. It's what we bring to our clients. If we were to be so arrogant as to mistrust a weird idea, or not give our people space to explore in a positive environment, we'd never be where we are today." An improviser's yes is exactly the same yes my client uses with its researchers. It encourages their best and brightest to run with new ideas and concepts.

That conversation felt so good, it was like being back onstage with my favorite improv ensemble. I was among friends. Consequently, my company went on to do very cutting-edge work with this scientific client over several years. Their sensibility for Yes! Space allowed us to take great risk and to enjoy great reward in our client-consultant relationship.

Now let me share what several of my other clients and friends said before we began working with this organization:

"Good luck with that one. Scientists are so linear; they'll never get your stuff."

"Are you kidding? You're working with them? I doubt the improv thing will go well over there."

"There's no chance those rocket scientists will want to step outside the box."

Sometimes I wonder how many people have been talked out of great accomplishments, great relationships, or great adventure because they couldn't get a simple yes. Let's take a look at how another company used Yes! Space to accelerate its business process. It was a simple change, a small change, and the benefits have been huge.

Yes! Space Case Study: NBBJ

NBBJ is a global architecture firm whose vision is to shape a future that enhances life and inspires human potential and spirit through design. Its U.S. division, Studio 20, engaged ImprovEdge over a number of years to lead team retreats and long-term leadership development programs for its architects, designers, and administrators.

The idea of Yes! Space, with its energy, humor, and power, really appealed to the studio's personnel. They are a collection of incredibly intelligent, creative people, and their grasp of the components of Yes! Space was impressive. They were able to immediately embrace the behaviors of saying yes, putting the critic on hold, and making it public. In fact, it became common language within the studio: "I need a little Yes! Space in this conversation" or "My critic is screaming. Could you help me put it on hold?" or "I need to make it public and bounce around some ideas. Can you share some Yes! Space with me?"

Saying Yes at NBBJ

One of NBBJ's Studio 20 core team members realized that the organization had an issue with its charrettes. A charrette is a public forum for an architect or designer to show his or her new work. Picture boards are displayed and people walk around looking at the designs and making comments. It's a key part of the process of reaching both client and design goals. This NBBJ leader had noticed that the architect or designer whose work was displayed often was silent for most of the charrette. He also began to notice that, following a charrette, the designer would return with work that had been totally redone, rather than preserving initial strengths and just fixing weaknesses. He watched and realized that, in the course of a charrette, 90 percent of the comments from attendees comprised criticism or suggestions for change. The architect or designer wasn't hearing about what he or she had done right!

It's an unfortunate assumption: We believe that if we don't comment on positive details a person will automatically understand that those parts are fine. However, after taking such a beating, the architect or designer often went back and changed everything, feeling he or she had been a failure. The leader realized that the organization needed to mindfully create some Yes! Space. He decided to say yes to recognizing the issue: Yes, there is something that we can change here.

Putting the Critic on Hold at NBBJ

The core team leader approached his colleagues and described what he saw. He made his concerns public. It was a little difficult for them to hear at first. Charrettes are an important part of their work, and the setup and process were quite ingrained. However, they put their critics on hold and realized exactly what they needed to do for their designers, who were suffering from a surfeit of criticism. Basically, the entire studio needed to put its critics on hold for the good of progress, design, and employee engagement. The studio's leaders entered into a collaborative conversation and came up with a solution.

Making It Public at NBBJ

Through executive collaboration, followed by all-studio collaboration, Studio 20 agreed to invoke an initial period of Yes! Space at the beginning of every charrette. Reviewers were asked to put their critic on hold and first to speak publicly about what they liked, the strengths, and the positive aspects of a design. This Yes! Space is a highly public exchange of support, encouragement, and focus on design strengths. The new process has built trust and communication within the team, and designs now move forward at a faster rate. Collaboration has improved, and the team has even introduced the concept of Yes! Space into its client meetings. Entire projects move forward faster.

All it took was a simple change. Just a few minutes of behaving like improvisers up front and then entire projects move forward more quickly and efficiently. So many people think that change has to be uncomfortable, time consuming, and difficult, but all it took at NBBJ was 10 minutes of group Yes! Space. They have saved hours of designer time, thousands of dollars of wasted effort, and have avoided many disappointed designers and clients.

Yes! Space Behaviors

It's time to think about the most basic behaviors we can put into place to practice Yes! Space. These are simple things you can do right now, today, to bring positivity to work.

- Say yes. Practice the reflex of responding with the word *yes* after contributions: "Yes, John. Tell me more about that."
- Put the critic on hold. Slow down and temporarily suspend judgment. Listen to conversations and stay with the speaker. Don't let your predispositions decide your response or take you out of the moment. If you don't like something you hear, just say yes and keep nodding and listening. Try to do it just once today.
- Make it public. If you like someone's work, tell them. If they exceed expectations, tell the team. If they make a superstar move, tell the organization.

It worked for NBBJ and it can work for you. The following exercise is another great way to bring Yes! Space into your everyday work.

Yes! Space Exercise—Fabulous Conference Calls[8]

Conference calls can be a great tool. Unfortunately, we know how common it is to multitask during a call—put it on mute, leave the room, write an email. So, how can we make conference calls more useful? It can be especially tough when you are the one in charge of organizing or leading conference calls. In this activity, you get to share the responsibility for the call. Participants will feel accountable and respected, and they'll see just how worthwhile the call really can be. Better yet, they may even stop checking email.

---

[8] Adapted from Karen Hough's Yes! Deck, available from www.improvedge.com.

Get Ready

1. Invite as few participants as possible. The fewer the people, the easier it is to engage everyone.
2. Engage the senses. Send something tactile through the mail for participants to hold. Or send a piece of candy to eat. Paint a picture with words. Use colors, describe things graphically, tell stories.

Get Set

3. Divide the agenda into parts and send a section to each team member. Brief them, give them time to prepare, then have them take ownership of that section. Remember, if 90 percent of your contribution is questions, then 90 percent of the call will be others talking.
4. Prepare a list of participants so that, during the call, you can call everyone by name and ask them to comment.

Go

5. At the beginning of the call, have everyone share something from work that recently has gone well. At the end of the call, have everyone commit to take an action based on the call.
6. Use Yes! Space. Whenever someone contributes, even in the slightest way, thank them, support them, respond positively. They will continue to contribute.

About the Author

Karen Hough is the founder and CEO of ImprovEdge and the author of *The Improvisation Edge: Secrets to Building Trust and Radical Collaboration at Work* published by Berrett-Koehler. You can find her website at www.improvedge.com. This chapter was excerpted from *The Improvisation Edge* with permission.

Chapter 26

Engaging Management: Put an End to Employee Engagement

David Zinger

Editor's Note

David Zinger is absolutely right when he suggests that managers put an end to employee engagement. We are programming the magic right out of work, and our emotions, passions, and drive are going right with it. In this highly useful (albeit counterintuitive) chapter, David shares ways that managers can emerge and move away from engagement programs and toward creating workplaces that draw people in.

> *"What we call the beginning is often the end*
> *and to make an end is to make a beginning.*
> *The end is where we start from."*
>
> —T. S. Eliot, "Little Gidding"

We need to put an end to employee engagement. I can imagine I hear a cadre of managers cheering at the suggested end of another task on their bulging to-do list, while another group of managers look quizzically at the statement because they are just launching employee engagement efforts in their organization after receiving dismal survey results paired with the strong business case for engagement. Employee engagement needs to end by becoming woven into the fabric of work so that it does not fade away when managers are cajoled by management consultants to jump on the latest and greatest new bandwagon.

Begin With the End

Stephen Covey has recommended that we develop the habit of beginning with the end in mind in his popular book, *The Seven Habits of Highly Effective People*. This chapter will help you develop the understanding and approach to end engagement well. There will be an outline of the current state of employee engagement, a definition fused with a model of engagement, and 12 steps you can take to ensure engagement ends well.

An Engagement Surge

There has been a surge of interest in employee engagement. As founder and community manager of the Employee Engagement Network, I have witnessed a rise in membership from a small group of about 10 in February 2007 to over 4,200 by September 2011. Every day in social media an author, a consultant, or a leader is extolling the benefits of employee engagement while tweets, blog posts, whitepapers, and workshops proliferate. Much of the former work on motivation, branding, and change management is being subsumed under the catchphrase of employee engagement. Meanwhile, skeptics have also pounced on employee engagement work as a fad, bandwagon, or scam (Harquail, 2010).

Successful Engagement

In the United Kingdom, David MacLeod and Nita Clarke completed a well-written, comprehensive report on *Engaging for Success: Enhancing Performance Through Employee Engagement* (2010). This comprehensive and informative report based on in-depth interviews and analysis embraced a variety of perspectives on employee engagement. In determining if employee engagement mattered they concluded:

> Our answer is an unequivocal yes. In the course of the past eight months we have seen many examples of companies and organisations where performance and profitability have been transformed by employee engagement; we have met many employees who are only too keen to explain how their working lives have been transformed; and we have read many studies which show a clear correlation between engagement and performance—and most importantly between improving engagement and improving performance.

This report led the British Prime Minister, David Cameron, to form a task force in 2011 led by MacLeod and Clarke to increase employee engagement throughout private industry and the government in the United Kingdom.

A Comprehensive Definition

We need a definition of engagement more aligned with the overall leadership, management, and functioning of an organization. An integrated definition would include engagement in results, strategy, and performance while also looking at community, development, and well-being. This is to ensure that engagement is not dismissed as buying donuts or having staff perform in a happy YouTube recruiting dance. One of the four drivers of engagement articulated by the MacLeod report was engaging managers who offer clarity and appreciation of employees' effort and contribution, who treat their people as individuals, and who ensure that work is organized efficiently and effectively so that employees feel they are valued, and equipped and supported to do their job. Here is a definition I crafted to embrace the integration of engagement into work and management:

> *Employee engagement* is the art and science of engaging people in authentic and recognized connections to strategy, roles, performance, organization, community, relationship, customers, development, energy, and well-being as we leverage, sustain, and transform our work connections into results.

The definition can also be visualized in the model (Figure 26-1). The definition and model integrate employee engagement into the normal practices of management, and high levels of employee engagement can be reached by practicing effective basic management.

Don't

Managers don't need additional engagement initiatives heaped on their plate of demands already overflowing beyond any reasonable ability for completion. They don't need to be told they are responsible for engagement of their staff and that low engagement scores are their fault. Managers don't need to fly to another initiative like moths to a light only to get burned when results are not achieved. Managers don't need another two-day workshop taking them away from their work and then telling them they have to do six new things when they return to work while their work falls further behind because they were at a seminar.

12 Invitations

Rather, here are 12 shifts managers can make to ensure engagement ends well. These shifts will help managers get things done through integration rather than addition, while offering a sustainable approach to work. I encourage you to slowly contemplate and judiciously practice this list of invitations rather than feel compelled to follow them as a quick fix or a tyranny of tips. The art of successful management is weaving together approaches, strategies, and tactics in your own mindful management tapestry that works for your reports, organization, customers, and you.

Figure 26-1. The Zinger Model

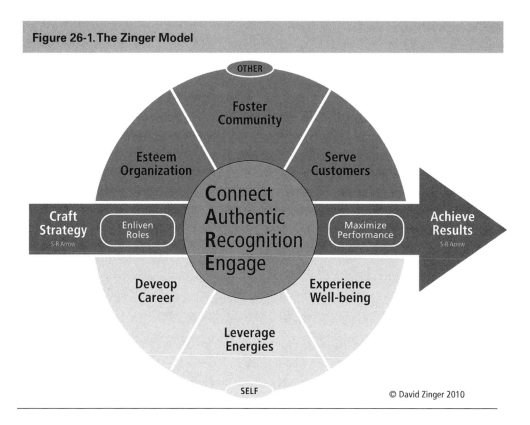

© David Zinger 2010

1. **Be the employee you already are.** Fully recognize that as a manager you are an employee. There is no "them" in engagement, so be cautious of creating a division between yourself and your reports. Engagement is connection, and connection is frayed by holding an us/them mentality. Accentuate the "we" in engagement and minimize the "me" by knowing who you are as a manager is co-created by whom you manage. You don't have to be best friends with the people who report to you. You need to foster mutual respect and interest while acknowledging that you are joined by your humanness as you fulfill different roles and functions within the organization.

2. **No problem.** Stop viewing employee engagement as a problem to be solved. Engagement is an experience to be lived rather than a problem that needs to be solved. Engagement is a human endeavor, and engagement can enhance not only productivity but employee well-being, community mobilization, and career development in the workplace. Problems are something we want to eliminate while engagement is something we want to integrate by being woven into work.

3. **Engage.** Transform the noun of engagement into the verb of engage. Engagement is not a score on an annual survey; engagement is the day-to-day connections all employees have with their progress, results, work, organization, customers, and peers. Look at daily actions and interactions as you concern yourself less with static state engagement and more with the everyday dynamic flow of multiple connections at work. Engagement is not something we finally achieve. Engagement is connecting daily to the key components of work.

4. **Replace imposition with invitation.** Command and control are well past their due dates. We need to see ourselves as management hosts. Hostmanship is the art of invitational welcoming based on serving, responsibility, wholeness, caring, knowledge, and dialogue (www.hostmanship.com). Managers have legitimate authority and the right to have expectations for performance. Make your requests less imposition and more invitation. Ask more and know less. Be tentative. Add more "white space" for employee input and responses. Offer compelling invitations and experience how work changes as you think of yourself as a host as opposed to a commander or guard. Of course employees can be invited to leave an organization when there is a poor fit or poor performance. Some people believe that employee engagement is exemplified by discretionary effort. I believe it is important to recognize that all effort is discretionary and that we play a role in helping all employees, including ourselves, to use good discretion in making effective and efficient work choices.

5. **Accountability on the level.** Managers are not responsible for each employee's engagement. Employees are responsible for their own engagement just as managers are responsible for their own engagement. Yet managers are accountable for results and relationships, so they need to check *in* with employees rather than check *up* on them. When we check in, we level with employees. When we check up, we tend to exercise a power differential, and employees will often feel micromanaged. In the age of engage we need to be on the level with people and to hold them accountable by checking in frequently and powerfully to stay connected to how they are performing and how we can help.

6. **Co-create work processes.** Work is co-created. To foster full engagement we need to draw out the creativity of the worker and to get full input about the work from the person closest to the job. With one billion mobile workers we need to know that we can't be on top of everything. If you are struggling to get everyone on the same page, ask yourself if you gave everyone an opportunity to write on that page. For example, have you considered having employees formulate the question on the next employee engagement survey? For another example of co-created work, the Center for Positive Organizational Scholarship has been advocating job

crafting where the nature of the job is co-created between the employee and organizations to best meet the needs of both.

7. **Strong management.** Peter Drucker, in a 2005 *Harvard Business Review* article, declared how important it was to manage ourselves and to know our strengths. Tom Rath in *Strengths Finder 2.0* declared that those who focus on their strengths every day are six times as likely to be engaged in their jobs, and that if a manager focuses on an employee's strengths the chance of that employee being actively disengaged is 1 percent. Do you know your strengths? Do you foster the strengths of those you manage? Are you leveraging your strengths on a daily basis in the service of others? Are your strengths woven into how you manage and work? Strong management is authentic strength-based management.

8. **Ensure progress.** Teresa Amabile and Steven Kramer wrote *The Progress Principle.* Progress is the alchemy that transforms work into engagement. Progress ranked higher than collaboration, recognition, and support for motivating knowledge workers. In their 2010 *Harvard Business Review* breakthrough idea, they conclude: "This brings us to perhaps the strongest advice we offer from this study: Scrupulously avoid impeding progress by changing goals autocratically, being indecisive, or holding up resources. Negative events generally have a greater effect on people's emotions, perceptions, and motivation than positive ones, and nothing is more demotivating than a setback—the most prominent type of event on knowledge workers' worst days."

9. **Hold frequent conversation.** Engaged managers hold conversations rather than issuing orders. Engagement is connection, and the glue of connection between people is conversation. Conversations can be as short as 45 seconds yet let the other person know you care about them and you care about what they are interested in while also offering your point of view. If you need to build your workplace conversation skills to handle variances, difficulties, and differences, I recommend two books: *Crucial Conversations* (Patterson et al., 2002) and *Crucial Confrontations* (Patterson et al., 2004).

10. **Energize through high-quality connections.** Dr. Jane Dutton demonstrated that the single biggest energizer for organizations is high-quality interactions. Douglas Conant, the former CEO of Campbell's Soup, outlined something similar in *TouchPoints.* Make the most of short interactions and you will find those interactions energize you, the other, and the organization. We do this even with brief connections with others through respectful engagement, task enabling, trusting, and minimizing corrosive connections. Never miss the opportunity to engage with others in the living moments at work.

11. **Foster organizational community.** Engagement has the chance to contribute to the shift we are seeing from hierarchical organization to community. Henry

Mintzberg (2009) believed that managers must lead, leaders must manage, and we are moving to "communityship." Our work is embedded in community, and engagement will be enhanced as we foster, build, and work through community. There is a strong power in a community mobilized to achieve goals that will benefit all.

12. **Practice engagement.** This has been a range of 11 potential invitations to put a good end to engagement. Do not accept all invitations at once. Engagement will end well when we take it one step at a time and our efforts are integrated rather than added. Can you say no to something you already do to say a bigger yes to engagement? Work with one invitation at a time by reading more about it, reflect on the implications and actions required, and ensure that you take action to engage. Small is the new significant when we fully stand for the significance of integrated and robust engagement at work.

Conclusion

Let's ensure employee engagement ends well. The term *employee engagement* was necessary as a focal point to move us toward more connected and integrated work. But ultimately, engagement is not an extra to be heaped on a manager's long list of duties; rather in this decade management is engagement, and engagement is work.

Management

Command and control
lose their seat
to conversation and collaboration.

Organizations humanize into communities
while impositions
quiet respectfully into invitations.

Hierarchy is redrawn on the napkin
into a matrix.

Leadership levels
while management spreads.

Our white space decade ahead
invites us to get more from management
than we ever imagined.

—David Zinger (2011, p. 9)

References and Resources

Amabile, T., and S. Kramer. (2011). *The Progress Principle.* Boston: Harvard Business School Publishing.

Amabile, T., and S. Kramer. (2010). What Really Motivates Workers (#1 Breakthrough Ideas for 2010). *Harvard Business Review,* 88:1, 44–45.

Conant, D., and M. Norgaard. (2011). *TouchPoints.* San Francisco: Jossey-Bass.

Covey, S. (1989). *The Seven Habits of Highly Effective People.* New York: Free Press.

Drucker, P. (2005). Managing Oneself. In *Harvard Business Review* (January). Boston: Harvard Business School Publishing.

Dutton, J. (2003). *Energize Your Workplace.* San Francisco: Jossey-Bass.

Harquail, C.V. (2010). 3 Reasons Why Employee Engagement Is a Scam. On "Authentic Organizations." Retrieved from http://authenticorganizations.com/harquail/2010/05/10/3-reasons-why-employee-engagement-is-a-scam/.

MacLeod, D., and N. Clarke. (2010). Engaging for Success: Enhancing Performance Through Employee Engagement. Retrieved from www.bis.gov.uk/files/file52215.pdf.

Mintzberg, H. (2009). *Managing.* San Francisco: Berrett-Koehler.

Patterson, K., J. Grenny, R. McMillan, and A. Switzler. (2002). *Crucial Conversations.* New York: McGraw-Hill.

Patterson, K., J. Grenny, R. McMillan, and A. Switzler. (2004). *Crucial Confrontations.* New York: McGraw-Hill.

Rath, T. (2007). *Strengths Finder 2.0.* New York: Gallup Press.

Zinger, D. (2011). *Assorted Zingers.* Winnipeg, Canada: self-published by David Zinger.

About the Author

David Zinger is a sought-after author, educator, coach, and consultant focused intently on employee engagement. David fuses a prairie presence with a global reach. He has worked from Winnipeg to Warsaw and Wales, from British Columbia to Barcelona, and from Saskatoon, Saskatchewan, to San Antonio, Texas. He is the founder of the Employee Engagement Network and has written *Assorted Zingers: Poems and Cartoons to Take a Bite Out of Work* and *Zengage: How to Get More Into Your Work to Get More Out of Your Work*. You can find his website at www.davidzinger.com.

Chapter 27

Creating Winning Teams

Vikram Bector

Editor's Note

I remember when I first met Vikram Bector at an ASTD conference committee meeting that I was impressed with his depth of knowledge about management. In this detail-rich chapter, Vikram offers a vision and blueprint for how you can build and develop great teams. Managers exist for their teams, to serve them, and to enable their results. And your team deserves your focus, attention, and best efforts.

In an organizational context, one starts thinking of building a team as the scope and size of work becomes complex, much beyond what an individual can do. As the work output of an individual or a group of individuals starts to improve in qualitative and quantitative terms, more work comes their way. As the quality and the value of the work output increase, the clients begin to see these individuals or groups as credible. This marks the beginning of a virtuous cycle as shown in Figure 27-1. This trend is seen across sectors, whether it is the work done by knowledge workers or those working in the manufacturing sector. This trend is also seen in case of work done for internal or external clients. It is common sense that top-quality work enhances the credibility of an individual or a group of individuals leading to more work.

There comes a point when there is a need to increase the team size as the flow of work to this group of individuals increases. There may be a few exceptions to this virtuous cycle, for example when the economy is in recession or when there are other factors that depress

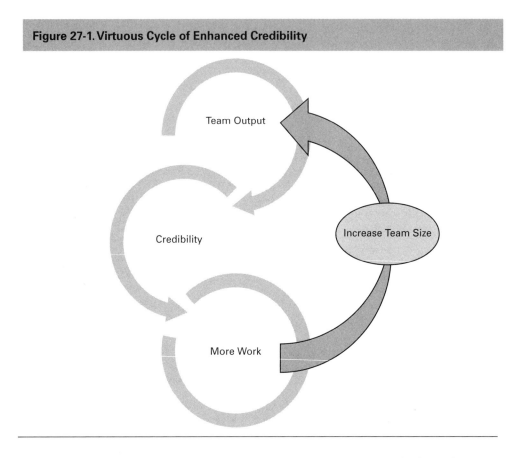

Figure 27-1. Virtuous Cycle of Enhanced Credibility

the demand of goods and services. Typically, as companies enter a growth phase, there is an increase in the number and size of these groups or teams.

Notice that we are still talking about a group of individuals and not a team. So let us examine the differences between the two social entities, that is, a group versus a team.

A Group of Individuals Versus a Team

I attend a yoga class in the morning, and so do 20 other insomniacs. Would you call us a team or a group? Merely referring to a collection of people or employees as a team doesn't make them one. The first question to ask is, Is this a team or a group? Typically, a team shares leadership and is interdependent, meaning team members depend on each other for information, services, or products to achieve a team goal. A leader (manager, supervisor) spearheads a group; members work on their own most of the time with little or no dependence on other members to do their job. All of us in the yoga class work on the postures together as a group, and yet each one is seeking a personal benefit. The collective following of instructions in a yoga class may be seen as a group effort, but it cannot be labeled as a team effort. Therefore, a group and a team are different and serve different purposes.

Stephen P. Robbins, author of *Essentials of Organizational Behavior*, talks about effective teams having a common and meaningful purpose that provides direction, momentum, and commitment for members. Many people use the words *team* and *group* interchangeably, but there are actually a number of differences between a team and a group in real-world applications. A team's strength and effectiveness depends on the commonality of purpose, the relationship between individual members, and the willingness of each team member to give his or her best. A group's strength may come from sheer volume or the willingness to carry out a single leader's commands. A group of rioters could be together to maximize their gains while there is anarchy in a city. It is often much easier to form a group than a team.

If you had a room filled with professional accountants, for example, they could be grouped according to gender, experience, fields of expertise, age, or other common factors. Forming a group based on a certain commonality is not particularly difficult, although the effectiveness of the groups may vary. A group's interpersonal dynamics can range from complete compatibility to complete intolerance, which could make consensus building very difficult for a leader.

A team, on the other hand, can be much more difficult to form. Members of a team may be selected for their diversity and complementary skills, not a single commonality. A business team during mergers and acquisitions may consist of an accountant, a business development person, a human resources executive, and an information technology professional. Each member of the team has a purpose and a function within that team, so the overall success depends on functional interpersonal dynamic. There is usually not as much room for conflict when working as a winning team.

Having made the distinction between teams and groups, let us delve into the recipe of creating a winning team. The recipe is based on my experience of over 20 years, having managed diverse global teams across multiple locations for a large global IT company, a large multinational consulting company, and a global Indian conglomerate. As a credentialed executive coach I have had the good fortune of coaching and leading diverse teams—diverse in all aspects such as gender, culture, race, and age. These winning teams have led their respective corporations to outstanding international and national recognition as best-in-class learning organizations. The recipe of success is based on a winning mindset, which is about recognizing and celebrating similarities between people.

Winning Mindset—Respect, Fairness, and Honesty

Daniel Gilbert, in his book *Stumbling on Happiness*, writes, "If you spent all day sorting grapes into different colors, shapes, and kinds, you'd become one of those annoying grapeophiles who talks endlessly about the nuances of flavour and the permutations of texture. You'd come to think of grapes as infinitely varied, and you'd forget that almost all of the really important information about a grape can be deduced from the simple fact of its grapehood."

My belief in creating and managing winning teams has been somewhat similar. I have always believed in understanding, appreciating, and celebrating similarities among team members as the winning mindset. It is so important to recognize and nurture this winning mindset. We spend so much time outlining and identifying differences between human beings that we have stopped understanding the underlying similarities. We miss the connections that we have with each other and the opportunity to leverage similarities for creating winning outcomes. This is the winning mindset that has helped me create winning teams and indeed is the vital difference between teams and winning teams.

There is so much management literature, consulting advice, and money riding on teaching us all how different we are from each other, and what I have outlined in the paragraph above may not find favor with all readers. This is truer today than ever before. In a party, we feel agitated if someone else is wearing the same tie or dress. In a team, we feel compelled to look for talent and characteristics that highlight our differences. Let me spend the next page or two sharing with you all how similar we are and how the underlying similarities can be leveraged to create winning teams. It is my belief that if a manager does not look for, nurture, or perpetuate these similarities within his or her team, there is virtually no possibility of creating a winning team.

We are more similar than dissimilar; we all breathe air, drink water, eat food, have lungs, and desire fame; and the list of similarities is endless. A manager with a winning mindset will be able to create a winning team where people would readily give their best. Let us spend some more time talking through these similarities.

Robert Bolton and Dorothy Grover Bolton researched hundreds of participants in their workshops and inferred that all people wanted to be treated with respect, fairness, and honesty (Figure 27-2).

My own experience in analyzing the employee engagement scores for hundreds of managers across three large corporations bears out the fact that managers who were exemplars score

Figure 27-2. How Everyone Wants to Be Treated

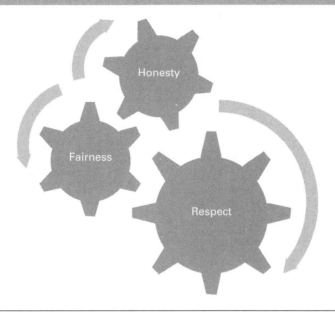

very highly on the above three attributes. It is well known that high engagement scores have a very positive correlation with higher sales, higher customer satisfaction, higher productivity, and lower attrition. Therefore, it makes business sense for managers to adopt a winning mindset and treat their direct reports with respect, fairness, and honesty. Here's what each of these attributes means.

Respect

Great managers treat all team members with respect irrespective of the work done, or the seniority or educational background of each team member. Respect is based on the fact that every other individual is, above all, a person. Respect is essential to building constructive ongoing relationships. The kind of respect we are talking about has nothing to do with competence or incompetence. Some managers feel that a person has to "earn my respect." Since few people live up to their high standards, the majority of people they know are devalued.

Have you ever faced a situation when you were trying to speak to your supervisor after she has given you an appointment, but during which she was busy doing something else, such as attending to emails? That is the moment of disrespect; one feels like a nonentity. Great managers treat everyone with respect and accord dignity. Respect is essential to building constructive ongoing relationships within a winning team.

Fairness

In his book *Conversations With God* (Book 3), Neale Donald Walsch (1998) talks at length about the basic instinct of human beings, that is, fairness. Fairness should not be confused with equality. It is not a basic instinct of all people to seek equality, or to be equal. Indeed, exactly the opposite of this is true. The basic instinct of all human beings is to express uniqueness and not sameness. Creating a society in which two beings are truly equal is not only impossible, but undesirable. We need to create conditions for everyone to excel but not be the same.

Equality of opportunity is what is required, and not equality in fact. This is fairness. Fairness is about mutually beneficial outcomes, about creating "win-win" outcomes or creating conditions that would lead the team and its members to win-win outcomes. After you have come up with what you think is a win-win approach, you can test its fairness by asking yourself a question. Immanuel Kant, a German philosopher and ethicist, taught us to test our behavior with the question, Would I be willing to be a recipient of my action?

Honesty

Honest managers consistently do three things. First, they steadfastly *refuse to make misleading statements*. They don't lie. They don't embellish the facts or twist the truth to their advantage. They do not say that the project is moving along OK when it is in fact behind schedule. This ensures that all members of the team receive the correct information.

Second, forthright people *do not withhold important information*. They don't conceal problems from their team members by a screen of silence. They give straight honest feedback on a timely basis. They are not selective in providing information to a few members and keeping it from others; they share all information that is important for the success of the team.

Finally, honest people are *genuine*; they have no false pretenses. You could use the acronym WYSIWYG for them, that is, what you see is what you get. They are down to earth and are "maskless"—you can see through their personality and do not have to guess their motives.

Treating team members with honesty, respect, and fairness is a winning mindset that provides a strong foundation of success for any manager—new or tenured. This winning mindset appeals to all human beings and builds trust between a manager and the team and within the team members as well.

Having explored the winning mindset let us discuss the other key ingredients of creating winning teams. The charisma of a manager is often cited as the key ingredient to attract people to a winning team. You may have heard or experienced how team members follow a manager to her new organization upon exit. We would try and demystify the charisma of a manager in creating a winning team in the following section. In my experience, behind managerial charisma there is a well-thought-out process.

The Process Behind Managerial Charisma

Creating effective teams has to be a carefully thought-out systematic process. Setting up a work team involves more than just putting together a few people and handing them a task. A team needs an effective team process in place for it to operate to the best of its ability. An effective team process involves providing clarity, proper guidelines for the teamwork, precise role definitions, adequate resources, well-thought-out appraisal systems, reward and recognition systems, and carefully designed training programs. Without a well-thought-out process, a winning team would be a pipe dream. Organizations have to focus on creating a whole system around a team in addition to identifying the right team mix. That's when a team can start functioning effectively. The following checklist is aimed at demystifying the process used by exemplary managers and provides a logical guideline for the steps involved in establishing a winning team. This 13-point checklist has been instrumental in building high-performance teams and has been very helpful and lucky for me, as lucky as the number 13.

13-Point Checklist for Creating an Effective Team Process

1. **Mission clarity:** What are the business objectives behind constituting this team? What do we want the team to accomplish? What should success look like?
2. **Skill set:** What are the necessary qualifications, experience, and expertise? What are the thinking patterns and personality traits necessary to accomplish this task?
3. **Identification and matching:** Who are the people who match the skills that we need on the team?
4. **Performance goals:** What are the specific goals and milestones that the team will work toward within the framework of the overall mission? What are the desired results from the team?
5. **Role definition:** What are the individual roles within the team? What are their responsibilities, and who is expected to perform them?
6. **Ground rules:** What is the day-to-day work system for the team? What is the system for sharing information? How often will the team meet? What is the method to be used for keeping each other informed? What are the procedures at an operational level?

7. **Performance assessment parameters:** What are the performance benchmarks for the individuals in the team and for the team as a whole? What is the appraisal system for the team as a whole and team members individually?

8. **Feedback and communication mechanisms:** What is the process for monitoring the progress of the team, and what kind of feedback is necessary to perform this? How do the members communicate, and what kind of conflict resolution mechanism exists?

9. **Organization input:** What kind of orientation program is necessary for the team? How do we crystallize and communicate the business goals to the team? What are team members' initial and ongoing training needs?

10. **Resources:** What is the support structure that this team requires to help members accomplish their task (financial, manpower, technological, software tools, expert guidance, etc.)?

11. **Recognition and reward:** What is the reward and recognition system for this team as a whole and for all members of the team?

12. **Team building:** What are the team-oriented programs that will be relevant for this team to create cohesion and enhance its performance? How often do we need to conduct these programs? Are the team members having fun, and do they feel energized and engaged while working together?

13. **Speed of decision making and collaboration:** Do the team members make decisions and build consensus, or are all decisions made by the manager?

The 13-point checklist outlined above is meant to help an organization facilitate the team effort and stimulate good work. Most successful teams thrive and excel when they have definite, meaningful, realistic, and measurable performance goals to work toward.

Meaning and Challenge

A manager needs to provide meaning. Each member and the whole team need to feel that they are making a difference in the lives of others. The efforts they make are not just about business success—they are about pride, about having their work mean something to someone. A good manager helps discover what that meaning is and magnify it. This helps the team members to clearly see the value of what they are doing and why it matters. The manager helps the team members feel the pride in their success.

Teams need to feel a sense of accomplishment; they need to see the end result of a project. A manager needs to assign whole projects, not pieces. She or he should let team members carry the project from start to finish. A manager needs to ensure that others know about the finished project and its importance. This would help team members feel the accomplishment of completing something significant. Everyone has limits. But how will team members ever know what their limits are if a manager never assigns them a project that is more difficult than they think they can accomplish? Team members need to learn and grow, to develop and improve. They need to be challenged. Once the challenge has been issued, they need to be assured of your support even if they fail.

Support Structure

Most teams need help in terms of resources, appraisal systems, team-building programs, and rewards, and all work in tandem to facilitate the output of high-performance teams. Assessment and reward are intrinsic to getting the best out of the team process. Any outstanding work done by the team has to receive due recognition. Monitoring individual progress is equally important. Many individuals who are put into teams have the fear that their work will not be noticed and that personal recognition may never come their way. It is therefore important for team leaders to keep track of what each individual is doing within the team.

Ground Rules

Setting the ground rules or team norms or a social agreement is an extremely useful method of organizing how the team members work together. The team members themselves can be encouraged to set out the guidelines before they kick-start the teamwork. Ground rules play a key role in ensuring that the team has certain procedures that all members agree upon and follow. It makes their work more organized, and more importantly, it minimizes the opportunity for interpersonal conflict.

Team Building

Team building has many elements, and some key elements beyond conducting training programs are being discussed hereafter. Laughter is a common language that everybody understands. So if a great manager legitimizes levity among team members, this is likely to reduce stress and build collegial bonds. Creating times for people to laugh together and loosen up also stimulates creativity. Celebration is another important dimension. This can be done by providing a meal or bringing food and celebrating for no special reason than to say thank you to the team. Identifying a theme and asking people to dress to the occasion could be another way to enhance team affinity. A manager should not expect employees to gather after work hours. Most people have family obligations and personal commitments.

Decision Making and Empowerment

This means full delegation. It is about not asking team members to explain every decision and every action. A manager ought to give the team full powers and outline its boundaries on budget, timetable, scope of responsibility, and authority. Beyond meeting with the team at agreed-upon times, and keeping his/her door open in case people need help, a manager gets out of the way.

Motivation and Reward

People do exactly what they are rewarded for. They don't respond to promises, requests, cries, screams, threats, or kindness. They respond to action. It is very important to reward individual members and the entire team for the results that are expected from the team members individually and collectively. When the team rises to the challenge and accomplishes something truly outstanding, a manger must show genuine appreciation for people's efforts, and reward the team accordingly. Let the team experience the respect that the manager has for these significant accomplishments, and make certain others see it as well.

The end goal for a manager should be to build a complete system as described above, which would ensure lasting success for a high-performing team. The 13-point checklist is intended to help create that complete system.

Best Practices in Creating Winning Teams

Given below are some exemplary best practices in my experience of over two decades as a manager and an executive coach. I am grateful to the many outstanding managers and leaders who have been an inspiration for this section. Their work and managerial style has helped many teams around the globe. I hope that these short best practices can serve as on-the-job aids for the readers.

Recruiting the Best Talent and the Right Mix in Your Team

Most great managers take great pains to hire the best possible talent. It is extremely important to hire people who are smarter than you and are experts in their domain. This is the first and the most important ingredient of success. This ensures that as a manager, you are able to focus on doing the work that you have been hired to do. I have often had leaders complain that their team members are not taking the action that they ought to take. As a direct consequence, each manager is doing the job one or two levels below what he or she is supposed to do. As an executive coach, I have often asked managers a simple powerful question, such as: Is he or she the best talent available in the industry for that role? I am alarmed at the number of times the answer is actually a no. I often wonder why these managers are unable to hire top-notch talent. Is it a lack of will, skill, or brand equity of the employer or an insecurity of hiring someone better than themselves? There is no common answer.

It is a known fact that the best talent would like to work for the best managers, and the best managers prefer to work with the best talent. Hiring the best talent takes time and effort, and yet the payback on hiring the best talent is very high.

Peers Choose Their Peers

This practice was widely leveraged by Ed Cohen, the chief learning officer of Satyam Computer Services (a global IT consulting company) and my boss. His contention, which proved right all the time, was that people should have a say in deciding whom they wish to work with. After all, we spend a major portion of our waking hours at work, and it is very important to have a positive chemistry with people who you work with. It is not about forcing friendships at work, but about working with people whom you respect professionally. It is about forging relationships where you could agree to disagree on issues, amicably. There were no surprise additions to the team. At any time, at least six to eight people were involved in the hiring of a peer and would be involved in his or her onboarding. It was no coincidence that the peers would invariably sign up as buddies for the new joinee. Being a part of this learning team was an awesome experience. This is one of the factors that helped the Satyam Learning team win awards such as the ASTD BEST award in 2007, the *Training* magazine Top 125 award, and many more.

While onboarding the best talent, the key is to have the right mix of personality traits and skills on your team. The right mix comes from a mindset of bringing in talented people with diverse strengths.

Leverage the Personality Styles

To be a great manager and create winning teams, a manager needs to understand his or her strengths and personality type. There is a very useful and practical tool based on the research on four personality types by Robert Bolton and Dorothy Grover Bolton. The details of this tool can be found in their book titled *People Styles at Work: Making Bad Relationships Good and Good Relationships Better* (2009).

According to Bolton and Bolton, although every individual is different, most can be grouped into one of four groups: analytical, driver, amiable, and expressive. Here are some basic characteristics of each of these personality styles as shown in Figure 27-3.

> **Analytical:** Analytical people are known for being systematic, well organized, and deliberate. These individuals appreciate facts and information presented in a logical manner as documentation of truth. They enjoy organization and completion of detailed tasks. Others may see them at times as being too cautious, as overly structured, or as people who do things too much "by the book." The words that you could use to describe them are *controlled, orderly, precise, disciplined, deliberate, cautious, diplomatic, systematic, logical,* and *conventional.*

Driver: They thrive on the thrill of the challenge and the internal motivation to succeed. Drivers are practical folks who focus on getting results. They can do a lot in a very short time. They usually talk fast, direct, and to the point. They are often viewed as decisive, direct, and pragmatic. The words that you could use to describe them are *action-oriented, decisive, problem solver, direct, assertive, demanding, risk taker, forceful, competitive, independent, determined,* and *result-oriented.*

Amiable: They are dependable, loyal, and easygoing. They like things that are nonthreatening and friendly. They hate dealing with impersonal details and cold, hard facts. They are usually quick to reach a decision. They are often described as warm and sensitive to the feelings of others. At the same time they may come across as wishy-washy to some. The words that you could use to describe them are *patient, loyal, sympathetic, team person, relaxed, mature, supportive, stable, considerate, empathetic, persevering, trusting,* and *congenial.*

Expressive: They are very outgoing and enthusiastic, with a high energy level. They are also great idea generators, but usually do not have the ability to see the idea through to completion. They enjoy helping others and are particularly fond of socializing. They are usually slow to reach a decision. They are often thought of as talkers, overly dramatic, impulsive, and manipulative. The words that you could use to describe them are *verbal, motivating, enthusiastic, convincing, impulsive, influential, charming, confident, dramatic, optimistic,* and *animated.*

Figure 27-3. The Four Personality Types

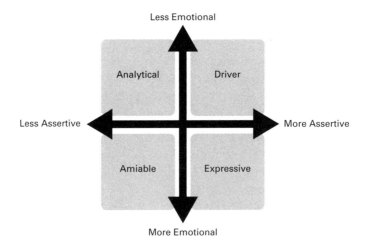

In most cases, you would be able to quickly identify the personality style given the above cues.

If you don't feel that you belong to any one group, don't worry. Many of us don't fit squarely in one group or another. However, we do have one dominant personality style that we use day to day.

A manager needs to know when to leverage the strengths of each type. Recognizing the pros and cons of a specific personality style can help you understand how to better deal with others on the team. Versatility is the ability to communicate with someone else based upon the other person's comfort zone. As a manager you have to master "style flex," which involves tailoring your behavior so the way you work fits better with the other person's style—like a baseball player swinging at different pitches. Style flex is a temporary adjustment of a few behaviors at key times. Style flex is not about conforming to the other person's point of view, giving up your goals or withholding your opinions, or changing the other person. It is about changing yourself for better outcomes. As a manager of a winning team, the primary leverage you have for improving a relationship is your own behavior.

When done in a team, this exercise illuminates each member's style preferences and gives everyone information to adapt and work together more effectively. For most people this creates an "aha" experience that is pivotal in fostering understanding and communication in a winning team.

A Periodic Team "Pulse" Survey

Many winning teams invest the time and effort in generating a team survey. This happens in a couple of different ways. One way is through an initial team survey that generates data on how members perceive team functioning and interactions. A survey could include topics such as commitment, trust, communication, and conflict resolution. The survey is administered at a pre-agreed frequency (say quarterly) to determine progress and team development priorities. Another way to take a team "pulse" is to have periodic frank discussions about what is working and what is not. Managers of large teams often practice regular, informal conversations that keep communication channels open or regularly conduct skip-level meetings.

Navigating the Five Stages of Team Development

You can't expect a new team to perform exceptionally from the very outset. Team formation takes time, and usually follows some easily recognizable stages, as the team journeys from being a group of strangers to becoming a united team with a common goal.

Whether a team is a temporary group or a newly formed permanent team, by understanding the five stages a manager will be able to help it quickly become productive. Psychologist Bruce Tuckman first came up with the memorable phrase "forming, storming, norming, and performing" back in 1965. He used it to describe the path to high performance that most teams follow. Later, he added a fifth stage that he called "adjourning" (and others often call "mourning"—it rhymes better!).

Teams initially go through a "forming" stage in which members are positive and polite. Some members are anxious, as they haven't yet worked out exactly what work the team will involve. Others are simply excited about the task ahead. As manager, you play a dominant role at this stage: Other members' roles and responsibilities are less clear.

This stage is usually fairly short, and may only last for the single meeting at which people are introduced to one another. At this stage there may be discussions about how the team will work, which can be frustrating for some members who simply want to get on with the team task.

Soon, reality sets in, and your team moves into a "storming" phase. Your authority may be challenged as others jockey for position and their roles are clarified. The ways of working start to be defined and, as manager, you must be aware that some members may feel overwhelmed by how much there is to do, or uncomfortable with the approach being used. Some may react by questioning how worthwhile the goal of the team is, and by resisting taking on tasks. This is the stage when many teams fail, and even those that stick with the task may feel that they are on an emotional roller coaster, as they try to focus on the job in hand without the support of established processes or relationships with their colleagues.

Gradually, the team moves into a "norming" stage, as a hierarchy is established. Team members come to respect the authority of the manager, and others show leadership in specific areas.

Now that the team members know each other better, they may be socializing together, and they are able to ask each other for help and provide constructive criticism. The team develops a stronger commitment to the team goal, and starts to see good progress toward it. There is often a prolonged overlap between storming and norming behavior: As new tasks come up, the team may lapse back into typical storming stage behavior, but this eventually dies out.

When the team reaches the "performing" stage, hard work leads directly to progress toward the shared vision of its goal, supported by the structures and processes that have been set up. Individual team members may join or leave the team without affecting the performing culture.

As a manager, one can delegate much of the work and can concentrate on developing team members. Being part of the team at this stage feels "easy" compared with earlier on.

Project teams exist only for a fixed period, and even permanent teams may be disbanded through organizational restructuring. As manager or team leader, your concern is both for the team's goal and for the team members. Breaking up a team can be stressful for all concerned, and the "adjourning" or "mourning" stage is important in reaching both team goal and personal conclusions.

The breakup of the team can be hard for members who like routine or who have developed close working relationships with other team members, particularly if their future roles or even jobs look uncertain.

Using the Tool

As a manager and a team leader, your aim is to help your team reach and sustain high performance as soon as possible. To do this, you will need to change your approach at each stage. The steps below will help ensure you are doing the right thing at the right time.

Identify which stage of the team development your team is at from the descriptions above. Now consider what needs to be done to move toward the performing stage, and what you can do to help the team do that effectively. The table below (Figure 27-4) helps you understand your role at each stage, and think about how to move the team forward.

Schedule regular reviews of where your teams are, and adjust your behavior and leadership approach to suit the stage your team has reached.

Some Tips for Managers

Tip 1: A manager needs to ensure that there is plenty of time in his or her schedule for coaching team members through the "forming," "storming," and "norming" stages.

Tip 2: A manager needs to think about how much progress is expected toward the goal and by when, and measure success against that. Since the team has to go through the "forming," "storming," and "norming" stages before the team starts "performing," there is a possibility that there may not be much progress during this time. Communicating progress against appropriate targets is important; otherwise the team members may feel frustrated.

Tip 3: A manager has to ensure that people don't use knowledge of the "storming" stage as a license for bad interpersonal behavior. A manager could institute an award for individuals who conform to team norms and support others in the achievement of team goals.

Figure 27-4. Activities of a Manager at Different Stages of Team Development	
Stage	**Activity**
Forming	Direct the team and establish objectives clearly. (A good way of doing this is to negotiate a team charter or a social agreement.)
Storming	Establish process and structure, and work to smooth conflict and build good relationships between team members. Provide support, especially to those team members who are less secure. Remain positive and firm in the face of challenges to your leadership or the team's goal. Perhaps explain the "forming, storming, norming, and performing" idea so that people understand why conflict is occurring, and understand that things will get better in the future. Consider teaching assertiveness and conflict resolution skills wherever necessary.
Norming	Step back and help the team take responsibility for progress toward the goal. This is a good time to arrange a social, or a team-building event.
Performing	Delegate as far as you sensibly can. Once the team has achieved high performance, you should aim to have as "light a touch" as possible. You will now be able to start focusing on other goals and areas of work.
Adjourning	When breaking up a team, take the time to celebrate its achievements. After all, you may well work with some of your people again, and this will be much easier if people view past experiences positively.

Teams are formed because they can achieve far more than their individual members can on their own, and while being part of a high-performing team can be fun, it can take patience and professionalism to get to that stage.

Effective team leaders can accelerate that process and reduce the difficulties that team members experience by understanding what they need to do as their team moves through the stages from forming to storming, norming, and, finally, performing.

I hope that the experiences shared in this chapter about some of the well-established and researched models will serve new and tenured managers in creating winning teams.

References and Resources

Bolton, R., and D.G. Bolton. (2009). *People Styles at Work: Making Bad Relationships Good and Good Relationships Better.* New York: AMACOM.

Gilbert, D. (2006). *Stumbling on Happiness.* New York: Random House, Inc.

MindTools.com. (2012). Forming, Storming, Norming and Performing: Helping New Teams Perform Effectively, Quickly. Retrieved from: www.mindtools.com/pages/article/newLDR_86.htm.

Robbins, S. (2009). *Essentials of Organization Behavior,* 10th edition. Upper Saddle River, NJ: Prentice Hall.

Team Building.com. (2009). The Secret to Creating Winning Teams. Retrieved from: www.teambuildingportal.com/articles/effective-teams/creating-winning-team.

Walsch, N.D. (1998). *Conversations With God: An Uncommon Dialogue* (Book Three). Charlottesville, VA: Hampton Roads Publishing.

About the Author

Vikram Bector is the chief learning officer of Tata Motors Limited. Tata Motors Limited is India's largest automobile company, with consolidated revenues of $27 billion (USD) in 2010 to 2011. It is the world's fourth largest truck manufacturer, and the world's third largest bus manufacturer. Vikram has over 22 years of diverse experience in business functions and geographies. Vikram is a credentialed executive coach with the International Coach Federation (ICF) and is widely regarded as a thought leader in the learning and organizational development area, and has led some of his earlier companies to outstanding international recognition as best-in-class learning organizations. He has conducted workshops and consulting assignments from Japan and China in the East, to the United States and Brazil in the West.

Chapter 28

Co-Create: Building a Successful, Enduring Organization One Project at a Time

Steve Martin

.... **Editor's Note** ....

This chapter offers a great case study for a compelling approach to project management. Steve Martin, along with his Hubert colleagues, created and have used the Co-Create Model for years, to launch and manage project teams that produce extraordinary results. Much more than a new business process, Co-Create is a way of working, and a culture that enables growth and personal bests. I am thrilled that Steve agreed to share his proven approach with you.

The Co-Create Model is a small-group engagement method for project management and change designed to improve organizational outcomes. But before we can get to a serious discussion of the model we need to take a step back to provide some context. This story begins with a map of how organizations develop and what it takes to create and sustain exceptional results. What I've created is a very high-level view of the work. It travels through a number of connected "stages" or activities.

An Organizational Development Map

Below is an outline of the stages:

- **Thought Leadership:** the core ideology (core values and purpose), mission, strategy, value proposition, and goals.
- **The Giant "What Is" Hairball:** the myriad of components that interact and must be analyzed by the organization's leadership to create projects that matter. These areas represent opportunities to pursue, issues to be solved, and forces (energy) needing management.
- **Activation Mechanism:** The Co-Create Model. This is the *how-to* vehicle for employee engagement, project management, and change.
- **The Results:** This depicts a virtuous cycle—what ideally happens over time if all is working well.

Stage 1: Thought Leadership

The foundation for any organization is its *core values and purpose*. This subject area was extensively written about by Jerry Porras and Jim Collins among others. The essence of this work is for an organization to know, at its most base level, what it believes to be true. These beliefs are so fundamental to the organization's identity that people would maintain them even if they became a detriment in certain circumstances. Successful organizations live these values, and the culture within the organization becomes very strong—some individuals fit, and others do not.

Mission identifies the business an organization is in (and conversely the business it is not in), its products and services, the market, and the point of competitive differentiation.

The *purpose* identifies the value the organization brings to the greater society. It is not a goal or something that is ever achieved—it is something forever pursued. It provides the highest expression of contribution and meaning.

The *strategy*, depending on the model used, describes how you intend to compete. Note this is a complex question and in practice can look very different. It might begin if you use some of Michael Porter's early work as a choice between a value-added strategy (goods *and* services) or a low-cost orientation (lowest price). It could be expressed in the type of market you are going after—a broad or a narrow slice. None of this is either/or—many variations are possible depending on the specific situation.

The *value proposition (value chain)* speaks to a level of detail underneath the strategy. It more specifically identifies the customers or the market value and how their interests link to your strategies. Examples may include innovation, or product assortment depth, or ease of ordering, or the customer experience—focusing on one or some combination. It also becomes a way to look at the organization—how are we performing on those expectations? What are we doing to enhance them? Do we have the capabilities we need?

The *goals* express where the company is going. They can include goals about size, market share or position, financial return, employer of choice, and so on. The purpose of the goals, however big or small, is to create energy to move forward.

Stage 2: The Giant "What Is" Hairball

This area represents critical variables the leadership of the organization strives to understand. It's very challenging because they are both internal and external and are constantly changing. Another factor is many are interconnected—so messing with one can affect another. Understanding what's going on at any point in time is the fundamental responsibility of top leadership. How well an organization performs over time is largely dependent on the job done here. But understanding is not enough. They must also translate what they've learned into projects that will move the organization forward. They must be able to frame the opportunity and issues in a manner allowing those deeper in the organization to figure out the best response.

Stage 3: The Co-Create Model—An Activator

This is the small-group engagement model that translates the projects into processes, systems, structures, and so on that move the organization forward. It is where members of the team turn the thoughts into tangible elements that are implemented.

Stage 4: The Results

If all is working as it should, the organization can begin a journey upward. Each project becomes a step to higher levels of being. No one project creates a breakthrough—rather each plays a role in moving it forward. What does happen is successful completion of the right projects creates a critical mass over time. When that point is reached the organization finds itself in a better place. Customers are coming back more frequently and buying more. Employees are busy and engaged in the task. The supplier community is humming bringing new ideas to the table. The owners are happy because financial results are trending upward.

As you can see, organizations are complex creatures living in a dynamic environment. A lot has to go right for success to happen and be sustained. This chapter focuses on the Co-Create Model—an approach our organization uses to translate our best thinking into tangible results. The essence is about getting the right group of people working on projects that matter.

Following are excerpts from the book, *Co-Create: How to Make Big Changes With Small Groups One Project at a Time*. This book was published on Lulu in 2011.

There's a moment during a successful project when things come together, the team gels, and their energy soars. It feels magical. The day-to-day work they have done and the time they put into the project have come together to generate clarity and momentum. Pieces of the project puzzle emerge and the team understands how their parts fit together and something new and useful is created. It's a beautiful thing!

If your company is like mine, a lot of work gets done through teams and projects. Over the last 20 years, my colleagues and I at The Hubert Company have been honing and using a system we call the Co-Create Model. This chapter describes the model and tells our story. We use the Co-Create Model for all our large projects. Our employees participate in meaningful conversations about how to improve our business—they are deeply engaged in creating a better future. The model establishes a framework from which team excellence can flourish.

Why Co-Create?

Our Co-Create Model is dynamic and still evolving as we apply it to increasingly complex projects. Each major project we launch creates an opportunity to try different approaches and experience success and failure. Our success rate has been excellent although we have had a couple of flaming failures that were humbling, painful, and very instructive. So based on our experience we believe this system offers several benefits including:

- Excellent project execution—Co-Create is an integrated process that helps team members 1) focus on their purpose and goals, 2) manage tasks, and 3) build collaborative relationships. Co-Create helps teams set up and run their projects well.
- Change leadership and agility—Co-Create uses the best change management principles to enable team members to cope with the fast pace of change and build agility into their work regimens. There are no magic bullets—no single leadership act—that enable sustained high levels of performance. Changes occur and organizational agility is developed one team and one project at a time. We use the co-create process to lead change and help employees engage by playing an important part in our strategic manifestation.
- Employee engagement—The model is participative and engaging. Our team members grow with each project they complete and co-own results with fellow

team members. Process steps prompt the team to think deeply together, be open to diverse possibilities, and collaborate well.

■ And finally we have no choice but to co-create. We are forever connecting and creating with others. Organizations exist to do what no one individual can. So the choice is whether or not we co-create *intentionally*. The Co-Create Model provides a path to help teams develop solutions that create value for all.

When we use the Co-Create Model, our teams experience high engagement and energy, clarity of purpose, and team member cohesion. They create high-quality plans that reduce downstream issues and improve results.

You will likely recognize some of the processes and tools included in the Co-Create Model. We have pulled from the "best of the best" to create the system. The combination and integration of these methods is unique and our results are extraordinary.

Energy Generation Is Core to the Co-Create Model

Our purpose, the organization's purpose, and meaning we derive from our work enhances our experience, motivates us to do our best, and helps us be more nimble and responsive to change. It is from deep within that we connect with the energy we need to make great things happen. When was the last time you used a project management process at work that reached down to your core and made you feel more alive and interested in the task? Until I experienced the power of the Co-Create Model, I did not think it was possible to find a business practice this pragmatic and inspiring. I now know that it is possible.

Throughout this chapter you will see me refer to purpose, truths, and energy. I believe that there is a positive creative force that influences all we do—both at work and in the rest of our lives. It relentlessly urges us forward—moving us toward a more fulfilling life. When we align ourselves with this energy, good things happen. One might attribute this to good luck or chance. What we've experienced is that great outcomes are not random events and that we can call forth this energy. Later in this chapter I will discuss four underlying truths that will explain our thinking in more detail. I will also share with you how we invite this energy into our work. This is a unique element in the Co-Create Model.

Comprehensive and Integrated

The Co-Create Model is comprehensive. It recognizes our work is complex, interconnected, and influenced by many elements and people. Most of our projects are neither simple nor linear. Project leaders and team members attend to overlapping work components and group and individual experiences during the project. Change unfolds in stages based on individuals contributing their unique talents and gifts.

Co-Create also integrates our individual and organizational goals and visions. It brings to the fore the idea that we are all working for something greater than a numeric outcome and that we are working for something greater than ourselves. Each contribution makes a difference—it changes the world bit by bit.

What's Next?

The Co-Create Model offers a way of working that will connect with those sitting in the boardroom and in the lunchroom. Our leaders love it because our projects are well thought through, planned, and executed. Our team members love using the model because it enables them to do their best work, experience meaning and purpose, and participate, collaborate, and create every day. The outcome is something that's true, good, and beautiful.

Crafting and using the Co-Create Model has changed my life and filled my work with purpose. I hope you and your teams try our process and enjoy the same benefits of its use.

> *"Never doubt that a small group of thoughtful, committed citizens can change the world. Indeed, it is the only thing that ever has."*
>
> —Margaret Mead

Underlying Truths

To understand any model, you need to know the basic assumptions that govern it. The Co-Create Model was developed to align our actions with four universal principles. We call these principles the underlying truths and they connect directly to specific stages of the Model and provide teams with a source of inspiration, energy, and focus they will need to complete the work. The underlying truths are the "soft stuff" that supports the manifestation of the "hard stuff." The work and magic happen in this container.

Underlying Truth #1: We are here to serve something greater than ourselves.

Life inside any organization is a challenge. So much of our day-to-day existence revolves around working a long to-do list, responding to countless emails and attending too many boring meetings. For many of us it requires a tight focus on what needs to get done to meet the goals and objectives of the job. Our performance is often measured based on how well we deliver tasks—check marks in boxes. This individualistic perspective, while great for task accomplishment, can cause us to lose sight of the bigger picture. It can isolate us and make us think that our purpose is to accomplish tasks. But no matter how task-driven your workplace is, we know that there is a more compelling reason we do the work. We are part of an unfolding story.

We are here to serve something greater than ourselves by co-creating a better world. In the broadest sense it is a universal purpose. *Better* can be defined in many ways—it may look like a more effective process, product, department, or organization. Or it may look like a productive meeting between two departments where there have been past tensions. Or it may be an authentic and caring conversation between two people. Whatever form it takes, *better* is any improvement in the current state.

We also endeavor to extend a better world and this concept speaks to the natural law of relentless forward movement. Nothing in nature stands still. We live in an expanding universe and our natural systems reproduce and expand. And while we sometimes use a machine metaphor to describe organizations, they are essentially organic and naturally want to expand and extend. Expanding is a sign of health—it is what we do.

There is an intentional organizing principle or energy at work and we each have an opportunity to participate in creating something better and extending it into our piece of the universe.

But what about when things don't go so well? How do we deal with problems? Problems are a natural disruptive force or energy and essentially feed the creative process by communicating the need for change. They indicate a situation requiring our attention. Problems present an opportunity to continue the movement forward by telling us where we have work to do.

What does it look like to be operating from a mindset of creating a better world? Outside of business it's about how we help people, the environment, and creatures of all types. In the language of business we are here to bring increasing value to all stakeholders. How can we improve the outcomes for our customers, owners, employees, suppliers, and the community? When we do this, our work makes a difference and has purpose.

The Co-Create Model uses the power of purpose by exploring goals and tasks several layers deeper than their logical surface. We ask and answer "Why?" and we create a vivid picture of how success will look and feel. There are several times and ways that we focus on purpose and we ensure that our plans are generative and creative—always moving forward and extending. Our teams know that it is their goal to align their work with their and the organization's (and this project's) greater purpose. When we do this, we see increases in focus and energy and amazing things happen.

Underlying Truth #2: We are connected and interdependent—existing in complex systems.

There is no *them*. This is one of the hardest concepts to grasp and apply in organizations experiencing nonstop change, particularly when employees are feeling guarded or insecure. When we are stressed, overwhelmed, and/or worried, we feel vulnerable. Working in a way that is connected can be hard! It's often difficult for us to clearly see how what we do impacts others. It takes time to understand and include our upstream and downstream internal customers. It may also be difficult to move beyond self-interest (many of us don't even realize that this motivation is driving our work).

The truth is we do not exist in isolation and can't accomplish anything significant without others. Our thoughts lead to actions. Actions occur within processes, which are part of systems, and which connect to other actions, processes, and systems. We are all intertwined!

Like a pebble thrown in the water, every action reverberates and causes ripples. What we do WILL result in intended and unintended consequences. Sometimes we are aware of the impact of our actions and sometimes we are not. Either way, the impact occurs. That is why believing and working in alignment with this principle is critical. To be successful, we need to become a lifelong student of connections and their consequences.

At work, this education begins with understanding how your individual job creates value to your immediate co-workers or department. It then extends to how your department contributes to other departments and the work they do. It continues outward by an understanding of how all departments come together to create value for key stakeholders. It extends further by understanding how your contribution connects to the stakeholders of your stakeholders.

So what happens when you are not happy with the results of a particular process or system? Every system is perfectly designed to give you the results you are receiving. To change the outcome, change the system. To change the system, it is critical to consider the interconnected and interdependent parts. As part of the Co-Create process, our team members explore the following questions:

1. Are we thinking about this appropriately? What mental models are we using? What beliefs or assumptions are under our actions? Are they still valid or do we need some new thinking? It always begins with thoughts—are the thoughts you are using serving you or do they need to be released and some new thoughts chosen?
2. How have the thoughts been translated into processes?
3. How have the processes been grouped into systems?

Another benefit of aligning our actions with this underlying truth is that it changes the nature of the conversations we have when we are dealing with change projects where there is serious pain. It is easy to place blame on others—feeling that if they only would do their job our problems would go away. Systems thinking—awareness of complexity and connections—helps us let go of dysfunctional blame or judgment.

The structures and processes within the Co-Create Model ensure that team members work in ways that recognize and utilize their interconnectedness. They know that each connection is vital for the whole to function optimally and that their work is part of a complex system. The best way to alter and improve outcomes is by working within the context of the system.

Underlying Truth #3: We are here to engage.

Given that we are here to make the world a better place and are interconnected, it is important that we believe in the power of making progress as individuals and as a team. Individually, we have the opportunity and responsibility to say, "yes" to change and to move beyond the past and the comfortable status quo. Engaging in the work can feel like leaning into a high wind and stepping forward. Do we do this or do we seek shelter when conditions get tough? The Co-Create Model helps individuals identify, explore, and move past sources of resistance and barriers to moving the work forward.

Engagement is also invaluable at the group level. Our teams know that contribution occurs when they engage, struggle, and learn as they improve our business and the world. We use the Co-Create Model to ensure that the right people are engaged with the right tasks. This helps us stay grounded on our purpose and increase participation, collaboration, and diversity of thought. When the right group engages in great dialogue, they figure things out! In his bestselling book, *Good to Great*, Jim Collins suggested that you "put your best people on your biggest opportunities, not your biggest problems." We believe this and are guided by it when we make team assignments.

Saying yes to engagement is not always easy. We might feel fear, worry, or mistrust when faced with a lot of changes. We worry whether we will be successful and whether our skills will still be needed and valued in the new reality. We may worry that we won't continue to measure up. The Co-Create Model phases help team members identify their fears, discuss them, and build confidence about what they will be able to contribute as things change. We believe this is a critical part of the project implementation process and every bit as important as creating a robust timeline or task list.

Our system also invites teams to deal openly with their concerns. If they disagree with the assumptions that define a goal, the process offers them a safe and consistent way to bring their ideas and apprehensions forward. Because it is a regular part of implementing the project, teams tend to be more candid and comfortable to challenge ideas.

Can you say "No"?

We always have the choice to say yes or no to what life presents to us. This conscious choice is essential to making any commitment and having the energy to follow through on the work. In a business setting, the expectation is for key employees to support the on-going development of the organization. If the executive leadership team has done their work well it should be readily apparent why a project is important to maintaining or improving the organization's ability to compete. If for some reason an individual disagrees with or finds themselves working on a project that violates their values then the choice they should make is to say no to being involved. Depending on the circumstances it may be acceptable to decline or it may require them to find a new employer more aligned with their values and vision where they can say yes. At the end of the day we must all be keep our integrity *and* be moving forward.

This underlying truth asks us all to engage and say "yes" to progress. And the processes we use as part of our Co-Create Model help structure a higher level of team engagement where it is both safe to be candid and where teams are expected to articulate and think through concerns.

Underlying Truth #4: We are here to contribute our gifts.

You can't create anything good with gifts you don't have. When we use our talents and are fully engaged, however, we can and do change the world. Every member of the team is amazing and wants to make a difference—we know and see this every day! The Co-Create Model starts with this belief and then helps our employees bring their talents to the project. Our process identifies more possibilities from which to determine solutions and create action plans. We solve problems every day, but without getting into the rut of a problem solving mindset.

Many of us are born problem solvers and it feels quite normal to focus on what's wrong. Our schools and the news media reinforce this view of life and work. The evening news bombards us with stories about pain, suffering, or unethical behaviors. Stories about politicians, sports figures, and business or religious leaders who have failed in a grand fashion get the most clicks and tweets and YouTube views. Good news, if any is included, appears in the last 15 seconds of the broadcast. At one point, our local Channel 5 in Cincinnati renamed their weather department the *Storm Center*.

What's the point? If you bring the same problem-centric thinking into your projects, you will hurt your results. You know this. We have learned this, too, and we have created process steps as part of the Co-Create Model that help remind us to think first about possibilities and talent (not problems and skills deficits). We may need to understand what's causing the pain or problems but we can't make it better until we shift our minds to the assets we have to work with to make it better. We create a better world with our gifts not our failings.

The most basic unit of change is the individual. It all starts there and flows outward. We focus on what people do well and can bring to the task. Focusing on what may be missing makes no sense because you cannot create with something that does not exist. When you multiply this way of working across a team of individuals, the results are amazing. Our model is designed to combine the gifts of multiple people in order to create something no one individual could have on their own.

You could go onto Amazon.com and find dozens of books about the importance of focusing on strengths versus weaknesses. This idea is not new at all. We pay homage to the founding theorists by building this powerful belief into our day-to-day project management processes. It's the structure and discipline that helps busy and well-meaning professionals do the right things for the right reasons. As natural born problem solvers, the built in processes make all the difference in the world!

We also help our employees discover and understand their unique talents. When we first started using the Co-Create Model, we were surprised by how many people had trouble articulating their strengths. When we are conscious of our gifts, we can use them more often and more flexibly.

At Hubert, we take the time to be sure we have the right group of people (with the right gifts) working on the right project. I will share examples of how we do this later in the chapter. Our team selection and assignment process creates an environment where diverse talents come together and create an environment of respect, collaborations, and results orientation. We need everyone's skills to remain competitive and to succeed.

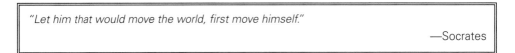

"Success means we go to sleep at night knowing that our talents and abilities were used in a way that served others."

—Marianne Williamson

Summary

The four underlying truths bring the Co-Create Model to life. Our culture is honestly aligned with these beliefs. If you spent a day with any of our project teams, you would see actions and hear conversations that would tell you these assumptions are alive and well in our culture. This is perhaps the most important distinction between the Co-Create Model and other systems for project and change implementations. That said, I know you are likely eager to learn more about how Co-Create works. Next I will describe the six phases of the model and give an overview of how we use it to accomplish our goals.

"Let him that would move the world, first move himself."

—Socrates

The Co-Create Model

The Co-Create Model starts with the four underlying truths and then uses six distinct phases to help teams launch and complete projects. When we were developing our system, we asked ourselves how we could combine what we felt was most important (the truths) with best practices from project management, change management, and team development. We continued to tweak the model until we felt we had an excellent practice that produced great results. In this section, I will cut to the chase and show you the model and explain how it works.

Figure 28-1 offers a visual description of the Co-Create Model. At first, it might look a bit complicated, but it is actually very straightforward. There are six phases that our teams use to launch and complete projects and produce results. These six phases are highlighted in Figure 28-2 and include defining, discovery, Co-Create the ideal, implementation planning, execution, and fine tuning.

The project phases help us build robust solutions to new opportunities. These six phases keep us on track and remind us to spend time where it will be most beneficial.

People, not machines or software, complete projects, so during the project we attend to two types of experiences, the team or group experience (highlighted in Figure 28-3) and each individual's experience (highlighted in Figure 28-4).

Figure 28-1. The Co-Create Model

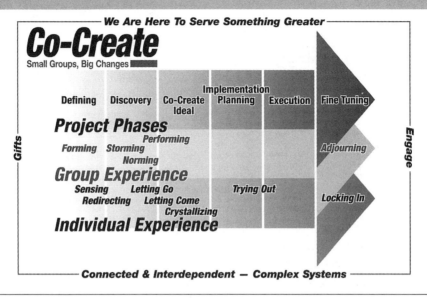

Figure 28-2. Highlighting the "Project" Phases

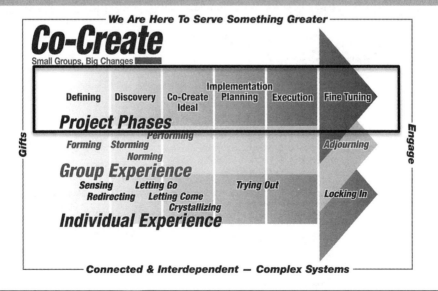

The Six Project Phases

The six project phases represent a process for individual engagement, team creation, and project execution. Here is a brief description:

1. *Defining:* We spend a lot of time at the beginning of each project to ensure we adequately define and describe what we want the project to accomplish and the roles people will play in helping to support and manifest project goals. During this critical first phase, every project owner creates a whitepaper for their project. That's right, a whitepaper. We have found that the time invested upfront improves everything that happens throughout the project.

2. *Discovery:* During the discovery phase, the team creates a robust and detailed picture of the current state. All team members participate and this tends to be a very energizing process. The information they generate is critical to creating solutions that work as well as being therapeutic.

3. *Co-Create the Ideal:* The team leader guides the team through creating a plan for a forward path based on the whitepaper from Phase 1 and the current state analysis from Phase 2. They discuss, agree upon, and document the conditions for success for the project.

Figure 28-3. Highlighting the "Group" Experience

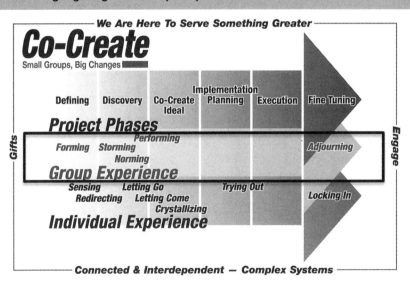

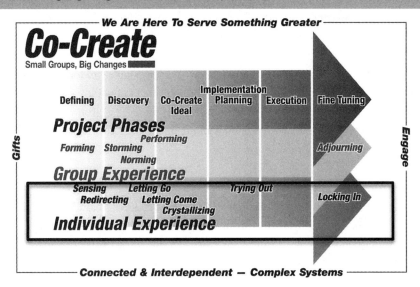

Figure 28-4. Highlighting the "Individual" Experience

4. *Implementation Planning:* During Phase 4, the team gets into the nitty-gritty to determine what needs to happen, by when it should be completed, and by whom. This phase is the most similar to traditional project planning processes. However, our action plans are much more than a long list of to-dos.

5. *Execution:* The team gets the work done and because their conversations have been open and collaborative thus far they are able to flexibly implement the project plan and meet or beat their milestones and desired results.

6. *Fine Tuning:* As the name implies, this phase of the project enables the team to make additional adjustments (they measure and adjust throughout the project) and tie up any loose ends. The team closes out the project.

These project phases ensure that our projects are well planned and executed. In my experience, most organizations focus on Phase 4 and Phase 5, but fewer start and end with the deliberate and open project management practices like we use in the Co-Create Model. The extra work we do up-front serves several important purposes and improves our results. Do our projects take longer? No. We start slower and with more initial discussion, but this work paves the way for a less troublesome project implementation with fewer post-implementation changes.

At the same time the team is working through the six project phases, they are experiencing their work as a team and as individuals. How people work together and experience change is important. Until we developed the Co-Create Model we did not have a way to proactively help our team members do their best work throughout a project.

You can probably recall a situation where a well-planned project underperformed because of poor team dynamics or low collaboration. And you may know individuals who are more talented than is evident by their contribution to the team. The group experience and individual experience elements of the model build in the structure we need to ensure we consider the people part of project excellence.

The Group Experience

To build a great team experience, we use the Tuckman Model of Team Development (Tuckman, 1977). Teams go through recognizable stages of development—and they go into and out of these stages many times during their work together. Dr. Bruce Tuckman presented a model in 1965 that identified five stages that teams experience. Figure 28-5 shows the stages of the Tuckman model, which are: forming, storming, norming, performing, and adjourning. Tuckman's model explains that as the team develops maturity and ability, relationships and coping skills strengthen. Project setbacks or victories will also affect how the team works together. For the Co-Create Model, we have overlaid the stages of team development with

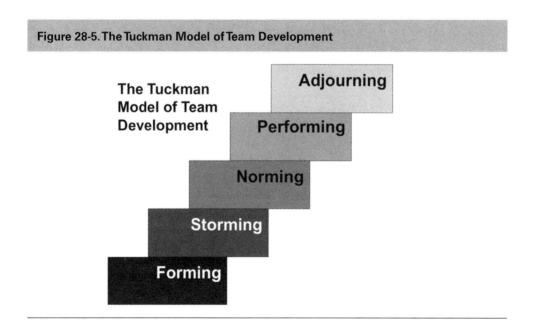

Figure 28-5. The Tuckman Model of Team Development

The Tuckman Model of Team Development

Adjourning

Performing

Norming

Storming

Forming

our six project phases. We do some very specific things throughout the project's life cycle to help our teams work well together and quickly identify and deal with any setbacks.

I am frequently asked whether the need to do team development is reduced as team members work on more than one project together. The answer is yes and no. We certainly benefit from the synergies, relationship building, and learning that have occurred on previous projects. That said, every team is a new team and project roles and tasks are different. Sources of potential conflict or discomfort are often tied to particular topics or tasks, and so we need to attend to the team's developmental stages—in some degree—on every project. By understanding the stages of team development and the corresponding team leadership and executive support actions that best support each stage (and movement to the next), we have found that we can better help teams do their best work. Here is a brief description of the stages of the Tuckman Model of Team Development:

1. *Forming:* The initial stage of team development where members are getting oriented to one another and seeking to understand their roles and boundaries.
2. *Storming:* This stage of team development is characterized by style clashes, conflict, and working points of differentiation out. We find that familiar team members can go back to this phase when a new project or task brings disagreements to the surface.
3. *Norming:* The team is getting to know each other and is working through how to work well together. Their efforts look and feel more cohesive.
4. *Performing:* The team is utilizing the strengths of their relationships to get more done. Their ability to collaborate and solve problems is a competitive edge. Roles are flexible but clear.
5. *Adjourning:* The team creates closure for their work and feels complete in the task of marking the project's end.

Teams can skip forward or backward in development when new members join when they are affected by unsettling changes. In addition to group health and drama, we also need to deal with how each team member is experiencing the demands of the project, interactions with his or her colleagues, and the work processes.

The Individual Experience

To help our employees do their best work, we draw upon the work of Peter Senge, Otto Sharmer, and Betty Sue Flowers. In their 2005 book called *Presence: Exploring Profound Change In People, Organizations, and Society* (Senge, 2005), the authors offered a model of individual development called the U Model that we use throughout the six project phases of the Co-Create Model. Here is a quick review of the elements of the U Model:

1. *Sensing (suspending):* Gathering and considering information and mental models about the current state.
2. *Redirecting:* See things from a systemic and holistic way. Become aware that we may need to think about things differently.
3. *Letting go:* Letting go of definitions of success and mental models that no longer serve our goals. Opening up our minds to new possibilities. Being more coachable.
4. *Letting come:* Authentic work that comes from the heart. Having confidence in the rightness of right things. The essence or seed of the solution becomes conscious.
5. *Crystallizing:* Bringing together learning and confidence to build an agile path forward.
6. *Trying out (prototyping):* Experimenting with new approaches. Learning from the process of trying.
7. *Locking in (institutionalizing):* Adopting and forming new habits and regimens. Something becomes your new natural way.

The U Model helps us understand and improve individual growth and development. And it's the fact that we encourage our team members to explore their learning that it gets done. I am convinced that if we did not include the Individual Experience Phases as part of the Co-Create Model, our learning rates and success would be much lower and the model would be incomplete.

The practices we use as part of the Co-Create Model reinforce the importance of paying attention to the project, the group, and individuals. Ignoring or skipping any of the work will reduce our results. We have even had teams fail because some part of the model was not adequately addressed. The task of the team leader is to be conscious of and working the project from all these three perspectives simultaneously. This is where the art and science of team performance converge.

Roles and Responsibilities

Many people, united by a purpose, help ensure team performance and success. Each project is different, but we typically define the following roles. These folks ensure that each project is well defined, aligned with Hubert's strategic plan, and executed well.

- **Executive group:** This is typically the president and the vice presidents who are responsible to identify the major issues or strategic opportunities facing the organization. Their job is to provide high-level direction about what needs to be developed to support the strategy.

- **Sponsor:** The sponsor is a vice president who translates the strategic direction into a project. When projects span functional areas, either the two VPs co-sponsor the project or the president will serve as the sponsor. The sponsor secures the required resources—people, money, time, etc.—and works with the project owner to write the project whitepaper. Once the work begins, the sponsor and project owner monitor the project to ensure alignment and are available to help with critical decisions as appropriate.

- **Project owner:** Most often this is a director level manager who has responsibility for the functional area where the majority of the project is taking place. They write the whitepaper with some help, attend all team meetings and actively participate in the work as a team member. This person is the primary contact for, and co-worker of, the team facilitator, who work closely together regarding approach, specific meeting agendas, and through the many details of the project. The day-to-day leadership is shared by the project owner and the team facilitator.

- **Team facilitator:** For major projects this role is fulfilled by someone from a corporate organizational development or HR function or an outside consultant. For smaller projects, the team facilitator is someone from a functional area who has been trained in the Co-Create system. This person is responsible to facilitate the team's process. This includes leading team meetings, developing meeting notes, and working with team members as they develop the discovery (Phase 2) visuals and design implementation communication or training programs.

- **Team members:** The team is comprised of frontline employees who represent key stakeholder groups and bring specific expertise to the work. Their job is to provide information and input and to participate in the implementation process.

- **End users:** The people outside the team who will be receiving or using the project output, which could be a new workflow process, software changes, or a new structure. The team may consider input from this group during the project. The team keeps this group updated on the progress of the project.

- **Outside vendors:** External partners who provide products or services to the group. Examples include software vendors and legal advice.

These roles, and any others as applicable, are specifically identified in the project whitepaper, which is completed during Phase 1 of the project.

Frequently Asked Questions

Here are the answers to the questions I most get from people when they first learn about our approach.

Q: How long are the projects that you use this for and how large are the project teams?

A: The major projects have ranged from three months to two years in length. The average project is nine to 12 months long. The team size typically ranges from six to 10 members.

Q: What about everyday projects, how do you handle these?

A: What typically happens is the model can be scaled down for smaller projects. The key is that the principles and phases apply but how they show up could be different based on the need. We also have an intensive version of the model that we use when the project is complex but the timeline is short.

Q: How long did it take for you to get buy-in from senior leader on the more "touchy-feely" aspects of the model?

A: The soft side of the model is very consistent with the Hubert culture. Also, when properly explained, the business case for the soft side is readily apparent and hard to argue. The model was ultimately embraced because of the results we achieved.

Q: Does using the model pay off financially?

A: Yes it does. Two of the clearest examples occurred when we used the model to run projects that 1) reduced our cost of goods by $1 million and 2) acquired $10 million in business, which had to be completed in a 60-day period. It's difficult to estimate the total financial contribution of all the projects using this model over the years. If I had to venture a guess about either the total sales or profit impact it would be somewhere between $50 and $100 million.

Q: How much training do your facilitators need to effectively help teams through the process? Do they need a particular skill set?

A: Team facilitator training takes about 45 hours. We cover the conceptual framework and actively work on skill development. The desired skill set is:

- communication—the ability to convey and listen
- interpersonal relationship building
- conceptual thinking
- ability to balance theory and practice
- emotional intelligence—being well grounded
- credibility
- results orientation
- detail management
- inquisitive
- ability to get results without having control
- ability to use Microsoft Word and Excel.

Q: What if I am worried that my organization is not ready for something like this?

A: You will find an organization readiness checklist in the Conclusion.

Q: How is participation on a team connected to your performance management system?

A: For many of our key positions project participation is listed as one of the responsibilities on their performance management document. We use a Mercer System and the individual performance is rated there. The performance ratings become part of a calculation effecting adjustments to their base compensation. For individuals who participate only occasionally on teams it is not formally listed as a responsibility and would be acknowledged in the comments or as an addendum to the performance management document.

Q: How does a team member balance day-to-day responsibilities with project work?

A: Our expectation is for the individual to figure out how best to balance their overall workload. For example, they may be able to juggle it all successfully and meet their obligations. They may approach co-workers and ask for help to cover some aspect of their responsibilities for a period of time. Or they may negotiate with their boss about delaying a certain task until a project is over. The bottom line is the individual is responsible to figure out the plan—to use their creativity to see what's possible and to ask for help. I would encourage them to begin with the question "How will I meet my daily obligations *and* participate on this team?" In our culture we have a core value around service to others—this is a perfect opportunity for a co-worker to lend a hand.

Q: Do team members follow through on their project assignments? How do you ensure accountability?

A: This has not been a major issue for us. Situations do come up that require flexibility but overall the use of simple project management techniques works well. For instance the facilitator captures all the action items at the end of each meeting along with the responsible party and due dates. This information is documented in the meeting minutes and sent to all team members. The facilitator then begins the next meeting by reviewing the action items from the previous meeting. If someone is having difficulty getting an action item done we use that as an opportunity to explore the issues. In the rare case where an individual continues to miss deadlines I've seen the group exert pressure on them or if the problem is legitimate invariably someone will volunteer to help out.

Conclusion

The Co-Create Model helps us bring out the best in our teams and ourselves. The process itself is only as good as its values, purpose and underlying beliefs are profound.

> *"I couldn't have laid out a strategy that would have led to the partnerships that the orchids have made real. I couldn't have mustered the cleverness and foresight to look into the future and see these things as goals. But my point is, I didn't have to. All I had to do was trust my intuition that there was something powerful in the beauty of a flower."*
>
> —Bill Strickland

The power of engagement is immense and will change your business when you focus this force on important change projects. So where do you go from here? Are you ready to give the Co-Create Model a try? I hope so! When I talk to colleagues in other companies about our approach, the conversation invariably turns to a discussion of readiness. Is your organization ready to turn on the spigot of change and engage team members fully? Here are several questions that can help you determine your organization's readiness for change and for using an integrated team project model like ours.

Is the organization ready?

- Is there dissatisfaction in the organization about how change was managed in the past, or are people generally happy with your current project management and change methodologies?
- Have there been any recent (or memorable) spectacular project failures or successes?

- How has the business performed—sales, profitability trend—over the last three to five years?
- Are your processes and systems highly developed, efficient, and aligned with the business requirements?
- Is your project implementation model sound or does it need to be modified or overhauled?
- How are customers responding to the value proposition?
- Are key stakeholders happy with the results or would they like to see improvement?
- Are the employees empowered and involved?
- Do employees have the technical and interpersonal skill required to complete great project work?
- What is the employee turnover rate?
- Do you have current employee satisfaction data? What does it tell you?
- Is the organization meaningfully involved in the community?
- Are your suppliers partners or adversaries?

Is the executive team ready?

- Are leaders able to clearly articulate the current state of the business—what's working and what's not?
- Can they translate that into a vision for moving forward including the projects, competencies, or changes required to make it happen (at a high level)?
- Will they empower employees to figure out solutions?
- Are they willing to invest the time required for the teams to do it right?
- Are they willing to fund training for the champion to learn the process?
- Are they capable and willing to make tough choices?

Do you have change champions?

- Is there someone internally who will champion this work?
- Do they have the necessary skills and influence in the organization?
- Do they see the need for a new way to manage and launch projects and have an interest in this work?
- Do they have the time to devote to championing work?

Answering these questions, and others unique to your situation, will give you a good idea as to whether or not a process like the Co-Create Model has application in your organization.

While we believe that all organizations will benefit from a strong team-based approach to project implementation, readiness and interest are critical.

The Ready Organization

I am often asked what I believe are the hallmarks of a ready organization. To use an inclusive and integrated approach like Co-Create, an organization needs to have:

1. Competent leadership (sponsors and owners) with a grasp on the issues and opportunities facing the organization.
2. The ability to translate the issues and opportunities into manageable projects—with enough detail for the group to engage.
3. A functional culture that supports the sharing of power with others. The group working on each project should possess a medium to high level of decision-making power.
4. Capable team members—they know their stuff (technical), have the interpersonal skill required to effectively play nice in the sandbox, and the willingness to accept the challenge.
5. The organization and leaders must have the discipline to give the work the time it needs. The process needs to play itself out.

Here's to Success!

I wish you the best of success and I hope that this information helps you and your peers unleash the talents and potential of your employees and generate great results. At Hubert, we have discovered that when our beliefs are aligned with how we work, we are able to grow the business and keep all stakeholders—owners, leaders, customers, partners, and employees—happy.

References and Resources

Block, P. (1981). *Flawless Consulting*. San Francisco: Jossey-Bass.

Block, P. (2002). *The Answer to How Is Yes*. San Francisco: Berrett-Koehler.

Bridges, W. (1991). *Managing Transitions* (2nd ed.). Cambridge, MA: DaCapo Press.

Collins, J.C. (2001). *Good to Great*. New York: HarperCollins.

Herold, D., & Feders, D. (2008). *Change The Way You Lead Change: Leadership Strategies That Really Work*. Stanford, CA: Stanford University Press.

Kotter, J. (2008). *A Sense of Urgency*. Boston: Harvard Business Press.

Kotter, J. (1996). *Leading Change*. Boston: Harvard Business Press.

Lewin, K. (1947). Group Decision and Social Change. In T.M. Newcomb, E.L. Hartley, et al. (Eds.), *Readings in social psychology*. New York: Henry Holt.

Lippitt, R., Watson, J., & Westley, B. (1958). *Dynamics of Planned Change*. New York: Harcourt Brace.

Project Management Institute. (2008). *A Guide to the Project Management Body of Knowledge*. Newton Square, PA: PMI.

Schein, E.H. (1987). *Process Consultation: Vol. 2 Its Role in Organization Development* (2nd ed.). Reading, MA: Addison-Wesley.

Scholtes, P.R., Joiner, B.L., & Streibel, B.J. (2003). *The Team Handbook* (3rd ed.). Madison, WI: Oriel.

Senge, P., Scharmer, C.O., Jaworski, J., & Flowers, B.S. (2005). *Presence: Human Purpose and the Field of the Future*. New York: Crown Business.

Tuckman, B. (1965). Developmental Sequence in Small Groups. *Psychological Bulletin, American Psychological Association, 63(6)*, 384–389.

Tuckman, B., & Jensen, M. (1977). Stages of Small Group Development Revisited. *Group and Organizational Studies, 2*, 419–427.

Tuckman, B. (1984). *Citation Classic-Developmental Sequence in Small Groups, Current Concerns*. Retrieved on April 24, 2011, from http://www.garfield.library.upenn.edu/classics1984/A1984TD25600001.pdf.

About the Author

Steve Martin's professional passion has been to explore the intersection of educational theory, psychology, and business. He is curious and especially loves connecting new learning to practical outcomes. At Hubert, Steve leads the organization development and human resources functions. Steve earned a bachelor's degree in psychology from Northern Kentucky University and master's and doctorate degrees in education from the University of Cincinnati. He is a lifelong resident of Cincinnati, Ohio, and is married to Mary. They have one son Joe, and three grandchildren—Julia, Joseph, and Edyn. Steve can be contacted at smartin@hubert.com.

Chapter 29

You're Not the Boss of Me

Jodee Bock

················· **Editor's Note** ·················

This is a short and sweet essay from Jodee Bock. Jodee has helped thousands of professionals shift their mindsets to places that better serve their goals. This piece is a great story that might help you or someone you know who is struggling with having a positive and sustainable impact at work.

"You're not the boss of me." How many times have you heard little kids say that? Where do they hear that phrase? And why is it so universal?

Maybe it's because somewhere in our human DNA, even as little kids, we want some level of independence in our lives. When we're toddlers, they (the former children who now are adults with poor memories) call that the "terrible twos" and just wait (im)patiently for us to "grow out of it." And then they domesticate us into believing that we should do what they tell us "because I'm the parent/teacher/authority figure."

Why is it so surprising that we have a certain level of defiance in our organizations? We've been trained throughout our lives that to speak our mind is somehow "wrong" or "bad," and we've been waiting all our lives with some pent-up resentment we don't even know about to say what we think. And then we have a real boss who we fight because all we can remember is that time we said "You're not the boss of me" and got punished.

Employees don't want to be told what they should do or have to do or must do. How does "boss-ship" work in our lives? That's the "do as I say because I'm the boss" mentality.

Employees are not toddlers anymore, although some may act like it because they haven't yet realized that all their pent-up anger from their toddler years is still in there somewhere. They're still resisting and defying and sometimes even sabotaging those bosses—and often the bosses are reciprocating, and it becomes a drama of collusion. What we resist persists, and that causes even more anger and frustration.

The Gallup organization says that "employees leave supervisors, not companies," but how often does that employee find another supervisor just like the one he/she left because "wherever you go, there you are"?

From the perspective of the manager or leader, this might look surprisingly similar. You may have heard of the Peter Principle where people are promoted to the level of their incompetence. In their book *The Peter Principle*, Dr. Laurence J. Peter and Raymond Hull assert that in a hierarchy, members are promoted so long as they work competently, and there comes a point at which they are no longer competent, and thus must be managed by subordinates in such a way that the damage they might do to the organization is minimized.

When it was originally released in 1969, *The Peter Principle* was supposed to be a humorous treatise. But today it seems the work has more than a subtle degree of truth. However, given the opportunity to develop higher levels of awareness along the journey, leaders and managers might hit that level of incompetence with openness and vulnerability that allows for higher employee engagement. With increased awareness, perhaps *The Peter Principle* might really be treated as the satire it was originally intended to be.

The only way to stop the game of collusion is to stop. And someone has to be the adult. We already know that it doesn't work to try to change someone else. So when an adult chooses to stop playing the game, he or she does it to alter his or her *own* behavior, not someone else's.

And now there's no game to play. When one side concedes, the game is over. If we as adults are still caught up in our childhood game of "king of the mountain," we will all lose.

I'm not blaming anyone here—employees or bosses. In fact, blame is probably the most useless emotion there is. But I am saying that in my experience, when things weren't working in my life the way I wanted them to, I got the best results when I looked in the mirror.

When I realized that I'm not the boss of anyone but myself, that's where the magic began to happen.

You don't have to be the boss to be the adult. What do you have to lose?

About the Author

Jodee Bock is the owner of Bock's Office Transformational Consulting in Fargo, ND. She has more than 15 years of experience in the areas of corporate communication, media relations, executive coaching, and training and development. She is the author of *The 100% Factor: Living Your Capacity* and co-author of the books *Inviting Dialogue* and *Don't Miss Your Boat: Living Your Life With Purpose in the Real World*. Her blog is called You Already Know This Stuff, and you can find her website at www.bocksoffice.com.

Make Talent Your Business

Wendy Axelrod and Jeannie Coyle

---------------------------------- **Editor's Note** ----------------------------------

Are you a talent builder? Helping individuals and teams grow is at the core of what great managers do. Wendy Axelrod and Jeannie Coyle help shine a light on this potential and managerial actions that help people learn and develop. Our team members want to grow—we want to grow, too. But in a world where we check emails 24/7 and march to the drumbeat of a mile-long to-do list, we might not be doing everything we could to enhance learning.

Wouldn't it be terrific if the people you manage were developing new skills while they delivered results every day? They would be more productive, happier, *and* less likely to leave. You would get a kick out of seeing their personal and professional growth and building the "human assets," not only for your department but also for your company.

Yet for most managers this seems far out of reach. We have seen this dozens of times. In one company, where we asked to uncover why their high-end talent management tools were not delivering the substantial talent development they expected, managers gave us great insights. During multiple focus groups with managers we learned that they felt left out of the talent development process. Though they were chomping at the bit to make their mark, these managers were unsure of how to connect with the company's sophisticated efforts. And, despite their interest to take part, no one was expecting them (or equipping them) to play a significant role in talent development.

If you are wondering how your company's approach to making managers a force for talent development stacks up to others', read on. Surprisingly, any extensive research study shows that fewer than 10 percent of managers are held accountable for developing employees in significant ways and fewer than 5 percent are deemed good at it (Hewitt and Human Capital Institute, 2008). Instead, because managers are required to focus on this quarter's numbers, they often focus myopically on performance management, helping their employees get more effective in their current role and little else. Longer-term and more sophisticated development is pushed to the sidelines, with heavy reliance on the human resource and training departments. What a shame. Positioning the manager to provide significant development seems obvious and optimal—managers continuously communicate with employees, delegate work, identify resources to get the job done, and guide employees' performance (Hill, 2007; Tulgan, 2007). They are the prime channel for acting on the decades of research confirming that most development happens by learning through work experience.

In Search of a Solution

Inspired by those managers who develop their people in significant ways, while reaching or exceeding their numbers, we explored what they did so it could be done by other managers. During our research we conducted in-depth interviews with prequalified "exceptional development managers" (EDMs) and "exceptional developmental employees" (EDEs). While research participants represented their own views, they came from great firms such as Corning, Adidas, Siemens, Marriott, Xerox, Merck, and Kraft (28 companies in all). The research objective: to understand exactly how EDMs so notably grew employees' capabilities for the long haul—capabilities that matter most to business results such as handling sensitive client interfaces, influencing others to accept change, and leading diverse project teams.

A Manager Who Grows People Like Crazy

What we uncovered was revealing (Axelrod and Coyle, 2011). These managers went well beyond coaching and performance management that get immediate results. Take Lori for example. A manager at a large consulting firm, she views developing people as an integral part of her job. She deliberately staffs high-impact project teams with people who have diverse skills and learning needs. For example, you are likely to find professionals who possess great client interface skills mixed with those who are technically competent but not so good with clients. As people implement the project, they are expected to help each other close skill gaps.

Lori gets a good read on people and develops trusting relationships. She knows just how far to push them, but stands in the wings to steer them clear of career limiting mishaps. The high trust she has built allows her employees to open their minds and hearts to exploratory conversations in which she provides hard-hitting feedback. In some of these conversations she makes sure they understand how to navigate the complex organizational environment, helping them to deliver the full impact of their work with clients. Plus, she directs them on how to tap others in the work environment who might help deepen particular, complex skills.

Lori infuses the environment with learning and growth for everyone, not just a few, and her staff loves it. Her people have developed comprehensive skills that can take them well beyond their current responsibilities. She is a true talent magnet. Is it more work for Lori? Not really—once she learned how to do this, it became just *different* work, a new blend of management work that is deliberate, resourceful, and continuous when it comes to developing talent.

Lori's approach embodies all five practices of EDMs that we uncovered in our research. Let's take a deeper look at each of them. Like Lori, though their names have been changed, and their actions seem heroic, the EDMs we cite below are based upon real managers who participated in the research.

Make Every Day a Development Day

Focus people on results and development simultaneously using "stretchy" work and continuous and daily support to help them develop more and get bigger and better results.

Consider the example of Juan Carlos whom we know from a West Coast high-tech design and manufacturing company. He takes risks with people by giving them the latitude and explicit requirement to learn. He thoughtfully picks the right new experience to tuck into the crevices of their work—with just the right degree of stretch. He determines that right degree of stretch by knowing his employees so well. Since he knows not only their current skill level, but also their level of resilience, he is able to help stretch them without breaking them. He then puts a double requirement into place to require both results and a new level of capability. At the finish line of the assignment, employees are expected to break through two ribbons—one for results and one for development.

But, he does not stop there. Juan Carlos is close by every day. This proximity positions him to see and seize developmental moments—asking thoughtful questions and providing on-the-spot observations that get people thinking and acting differently. So instead of saying, "Do it this way," he prompts new insight with a question such as, "How can this action link with other things we do for offer clients, rather than being a stand-alone?" He also bolsters development in the special way he staffs work teams. He is very purposeful in the way he shapes assignments in team projects to allow for peer coaching while insisting the team make progress in both results *and* learning. Juan Carlos says, *"It is a matter of seamlessly merging results and development and making it an everyday occurrence."*

Tap the Psychological Side of Development

Create a trusting relationship that makes it safe for employees to hear and act on feedback, take risks, and become more aware both of what's driving them and of their impact on others. Often, smart people think they know the answers. And when it comes to the toughest things, like increasing self-awareness, understanding how their behavior impacts others, and the best ways to influence others—it is a real challenge for them to open their minds enough to develop.

Consider EDM Ravi, who is even smarter. He gets to know his people and takes the time to build trusting relationships with them. Though many managers believe employee trust comes with their title, research shows otherwise. By building trust through explicit actions (e.g., fulfilling commitments made, being transparent in communications, showing faith in their abilities), Ravi opens employees' receptiveness to his questions and feedback. Unlike many other managers, he is then in a position to hold up a mirror and help employees look at their own emotions and behaviors during very difficult situations (e.g., when they have had a setback or received surprisingly negative feedback from others). They gain new insights that help them manage their emotions rather than be controlled by them.

He also has the guts to hear and act on the truth about *himself* as others see it. He even shares how he adjusts his own inner struggles (e.g., "I was angry, but realized I could rise above that and find a win–win"). This openness gives him the platform to cultivate great relationships with his employees. Getting to know his people well gives Ravi a few advantages. They know they can come to him when things go off track, rather than covering over their mistakes. He can also make good decisions on how far out to push people. He keeps a watchful eye, but allows them to experience some minor bumps and bruises knowing that is part of spreading their wings. Often, the scarier the experience, the more development it packs. One of his direct reports said, *"The greatest development I ever had came when my manager really pushed me out on the ledge …but quietly had my back the whole time."*

Connect People With Development Partners

Open up the door to help people connect with a rich network of people who have the expertise people need to learn. Then teach them how to get the most learning from the relationship and be there to help employees transfer that learning to their work.

Having a mentor is great, but having a good boss and mentor is not enough. And for many managers developing all their people can be overwhelming. EDM Linda connects people to several development partners, knowing full well she doesn't have to do all the development herself. She relishes the wonderful multiplier effect of hooking people up with the right source of learning at the right time, which also lightens her load.

She found she needs to help people understand the value of this approach so they don't just stick close to home but venture out to find the right partners. Linda lets them know that there are better experts out there than herself, and that she is not always available when they need it. Then, she helps employees get crystal clear about what skill they need to learn, so they can narrow the search for those who both have the targeted skill and have the willingness to be a development partner. Other managers might keep the development goal too vague (e.g., "improve sales approach"), but Linda guides employees to get exactly what is needed (e.g., "learn how to close the sales presentation and follow up"). Linda then provides employees specific guidance for structuring the development partner relationship for mutual satisfaction and best learning. After all, the development partner's motivation to do this volunteer work may well come from feeling respected and seeing some mutual value derived from this developmental partnership.

Ensuring her employees use development partners does not mean she is missing in action. Linda ties the effort together by asking what the employee has learned, and how he or she is applying the new skill. She also helps employees look at ways they can hone the new skill by using it in a variety of situations.

Teach Skills to Navigate Organization Politics

Help people map the political terrain and enter it prepared to not only survive but thrive, producing results that stick while reducing the time managers spend cleaning up political missteps.

Political naïveté has killed more good ideas and careers than we care to recall. Many people avoid the very notion of what they consider "dirty" politics. Without realizing it, employees who want to keep their heads down in their work without venturing into the organization's political landscape limit their effectiveness. Their efforts, while seemingly correct, are not shaped to be applied well in their environment (e.g., an employee-designed system that has tons of technology features but does not align well with other company processes because the employees did not check in with stakeholders or those who had objections). But EDM Jared from a global company in electronics and electrical engineering knows in his bones that politics is about the power to positively make things happen. He says, "I've gotten really good at spotting when people don't 'get it' and have lots of ways to help them embrace the importance of mastering politics."

Jared takes a learn-by-doing approach and helps them map the political terrain they are traversing. He helps them see that the terrain often has invisible bumps and obstacles, such as another team angling to dominate available funds, or an executive who can influence the outcome but is unimpressed with the direction of Jared's team's project. Then he works with them to put strategies and skills in place to get through the terrain with results, not injuries. Tools such as force field analysis or stakeholder interviews can suddenly come to life for employees whose success depends on getting the right decision makers onboard. One technique Jared often uses is to rehearse people for delicate high-stakes presentations or discussions with powerful players. He says, "I try to make my staff the Indiana Jones of the political jungle!"

Shape Your Environment to Drive Development

Weave development into the very texture of the organization, making it an ongoing expectation and abundant reality, not just for high-potentials, but for all. Master ways to manage the interface between your group and the broader organization. Create the space to take risks to put people in developmental work and to increase the value of development tools the company offers. This EDM practice is a bit different from the four others because it focuses on the department surroundings rather than the direct interface with employees.

Consider the case of EDM Ellen who is a master weaver of development environments. She is adept at doing lots of small things regularly that create the demand for learning, and then she applies just the right touch (after-action reviews, questions to spur next steps, etc.) to make it stick. But it is the volume and consistency of these actions—applied abundantly to all staff, not just high-potentials—that creates a self-sustaining environment, rich with development. Employees are drawn to the reputation of her shop because they know they will learn and thrive there.

Ellen also leverages company tools to positive effect. Knowledgeable about structured programs (e.g., development planning, 360 feedback, and coaching programs), she has worked with the HR department to gain the situational leeway to match the right tool to the right person at the right time. It does not work out every time, but HR often supports her by integrating its offerings into her practical development game plan.

Ellen is also a savvy activist when it comes to managing the risks of interfacing with the broader environment. She lives in a company that exhorts managers to develop people, but truth be told, the culture does not accept the risk of failure that comes with learning from experience. She has learned when and how to fly below the radar, and when to assert the development interests of her people with upper management, negotiating how she will provide cover for individuals' regular duties while they take on stretch assignments. No matter which approach she takes, her department always delivers results gaining her more political capital to take reasonable developmental risks. We were a bit surprised by the tales from the front line of managers like Ellen, who valiantly face these risks. One told us, *"People have no idea how bloodied I get standing up for their development in the face of pressures for short-term results."*

A Call to Action for All Leaders: Make Talent Your Business

Mostly, we have been directing our conversation to managers in the hopes that they will increase their use of these five exceptional development practices. If more managers in the company use these practices, it will make a difference. But to make a big impact it will take an organizational effort. Just imagine the benefits of having an organization full of EDMs. Your company would attract and retain spirited employees who love striving for higher levels of performance. Managers would continuously prepare employees for more complex and changing work, expanding your company's capabilities to innovate and stay in front of competitors. We believe that training and development leaders can lead the charge to grow the supply of EDMs systematically. Our call to action to training and development leaders is to start with these four practical actions:

- **Influence the resetting of managerial expectations.** Work with company leaders to reshape the role of manager as talent developer, not as an "add-on" but as central to their role. Help eradicate the philosophy that attaining results drives out all other objectives. Instead, communicate that continually growing the business means striving for a double ribbon at the finish line—both results and development, seamlessly integrated as part of daily management. This means a recalibration of their current roles to take off some operational pressure (and to stop piling on all those extra projects) to make space for these developmental duties. As proof that it can work, seek out examples in your company where managers with developmentally focused departments get better results, retention, and increased capability to take on more complex efforts.
- **Build demand.** Create a groundswell from the managerial ranks of those who see the value, are developing employees beyond their current roles, and want to learn how to significantly grow talent. Our research indicates the abundant benefits of being EDMs. Their employees will expand their approach to learning, take on more challenging assignments, work more independently, and require less of

managers' time to clean up mishaps. EDMs also told us their teams were higher performing, their professional reputations were enhanced, and perhaps most importantly they felt the deep personal gratification of growing others.

- **Determine delivery methods for managers' development.** Develop managers so they, in turn, can intentionally develop others. The usual development workshops, particularly coaching, feedback, and delegation, will be a part of this but not nearly sufficient. Find ways to include learning about the five practices of EDMs. Invest in approaches to develop the skills of managers to amplify learning from their work experiences, orchestrate their peer mentoring and access to others, gain greater self-awareness, increase their repertoire of influencing others, and, where appropriate, provide expert coaching.

- **Create the most compelling results.** Savvy learning and development leaders know that measures of attendance in development programs hardly scratch the surface. Create measures that will help validate why these EDM practices are essential for your organization. Determine the appropriate Kirkpatrick level three and four measures. For example, add three questions to your employee engagement survey to measure how well employees are developing through experience with hands-on help from managers.

Enhanced capability to develop your workforce equals better bottom-line results with intervening benefits for the business such as attracting and retaining talented employees, managers better positioned to address change, and increasing capabilities to outpace the competition. The five proven practices for making talent your business will not only give you enormous satisfaction but also help transform your employees and the business.

References and Resources

Axelrod, Wendy, and Jeannie Coyle. (2011). *Make Talent Your Business.* San Francisco: Berrett-Koehler.

Hewitt and Human Capital Institute. (2008). The State of Talent Management: Today's Challenges, Tomorrow's Opportunities. Retrieved from www.hci.org/files/portalupload/hci/hciLibraryPaper_79300.pdf.

Hill, Linda. (2007). Becoming the Boss. *Harvard Business Review, 85*(1). Boston: Harvard Business School Publishing.

Tulgan, Bruce. (2007). *It's OK to Be the Boss.* New York: HarperCollins.

About the Authors

Wendy Axelrod, PhD, is managing partner of Talent Savvy Manager and co-author of *Make Talent Your Business: How Exceptional Managers Develop People While Getting Results.* A recognized thought leader in talent development, Wendy works with line and HR executives to heighten the organization impact of their talent management, leadership development, and executive coaching efforts. Some of her past clients include Deloitte, Vanguard, Novo Nordisk, Occidental, Sanofi, Shire, and Merck.

Jeannie Coyle is managing partner of Talent Savvy Manager and co-author of *Make Talent Your Business: How Exceptional Managers Develop People While Getting Results*. Jeannie is a trusted advisor to business leaders as an executive coach and partner in the design of organizations and leadership development systems. Her clients include 3M, Intel, Nike, American Express, GE Capital, and Wells Fargo.

You can find Wendy and Jeannie's website at www.talentsavvymanager.com/.

✎ Section IV

Management Is a Social Act

"Relationships are all there is. Everything in this universe only exists because it is in relationship to everything else. Nothing exists in isolation. We have to stop pretending we are individuals that can go it alone."

—Margaret Wheatley

Chapter 31

Unmanaging the Network

David Weinberger, PhD

······························· **Editor's Note** ·······························

David Weinberger is an amazing thinker and synthesizer of meta and micro trends and data. His observations about technology—and the sociological shifts that are occurring—are insightful and game changing. My reaction after reading one of his posts is often "whoa." I am so pleased to be able to share several of David's pieces with you and hope that you will find them a source of inspiration, discomfort (learning dissonance), and then a catalyst for action.

Lisa Haneberg asked me if she could reprint several of my columns from *Knowledge Management World* for this management handbook. Together we selected the columns we felt might be most useful to managers.

They try to provide some context for the changes we're all confronting in our business environments. Their overall point—or at least their starting point—is that these changes are even more pervasive and fundamental than we often think they are. So many of our practices are built on assumptions already being overturned by the Net, for the Net is providing new ways for us humans to connect with one another and with our ideas. Until the Net arrived, not only had we been moving at the pace of paper, but we'd accepted the limitations paper has imposed on everything from who gets to speak to what constitutes being done with a project. Because every aspect of business has to do with humans connecting with one another, the Net opens an opportunity to reinvent ourselves and our businesses as deeply as we want to go—beginning with how we make sense of our environment, and how we do so together, which is the basic theme of these columns.

I hope you find them helpful. Either way, feel free to let me know at self@evident.com.

September 29, 2008: The Ambiguity of Information

We are very confused about the meaning of the word "information." And that's for two good reasons.

First, it's a really important word, and important words are almost always stretched to the ripping point as they struggle to cover topic after topic after topic. (Perhaps this indicates that topics are more different, and less susceptible to uniform explanations, than we think.) Second, the word "information" became important because a particular genius—Claude Shannon—took it out of everyday parlance and used it in a very different way in his theory. It's as if Einstein had used the word "deliciousness" instead of "relativity," so now when we talk about Swiss Chocolate Almond ice cream we're not sure if ….

OK, skip the analogy. The point is that Shannon gave "information" a mathematical, probabilistic sense that had little to do with what we'd meant by the term before that. His theory was so powerful that it got applied to everything from DNA to black holes, and thus the term "information" got spread around and intermingled with the ordinary sense, along with the communication theory sense and the computer science sense, until it became a hodgepodge word. It has some precise meanings within particular limited fields, but if you try to define the term as it's used in the phrase "The Information Age," I bet you can't in a way that covers everything we mean by it.

Throughout the Information Age, however, the term has also retained its original meaning. That meaning is hard to pin down, too, but only in the usual way that words escape their definitions. Its normal sense hasn't changed much in the past 150 years. In fact, the memoirs of Charles Babbage are a good place to use as a source. Babbage is the English inventor and mathematician who is credited with designing gear-based computers, starting in the 1820s, that anticipated the modern computer with eerie precision. In fact, that's a very bad misreading of Babbage, in my opinion, but that's a different hobby horse to ride.

In his memoirs, written in the 1860s, Babbage uses the word "information" 28 times. In most of those instances, he means something quite ordinary, such as when he says he asked some young classmates how to invoke the devil, and they gave him that information. We can get all twisted up in trying to figure out what are the defining characteristics of the class of statement called "information," but it's really much simpler than that. In most of those instances, Babbage means information to be simply something about the world that he did not know before. And that remains one of our usual senses of the term as well.

But a second meaning shows up in Babbage's memoirs. For example, to help the British railway system decide what the distance between the rails should be, Babbage set up a metering system to measure the sway of railway coaches. The data that his instruments produced he casually refers to as "information." And that does indeed refer to a special class of knowledge: what fits into a table.

The importance of table-based information cannot be over-emphasized. Before computers, tables of numbers were crucial to applying mathematics. If you wanted to know the angle at which to aim your artillery, you had to look it up in a table. Galileo himself created and sold artillery tables. In fact, tables could themselves be an instrument of computation. For example, in 1684, Edmond Halley noticed a pattern of recurrence in the appearance of a comet. Yet it didn't come back as regularly as it should. Halley thought that perhaps this was because of the subtle gravitational forces of the planets. But he couldn't figure out how to calculate that, so he went to Newton himself. The "three body problem" was too hard, Newton said, demurring. It took three French aristocrats spending an entire summer filling in a table, manually calculating the gravitational forces' effect on the comet at step-by-step intervals, to confirm that Halley's comet was indeed a single heavenly object.

But there was a problem with tables. Because they were created by humans, they were error prone. They'd issue errata sheets, and then errata sheets for the errata sheets. In fact, the French tables that predicted Halley's comet's return only worked because—it was discovered later—the copious errors canceled one another out. Jonathan Swift declared mathematics to be a dim science precisely because we would never get the tables right.

But Swift didn't count on Adam Smith. When the French government, after the Revolution, ordered new logarithmic and trigonometric tables created to reflect the new metric system, Gaspard de Prony used Smith's description of the division of labor to structure the process. De Prony broke down the task of computing tables into a few simple steps, most of which could be performed by workers who only had to know how to do basic math. In fact, many of the people he hired were former hairdressers to aristocrats who had lost their hair because they had lost their heads. De Prony manufactured tables the way factories manufactured pins, he said. Babbage explicitly characterizes his own mechanical computers the same way: They were intended to be factories for the complete and error-free manufacturing of tables. (David Alan Grier's *When Computers Were Human* is a terrific history of tables.)

Tables-based information is familiar to us. Tables pare a topic down to a simple set of repeating parameters. They are designed for fast retrieval. They are unambiguous. They are intensely useful. They are basically what we find in computerized databases. But if information stayed that simple, we wouldn't be calling this the Information Age. For that, we had to take information as standing for something far more important. In the Age of Information, information becomes the very stuff of consciousness and even (according to some) of physics. Tables are too humble to carry such a burden.

So, we know what information was. We know what it still is, within circumscribed areas. But this is the Information Age, not the Age of Electronic Tables. Information means something much more than what it meant to Babbage. The problem is that we have an entire age named after it, and we still can't say what it is. We have reconstructed our understanding of our world and ourselves using a term we don't understand and don't agree about.

What a species.

January 2, 2009: What Crowds Are Wise At

Meme used to mean something very specific. It came from chapter 11 of Richard Dawkins's book on genetics, *The Selfish Gene*: "Just as genes propagate themselves in the gene pool by leaping from body to body via sperms or eggs, so memes propagate themselves in the meme pool by leaping from brain to brain ...."

When the term jumped kingdoms and took root in the world of the Internet, it still signified something fairly confined: an idea that had taken on a life of its own. "Meme" had indeed become a meme. But over time, it's lost its original significance. Now the term means something like "an Internet fad." It's become sloppy and loose-edged. Richard Dawkins may or may not like what's happened to his coinage, but he should. It's a sign of the term's success.

The same has happened to James Surowiecki's phrase "the wisdom of crowds," which was the title of his 2004 book. Surowiecki meant something quite clearly defined by it: There are situations in which little bits of evidence from lots of people, when properly processed, create results more accurate and reliable than the estimates of experts. Surowiecki's lead example is Francis Galton's surprise that you get a closer estimate of the weight of an ox by averaging the guesses of people at a county fair than you do by relying on an expert at oxen.

Surowiecki's book is quite methodical. He breaks the wisdom of crowds into three types. First, there are *cognitive* questions with precise answers, addressed by (for example) prediction markets. Second, there are issues of *coordination*, such as the way sidewalk traffic optimizes itself without any top-down plans, simply because each person acts in her own self-interest. Third, there are times when you want individuals to *cooperate* in ways that create mutual advantages by seeing beyond their own immediate interests, such as paying taxes.

In his book, Surowiecki carefully looks at the conditions for success of each of these three types. He is an economist and a careful thinker. But, the title of his book is so good that it quickly escaped him, just as the "meme" meme escaped from the godless hands of Richard Dawkins. (Note: "Godless" because Dawkins's most recent book is an argument against God. So that wasn't as random an aspersion as it may have seemed.)

The phrase "wisdom of the crowd" now seems to refer to anything a bunch of people can do better than people alone, especially once it gave birth to the term "crowd sourcing." Sites that let citizens report burned out streetlights are now examples of the wisdom of the crowd, as are sites that let citizens upload videos of their government representatives. At some point, I expect that Texas Hold'em sites will be put forward as examples of the wisdom of the crowd because they let good players succeed … a type of wisdom of the crowd that joins it with Dawkins's evolutionary sense of "meme."

The term is being stretched and pulled until it's just about unrecognizable. That is, it's succeeding.

But why? When a phrase gets noticed and then gets so widely applied, it's because it—perhaps inadvertently—calls attention to a phenomenon that we want to be able to note and talk about. In this case, we seem to be eager to point out all the ways in which groups of people do better than individuals. It's as if we have a case to make. Historically, we'd been told that individuals are the source of real value, that groups are at best suspect and at worst mere abstractions, that if you set individuals free they will automatically build a fair world.

We didn't have to wait for the failure of deregulated markets and Alan Greenspan's dismal apology to start recognizing that competitive individuals are not the answer to every problem. So, now we slap the "wisdom of the crowd" or "crowd sourcing" label on everything, as if to say: "Nope. You got your assumptions wrong. Get 'em right, and we can build the world's greatest encyclopedia, replace network TV, and find lost cufflinks." It's not always true, but the challenge to our assumptions is just about always welcome and helpful.

If you want to see how eager we are to make that case and to challenge those assumptions, just look at all the places we are applying those "crowd"-based labels. The thinness to which we've stretched the term is a measure of how eager we are to show the power and value of connecting with one another.

And please note that taking the range of ways in which we've applied the term as evidence for a desire to connect is, yes, a type of crowd sourcing.

April 1, 2009: Knowledge and Understanding

There are things I know and things I understand. The distinction is blurry, but real. And crucial.

Rather than simply trying to think our way into the definitions, let's look at some cases where we use the words. For nontechnical terms, that's often the surest way to proceed.

Here are some things I know (or at least think I do): The names of the twentieth century U.S. presidents, in order. The capital of New York. The name of the waitress at Mandy & Joe's. How malaria is transmitted. When *The Daily Show* airs. My waist size in inches. Which of our children was born with black hair. Where the #66 bus stops in Cambridge.

Here are some things I think I understand: Why Pluto was demoted from its status as a planet. How simple electrical circuits work. The effect federally mandated testing has had on our local public schools. Why John McCain chose Sarah Palin. Why one of our children chose not to go to college.

What's the difference? For one thing, what I know isn't as open to argument as what I understand. If you want to insist that Hubert Humphrey was a twentieth century president, I'm not going to argue with you much. I'm going to look it up and prove that you're wrong. If you don't accept the evidence, I'm going to break off the conversation because we don't agree enough about the rules of the road to safely share a highway. If, however, you disagree with me about why McCain chose Palin, the argument is likely to be much longer. Furthermore, it's entirely possible that you and I will end the discussion without feeling the need to resolve the issue.

In fact, we may leave the Palin discussion each acknowledging that there's a possibility that the other was right, or that the other person's explanation could be part of the overall explanation. That's unlikely to be the case about our dispute over President Humphrey. If you don't change your mind by the end of it, you will not have affected what I know about Hubert Humphrey, although you may have changed my understanding of exactly what sort of pig-headed, !$#%#-ing ignoramus you are. For the same reason, I can reasonably claim to understand the effect of federally mandated testing on our schools without thinking that

I've grasped it as fully or as certainly as my knowledge that Hubert Humphrey was not ever elected president. Understanding allows for more nuance, probability, and multiplicity than knowledge does.

There's a third distinction. The examples of knowledge that I gave are fact-based. Each could be phrased in a sentence: "Here is the list of twentieth century presidents: ... " or "Malaria is transmitted by mosquitoes." The examples of understanding, on the other hand, would all require longer statements, and those statements may themselves need yet more explanation: "Pluto was demoted because an international body of astronomers voted on a definition of planets, which they had to do because of discoveries of large bodies in our solar system that ... " etc. Understandings take longer to explain because they connect multiple ideas in ways that go beyond the ideas themselves. That's why we can test someone's understanding by asking questions that go beyond what is explicitly known in the understanding: "So, if you understand why Pluto was demoted, why did it take so long? Why was it done by vote? Could geographers get together and demote some mountains?"

Although knowledge and understanding are different sorts of things, they are, of course, related. My understanding (which is shaky) of McCain's choice of Palin is based on some of what I know about the case and could be changed if I read the transcripts of the confidential phone calls between them. Similarly, my knowledge of the list of twentieth century presidents only counts as knowledge, and not as empty phrases, because I *understand* that we live in a country that elects presidents every four years and has done so for hundreds of years.

Now, ask yourself which you would rather have: knowledge with no understanding, or understanding with no knowledge? Knowledge with no understanding gets you nowhere. Plus, it makes you a bore at parties. Understanding with no knowledge is of no use. You need both.

But we have put such a premium on knowledge in our culture that we sometimes forget that the point of knowing is to understand. Perhaps that's because knowledge is easier to evaluate and to manage—you don't see a lot of "understanding management" systems around, thank heavens. Knowledge also doesn't have the squishiness of understanding, a squishiness that is in fact understanding's strength: Multiple ways of understanding can enrich one another. For whatever reason, understanding has gotten short shrift.

It's time to lengthen understanding's shrift.

Feburary 1, 2010: Bring on the Info Overload

Information overload isn't the problem we once thought it was. In fact, as the Internet Age got started, it renounced its entire heritage, and even changed its basic character. It's as if Jenna Bush changed her last name to Gore and then transformed from a person into, say, a climate. In the case of info overload, the change tells us a lot about our current age.

The term "information overload" was coined as a follow-on to "sensory overload," a term with a related and revelatory history. The first use of the actual phrase that I can find was in a paper by Donald B. Lindsley at a conference at Harvard Medical School in June 1958. But it entered popular use in the mid-1960s. For example, an article in *The Nation* in 1966 introduces the phrase as if it were unfamiliar to readers: "Recent experimentation, however, has confirmed the significance of the problem of sensory overload; that is, of an inability to absorb more than a certain amount of experience in a given time." In 1968, in testimony to a Senate panel on drug experience, a witness used the term and again had to explain what it means. So, we can put the phrase's rise into ordinary usage right at the beginning of the popular career of psychedelic drugs.

Sensory Overload Concept

The concept of sensory overload (not the phrase) is usually traced back to an article by Georg Simmel, "The Metropolis and Mental Life," written in 1903, when we didn't yet know about the joys of LSD and the Grateful Dead. Simmel points to the effects the onrush of sensations have on the mental life of city dwellers. "Man is a creature whose existence is dependent on differences, i.e., his mind is stimulated by the difference between present impressions and those which have preceded," he wrote. Put us in a city, and we'll cope with the onrush of "violent stimuli" by becoming more head than heart, by becoming indifferent, by becoming numb.

This psychological observation was in sync with what people had seen happen during World War II. Soldiers were known to sleep through artillery attacks, so numbed were they by the overwhelming landscape of sensation.

Our "Channel Capacity"

Simmel's article was translated into English in 1950, and it began to have an effect, in part because it rode on the back of the burgeoning new science of information. The brain started to look like one end of a communication system, connected by "channels" that could get overloaded the way a telephone wire could have so many inputs that all you got at the other end was noise. That's exactly how Alvin Toffler explained the notion of information overload in his 1970 bestseller, *Future Shock*. Suppose we were being overwhelmed not by mere sensations—the constant sounds of cars, the mingled smells of multiple sidewalk carts—but by information? Toffler is thinking of information here not as an information scientist—sequences of bits with varying degrees of predictability—and not as mere sensation, but as small, intelligible facts about our world. In explaining information overload, however, Toffler uses the concepts of information science: The amount of information we're given in the modern world can exceed our "channel capacity" and our brain's processing power.

When information overload started off, it created the same sorts of difficulties as sensory overload: Info overload was a psychological syndrome in which we lose our ability to act rationally. Overload us with information and we won't be able to make good decisions, we were cautioned. "Sanity itself thus hinges" on avoiding information overload, Toffler warns.

Remarkable Adaptation

But that's not how we think about information overload now, even though the amount of information far outstrips what Toffler feared would unhinge us. (It's actually quite amusing to read the research from the mid-1970s that thought that consumers faced with 16 different fields of information on the labels of competing products would suffer from information overload. Sixteen? Hahahaha.) We now think of information overload as a social issue, not a psychological one. We do not worry about losing our minds so much as not being able to find the information we need.

This is a remarkable story of adaptation. What we thought was a predicament that would destroy our ability to make rational decisions and might even drive us mad has now become simply our environment. It's where we live. Rather than fleeing from the overload of information, our concern is that we're not getting enough of it. We have adapted well. Or, perhaps, gone mad.

May 28, 2010: *A Lot to Hate...* But PowerPoint Brings Order to Unruly Thoughts

People hate all sorts of software because it's hard to use, under-featured, or just plain irritating. But they hate PowerPoint for deeper reasons—for what it does to meetings, for what it does to social interaction, for what it does to how we think. Yet that blind fury can bring us to forget that PowerPoint took us a big step past where we were.

The question whether PowerPoint is a merge scourge or a harbinger of the Apocalypse arose again recently because of an article in the *New York Times* by Elisabeth Bumiller

(April 26, 2010) about the Army's newly kindled hatred of PowerPoint. Apparently Gen. Stanley McChrystal was shown a PowerPoint slide "that was meant to portray the complexity of American military strategy," and replied, "When we understand that slide, we'll have won the war." We are told that the "room erupted in laughter," which I imagine is what usually happens when four-star generals make jokes.

Interconnections, or Not?

The article uses that anecdote to open a wider front in the war on PowerPoint. The military is apparently fed up with the amount of time spent on generating graphs and other visual aids for slide shows. And, PowerPoint inculcates the illusion that all the world's problems are "bullet-izable." Bullet points, says Gen. James Mattis, don't show the interconnections of "political, economic, and ethnic forces." Further, PowerPoint stifles discussion.

Wow, that's a lot of anger. There's so much anger that the complaints aren't even consistent: The article opens with a criticism of a slide that was too complex and showed the interconnection of lots of different elements, but quickly moves to criticizing PowerPoint slides for not showing complexity and interconnections. PowerPoint stifles discussion, we're told, although surely that's the fault of the guy in the suit at the front of the room who refuses to take his hand off the clicker.

Synthesis Is Important Too

So, let me say one positive thing about PowerPoint. In my limited experience, the introduction of PowerPoint (which depended upon the introduction of laptop projectors as standard gear for conference rooms) improved the logic of business presentations. Before PowerPoint, business managers would stand up in the front of the room and give rambling presentations that lacked coherence but demanded our attention. After PowerPoint, those presentations had more structure and more focus.

That's because PowerPoint requires you to break your ideas down into a series of points, one after another. Each point gets a slide. And on each slide, points get bullets that explain them or support them. PowerPoint forced business presenters to become more analytic.

Now, there are problems with how PowerPoint expects us to think. Analysis into chunks is important, but so is synthesis. When you've broken your ideas down into a series of slides, one after another, it's important to keep in mind what the overall context is; PowerPoint gives us no tools for that. It does nothing to connect the slides logically or thematically. Instead it gives us fancy transitions that, if they're effective, make us say, "Oooh," and forget the point the presenter was trying to make. Putting eye-candy between slides tells us nothing about the relationship between the slides, much less remind us where we are in the overall arc of the story or argument.

A Measure of Order

This is one of the ways that Keynote—Macintosh presentation software—is superior to PowerPoint. Keynote has a transition ("Magic Move") that automatically moves and sizes elements seamlessly from one slide to another, so at least you can knit together two slides in a meaningful way. Aside from that, Keynote is as bad as PowerPoint at giving easy ways for presenters to show the overall arc.

Sure, there's lots to hate about PowerPoint, some of which is genuinely a part of the product (such as the discreteness of the slides) and some of which is merely enabled by the product (such as decks with 100+ slides, each with 15 bullet points in colors that can't be discerned against the background, and each read by a guy who thinks he's clarifying important ideas). But we should also take a brief moment to remember that PowerPoint brought a measure of order and logic to our unruly thoughts.

May 1, 2011: The Human Drive of Tech

I've been thinking a lot about technodeterminism these days, for two primary reasons.

First, I've seemed to side pretty heavily, in my "career," with the technodeterminists, that is, with those who think that the Internet has an effect on us, and that that effect has a certain inevitability. If you say, for example, that the Internet will change business or politics, you are saying that technology itself has a determining effect, and you are a technodeterminist. I have been that person.

Second, technodeterminism is quite possibly quite wrong. If it means that we are helpless pawns in the hands of our tech, it is certainly wrong. If it means that technology has the same effect on all people regardless of their culture, socioeconomic class, or personality, then it is certainly wrong. If technodeterminism means that our technology once spawned will overcome all obstacles, we are now witnessing the terrible disproof of that as we hand our Internet to providers who want to turn it into something tame, dumb and lucrative for them.

The fact that technodeterminism is a false doctrine (#2) has made me feel fairly foolish for my earlier espousal of it (#1). But I realized something obvious recently that makes me think the focus on technodeterminism itself is misguided.

I came to this obvious realization because someone asked me to write something about how *The Cluetrain Manifesto*—a book I co-authored with Rick Levine, Christopher Locke, and Doc Searls—is standing up 12 years after the Cluetrain.com site went up. Ever since the tenth anniversary, the authors have been asked that question with some regularity, so I've got an answer down. It includes an early acknowledgement of the book's technodeterminist triumphalism.

But, this time I realized that I don't fully believe that criticism. Sure, technology is just a tool, and you can use an oar to propel a boat or to fuel a campfire. But the real question isn't whether the Internet taken by itself forces certain effects on us, but whether the Internet (plus we users) has determinative effects.

The answer to that question is, I believe, still yes. But the determinative power of the Internet does not come from its technology. It comes from the humans who use it. That's in fact what *Cluetrain*—and much else I've written since—says. It's also why I love the Internet: It provides an opportunity for some frustrated and worthy human traits to flourish.

Technology already reflects our interests, of course. For example, the uber-geeks who created the Internet built it as a protocol for the movement of bits without discrimination among the bits because they thought that would help fulfill the human need for open information and the human urge to innovate. If they had had in mind a different set of human needs and limits—say, to protect copyright owners—they would have created a different piece of technology. So, tech already reflects ideas about who we are and what we want.

Of course we can use tech in ways its creators did not envision, just as Pringles cans turn out to be pretty handy for focusing and directing Wi-Fi signals. But that's just to say that the tendencies we build into technology can be overcome by the determination of humans.

But are humans determined? As President Obama once said about the question of when life begins, that's beyond my pay grade. Nevertheless, there are some broad generalizations about us that seem not only to be generally true, but that are good to believe because they move us toward better policies and more happiness. For example, I'd be OK saying that we humans are social creatures, that we are all interested in what happens to us and to our fellow creatures, that we are explosively creative, that language is fundamental to who we are, that we all have an equal right to life, liberty, and the pursuit of happiness.

From these truths—assuming for the moment that you accept them, and if you don't, I have no Plan B for convincing you of them—come few determinant actions. But, they let us make some general statements about how we'll use the Net. We'll use it to be social, to pursue our interests, to engage with others, to be creative. If that's determinist, it's not because the technology is forcing us to use itself one way and not another. The determinism comes from the human side of the equation. And that's also exactly where the hope comes from, too.

September 1, 2011: The Wisdom of Impractical Knowledge

In the 1980s, when the idea that data, information, knowledge, and wisdom formed some sort of pyramidal value chain, knowledge started to get redefined as "actionable information." This was not the first time in Western history that knowledge was tied to the practical as opposed to a purer understanding of the cosmos, but within the business world it seems to have stuck. Knowledge that does not help you make better decisions is not knowledge worth having, or possibly is not knowledge at all.

This idea would be dangerous if put into practice.

Let's say your company is trying to decide if it should acquire a promising start-up. Sure, there is a set of numbers you'd better pay attention to. That's the easy part. But you can't possibly predict what it is you need to know to make the decision, and any attempt to do so could have disastrous consequences.

For example, let's say the start-up has a new way to make contact lenses. Let's say one of your engineers wants to go to a video game conference. Under the rule that says that it's only knowledge if it leads to making better decisions, the engineer should not be enabled to go to the conference. She, therefore, fails to attend the session on new video card technology that compensates for the ocular weaknesses of individual users, and thus the company fails to anticipate the breakthrough that obviates the need for contact lenses.

The problem here is not with the redefinition of knowledge as actionable information that leads to better decisions, for what your engineer would have learned certainly would have affected your company's decisions. The problem is that acting on that definition of knowledge would keep your company from sending your engineer to a place where it is unlikely she would have acquired what turns out to be actionable information. This seemingly hardheaded, pragmatic view of knowledge, if put into practice, can lead to less knowledge and worse decisions.

In fact, if you want knowledge that leads to better decisions, you need a way to include more. Indeed, you need to know more than any one individual can know. Fortunately, we now have technology that makes us better at that than ever: networks. Social networks have always enabled this: One of your VPs is in a knitting circle with (I'm just trying to get away from saying "plays golf with") a product VP at a chip company who mentions a new vision-correcting algorithm rumored to be under development—or, more likely, whose teenage child has read about it in a gaming magazine—and now you've learned some "actionable information." Our new technological network enables those social networks to extend around the world, to post information in ways we can reference, to filter and forward information with surprising efficiency, and to build the trust that enables even competitors to share what they're thinking about. Knowledge now lives in networks.

The irony is that the view of knowledge as actionable information that leads to better decisions was initially suggested as a heuristic for reducing information: In the sea of information, knowledge supposedly consisted of the few islands that actually have practical implications. Knowledge thus seemed manageable. The problem is that you can't tell the islands from the oceans ahead of time. Telling one from the other, in fact, requires making decisions.

The greatest irony is that in this view, just as knowledge is a reduction of information down to what matters, wisdom is proposed as a reduction of knowledge. That's why data, information, knowledge, and wisdom arrange themselves into a pointy pyramid. But wisdom is not really knowledge filtered and condensed into a bouillon cube. Instead, wisdom often starts with an openness to the farthest reaches of the sea of possibilities—seen from a vantage point that defines the person and gives coherence to her vision.

That is a very different model of data, information, knowledge, and wisdom than the pyramid suggests. Each layer is not a reduction of the other. And they are not a mere sea of equivalent molecules. They are more like a primordial soup. The wise person comprehends broadly and is able to bring molecules into connection. Knowing is creating. Deciding is affirming creation.

Conclusion

What practices and behaviors might the ideas in these columns lead to? Here are some ideas.

Let data get complex. There's tremendous value in the complex relations that will emerge from a data set that is not kept arbitrarily simple.

Get the balance of chaos and order right. If order always wins in your environment, you're missing out on opportunities.

Do not assume that the Net builds culture. It won't happen by itself. It requires patient, gentle gardening...and the occasional bold action.

Similarly, do not assume that all members of your team (or, more exactly, your extended network) are equally at home on the Net. Some people are shy; some people feel intimidated; some people don't type very fast. If you are not careful, the old inequities (and some new ones) will re-emerge on your network.

Businesses often are tempted to view decisions as the most important act. Decisions are obviously important, but they are not isolated nodes. They occur within networks that lead up to them, carry them out, and appropriate them.

Most important, the Net gives us the chance to build smart networks—networks that are smarter than their smartest participant. It takes work and care, but it's crucial both because of the benefits a smart network brings, and because it is also possible for networks to make us dumber.

Do not assume you can do any of this alone. Build a smart network to help you build a smart network. And have the fun of creativity and collegiality as you do.

About the Author

David Weinberger, PhD, is the co-author of the seminal web business book, *The Cluetrain Manifesto,* and is the author of *Small Pieces Loosely Joined, Everything Is Miscellaneous,* and *Too Big to Know* (January 2012). He has been a marketing vice president and marketing consultant since the mid-1980s He is a senior researcher at Harvard's Berkman Center for Internet & Society. You can find his work at www.hyperorg.com.

The columns included in this chapter have been reprinted from *Knowledge Management World* with permission.

Chapter 32

How to Fascinate

Sally Hogshead

-- **Editor's Note** --

Stick with me, here. Sally Hogshead is an advertising and branding genius. This is a book about management. Huh? To manage well, we need to inspire, excite, and grab the attention of our employees. I asked Sally to share her work on how we can utilize our strengths and natural style to fascinate those we work with and must influence. She created this chapter geared for managers just for you! Have some fun with this and engage your team in taking Sally's F-Score test. It is free and will lead to an illuminating conversation and deeper understanding about each other's gifts. If you struggle to have impact with others, this chapter might help you the most of all.

A hundred years ago, you didn't need to fascinate.

Back then, the average attention span was about 20 minutes long (an estimated one minute for each year of age, up until age 20). But then, a little thing called "The Internet" happened. Now people are overwhelmed by messages: voicemails and videos, emails and apps, updates and upgrades, tweets and retweets. So how do our brains respond to all this stimulation? Turns out, we're learning to think differently. We think *more quickly*, and get distracted *more easily*. The BBC announced: "The addictive nature of web browsing can leave you with an attention span of nine seconds—the same as a goldfish." *Nine seconds!*

That's all we get before our employees and customers can get distracted. We might only get nine seconds before their brains make an unconscious decision to either stay focused, or relocate to a new topic. If you fail to create connections, your co-workers and customers will swim away like the goldfish. You'll be forgotten—or worse, ignored.

In today's distracted and competitive environment, you must immediately spotlight your own unique competitive advantage. Only the most persuasive and influential managers will triumph.

In this battle for attention, fascination is your weapon.

Fascinating managers win. They have the ability to quickly start relationships. They create connections. They earn respect. They build better relationships, bigger networks, and deeper trust. Here's the bottom line. If you fail to immediately fascinate, you will lose more than attention. But if you tap into what makes your personality uniquely fascinating ... you win.

The reality is: You're already fascinating. My research proves it.

I'll explain why your personality is already fascinating. But first, let's explore the science of fascination, and the way in which it controls our decision making. What is "fascination," exactly? *Fascination is an intense emotional focus.* When you fascinate people, they become totally focused on you and your message. They stop fidgeting. They stop texting. They stop thinking about to-do lists and Facebook updates and what to feed their kids for dinner. Your message becomes more important than all the other things competing for their attention. When you achieve this level of intense emotional focus, your listeners become more alert and focused. Instead of being diverted by meaningless distractions, now, your message is their priority.

Think back to a time in your life when you were leading a presentation or expressing a point of view, and your audience was completely focused on you. They weren't just *listening*, and they weren't just *paying attention*. Your message was intensely captivating to your audience. Here's what was happening in this moment. Your members were opening themselves up to you, and your message. They were absorbing your ideas. They were lowering the barriers of cynicism and inertia. They stopped merely *listening* to you, and started *connecting* with you. This moment—this moment of intense emotional focus—is when you have an opportunity to persuade. In these moments, your audience is at its greatest likelihood of:

- making a purchase
- changing an opinion

- following your lead
- falling in love (and not just romantic love, but all kinds of love).

When you can create more opportunities to *fascinate*, you create opportunities to *sell, convert, lead,* and *connect*. In my research, described at the end of this chapter, I'll give examples of the qualitative studies behind this. Yet these opportunities are rare, because we live in a distracted world. As a result, the ability to fascinate is seen as a matter of luck, or raw charisma, or saying just the right thing. However, fascination is not luck. It's not a matter of being "in the zone" or any other circumstance left up to chance.

- Fascination is a scientifically proven, neurological response.
- The ability to fascinate is a choice.
- You can create the moments at will.
- You can create intensely emotional focus.
- You can do it with your own natural, hidden strengths of persuasion.
- And you can do it today.

Fascination is instinctive. It's born from a natural instinct to influence the behavior of others. But the key to mastering fascination is a conscious, strategic process of effectively activating what I call "triggers." You can become a more persuasive manager, once you understand how to apply the seven triggers of fascination.

The Seven Triggers of Fascination

There are exactly seven different types of fascination. I call these "fascination triggers." When it encounters a fascination trigger, your brain snaps into that intense emotional focus I described earlier. Fascination triggers are the key to creating persuasion. Your seven hardwired triggers of fascination are:

- **Power:** Take command.
- **Passion:** Attract with emotion.
- **Mystique:** Arouse curiosity.
- **Prestige:** Increase respect.
- **Alarm:** Create urgency.
- **Rebellion:** Change the game.
- **Trust:** Build loyalty.

You have all seven of the fascination triggers built into your personality. (In fact, you're already using these seven triggers at different times through the day.) Whether you realize it or not—whether you intend to or not—you're already using the seven triggers in management. The question is Are you using the right triggers, in the right way, to get your desired result?

The F-Score Personality Test

Based on my research, I developed a free, fast tool to evaluate how you are most likely to persuade others: the F-Score test. You can take the test at www.FScoreTest.com. The test was developed based on proprietary studies, which I outline further at the end of this chapter. The F-Score test identifies seven main personality types, according to the seven triggers of fascination. It's not about how you see the world, but about how the world sees you. Over 50,000 people have taken the test so far. In about three minutes, the test tells you what makes your personality most persuasive.

Your primary and secondary triggers: You use all seven triggers in work and life. But you have one that's your main talent for persuasion: your "primary trigger." *Your primary trigger is the way in which your personality most effectively persuades others.* You also have a second trigger that you use, which layers underneath the first one. This is your "secondary trigger." Your secondary trigger is the way in which your personality applies the primary trigger. Together, your primary and secondary triggers identify the way in which your personality is hardwired to connect and communicate with others. I call this your "personality brand" (see Figure 32-1).

Unlike a personal brand, which can be artificially manipulated, your personality brand is an innate way in which you project yourself to the world. It's based on how your personality uses and applies the seven triggers in daily work and life. Your personality brand represents your natural, built-in talent for persuasion. Once you discover your own natural talent, you

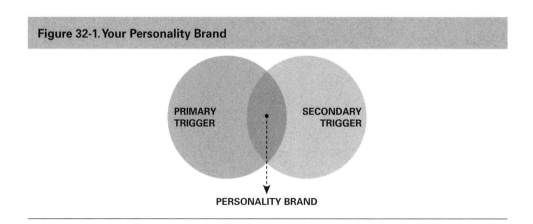

Figure 32-1. Your Personality Brand

PRIMARY TRIGGER

SECONDARY TRIGGER

PERSONALITY BRAND

can heighten it to its greatest competitive advantage. Identify your personality brand at www.HowToFascinate.com. If you want to influence employees and customers, you must understand which triggers drive their individual personalities. But first, you must understand which triggers drive *your own* personality. Take the test online, and then read on to learn more about what your results mean about your style of persuasion.

We'll review each of the seven triggers of fascination, one by one, starting with the one most commonly applied in leadership and management: power.

Power Trigger Overview

People who use power as their primary trigger fascinate us with authority and control. They dislike following someone else's rules, and prefer to actively lead. They persuade others with their strong opinions and bold actions, often instantly sparking a response from others. Here is how the power trigger affects our opinions and beliefs: The power trigger fascinates us by commanding and controlling the situation. Companies that fascinate communicate their message with power and use strength and authority. This trigger weaves itself throughout our life every day, guiding our behavior. Used intelligently and selectively, this trigger strengthens your reputation and earns respect.

POWER ◄ Take command

Power can motivate others to rise to their best. Authority figures use power to control. But power isn't necessarily *overpowering*. It can guide gently, even lovingly. It's a necessary ingredient in many forms of structure, training, and motivation to achieve higher results. A parent uses power with an infant by shaping sleep patterns, feeding times, and language development. A parent might also use this trigger with a high school student through a weekly allowance or use of the family car. Either way, the goal is not to defeat the child, but to make her stronger.

As the alphas of the pack, powerful people control our behavior in a myriad of ways. Who's powerful? CEOs and prime ministers. Black belts and Boy Scout leaders. Terrorists. Oil sheiks, film critics, and teacher's pets. Firstborns, matriarchs, and Big Brother. Though their leadership differs, powerful people share an ability to both *make* decisions and *influence* decisions. In fact, studies show that the serotonin levels of our brain literally shift in the presence of a powerful person, or when we ourselves are feeling a surge of power.

Passion Trigger Overview

People with passion as a primary trigger have a talent for immediately creating connection. They use warmth and emotion to draw others closer. They're intuitive and creative, often making decisions on gut instinct rather than cold facts or rational data. These personalities captivate others through participation, enthusiasm, and optimism. Here is how the passion trigger operates in our daily lives: Passion fascinates us through the experience of emotion and feeling. It fascinates us by attraction and warmth and closeness. This trigger can focus on an object, an experience, or a person; it might last moments, or a lifetime; yet in every case, passion captivates our desire for sensory fulfillment.

PASSION ◀ **Attract with emotion**

Facts create alarm, and opinions stem from power. However, passion is different. It doesn't involve reasoning. It's not sensible. For example, when you're on a diet, you can't help but be fascinated by your favorite junk food. It's not a rational choice on your part. Whether we *should* crave cheesy Taco Bell nachos rarely determines whether we *actually do* crave them. Passion is not about utility or function. A product does not become more passionate by adding more data to the instruction manual, or more product description on the product label. (Compare Microsoft's packaging to Apple's, and you'll see why.)

Do you want to connect more quickly and emotionally with people? Do you want them to respond with feeling to your message? Do you want to add warmth to an otherwise cold presentation? Do you want to pull customers into stores, magnetically drawn to look at and touch your product? Passion builds the allure of this interaction.

Mystique Trigger Overview

People who use mystique as their primary trigger are intriguing and complex. They reveal little about themselves, preferring instead to selectively cull down what they express. They influence others by not revealing everything that's under the surface. When they speak, for instance, people are more likely to pay attention. Here's how the mystique trigger affects our daily opinions and ideas: Mystique arouses our curiosity to learn more. Of the seven triggers, mystique is the most nuanced, and perhaps the most difficult to achieve. Mystique invites others closer, without revealing everything at once. (The magic trick ends if you find out how the white rabbit appears from the black hat.) A delicate balance to be sure, but successfully achieved, it's fascination's exemplar.

MYSTIQUE ◀ **Arouse curiosity**

Mystique can add anticipation and curiosity to any relationship, from new business pitches to social invitations, by motivating others to return for more. When a product has success-fully fascinated us through mystique, we might ask friends about it to hear their experi-ences, research it online, read the manual, spend time learning about its history and pro-cess, and spend time in the store. If we're deeply fascinated by a brand, we might join hash groups on Twitter, or travel to a conference where it's featured.

Intriguing people make us curious to learn more. We think about them, we talk with our friends about them, we might research them, and we want to be close to them emotionally, intellectually, or physically. If you fascinate others with mystique, they'll want more infor-mation. Reveal that information very carefully, if at all.

Prestige Trigger Overview

People with the prestige trigger earn immediate respect with their higher standards. Dis-cerning and ambitious, they push us to achieve the next level. They are motivated by admi-ration and concrete achievements. These personalities fascinate us with their aspirational ideas and actions. They constantly elevate their own performance, and that of the people around them.

PRESTIGE ◄ **Increase respect**

Prestige increases respect. Fancy logos, designer brands, and famous European hotels might come to mind. But that's merely the obvious side of prestige. This trigger applies to many kinds of achievement. Bake-off champions show off blue ribbons. Mary Kay's top employees drive pink Cadillacs. Children collect autographs from Mickey and Minnie at Disney. Scholars frame Phi Beta Kappa keys. Girl Scouts wear merit badges on uniforms. Proud fathers of newborns have hospital bands.

Prestigious people evoke admiration, and even envy. Among corporate circles, a person might earn the prestige fascination trigger with a framed Princeton diploma or an invitation to speak at a conference. In a second-grade classroom, the same status might mean winning a video game. Both represent achievement, and carry implied "value" to the group.

Limiting availability requires exercising some degree of restraint. In a culture obsessed with larger portions, mass production, and a store's cubic footage, prestigious people and companies know when to decline the supersized in favor of a single mouthful of perfection. Quality, not quantity. Repeat after me: No thank you, Sam Walton.

Alarm Trigger Overview

People with alarm as their primary trigger protect us from negative consequences. They're naturally oriented toward caution, and as a result, are often highly skilled at preventing undesirable outcomes. These personalities influence others by pointing out problems. They are sensitive to demands of others, often highly structured in their deadlines and deliverables. They focus on ways to avoid conflict (or more specifically, losing a conflict). Alarm creates urgency with a threat of negative consequences. Applied positively, with constructive goals, most people respond quickly.

ALARM — **Create urgency**

This trigger has a unique ability to urge people to do things they otherwise don't care to do, in order to avoid consequences. Tax forms are not considered widely fascinating. However, if you haven't completed them, they become positively riveting on April 14. How does the IRS convince you to willingly hand over a percentage of your income? It clearly defines the consequences. When you're driving along and you see blue lights in your rearview mirror, it immediately creates a strong response within you.

How can you apply the alarm trigger? Define consequences and create deadlines. By more clearly defining consequences associated with your message, you can more specifically shape behavior around them.

Do customers drag their feet to sign your contracts? The greater the resistance to a task (e.g., paying taxes), the greater the consequences must be to compel us to do it (e.g., prison). For a customer waffling about a decision, a message with alarm can tip him over to your side.

Rebellion Trigger Overview

Rebellion is about rejecting the traditional way of doing things, and instead, creating a new path. Individuals who use this trigger tend to be bold, daring, and original.

REBELLION — **Change the game**

We're fascinated by rebellion personalities because they constantly innovate fresh ideas. They reinvent old systems, and solve problems with an unexpected perspective.

In marketing, the purpose of rebellion isn't to lure your audience to rebel—but rather, to lure people away from the alternative—especially if you're marketing a small business, a new product launch, a niche category, or yourself. Your survival depends upon your ability to change behavior.

Even if your audience isn't *deviant*, you probably want people to *deviate* from their current behavior. Entrepreneurs rely on rebellion. For instance, Richard Branson uses it to differentiate Virgin from Delta. Steve Jobs used it to position Apple apart from Microsoft. A whit of rebellion can transform a humdrum conversation or an ordinary idea into something far more interesting, making this trigger a favorite of unconventional thinkers everywhere.

Trust Trigger Overview

Finally there's trust: the seventh and most important trigger. This trigger is harder to earn, easier to lose, and the most valuable to hold. Personalities with a primary trust trigger are stable and reliable. Because they're so dependable, they rarely surprise or disappoint us. They dislike feeling off-kilter, and work hard to reach a level of consistency in everything they do.

TRUST　　◀　　**Build loyalty**

Trust is unlike any of the other six triggers. The other triggers can fascinate us in a short timeframe: The sound of an ambulance siren instantly triggers alarm. A magazine article's provocative title sucks us in with mystique. One glance at the latest Maserati summons passion. But the trigger of trust, however, is fascination of a different sort. You can dabble in prestige, or experiment with power, but you can't dip in and out of trust. It must be established consistently.

We're living in a distracted and stressed-out ADD-style world. Even if we ourselves don't have ADD, we have to deal with fragmented schedules, competing demands, and priorities pulling our attention in different directions. Even our relationships change more frequently, making everyday life feel more scattered. In the face of overwhelming stimuli, the most trusted options relax and reassure us.

Neurologically our brains are hardwired to try to find consistent patterns. So when we see something that we recognize, we feel an affinity for it. We gravitate toward it because we don't have to make any decisions about it. It's why you love your favorite pair of old cozy jeans or reruns of the same show or your mom's spaghetti sauce—those things that we know as traditions or that we feel become so part of us over time that they literally change the hardwiring of our brains. And so when a message gives us trust it comforts us because we feel as though we can relax and rely on it.

Trusted companies reliably deliver specific qualities: In the morning, we can wake up and put on a navy blue Brooks Brothers jacket knowing it won't look passé, get into our assuredly safe Volvo, and drive to any Starbucks in the country to enjoy the same cup of coffee. At work we can sit at an ergonomic Aeron chair and stylish Herman Miller desk, writing with the Sharpie pen that won't wash off. On the way home from work, while listening to a Miles Davis song that we know will be cool, we can pick up a dinner we know will be healthy at Whole Foods. We order the same dish in a restaurant over and over not because it's surprising, but the opposite: We know and love it. Once we know what to expect from a brand, they've already done much of the decision making and heavy lifting for us.

Earning trust is easier said than done, because trust demands an investment of time and effort. Predictability requires a guaranteed certainty. Trusted individuals carefully pay attention to detail, reinforcing consistency between expectations they set and results they deliver. In return, the reward for earning trust is a big one: loyalty.

Loyalty acts as a rudder of decision making, because in certain circumstances, we want to know exactly what to expect. Surprises aren't fun when it comes to an auto manufacturer's warranty, auto-deposit of a paycheck, or the skill of our cardiac surgeon. In these types of relationships, we seek reliable options. Safety is paramount and excitement is bad, so we're drawn to stability. Year after year, we might return to the same accountant not for her keen fashion sense or witty banter, but because we don't have to worry if our 1040 form will pass muster.

How Your Own Personality Uses the Seven Triggers

Once you understand and apply your primary and secondary triggers, your ideas become more memorable, your conversations more persuasive, and your relationships more lasting. Your primary trigger is critical to understanding what makes you fascinating. But it's the secondary trigger where things start to get interesting.

Originally, we assumed the primary trigger was the crux of the personality. But as we continued our research, we saw that the secondary trigger has a significant effect on how a person will fascinate others. For instance, a passion/power personality is very different from a passion/mystique. After watching the data of all these participants, my company has developed an in-depth personality report. You can learn more about your personality at our site, www.HowToFascinate.com.

With our assessments, we can make a range of predictions about an employee or a potential hire, based on his or her primary trigger. But the secondary trigger is where we refine our vision of that person. That's when we can begin to identify and understand that person's personality brand.

Every Personality Brand Has Differentiating Strengths

Each personality brand will persuade and captivate in a uniquely specific way. Each has a different communication style, a different relationship approach, and different professional priorities. By learning what makes you fascinating, you can sell more, create better relationships, and become more effective in all your communication. You become more valuable to your company, and to your clients. You earn greater respect and receive more acknowledgments with higher esteem. You have a stronger ability to connect with people because you understand your own personality, and their personalities, better than ever before.

You already have a specific talent to be a powerfully influential communicator. Whether or not you realize it, you've probably had it your entire life, untapped, ready for you to discover and use. The more you can amplify your personality brand, the more likely you are to be heard and remembered. But it's more than that. This is bigger than management. Once you understand your personality brand, you can more meaningfully connect with the people around you who matter most. You can develop more lasting relationships with customers, more authentic relationships with friends, and closer bonds with family.

How to Apply the Triggers for Persuading Your Employees

Your leadership style should adapt somewhat, depending on your employees' triggers, in order to get the best out of them. For instance, someone with a mystique primary trigger will respond to a performance review or unforeseen deadline very differently than someone with a passion trigger. Below is a list of primary triggers, and how your management can best help people reach their potential.

Power: Taking Control

Employees with a primary power trigger can be most easily groomed for future leadership, because they're probably already envisioning themselves in a position of greater control than they currently enjoy. Do not micromanage these people unless you want to see them either backlash against your grip, or leave for another boss. Instead, give them a little bit of room to prove themselves, and then evaluate results together. The more you can grow their sense of collaboration and support, the more they will reward you with strong performance.

Passion: Connecting With Emotion

Employees with a primary passion trigger want to be right in the heart of the activity. Properly motivated and coached, they'll give outstanding customer service, because they naturally understand how to relate to people's emotional needs. They excel in introductions and pitches, because they can form bonds more quickly than triggers such as mystique and alarm. Make sure that they understand your expectations, because their expressive nature and intuitive skill means they might tend to "wing it" rather than follow protocol.

A recommendation: They thrive on direct face-to-face human contact, so give them plenty of opportunity to interact with customers, with you, and with each other. Ignored, their naturally high energy will putter out.

Mystique: Prompting Curiosity

Mystique as a primary trigger means that this employee wants to focus on the results. You won't always know what this employee is thinking or doing; however, you will see all the "proof in the pudding." As is the case with the power trigger, you should stand back, advise employees as needed, but direct them with a light touch. For these people, their purpose is to reach a successful conclusion.

Aside from those with primary passion or rebellion triggers, these employees don't want to belabor discussions about process, and usually dislike group brainstorming. Their skill at complex mental assignments means they often excel in information-driven roles, usually behind the scenes.

Prestige: Increasing Respect

An employee with a primary prestige trigger is similar to the one with a power trigger, except these employees do not need to be in control. Rather, they seek consistent improvement, higher goals, and tangible evidence of their success. Because they seek to exceed expectations, it's important to give them clear goals, with clearly outlined expectations, and a way to self-check their own progress. Incentive programs will work extremely well to inspire exceptional efforts; these don't necessarily need to be extravagant, but rather should be symbolic demonstrations that the employee is overdelivering for you.

One last word of caution: These employees will be demoralized, if not wounded, by public criticism. Reprimand them carefully, and praise as often as warranted. You will see the results in their performance.

Alarm: Inciting Urgent Action

For employees with the alarm trigger, you'll want to give plenty of structure with predictable schedule and policies. If you suddenly change your own vacation plan, or schedule a last-minute presentation, you might see these employees feeling flustered to regain balance long after someone with the passion or rebellion trigger has accepted the change.

They succeed magnificently when they can map out a plan, with desired results and contingencies, and then get a group to adhere to the plan. These employees often work well in human resources, billing, and other jobs that require tight control of company details.

Rebellion: Changing the Game

Want to empower employees with a primary rebellion trigger? Steer their natural creativity in the most productive innovation opportunities. Coach them with clear rules when necessary, but also give room to explore. Give them space to show you what could be improved, and how you can rethink your company's old habits.

These employees will not be 100 percent accurate every time (unlike someone with a primary trust or alarm trigger); however, when well informed, they will give you solutions you'd never have dreamed possible. They'll work best in a role such as marketing.

Trust: Building Loyalty

With a primary trust trigger, employees want to buy in for the long haul. They seek daily routines, consistent co-workers, and steady improvement. They are not looking for the quick fix at work; they desire stable, lasting relationships with their employer.

While their personalities might not be as expressive as those with the passion or prestige triggers, they do exude stability, so customers become comfortable with them. These employees will deliver dependable results, on time, as planned. You might find, however, that they are uncomfortable with change, or with being pushed to perform at a higher level. They're built for consistency and repetition.

Research on Fascination

To better understand fascination, we've already led over five years of proprietary research on the subject, including the first-ever marketing research study specifically on how people and brands become more fascinating.

The Kelton Fascination Study

Kelton Research is a global public opinion company, leading research with more than 30 of the Fortune 100 corporations, including McDonald's, Target, and Pepsi. Twice it has been named "fastest-growing market research consultancy" by *Inc.* magazine. Kelton led Sally Hogshead's deep-dive analysis of 1,059 Americans on fascination. The survey included a lengthy list of questions on the relationship between fascination and decision making: brand choices, careers, relationships, and personal branding. Our goal was to define the role of fascination in people's lives, and measure it in tangible terms. We set out to understand the ways in which fascination is a shortcut to persuasion, and the return-on-investment (ROI) of making a brand more fascinating. The Kelton Fascination Study included:

- How much is fascination actually worth, in dollar amounts?
- How much more are people willing to pay for fascinating products?
- Which employees are most engaged and engrossed at work?
- How can leaders fascinate their employees?
- What exactly determines if a message, or product, is fascinating?
- How do demographics affect a person's levels of fascination?
- What behaviors and actions do people exhibit when fascinated?

The resulting research offers a breadth and depth of insight (a four-inch-thick binder of exceedingly small type, to be exact). Here are sample key findings on fascination and branding:

- *People will pay a great deal of money if you can help them become fascinating.* On average they will pay $288/month to be the most fascinating person in a room (5 percent will pay more than $1,000/month). In addition to paying more, they'll invest more energy in you and your product.
- *People will pay a great deal of money if you can help them feel fascinated.* A fascinating brand can charge more than an unfascinating one. People also will pay a premium for brands that activate desired triggers.
- *Women will spend more to be fascinating then they spend on food and clothes combined.* They will pay an average of $338 per month to become the most fascinating person in the room, roughly 15 percent of their net income.
- *Fascination is an intellectual, emotional, and physical response.* In the presence of a fascinating product, people report a physical, intellectual, and emotional response, and sometimes even an "adrenaline rush."
- *People will go to surprising lengths to have a more fascinating life.* They will spend a sizable percentage of their take-home pay, and go to surprising lengths, to feel more engaged and immersed. This represents a tremendous finding for brands. If brands can help consumers have a more fascinating life, they can charge more.

◼ *Brands should make the truth fascinating, rather than fabricating a myth.* In our study we saw that 64 percent of people are more interested in fact than fiction.

Fascination at Work: For Managers, Employees, Co-Workers, and Clients

◼ *Fascinated employees are more engaged with their work, and more loyal to their bosses and companies.*

◼ *There's no such thing as "one-size-fits-all" fascination.* Different employees are fascinated based on their personality triggers.

◼ *We're at our peak of fascination with work while in our 40s.* Members of this group say they become the most engrossed in their work, compared to the rest of the population. Of these, 55 percent are fascinated at least once a day and sometimes more. (Replacing your more "expensive" employees with cheap young talent could end up costing more than enhancing the workplace experience for experienced players.)

◼ *Only 9 percent say their bosses are "extremely fascinating."* The majority of people don't find their bosses even mildly fascinating. Management training to help leaders engage and inspire might help workplace morale.

◼ *There's a direct relationship between income and the power trigger.* People who make under $50,000 a year are half as likely to be fascinated by the power trigger as those who make over $50,000. (This is important for leaders to know if they're trying to influence younger employees and administrative staff—and we can show you how to use methods beyond the standard power trigger.)

◼ *The trust trigger shapes relationships, but does not necessarily shape decision making.* Mid-level managers, for instance, are less worried about telling the truth than other professional segments.

◼ *Fascination changes by generation at work.* Generations are fascinated differently by work, and by personal life. It's important not only to evaluate which trigger to use with your groups, but, to persuade and influence behavior, you must also customize for their age and professional level. Our priorities change throughout our careers. For instance, 18- to 29-year-olds think having a fascinating career is more important than a fascinating personal life. Looking at the older set, C-level employees say they're more fascinated with their spouses than any other group.

◼ *One last interesting bit.* People would rather be fascinating on a job interview than a first date. Yet married employees are more likely to be "extremely fascinated at work" than their unmarried counterparts.

Looking Beyond the Numbers

Within the four-inch-thick binder, when we looked deeper than the numbers, the study revealed more. What began as a quantifiable study about the ROI of fascination became a look at how people feel about themselves and their lives in general. The numbers tell us the role of fascination in people's ambitions and insecurities, love lives and work lives, private lives and personal brands, their respect at work and their passionate connection to their children.

On the very first page of the Kelton Fascination survey, at the top of the first page, participants read the following opening statement: *For the purpose of this survey, we are describing fascination as an intense captivation. When something is fascinating, it captures your attention in an unusually intense way. It's more than "interesting." It distracts you from other things around you, and makes you want to pay complete attention. You might be fascinated by a favorite book, a project at work, or even a new love. Note that when something is fascinating, it is not inherently good or bad, only that it captures your full attention.*

By the end of the research, it became apparent that in terms of the role fascination plays in our lives, it's more than described above. The respondents told us that fascination is a fundamental part of our relationships and our quality of life. It affects how hard we work, who we marry, even how we feel about ourselves. When fascinated, we're more likely to learn new ideas, love our work, and live more fully.

In today's nine-second world, you must wield your personality's competitive advantage—the way in which you naturally fascinate. By identifying and applying your own personality brand, you build relationships, nurture employees, motivate teams, and reach your personal potential.

In a world with a nine-second attention span, that's how to fascinate the goldfish.

About the Author

Sally Hogshead is a keynote speaker, an author, and chief fascination officer of Fascinate, Inc. She teaches audiences how to persuade and influence in a world with a nine-second attention span. Sally's second book, *FASCINATE,* has been translated into 14 languages. She's helped clients such as Nike, MINI Cooper, Aflac, Target, and Godiva to develop messages that persuade and captivate. Sally's work and insights are profiled by the *New York Times* and NBC's *Today* show, and she is described by the press as "the marketing mistress of fascination." Find out how to fascinate at www.HowToFascinate.com, and learn more about Sally's speaking at www.SallyHogshead.com.

Chapter 33

ValYouCasting: The New Workforce Social Competencies

Terrence Wing

Editor's Note

If management is a social act and managers exist to help their team members do their best work, then great management goes hand in hand with social learning. In this chapter, Terrence Wing brings vision and depth to an exploration of social learning and how managers can use it to enable team excellence. In December 2011, the world tragically lost Terrence, and I am honored to be able to share some of his work here. He was a rising star in his field and will be missed.

This day was no different than any other. Crystal came in to work and sat behind her computer to do her daily tasks. She worked for a leading automobile manufacturer. Her day consisted of processing orders from the dealerships and providing basic support to help them manage their inventory levels. The process, like most in the company, was automated through a series of connected software applications. Crystal was effective at her job but, like everyone, found limitations to her expertise with the system.

Routinely, Crystal would find herself in the break room chatting with her co-workers about some of the limitations she was experiencing with the software. Many of them had the same problems. They would volley insults toward the system and at times spontaneously brainstorm a hack to work around the system's limitations. These hacks at times became standard operating procedures when management would notice the new practice and its positive impact on work flow.

The proverbial water cooler became a beacon for Crystal and her peers to socialize, collaborate, and solve problems. Unfortunately, management became privy to the spoils of these conversations only by chance. Nonetheless, these informal meetings were embedded in the company's culture. They became a standard of practice for solving problems. Their efficiency may be questionable, but many of the ideas generated informally here were adopted for mainstream use throughout the company.

We all have probably witnessed or participated in "water cooler culture." Perhaps in some organizations there is greater potential to hear more gossip than solutions. However, it is still a common workplace practice that doesn't show any signs of disappearing. But do we want it to disappear? Many managers and human resource professionals have stared through the break room window wishing they could be a fly on the wall to hear all the "goings on" from the perspective of the workforce.

Let's give that some thought. Why would we, as managers, want to bug the water cooler? Sure, some of the gossip could be juicy. However, as you read between the lines you gather information about employee sentiment. This could be toward the company, a process, a policy, or even toward you, the manager. You gain a certain level of transparency into the mind of your workforce. You also hear about solutions and workarounds (or hacks as they are often referred to). I am not suggesting you bug your water cooler, but imagine the possibility of capturing the spoils of socialization. These two opportunities, witnessing sentiment and capturing best practices, are just a few of the advantages of digital social learning (social learning 2.0).

This chapter is about an emerging set of competencies for the 2.0 (a numeric identifier associated with the incorporation of semantic or social media technologies) workforce due to the digitization of social learning. A social learning culture has implications for both the workforce and management at all levels. Social learning is a process that demands careful facilitation and encouraged participation. In their book, *The New Social Learning*, Tony Bingham and Marcia Connor explain, "*Social learning is participating with others to make sense of new ideas, what's new is how powerfully they work together. Social tools leave a digital audit trail documenting our learning journey—often an unfolding story—and leaving a path for others to follow.*"[1] Although social learning is not a new phenomenon, the

---

[1] *The New Social Learning,* Tony Bingham and Marcia Connors, p. 9.

emergence of social media has stimulated a transformation of social learning into digital form giving rise to a new worker and new competencies. I call this group of competencies ValYouCasting™.

ValYouCasting Defined

ValYouCasting (www.valyoucasting.com) is the art of social broadcasting. It is the exchange of information for social currency and equity. When we ValYouCast, we are sharing information, knowledge, or expertise for a new form of currency—although calling it new may be a bit pretentious. Social currency is more of an emerging brand. It's been around as long as we have walked the earth. Its value had been somewhat minimized throughout history. However, modern technology and the growth of social media have elevated its status and created a form of commerce around it. Organizations who have embraced social learning engage in this new type of information marketplace.

Social commerce is the exchange of some form of information or useful conversation for followership. Think about how you keep track of what is going on in your world. The marketplace is saturated with newspapers, magazines, television, and radio broadcasts. After scrutiny, you decide which of these (or combinations of them) hold enough value for you to tune in. Once calculated, you integrate them into your schedule. You watch the local morning news for weather and traffic. You grab a cup of coffee and the *Wall Street Journal* on your way to work. Perhaps in the car you turn to your favorite talk show to heckle the opinions of callers who clearly have way too much time on their hands. These media and the authors of the content have established an exchange of social currency with you. You watch, and they will continue to deliver content. This symbiotic relationship is similar to the exchange with social media and social learning.

It's important to explain social media and draw a line of distinction between it and social learning. Wikipedia defines social media as "a group of Internet-based applications that build on the ideological and technological foundations of web 2.0 and allow creation and exchange of user-generated content."[2] I will elaborate with more detail later in the chapter about many of the social media tools available. They include sites like Facebook, Google+, LinkedIn, Twitter, Blogger, Wordpress, Digg, YouTube, and literally hundreds more.

The popularity of social media at the time of writing this chapter has been on a steady upward climb. The following data come from the PEW Research Center:[3]

---

[2] www.wikipedia.org/wiki/socialmedia.
[3] PEW Research Center, http://www.pewinternet.org/default.aspx.

- 51 percent of college students say an online course provides the same value as the classroom.
- Three-quarters of colleges in the United States offer online classes.
- 28 percent of adults do at least one social activity using phones or computers.
- 83 percent of adults own a cell phone. Of that, 35 percent own a smartphone.
- 92 percent of adult smartphone users use their phones to send text messages and take pictures.
- 59 percent of adult smartphone users use their phones for social networking.
- 15 percent of adult smartphone users use their phones to access Twitter.

These are not isolated findings. More and more studies are reinforcing the dominance of social media in our lives. As technology evolves and access increases, social media and social learning 2.0 will be the norm for how we learn and communicate.

The line of distinction between social media and social learning is that social media is the tool. Social learning is the activity. We use social media to learn. For example, the Facebook Fan Page, ISD 2.0 (www.facebook.com/ISD20) was designed to gather and engage a community of instructional designers (IDs) and learning professionals. The content on the site is relative to the group. The site creator's vision is to help IDs fuse the semantic technology of social media with instructional systems design.

In the ISD 2.0 example Facebook is the social media tool. The fans of the page engage in social learning by tuning in to status updates from the page administrators and other users on newfound social media tools that can augment their efforts with instructional design. The site also features a series of screen casts on designing PowerPoint presentations and even hosts e-learning programs as a demo of what could be done with Facebook.

The value this site brings to the users is its social currency. As more followers join the page, it gains not only popularity but also leverage to Facebook and other third parties who want to access this community. The ISD 2.0 fan page is designed to be free of solicitations, but there are plenty of sites on Facebook that do take advantage of their popularity to exchange their social currency for real currency.

This brings us full circle to our early point of social commerce. As the workforce engages in social learning, people are exchanging social commerce with each other. The "like" and the "share" actions on many sites have become the modern point of sale (POS) of social learning communities. You could be thinking, How impactful is a "like" or a "share" button (a feedback vehicle on social media sites) to corporate objectives? As you read further into the chapter, I am convinced their value will become even more relevant. For argument's sake, let's use an example.

You remember Crystal from the beginning of the chapter. Crystal engages on social learning platforms at her organization. The automobile manufacturer realized that encouraging employees to comment and contribute on the platform would unleash the power of social learning. It removed the "Big Brother is watching" mentality and accepted that the content will yield the good, the bad, and the ugly about the company. Crystal decides to start a discussion on the platform about the software training. She is less than complimentary but is fair and professional. Her peers agree with her, and suddenly the discussion goes viral with "likes" and "shares." An evolved organization doesn't see this as a problem but instead a great opportunity.

The popularity of the post and the stream of feedback enable the company to address the issue and applaud the employees, especially Crystal, for courageously discussing it. This creates that "fly on the wall" opportunity. Also look at the social currency Crystal gained. Amongst her peers she gains the rank of "voice of the workforce." They inevitably will follow her posts more frequently if they see value. This creates a level of relevance that Crystal can cash in on when applying for that next promotion and other opportunities that may arise. She becomes somewhat of a celebrity employee as long as she contributes value to the network.

This same scenario is happening at Creative Channel Services. The company uses a social learning platform called Wisetail. Employees are encouraged to post instructional videos and other content. Their engagement is measured by their interaction with other users and the completion of courses. The users score points based on their activity. Those points have multiple purposes, but one is that the user can exchange them for rewards. This function at CCS is similar to the data collected via the "share" or "like" button we see typically in popular social media sites.

Crystal and the active contributors at CCS are examples of knowledge workers. Not everyone in the workforce is one. However, the ranks of this group of employees are growing dramatically. Parallel to that growth is the ease to capture and share information and data even across distant borders. This exchange is also instant. A problem can be noticed in one department and instantaneously shared throughout the entire organization. Finally it could be solved by an employee, a customer, or a vendor from another department even on the other side of the world. All this can happen in an instant. Our access, speed, and ability to share information today are unprecedented.

Enter the Knowledge Era

Knowledge is the new currency, and the knowledge worker is the new broker. Peter Drucker defined the knowledge worker as one who works primarily with information or one who develops and uses knowledge in the workplace.[4] As simple as that definition is, it gives us a starting point to explore the DNA of the knowledge worker to identify the competencies needed to be successful.

The modernized workforce has always been inhabited by knowledge workers. However, their numbers were smaller, and the class was more elite. Doctors and lawyers were types of knowledge workers. Today it is likely you are sitting in a cubicle surrounded by knowledge workers and perhaps are one yourself. With the emergence of social media, we now have a boom in the number of knowledge workers as well as greater access to them. We are in many ways taking a look at the emergence of a new future for our workforce. To understand our future, we have to take a brief look at our past and what brought us to this point.

Before we entered the Knowledge Era, there was the Industrial Era, which saw the rise of manufacturing and technology. Some historians say this started in Europe and migrated to the United States later in the 1800s. With the rise in industrialization there came a greater demand for a skilled workforce. The workforce was sculpted to perform repetitive tasks. Knowledge was still isolated to a select few. Managers weren't trying to build a thinking workforce. They were trying to build a mechanical workforce, and they were successful.

With the increased use of computers in the 20th century there came a greater demand for managing knowledge. The exchange of knowledge can't be credited to computers exclusively. Apprenticeships, on-the-job training, bulletin boards and forums, corporate libraries, and even mentoring programs gave rise to the exchange of knowledge, and then came the Internet. The Internet created access points to knowledge that had never before been seen in history (at least not to this extent).

As Internet technology advanced, users discovered new ways of connecting. At first, web 1.0 was more of a library of information. You could access it, but there was very little connection with other users. Web 2.0 connected the users. Not only were they accessing the information, but they were conversing, collaborating, editing, aggregating, and contributing to the existing information. This was enabled by the emergence of semantic technology.

Social media have opened access to knowledge even further. They have enabled the Internet to become the open-source platform of human intelligence. Essentially anyone with Internet

---

[4] www.wikipedia.org/wiki/knowledgemanagement.

access and a computer can learn almost anything, from how to tie your shoes to how to fix an engine. Simple to complex tasks are being shared across networks creating a database of information than no one organization could ever create to this extent in this amount of time. Simply having access to the information does not make us a knowledge worker.

Knowledge workers manage information and knowledge to help them and others access, recall, consume, and essentially apply knowledge to solve problems or improve a condition(s). This class of worker is unique from the workforce as a whole. Knowledge workers today are:

- subject matter experts
- mobile
- connected
- networked
- broadcast-ready
- trackable
- syndicated
- aggregators
- analysts
- facilitators.

Subject Matter Experts

Knowledge workers' expertise may not always be in the information they aggregate. Sometimes the expertise is their ability to aggregate information. For example, a knowledge worker like Crystal from the automobile manufacturer may be looking for answers. Her ability to gather information and compile it into a reference for her to use, as well as for other employees to use, makes her a subject matter expert. There are also skill sets Crystal has where she has a high level of expertise. Her deposits of knowledge based on that skill set also reinforce her status as a subject matter expert.

Mobile

A few decades ago, mobile wouldn't be part of this list or at least not to this degree. The technology today has greatly enabled the exchange of knowledge using mobile technology like smartphones and tablets. Knowledge workers are accessing, compiling, distributing, and consuming information from all points on the globe. Whether they are in their office or out in the field, the information and knowledge they discover is being pooled into the organization's knowledge database for all employees, vendors, and stakeholders to access, consume, and share with their networks. Mobile devices like tablets, smartphones, laptops, and other mobile devices unleash knowledge workers from their workspace and allow them to cultivate knowledge from anywhere.

Connected

The tether of time and space is an obstacle or a restriction of a past era. Knowledge workers remain connected to their knowledge management systems 24/7/365. That's not to say they never sleep. It just means that no matter the time or distance separating them from their workspace, they can access their knowledge base to deposit or withdraw information. Internet access is becoming more and more available too. Whether it is through hot-spot technology or mobile broadband cards, the knowledge worker is always connected and thus managing information at will.

Networked

Knowledge workers do have something they want and need to be tethered to. That's their network. Their network is their community of other knowledge workers. It's who they reach out to to get the answers and information they need. Their network is part of their equity. Having a diverse network gives them the ability to expand their knowledge base. This network is also only a few keystrokes away. If it is a strong network, it is also available 24/7/365.

Broadcast-Ready

Capturing information in various media forms has never been simpler or more economical. Tools are more accessible and cost-effective. Knowledge workers are equipped to capture information in multiple formats to include video, photos, documents, micro-statements, and more. They archive, tag, and share information in these formats with their network and anyone accessing their knowledge feeds.

Trackable

The priorities and efforts of the knowledge worker leave a virtual trail of information. There's the more obvious with geo-location. That lets you know physical locations where the knowledge worker has been. Beyond that is an arsenal of measurements that informs the manager and the knowledge worker of their progress and impact on their network and the organization. Knowledge workers can track their influence and evaluate their efforts through an array of analytics that are available on most web 2.0 platforms.

Syndicated

In the past, organizations dealt with a handful of communication channels throughout the workforce. With a learning network, those channels have become exponential. Every knowledge worker manages his or her channel. Each of those channels consists of some original programming and syndicated information from other knowledge workers. Knowledge workers will share information they've received from their and other networks within their channel. The process of syndicating information improves its longevity by affording it an opportunity to go viral.

Aggregators

A knowledge worker is constantly collecting data for personal use, future reference, and to distribute and share now or when it becomes more relevant in the future. All information is not relevant at all times. However, some information collected prematurely can be used later with foresight of its value. Knowledge workers will organize their findings for retrieval and consumption by them, their network, and the organization. They will aggregate information using tags (reference codes) that allow it to be clustered with similar data and information that is relative and retrievable.

Analysts

Not all data and information are created equal. Some hold more relevance and validity than others. Knowledge workers will filter the good, the bad, and the ugly. They take pride in building value to their network and organization. As that value builds, their relevance increases. To build that value, they must analyze what information and data are most useful to their network and organization. Aggregating too much irrelevant information into the knowledge base will have a negative impact on the knowledge workers' value and hence their relevance.

Facilitators

The arena of a knowledge worker in today's modern workforce is the social learning community. No one knowledge worker knows it all. That goes without saying. By drawing out other knowledge workers into discussion, information is exchanged, collected, tagged, and archived to be consumed as needed. As a facilitator, the knowledge worker fuels this social exchange.

A knowledge workforce sounds like a great thing. If managed correctly it is. The knowledge worker is an important commodity in the workforce. Perhaps at some point, knowledge workers may even find themselves factored into a P&L statement or listed as a condition of a merger and acquisition. A workforce without them in any industry is ill equipped for its future and potentially vulnerable to its own demise.

There are many benefits to an organization building its knowledge worker base and its social learning community. Some of the direct benefits are financial. Others may be less tangible than dollars and cents and more relative to many of the other elements that fuel a robust organization. The combination of both creates a value proposition for social learning worth exploring.

The Value of Social Learning

Chrysler Corporation

Chrysler Corporation identified the potential in social learning and incorporated web 2.0 technologies (social media) into its LMS (learning management system) creating the Chrysler Academy. The benefits of its program were both tangible and intangible. One element of its initiative converted a $100,000 cost for new product training into a $10,000 to $15,000 cost.[5] This saved the company $85,000 or more on every new product training program it created using its knowledge workers. Chrysler proved the financial spoils of social learning are abundant.

Chrysler was faced with a similar challenge that most organizations in today's modern business theater face. Its network of 160,000 global customer-facing employees needed to be trained more effectively and efficiently. The company set out to provide greater performance support, speed, knowledge sharing, cost, time (from production to getting in the hands of the learner), feedback relays, and collaboration. This effort was in part an attempt to equip its customer-facing employees with deployable knowledge to address a savvy customer base.

Chrysler was able to meet its objectives by infusing web 2.0 technologies into its LMS. The platform it created increased the company's knowledge base and resources through employees', specifically knowledge workers', contributions. Semantic technologies used at Chrysler included blogs, RSS news feeds, audio and video casts, polls and surveys, web-based courses, learning objects (like PDFs and documents), cloud-based applications, and others. Within the first six months of launching the site, 750 learner blog contributions had been vetted and published, 1,100 ad hoc survey responses had been received from the learners, and 9,000 weekly poll responses had been received and aided in resource development.[6]

Despite the financial benefits and cost savings, the greatest accomplishment was in the improvement in how the employees were able to meet the demands of their customers. The time between identifying a performance gap and addressing it was greatly reduced. Chrysler had quicker delivery of content, agile content management, efficient culling of impertinent information, and refined content development. Production of course content went from a two-week cycle to a rapid turnaround of one day via the company's social learning platform.[7]

---

[5] Chrysler Academy20.pdf, via Latitude Learning; www.latitudelearning.com, page 7.
[6] Chrysler Academy20.pdf, via Latitude Learning; www.latitudelearning.com, page 8.
[7] Chrysler Academy20.pdf, via Latitude Learning; www.latitudelearning.com, page 8.

Chrysler's story is one of many. Organizations large and small are embracing social learning. They see the rewards of this shift not only in how the organization learns but essentially in the evolution of their organizational culture to accommodate the growing number of knowledge workers. Dollars are part of the story, but there is so much more to gain through the adaptation of a learning culture.

Yum! Brands

Yum! Brands is another example of a large organization embracing social learning. Yum!'s objective was to open access and create a stronger collaborative environment amongst its employees. This effort would be nearly impossible, highly difficult, or costly with conventional methods. The company sought web 2.0 technologies to help it meet its objective.

The company's social campaign, iChing,[8] was part of an organization-wide growth strategy. The social platform connected its management teams, leading to aspirations for total inclusion of its workforce. The benefit of the platform was a faster and improved competitive position. Ideas across the organization were shared. These included innovations for a new pizza and breakfast ideas to name a few. Over 4,500 documents were uploaded, with over 26,000 downloads; 3,600 corporate users were actively using the system; and 645 groups had formed in the first six months.[9] Ultimately the platform enabled network-wide collaboration.

Cost savings is thematic throughout most cases of web 2.0-enhanced social learning. It has definitely become a bottom-line-friendly tool. The benefits of social learning don't stop there.

- **Harvest of intellectual property**: With the exit of the Baby Boomers from the workforce, there is also an exodus of decades of knowledge and experience that will leave with them. Social learning platforms allow organizations to capture that knowledge and convert it to resources that can be used indefinitely.
- **Satisfying the hunger from a tech-savvy workforce**: Outside of our organizations, we are engaging each other using web 2.0 technologies. The exposure, and in some cases dependency, to these technologies is greatest amongst the youngest of the generations entering the workforce. This style of communication is a norm to them and an expectation when they arrive at your corporate front door. To recruit and retain them, the youngest workers will demand a social infrastructure enhanced by web 2.0 technology. Despite your many career opportunities, the absence of web 2.0 infrastructure will literally "bore" these workers into seeking opportunities elsewhere.

---

[8] Case-Study-Yum-Brands.pdf, www.jivesoftware.com/customers/case-studies.

[9] Case-Study-Yum-Brands.pdf, www.jivesoftware.com/customers/case-studies, page 3.

- **Two-way transparency**: Social learning platforms create a "fly on the wall" level of transparency. As an employer, you gain insight and access into the social minds of your workforce. Their contributions and frequency of use will create a new form of metric that before long will find its way into the yearly performance review and almost every form of performance measurement.
- **The spread of engagement**: Social learning platforms and cultures are an open invitation to join the proverbial party. Although at some organizations, it is an actual party. Those so inclined will take new ownership in problem solving. With this new ownership comes a greater ability to actually solve problems through sourcing solutions from one's network.
- **The viral spread of ideas**: One voice can go viral in an instant, creating buzz and excitement around an opportunity. Additionally, that voice is simply the seed. As the idea travels through the network, it is nourished with improvements, changing from its infant stage to a mature concept waiting for implementation.
- **The fueling of conversation**: Every conversation essentially is the starting point of a future resource. As employees discuss problems, solutions, conditions, and so on, it ultimately is archived in a catalogue for others to view and learn. Talk is cheap, and now it is essential.
- **The augmentation of listening**: Social learning gives everyone a voice that can resonate throughout the entire organization. The life of any statement can live longer than if spoken to a small group. The community's engagement suggests people are listening to each other more.
- **The nourishment of inclusion and access**: Social learning platforms enable the rise of the celebrity employee. Every employee can access the system and share his or her value. In return all employees reap the benefits of inclusion. They feel part of something. That is usually positive energy toward productivity.
- **Channeling of solutions**: Chances are someone in the organization has experienced a problem that is now creating an obstacle for someone else. Social learning allows the seeker to find solutions from archives of discussion and other resources or through real-time coaching and support.

IBM

IBM has been pioneering social learning 2.0 since its early beginnings. Of course this would be naturally expected from a technology solutions company like Big Blue. Ann Dreyzin, enablement lead of the Social Software Adoption Program at IBM, and Khalid Raza, community manager of the IBM Center for Advanced Learning, explain how social learning has changed the workforce at IBM:

- There is an increase in educational content (via webinars, conferences, etc.).
- Communities of interest both private (behind the firewall) and public have been created and aid in solving business problems.
- Knowledge transfers across silos more frequently and can become a natural act in a socially empowered culture.
- Learning has moved from top-down training to lateral learning. This caters to the wants of the learners who typically are the subject matter experts. It creates a targeted opportunity to bridge a performance gap instead of broad strokes of enterprise-level training programs.
- Content delivery is streamlined. Users generate content. Users validate content. Users consume content. This reroutes the obligation of content development away from the central training role (partially) and places accountability in the hands of the end users.

Results at IBM and its clients are seen through a combination of return-on-investment (dollars) and intangibles like those previously mentioned. Social learning 2.0 or even learning without the technology is difficult to measure independently, admits Dreyzin. However, IBM's leadership is highly supportive and engaged in the success of a learning culture.

Of course the benefits of cost savings, improved performance and workflow, and speed to market are encouraging to anyone intimately connected to the organization's P&L. Social learning enables creativity to move from concept to creation, and this translates to dollars and cents.

The Socialization of Work

Every day we come in to work to accomplish specific tasks. The tasks vary depending on our profession. A laborer may have to create a product or fulfill an order. A manager has to oversee the processes of her department. An executive has to monitor the overall health of the organization. Despite the degrees of separation of all these roles, they each are being affected by the socialization of work.

The socialization of work is connection we all have with each other and the distribution of conversation, ideas, and solutions across the workforce. The word *conversation* typically does not conjure images of productivity, but that depends on the content of the conversation. When you look at some of the casual uses of social media, it is quite easy to draw skepticism as to how these tools can help you or your employees work. A typical Facebook news feed may contain images of dancing cats, giggling babies, and truth-or-dare victims, which end up digitally immortalizing their stupidity. Clearly these offer very little value other than the temporary reprieve from work. However, with the proper facilitation, an enterprise social learning community can yield productive conversations and harvest useful content. The key words in that last statement are "proper facilitation."

Think of a professionally run town hall meeting. People are gathered to discuss the state of the organization. The disclaimer I am giving here is that there are bad town hall meetings and there are good town hall meetings. Needless to say, I am calling on your memory of good town hall meetings. The presenter, like a president or spokesperson, announces to the group his or her goals for the meeting. Typically the goal, barring hidden agendas, is to gain insight from the community on an issue. There are a few unique dynamics at play. A strong presenter spends more time listening and fostering content from his audience. This audience, if chosen correctly, is the end users or the subject matter experts. Therefore it makes sense to listen. Rarely does a president have the skill set required to do the work of the employees he leads. That's not his role. He possesses a different set of skills.

During the meeting, the presenter has to facilitate the discussion, or it becomes a waste of everyone's time except the occasional saboteur or anarchist. This facilitation includes asking the right questions, listening, providing understandable responses, and so on. Overall, a good presenter will try to make it a safe place for the attendees to share their expertise. The safer it is perceived, the more feedback the organization will receive. That feedback is enabling. The subject matter experts will open up and share with the organization the possible solutions and sentiment about the goal that can lead to even greater innovations. That's not to say that every town hall meeting or social learning community will produce the next smartphone or tablet. But, discussion can be part of a blueprint toward innovation.

The reason I use the town hall meeting as a metaphor is because one aspect of social learning is conversation. The more your workforce is talking about solutions, the greater the opportunity to actually find one. The wisdom of the crowd usually is greater than that of one individual. That statement isn't an absolute because, let's face it, there are some crowds with absolutely no wisdom. However, for the typical workforce that is hardly the case.

On any given day, your employees are moving about the facility and engaging in social learning despite the presence of a web 2.0-based platform. Crystal from our earlier stories may have a question about her software nemesis. At this point she goes to a peer and asks for help. They discuss the problem and then ultimately find a solution amongst themselves or by pulling in other users to collaborate. The collaboration is a conversation. Now imagine the conversation being recorded, archived, and made ready for anyone in the organization who may be having the same problem. Social learning is happening in this situation. The web 2.0 platform is just enabling the conversation to be shared.

As I explained the town hall meeting, I expressed that the attendees would collaborate and share as long as they perceived it as safe. If your workforce is guarded and in fear of retaliation for contributing to the conversation, then you are fighting a potentially futile battle. Your workforce needs to feel safe. That doesn't mean ignore the social forum. To the contrary, you as the manager should be very much engaged. However, you should be more like a security guard and not a police officer. What I mean by this is a police officer will arrest while a security guard is more of a slight deterrent from malignant behavior. Governance is important to have, but if it creates a "Big Brother is watching" mentality, it will stifle the conversation. Michelle Winkley, a human resources consultant at OPHR Group, states, "to protect employees and your company, it is wise to establish and maintain a social media policy, whether or not you are utilizing these tools for communications."[10] Governance should be designed to protect everyone. Well-designed policy won't be intrusive but instead will actually reinforce the safety of the conversation.

The socialization of the workforce is not a new concept. Your employees have been socializing before you were managing them, and they will continue to socialize when you move on to the next promotion. Socialization is becoming a workforce feature that attracts the most tech-savvy employees. Those employees want to know they can reach into every corner of the organization to find the answers to their questions. They understand they don't know it all, and that is why they want and value their networks. Restricting the socialization of work will turn away some of the brightest and best talent your organization cannot afford to miss.

Social Learning Tools

Not every conversation is generated by a discussion thread. Social platforms have enabled an arsenal of media tools employees can use to broadcast their expertise and sentiment. Most enterprise-level platforms allow customization and integration of social media tools into existing IT infrastructure and learning management systems. These tools are the muse for your employees to share, collaborate, and learn.

Blog

Blogging is thematic writing that is digitally published. Like most of the tools we will discuss, blogging gained popularity as a public tool before organizations took it behind their firewalls. Blogging has created a voice for anyone who can type and access the Internet. Not

---

[10] "Using Social Media in the Workplace," Michelle Winkley, OPHR Group.

all blogs are worth reading, but there are many that are written well and contain extraordinary content. ASTD has a blog at www1.astd.org/blog/.

Many organizations have used blogging to communicate with their employees as well as allowing their employees to communicate with each other. Unlike traditional communications, blogging allows two-way feedback. Most blogs allow their readers to post comments and critique the content of the blog. This is different from raditional communications where the author has the last word. Now every blog post can potentially generate a never-ending discussion.

Wiki

Perhaps the most famous of these is Wikipedia (www.wikipedia.org). A wiki is a website that allows for a community to share information. This use of semantic technology has been so powerful that it has brought the Encyclopedia Britannica to its knees. In studies not only has Wikipedia contained more information, but the information was validated as more accurate than Encyclopedia Britannica.[11] We could speculate that this is because the editorial process is owned by the community and not an appointed few.

Organizations are using wikis to crowd source the intellectual capital of their workforce. This is extremely practical. In the traditional style of sharing information, it was sent from the top of the organization down. This style is lethargic and often distanced from the subject matter expert. In the past, we progressed as a learning community, but technology has allowed us to evolve the way we learn and share content.

Document Sharing

The cloud has enabled software and documents to be accessed in any location via the Internet. Think of the cloud as a floating hard drive that follows you wherever you go in the world. As long as you have an Internet connection, you can access the cloud. This has enabled organizations to share information across borders.

An organization can post the white pages to a relevant meeting. Since not every employee is able to attend, the information would be limited to a few. Document sharing allows every employee access to the information to learn more about the discussions and content of the meeting. Slideshare is a social media application that demonstrates document sharing (www.slideshare.com). Users can post their presentations for others to view, comment on, and share.

---

[11] *Socialnomics* by Erik Qualman.

Video Sharing

The cost of video equipment is the lowest today than it has ever been. This has enabled massive amounts of video content to be created. Look at YouTube (www.youtube.com). More video content is uploaded to YouTube in a 60-day period than the three major U.S. television networks created in 60 years.[12] YouTube reports that 48 hours of content are uploaded every minute.

In the tradition of YouTube, enterprise social learning platforms are inviting employees to share "how-to" videos and video documentaries of their expertise. The videos are then shared virally based on their value to the workforce, not the leadership. A training department could never match the production time and quantity of video sharing. However, the instructional value of these videos can be criticized in comparison to the formally produced videos of most enterprise training departments.

Photo Sharing

A picture is worth a thousand words. The popular photo sharing site, Flickr.com (www .flickr.com) is estimated to have over 51 million users. Today most social media sites have a photo sharing feature. This allows users to upload photos from either their phones, mobile devices, or computers to the site. Other users can then see, share, and comment on those photos.

Enterprise photo sharing can be both professional and social. Photos of equipment, displays, new products, organizational events, employees, and so on can be shared on the learning platform. The photo sharing features of an enterprise social learning platform enable the capture and sharing of this information.

Social Bookmarking

Every web browser has a "favorites" feature. This feature enables the user to save the links to webpages they wish to bookmark. On the browser, this feature is restricted to the user of the computer that is hosting the browser. Social bookmarking is similar to the "favorites" feature except it allows users to share their bookmarks with anyone in their network. Delicious.com is a social bookmarking site that enables you to socially share your favorite URLs.

Enterprise social bookmarking is similar. Employees can bookmark URLs they wish to share or reference later. The employee can also organize a series of URLs and tag it with a specific title. For example, if an employee is researching a project, he or she can gather

---

[12] http://www.youtube.com/t/press_statistics.

information on the organization's intranet, bookmark the relevant sites, and title it by the name of the project. Other employees can then review the same bookmarks, and contribute to the stream.

Microblogs

Twitter is the most popular of these. Microblogs enable users to exchange digital content with the constraints of a character limit. In the case of Twitter, that character limit is 140. Every post is shared on that network in 140 characters or less. Microblogs are usually media rich. Videos, pictures, and other forms of media can be exchanged via hyperlink. Sometimes the sites embed media players within the feed to avoid having to leave the page.

Microblogs within the enterprise often facilitate conversation. It is similar to instant messaging (IM) in that a conversation typically evolves. Microblogging's uniqueness is that unlike IM, everyone on the network can see the conversation. IM limits the conversation usually between two people. Microblogging expands it to the entire network. Filters can be applied to make the conversation streams more manageable and relevant to the user.

Live Streaming

With the growth in video production tools, it was inevitable that broadcasting live would soon follow. Live streaming is the broadcasting of live video content over the Internet. Streaming sites like Justin.TV, UStream, and Livestream allow users to broadcast a live show over the Internet. Today the quality is fairly good, and by the time this chapter is read, it will undoubtedly get even better.

Now employees in an organization can attend a live-streamed meeting. They simply need a computer and an Internet connection. The CEO can stream her state-of-the-company address around the world for a miniscule cost compared to traditional satellite feeds. The sky is the limit to what you can broadcast on your corporate channel. It'll vary depending on the culture. Some organizations will broadcast a weekly news show instead of sending out a newsletter. Creativity knows no bounds.

Social Reviews

Everyone is a critic. Sites like Yelp allow users to review venues. If you are at a restaurant and have a wonderful experience, you can pass that on to the Yelp network. The same goes for a bad experience. The reviews become part of a database that users visit to get the real scoop on that new restaurant down the street. Prior to social reviews, we were victims to the mood of critics who were given the privilege of broadcasting their opinions. The review process today has been totally liberated, and now we all have a voice.

Sometimes it takes a brave organization to open itself up to social reviews. This can be used to provide feedback to any number of corporate events. An organization can apply social reviews to things like its cafeteria management. Employees could critique everything from "Meatloaf Wednesdays" to the popular lobster bisque that is served before the eve of the shareholders' meeting. Social reviews alleviate the need for surveys that have varying response rates.

Location Sharing

Have you ever gone to a mall and bumped into a long-lost friend? Most people have at some point in their life. Location sharing minimizes chance. What if members of your network knew you were shopping for a new pair of shoes at your favorite store? If they happened to be in the vicinity, they could stop by and say hello. Or they could direct you to where the shoes are on sale. For us men, we can always post that we are watching the Steelers beat the Raiders in the electronics store while our significant other shops for shoes. It might turn into a tailgate party in Best Buy as your nearby buddies stop by the food court on their way to meet you.

Location sharing within the enterprise would work similarly. Employees can share their location as they move throughout the facility, campus, or even global satellite offices. Their network is notified that they are in proximity. Those notifications could turn into opportunities for employees to connect in real life as opposed to virtually.

Podcasting

Podcasting is similar to video sharing without the visuals. Podcasts are audio files that are available to download or access through the Internet. A podcast can be a recording of anything from a meeting, to a speech, to narration of an article or book, and so on. ASTD has a vast library of podcasts from its *T+D* magazine. Podcasts can be live too.

An organization can make exceptional use of the podcasting tool. Essentially anything that has sound can be recorded. An employee can record a presentation he or she delivered to a client and post the podcast (of course this is considering that permission was given to make the recording). Human resources can create a podcast as part of their new-hire orientation. A manager can record a podcast about himself as a way of letting employees know more about him. Podcasts are useful to train when a visual is not necessary or available. However, you can work around that by using a podcast and a document-sharing combination.

Augmented Reality

Augmented reality (AR) blends real-world conditions with some form of data. Let's say you are gazing at the beautiful starry night sky. Suddenly you wish you could remember all the constellations you learned in the Boy or Girl Scouts. Have no fear. You can use an AR application like Google Sky Map. This app utilizes the camera in your smartphone. As you move the phone (camera facing the sky), the constellations appear over your image. You can really impress your kids when they aren't looking—although, chances are they are already using AR.

With the exception of NASA employees, astronauts, pilots, naval sailors, and a few others, there are probably not many uses for the rest of us earthbound humans to recall the names of constellations. AR has other uses. What if you walked onto the floor of your factory and could instantly recall productivity numbers from each department simply by looking at your mobile device? As you walked the floor, the data would adjust based on what you were looking at. Maybe you wanted to know your payroll at this moment in the shipping department. Perhaps you wanted to know how many orders still needed to be processed in the stocking department. You could even look at a moving forklift and see the maintenance report for that equipment. The applications are incredible.

Customer Relationship Management

Perhaps the most popular of these tools is Salesforce. Customer relationship management (CRM) is sometimes a social platform by itself. In other cases it can be incorporated into the social information-technology infrastructure of your organization. CRM systems allow employees (typically a sales force) to share customer-centric data. In its simplest form, a sales rep can record notes from a sales call. Other members of the team can utilize those notes to build on the sales call when they interact with that customer.

Pharmaceutical sales reps use CRM systems daily. These reps are tasked with communicating their products' brand to medical professionals. In some cases, a pharmaceutical sales representative may visit a medical facility a few times per week or weekly depending on the buying or prescribing strength of that office. As reps make a visit, they record information they feel would be useful to their sales partners. They could use this information to build and plan their next call by recalling it prior to their next office visit. The management can access these notes, and often the company can track if its branding messages are being communicated effectively. The CRM system can also be a means for instant messaging, webcam-based communication, and other social features.

Virtual Worlds

Virtual worlds are animated environments the user can immerse in via an avatar. An avatar is a visual representation of you. It can be anything from an animal, to a three-legged alien, to a simple cartoon. The avatar moves throughout the virtual space and interacts with the environment. One of the most popular virtual worlds is Second Life. While in Second Life, you can meet with other avatars, shop, walk or fly around, listen to music, and essentially do many of the things you can do in the real world.

Organizations are using virtual worlds as learning platforms. Many conduct training and hold meetings in these virtual spaces. A virtual world offers a different level of interaction than a webinar would. The avatar can engage with other avatars and objects in the virtual space. You can do a team-building exercise where people from all over the world have to build something in your virtual space. You could even run a virtual ropes course. This would be difficult to do in a webinar and costly to do in real life. Some work groups are even meeting in popular games like *World of Warcraft* and using the collaborative spirit of this virtual game to learn. Virtual worlds give employees an opportunity to interact and build a relationship with the next best thing to a face-to-face meeting, an avatar-to-avatar meeting.

Crowd Sourcing

Brian Solis, author of *Engage*, defines crowd sourcing as online content communities that foster connectivity and interactivity around compelling content.[13] Sites like DIGG, Reddit, and Buzz are examples of this social media tool. Users can post content they find or create to the community. The community then votes on the content. The more votes a post receives, the greater the visibility of the content. Conversations also transpire based on the content that is being shared.

Organizations can use this to encourage the practice of curating content. This can keep relevant information circulating through the network. It can also keep visibility on hot issues either based on votes or based on a robust conversation stream. Every employee essentially has the ability (or obligation) to curate content, cull it, and share his or her voice with the network.

The tools are part of the equation to social learning. They enable and expand the conversation beyond a few people to many tapping into the wisdom of crowds. As you start to explore these tools, you'll discover a unique skill set for each of them. There's a dynamic that happens with video sharing that is different from mircoblogging and even email. Let's face it, email is a social learning tool as well but hardly needs mentioning beyond this sentence. Ian Bird of IBM stated in a webinar I attended that "email is the place that knowledge goes to

---

[13] *Engage*, Brian Solis, p. 52.

die." Although comical, I think he's being harsh on email. What's happened is we've abused it to the point where it's difficult to see it as an effective learning tool. As each of these tools find their way into your organization, your employees will need to adapt to a new skill set. That skill set is what I call ValYouCasting.

ValYouCasting

As technology emerges in a society, traditional practices, work flows, and even customs may become antiquated and extinct. New methods and applications emerge to replace the old and foster a stronger relationship with invention and progress. Social media has had the same effect on the workforce and how it learns and performs. As more organizations look to web 2.0 social learning platforms, their need for employee training will increase as well. As managers, your teams will be evaluated based on their ability to meet these new competencies.

ValYouCasting is the master heading of a catalogue of competencies enabling social learning. If we were to conduct a task analysis of ValYouCasting, it would contain an arsenal of subtasks that result in employees' ability to amplify their value to their network. The tasks have a strong social base and are rooted in the technology of social media. Following are many of the competencies.

Design

Content design traditionally was a top-down strategy. A problem would be identified in an organization. The training department would then design and implement the required or proposed learning activities. The problem with this approach is the training department is rarely the subject matter expert closest to the problem or solution. In many cases they may even be on the furthest edge of the needed expertise to actually solve the problem. To bridge this gap, a SME may be consulted and even used to implement the training. However, this is still lethargic and costly compared to its social learning alternative.

In social learning, the SMEs design the training. Design becomes a workforce competency instead of the competency of a supporting department. Now SMEs are expected to design their content for their networks. Depending on the platform and culture, the design and the SME's expertise are even evaluated by the users. Users will express the value the content has based on their social interactions with it. The modern workforce will need to gain proficiency in all the subtasks associated with design as well. This competency would include analysis, observation, research, and so on.

Produce

Production is a competency that transforms design into a usable media for consumption. Production can include authored courseware, videos, text-based resources, applications, and so on. The cost of production tools has been dramatically reduced. What cost literally tens of thousands of dollars (or more) in the past can be done today for a shoestring budget of next to nothing. This reduction in costs has enabled the technology of media production to reach access points to almost everyone and essentially everywhere. This access also has exponentially increased the amount of content (both good and bad) available. YouTube reported that "more than 13 million hours of video were uploaded during 2010 and 48 hours of video are uploaded every minute resulting in eight years of traditional content uploaded every day."[14]

As a manager, your workforce will be tasked with producing the learning content that will serve your organization's intellectual growth. Essentially this makes you a producer, not dissimilar to that of a broadcasting company. Your employees will design their content while you serve as quality control and facilitator. As your employees find a new solution to a workflow problem, they will communicate that solution through the network using the media tools available in your organization. Production value depends on the employee's competency in producing content.

Critique

Criticism may have negative connotations, but your employees' ability to critique content is important to a robust social learning exchange. Let's observe movie critics for a moment. These critics bash, banter, or praise films. Based on the critics' popularity, their opinions can sway box-office performance. The voice of the critic moves the performance analytics of the movie. If they liked it, more people could possibly want to see it. If they didn't like it, many fans would avoid it or at least patiently wait for the DVD or Netflix release. Social learning is similar.

Every employee will become a critic in social learning. It's essential to the viral spread of valuable content. As your employees rate the content they receive from their social feeds, most platforms will measure it. As the rating increases, the distribution increases as well. This is similar to search engine optimization (in the very basic sense of the formula). The more a website is visited or searched for, the more points it is given. The content or website with the greatest amount of points shows up first in the user's search. This competency is helpful for the organization in that it makes relevant information easily searchable spreading the solution.

---

[14] www.youtube.com/t/press_statistics.

Promote

The line between promotion and criticism may be thin, but they are two separate competencies. Promotion is not about spreading your opinions as the latter competency is. Promotion is more about supporting the viral effect or potential of relevant content. Some information will be pulled from the archives while other content will be pushed out to the network. Some social media tools act more passively in this regard. Others take a more active approach to broadcasting. For example, a social bookmark is a passive way of storing content that users can access when they want. Microblogging pushes content out to the network via a news feed, like a commercial showing up in the middle of your programming.

Promoting is more an active approach to sharing content. Your employees will be pushing content to their networks. They may broadcast a status about an upcoming organizational event in an attempt to raise awareness about it. They can also promote their content. If they just produced a video of a software work-around, they will want to notify their network the video is available. Producing the video is one competency. Promoting it to their network is another.

Aggregate

Every news show you watch on TV (or the Internet) or listen to on the radio is an aggregation of events, stories, and information formatted to a program. The news team filters through essentially a limitless amount of information to determine which is the most relevant for its viewing audience. The programming attracts a base of fans who find this information important to their lives. Some people will tune in to Fox News while others may find *Access Hollywood* more valuable. The competency of aggregation is now a new workforce competency.

Each one of your employees is essentially creating a program for his or her network. A sales rep may have one type of programming while an HR generalist may have another for obvious reasons. Sales reps may aggregate content about sales practices like how to close or how to probe more effectively. They can blog or microblog the content they find. An HR generalists may aggregate content on governance. Their approach may be to categorize and socially bookmark URLs or sites where they have found the answers too many of their HR questions. In both situations, the network now has a station to tune in to for the information people find most relevant at any given time. Successful knowledge workers will know how to find and archive information so they and their network can recall it when needed.

Converse

Who would have thought conversation would be an encouraged task and even a competency? In the world of web 2.0, it is essential. Much of the content that is aggregated, shared, and stored is a result of conversation. Social media enable "one-too-many" communication. With IM or email, the communication is self-contained. More socially open tools like Facebook, Twitter, LinkedIn, and similar enterprise-level programs allow a conversation to grow virally, tapping into the intelligence of crowds. A conversation can be observed by all and seen as an open invitation to join in and contribute. As a conversation of relevance grows, it begins to collect data, sentiment, and other information that is now digitally stored and if done correctly tagged for future retrieval through search.

In social learning, a conversation eventually becomes learning content. Rheinmetall, a German company ($4 billion in revenue), implemented an entire collaboration suite with IBM social tools. The company's community has grown to over 10,000 users. Rheinmetall built two social environments, one secure behind the firewall and the second incorporating vendors and customers who exist outside the firewall. Users are able to have conversations with each other to address obstacles and share solutions. Knowledge workers are able to productively participate in these conversations.

Collaborate

Collaboration is working together to achieve a goal. Collaboration and conversation have similarities. I'll draw a difference between the two by saying conversing is about developing a dialogue. Collaborating is about mapping and accomplishing a goal. Collaboration involves actions beyond a discussion. When individuals, teams, or companies are collaborating, they are contributing to the construct and execution of a plan to accomplish a goal.

NASA wanted to map the universe. It photographed hundreds of thousands of galaxies and needed to classify them by shape to understand how these clusters form. Due to social media, more than 250,000 volunteers have searched and categorized the cosmos. This wasn't simply a conversation. This collaboration was people moving and acting to meet a goal. The knowledge worker will lead and participate in collaborations.

Network

Networking has become an important career-building competency. With the connection of communities that is happening with web 2.0 technologies, it is emerging as a core competency. Networking is essential to collaboration. It is the art of building strong connections to others with expertise you may wish to tap into. In the web 2.0 era, networks are portable and can be accessed anywhere in the world. Often, a strong network can be accessed 24/7/365. To do this one must extend his or her reach globally. As a competency the knowledge worker will connect with other knowledge workers with the understanding that they will help in the solution of a problem or to collaborate on an idea.

At the enterprise level, knowledge workers will surf the feeds, stories, blogs, videos, and other media to not only aggregate content but also connect with people in and outside the organization who authored it. This network of expertise becomes a commodity. Other knowledge workers will also view someone's network to evaluate his or her expertise or to gain an introduction so they can increase their network. In the context of this chapter, we are talking about digital networking; but in reality, networking extends well beyond the digital space, and personal introductions and gatherings are just as important.

Consume

Knowledge workers cannot simply produce content, but they must be avid consumers of others' content. Imagine writing a screenplay without ever seeing a movie. It would be difficult, and chances are the reader would struggle to follow the author's intent. The reason for this is that content takes on the form of the culture. Compare the American blockbuster to an independent film coming out of Syria. The culture has dramatic influence on relevance, structure, and technique. Social content is the same. Knowledge workers are producers, so they must consume the content of others in the network to connect with what's important.

Some organizations use blogs as a preferred tool. Over time, employees acclimate to this tool. The more they acclimate by consuming content, the more they are prepared to contribute themselves in this format. Another organization may choose video or screen casts as its preferred tool. The same holds true for these employees. This is not to say you have one bullet to load in the gun. It simply means the users will gather around specific media, and their exchanges will be stronger at those points than with the other features of a platform. Over time this can change as content and value are collected in the different media forms. That is why consumption is a competency. The knowledge worker must acquire a taste for the media of the learning community.

Relate

Behind every avatar, profile, or user ID is a human being. Building and maintaining relationships in a digital space are just as important in the real world. Many times both can cross the threshold and move a good or bad relationship into the realm of the other. All the skills and competencies of relationship building apply in digital space. A snide remark will gain the same emotional charge in a virtual space as it will in the real world. The goal of digital collaboration is to build community. Part of that is the competency of users being able to relate to other users.

Enterprises must encourage their employees to form and grow relationships with each other and use the social platforms as a way to augment the relationship. Every act of consumption and production leads to a possible catalyst for building a relationship. Tone can play a major part. If an author uses his blog to distastefully slander a policy, another employee, or the company, this can resonate throughout the organization. Knowledge workers must ensure their consumption and production are done without malice or ill intent. Leaving a professional comment on another employee's blog is an opportunity to harness a fruitful relationship.

Management's Role

As a manager, this creates yet again something else that needs to fit into your daily to-do list. It may find itself in different places on the priority scale depending on the organization's culture. If the organization is looking to its future, it should be high on the priority scale. The increasing number of seasoned veterans leaving your organization for retirement and the growing number of tech-savvy rookies entering your organization should be alarming enough to put a priority on social learning 2.0.

The veterans hold the current intellectual capital. Their years of experience and knowledge are getting ready to leave your organization as they retire to their retirement homes on some sandy coast. Social learning 2.0 captures this otherwise lost wealth of social capital. The veterans need to be encouraged to produce content. Their digital footprint will serve as the training ground for their replacements.

Your new hires are more and more tech savvy. These digital natives know how to navigate your learning platforms to retrieve and access information because they do so in their social lives. They're even primed to contribute their own content. The challenge with the younger generation is their experience and knowledge with electronic learning platforms far outweighs their experience with the work you are hiring them to do. Ask them to do a database search and they'll probably retrieve content you didn't know existed. Ask them to apply what they found and you may get that deer-in-the-headlights look. That's not to say they won't become as proficient as the veterans. They will, and thanks to social learning 2.0, they may even get there faster and more efficiently than their predecessors.

These competencies now open the door to several considerations for you as a manager of social learning. Your competencies must shift as well.

- Managers will be tasked to motivate the workforce to engage in social learning.
- Managers will be tasked to train the workforce on social learning 2.0.
- Managers will be tasked with interpreting the vast amount of analytics from social learning 2.0.
- Managers will be tasked to govern social learning communities appropriately.

■ Managers will be tasked to participate as knowledge workers in social learning communities.

The burden of competency doesn't lie solely with the knowledge worker but lies with all those vested in the organization's success. That includes the management.

Social learning is an often overlooked managerial process. It is as native as financial management to every organization. An organization may not be vested in a web 2.0 platform. Nonetheless, social learning is happening. Web 2.0 enables the process of social learning to become more viral. It also enables an organization the opportunity grow its knowledge base for future generations of workers. ValYouCasting competencies are the mechanics behind the production of content that will enable questions to be answered, partnerships to form deep collaborations, and knowledge to fuel performance results for your organization.

About the Author

Terrence Wing was the founder of LIQUID LEARN™. He specialized in blended training design, delivery, and evaluation with a passionate interest in learning technology and its fusion with social media. Terrence wrote a monthly column for *Learning Solutions* magazine titled "App Fusion," which focused on learning technology.

Chapter 34

Using Social Media to Create Systems of Engagement

CV Harquail, PhD

Editor's Note

Management guru Gary Hamel said in his management 2.0 speech (see it here: www.managementexchange.com) that organizations should seek to develop some of the best qualities that we find on the web. In this chapter, CV Harquail offers managers a vision and meaty list of practices they can implement to use new technology tools (and the mental and social constructs they create) to build engagement. And she does this with a style that is fluid and a pleasure to read. I have often thought that managers have much more competition for their employees' time, attention, and intrinsic motivation—team members can go home and tap into networks of people who inspire and excite them. Being an "OK" boss who will occasionally ask for input at the end of a three-hour staff meeting is just not good enough any longer (OK, that was never good enough, but we tolerated it). After reading this chapter, you will be better able to compete for and earn the participation and commitment of your team members.

After all the acronyms, analyses, and advice that have been offered to managers who want to build employee engagement, it's hard to believe that there could be any new insight, new approach, or new tool set that promises to do anything different or differently from what's been done before.

And yet, there is.

Moving quietly into organizations is a technology—enterprise social media—that holds great potential for the proactive manager looking to increase employee engagement. This technology appears to be such a predictable evolution of current tools that many managers won't even see it as a different kind of opportunity to increase engagement. More savvy managers will recognize an opportunity but won't understand it fully. These managers will find it hard to maximize the positive influence of social media on employee engagement and organizational performance. The savviest managers will learn about the technology, understand what makes it different, and use social media technology specifically to enable, focus, and inspire people's contributions to the organization.

This chapter is for managers who aspire to be in the third group. These managers have the chance to lead a different kind of employee engagement initiative, one where social media helps employees meet deep-seated human social needs and, in so doing, motivates employee engagement.

In this chapter, I'll introduce enterprise social media and describe what distinguishes enterprise social media from communication tools that have come before it. I'll explain how enterprise social media creates an opportunity for each employee to become more engaged, because it helps employees meet five different needs that all humans have in social situations. By helping employees to 1) enable their full identity, 2) engage their distinctive voice, 3) activate their agency, 4) cohere into a community, and 5) catalyze their individual and collective sense of purpose, enterprise social media invites employees to engage their full selves in meaningful collective work.

Key features of enterprise social media—including its interactivity, its openness, and its multidirectional connectivity—have the potential to motivate employees to engage, but only deliberate leadership can turn these communication tools into "systems of engagement." I offer several questions to help the non-IT manager consider how to deploy enterprise social media as a system of engagement, and suggest four action steps to help managers get started.

Employee Engagement: A Quick Overview

Few managers reading this book will need an introduction to employee engagement. It's likely that you are already familiar with the concept at some level, because employee engagement has been management's "holy grail" for the last decade. Or two.

Employee engagement, simply defined, is the heightened emotional and intellectual connection that employees have with their work, their colleagues, their organization, and even the organization's stakeholders. This heightened connection leads members to voluntarily contribute more of themselves to their work and to participate more fully in the organization. Engaged employees exert more intellectual, physical, and emotional effort on behalf of their work and their organization than do less engaged employees.

Study after study demonstrates a link between increased employee engagement and positive organizational outcomes. And, research demonstrates that the innovation, collaboration, and creativity that organizations need to be competitive require employees who are motivated to go above and beyond what can be explicitly outlined in a job description.

For their part, individual employees aren't averse to being engaged in their work, their work relationships, or their organizations. Engagement can have positive outcomes for individuals, such as having their work feel more meaningful. It's just that employees want to get something back for this voluntary effort. Often there is too little for employees within the work or within the organization that makes increasing their engagement feel worth the extra effort.

Employee engagement is usually pursued because engagement directly benefits the organization. Although engagement can offer collateral benefits to employees themselves, most approaches to employee engagement focus on what the *organization* needs. Employee engagement initiatives seldom focus on what employees themselves might need to make engagement worthwhile for them.

Many people advocating for enterprise social media propose that it will increase employee engagement, and some can even cite the data that show a positive correlation between the deployment of these tools and employee engagement. However, they have a harder time explaining what creates this link, and how we might maximize its power. That's why it's important to understand that the quiet, powerful benefit of enterprise social media is that these tools offer individuals something that makes fuller participation and increased engagement personally worthwhile. Specifically, the features of enterprise social media offer ways for individuals to meet some human needs that they experience in social organizations but are often not able to fulfill. However, before we can talk about how enterprise social media can meet these needs, we need to know a bit more about enterprise social media and what makes it a distinctive type of communication.

What Is Enterprise Social Media?

Enterprise social media comprises digital communication tools used across an organization to support and drive the organization's internal activity. These tools and systems go by many names, including social business, enterprise 2.0, enterprise social software, emergent social software, social computing, and enterprise collaboration. Enterprise social media supports interactive communications among employees and between individual employees and organizational agents (e.g., the HR department), within the organization's firewall.

Enterprise social media includes tools like social networks, moderated communities, discussion forums, wikis, idea banks, blogs, social search, member profiles, collaborative planning programs, activity steams, social bookmarking, and microblogging. These tools have all the same qualities of social media platforms we use in our personal lives, like Facebook, Twitter, and LinkedIn. Enterprise social media helps employees coordinate activities and projects, build and share knowledge, and create and sustain relationships, all so that the organization's work gets done.

When we take a snapshot, surface-level view of enterprise social media, these tools look a lot like communication tools we're already familiar with. For example, posts on corporate blogs look a lot like emailed newsletters. Enterprise microblogging looks like the real-time, back-and-forth communication on instant message tools like AIM or ICQ. Internal employee profiles on platforms like SocialCast or IBM's Connections show the same information as the employee data summaries maintained by HR. Underneath these similarities in appearance, however, enterprise social media tools are distinct from conventional organizations' communication in three key ways.

Features of Enterprise Social Media

While each social media tool has specific features based on particular activities it is built to facilitate, these tools have three features in common: 1) dynamic interactivity among users; 2) constant streaming of public, searchable, and open contributions; and 3) multiperson, multidirectional connections among users. These features, taken together, make it possible for organization members to participate often, openly, where they want to, when they are needed, with people who share their interests and concerns, and irrespective of other organizational structures or boundaries like departments or location.

Dynamic Interactivity Among Users

Interactive communication makes it possible for users to respond to any communication someone else makes. The idea that employees might always be able to respond to someone else's contributions seems minor. But, keep in mind how many different types of conventional organizational communication are one-way, where one author speaks, everyone else listens, and no one is invited to reply.

With enterprise social media, no communication is presumed to go only one way or lead to a dead end. Because the tools are interactive, any user can initiate, participate in, or respond to a conversation. Users can shift fluidly from sending to receiving information, from speaking to listening, from author to reader, from instigator to follower. Thus, participation is not only possible, but it is presumed and even invited, simply because each tool has a facility for individuals to respond.

Constant Streaming of Public, Searchable, and Open Contributions

Organizational conversations that are public, searchable, and open are easy to see, easy to find, and easy to join. Employees can follow conversations, refer others to these conversations, and be persuaded by these conversations. Because public, accessible contributions can be seen, found through searches, retrieved, and reinserted into other conversations, one employee's participation in a conversation can influence how an infinite number of other employees think, feel, and react.

Multiperson, Multidirectional Connections Among Employees

Multiperson, multidirectional connections among employees create communication networks that circumvent and even transcend conventional communication channels, decision-making silos, and bureaucratic pyramids. Communication networks make it easier for employees to rise above the boundaries presented by physical location, departmental assignment, or status level so that they can connect with other employees based on interest or need.

And, the network of connections means that the effects of a useful or provocative contribution can be amplified. One person's contribution can take on the power of other employees' recommendation when he or she shares it with his or her connections. Being connected to people, who themselves are connected to others, makes it possible for employees to distribute an inquiry or a contribution far across the organization, outside their regular circle of influence into areas where their contribution otherwise might not venture.

Linking Enterprise Social Media and Engagement

When it comes to employee engagement, it's clear that enterprise social media supports the organization's needs. Consider how interactivity, openness, and connectedness support the practices for increasing employee engagement recommended by Richard Axelrod, in his

2000 book *Terms of Engagement: Changing the Way We Change Organizations.* Axelrod advises organizations to 1) widen the circle of involvement, 2) connect people to each other, 3) create communities of action, and 4) embrace democratic principles.

Interactivity and openness help to widen the circle of involvement by expanding participation to more members to include new voices and different ideas. And, they help organizations embrace democratic principles by inviting employees across the organization to participate in debates and influence decision making. Similarly, the multiparty, multidirectional networks of enterprise social media help to connect people to each other and to create communities of action.

What's surprising is how enterprise social media can also support what employees need to be fully engaged at work—the chance to fulfill our need for identity, voice, agency, community, and purpose. When we can be our full selves, share our perspectives and experience, influence the situation around us, join with and influence others, and be part of a meaningful, goal-oriented project, we can be fully engaged.

When social systems (be they digital or analog) make it possible for individuals to meet these social needs, individuals are more able and more willing to invest themselves into the social situation. By design, enterprise social media invites individuals to put more of their selves into their activity at work. These tools make it much easier for employees to 1) enable their full identity, 2) engage their distinctive voice, 3) activate their agency, 4) cohere into a community, and 5) catalyze their individual and collective sense of purpose, all while participating in the work of the organization.

Five Social Needs of Individuals and How to Meet Them

Need for Identity

We want to be who we are, and to be seen and affirmed for who we are. We want to bring our full selves to work and into our interactions with colleagues while we are working. When we are able to be "who we are" in specific, descriptive, textured, multiple ways, we can bring forward all the knowledge, insight, and ability that is linked to these different facets of ourselves. We can engage all the different parts of ourselves in our work.

How enterprise social media can enable identity: Enterprise social media gives individuals many different opportunities to define who they are at work, helping employees to be seen and be known for who they are. With organization-wide opportunities to publicly describe themselves and their interests, as well as to demonstrate what they have to offer through their visible participation and work activities, employees can present who they are as broadly and specifically as they choose.

For example, when employees have a company directory where employees write their own profiles, they are able to own, modify, and expand their self-description as they choose, allowing employees to reveal a fuller sense of their selves to each other. Similarly, employees can use microblogging to regularly share small bits of information about themselves and what they are working on. This sharing not only displays more employees to others, but it also makes it easier for others to discover them, to follow what they're doing, and to interact.

Zappos has a simple and fun way to help employees in a growing company keep learning the names, interests, and abilities of the other people who work there. Before Zappos employees are able to sign into their corporate computer system, they need to identify the name of a randomly pictured employee (choosing from three possibilities). Once they've chosen, that employee's self-created, self-expressive profile is displayed to tell the users more about the featured employee.

Social media tools allow employees to show and be seen as their fuller selves, which creates a multifaceted base on which co-workers can connect with each other and build collegial relationships. These richer connections help employees create personal meaning that engages them at work. Employees are more likely to engage because they have more ways to bring into the organizational conversation more of who they are and more of what they have to offer.

Need for Voice

In social situations, we need voice. Voice is the ability to speak out what we think needs to be said, in our own words and in our own style. Voice also includes being heard and being acknowledged when we say something. Voice puts into a situation our personal expression of who we are, what we think, and how we feel. When we have voice, we are able to offer ideas, share insights, offer feedback, have influence, and get acknowledged.

How enterprise social media can foster voice: Enterprise social media gives employees organization-wide access to places where they can speak, where they can spread their ideas, and where they can be listened to by others. Social media tools that invite us to add our voice allow us to contribute to work and to collaborate with each other.

When employees comment on blogs, participate in online dialogs, share links on microblogs, or edit a group document, their activities show their personal perspectives and unique knowledge. Perhaps no other enterprise social medium offers more room for voice than employee blogs. Blogs allow employees to write longer position pieces, and to follow their own information-sharing agendas.

Just think of the amount and potential value of employee voice at corporate giant IBM. With nearly 400,000 employees, IBM had about 17,000 employee blogs (as of January 2010) covering topics from service-oriented architecture to innovation management to working parenthood. On these blogs, employees describe their own projects, exchange ideas, advance conversations, and promote their successes and learning. About 100,000 other employees comment on posts, adding their voices to the conversations initiated by the bloggers. Because all the blog posts can be easily searched, any employees' expert opinions and arguments can be found by other interested parties, and come to influence business decisions.

Enterprise social media that promotes employee voice also dampens the influence of status level and role-based organizational power. Because employees' contributions are invited, regardless of the employees' status levels, employees' ideas come out from under the power structure. No single role holder or hierarchical level can control the dynamics and content of the conversation. Some tools are even designed to show the employee's name and small photo but not his or her job title. Employees at EMC noted because their social tools show the employees' names and photos but not their job titles, employees feel like they can participate based on the quality of their ideas and not the status of their formal position.

The more opportunities that employees have to participate, the more they exercise their voice. As employees exercise their voice, they contribute their unique perspectives and expertise to the organization's work, enriching the work and engaging more of themselves.

Need for Agency

Agency is our ability to act, to get things done, and to cause things to happen. We need to be able to make choices and to enact those choices. When we have agency we are makers, doers, creators, and innovators. We are able to use our unique insights to influence the world around us.

How enterprise social media can activate agency: Enterprise social media creates opportunities for agency because it gives employees more places where they can act and influence how others act. For example, interactivity invites every user to join conversations so that they can influence processes like discovery, discussion, decision making, and implementation. Employees can accept the invitation to add their unique voice and skills to the situation, and empower themselves.

At Vancouver's Mountain Equipment Co-op, an outdoor gear retailer, 15,000 staff members (both at headquarters and on the stores' sales floors) use the company's social intranet to negotiate their schedules, coordinate time off, reorder product, and take action on a range of business issues. They can send out a call to all employees to find someone who might have experience with a specialized piece of gear, and get a reply in time to share it with a customer. And, when another employee needs advice or assistance, they can volunteer to help.

Employees are also able to demonstrate that they are getting things done and that they are effective and influential, by using enterprise social media tools to publicly narrate the work they are doing. When employees explain what they are doing and why, they are able to demonstrate mastery of their work and lay claim to the contributions they are making. When their work is made visible this way, employees can be recognized for their contributions. They can get feedback, help, thanks, and recognition from colleagues across the organization, all of which helps to affirm their sense that their work matters.

Enterprise social media also gives employees the increased autonomy, responsibility, and accountability that engagement requires. The public nature and accessibility of conversations make it possible for employees to take charge of the location, the level, and the quality of their contributions on a wide range of work-related topics. Employees can participate in a peripheral way by reading a conversation, or choose to get more deeply engaged by actually joining it. They can track conversations that are interesting but not (yet) critical to them, as well as conversations that are directly relevant. Being able to decide where to invest their attention allows employees to shape their jobs to incorporate more of what matters to them. Even when they have only a small amount of discretion in their jobs, being in control of their participation lets them choose to engage in what is meaningful *to them*.

Need for Community

Communities are our connections with other people—not just one-to-one connections but also networked connections. People yearn to be connected with people who know them and who need them. When we are part of a community, we have a slew of direct and indirect relationships through which we can be supportive, helpful, and influential. Community gives us a way to matter to other people.

How enterprise social media can cultivate community: Enterprise social media helps employees find the people they need and who need them. Employees can search out people who are already engaged in issues that matter to them, and employees' own activities can draw others to join them.

With these tools, employees create small and larger online communities around shared interests and contribute to the work of that group. The array of interests can be quite broad, since anyone can create a group around an issue that matters to him or her. For example, France Telecom-Orange has 900 communities, many but not all of which are business focused, centered on specific job activities or career paths such as marketing, human resources, or research.

Intrawest Placemaking wanted to gather the company's intellectual capital and strengthen the sense of community across their 250 employees at seven offices on two continents. Placemaking created a wiki to capture its entire real estate development process—from land acquisition to building conception to homeowner delivery. Now, on more than 500 different pages and topics, anyone at the company can annotate or edit the page with his or her ideas and suggestions. Although the organization benefits from the communities and the information resources that have been created by groups of employees, each employee has also benefitted from the chance to contribute his or her own expertise to the company's shared knowledge.

Need for Purpose

Purpose is our reason for being. Beyond our individual self-interests, human beings search for purpose, a cause or goal outside themselves that focuses their contributions to the larger social community. When we share a purpose we can have commitment, vision, motivation, collaboration, and accomplishment. With shared purpose, our social activity has meaning.

How enterprise social media can catalyze purpose: Enterprise social media catalyzes purpose by creating a sense of the "whole" organization working together, by keeping collective goals in focus, and by making visible all of the small pieces of work as they fit together and build toward the collective goal.

Enterprise social tools like intranets and discussion groups give individuals a place to talk about "work" and "the organization." They can tell stories that demonstrate who the organization is, they can deconstruct activities to understand why the organization does things, and they can share with each other what they'd like the organization to do. All of this conversation helps to form a sense of the organization as a coherent thing that they are each part of. It allows employees to construct a meaningful sense of collectivity.

At eHarmony, employees use their intranet to create a meaningful sense of collectivity, by keeping the entire company up to date on corporate activities. The HR group posts current and upcoming events, monthly updates on company performance, messages from the CEO and COO, pictures from the latest company event, and changes to the employee manual. This information often begins as a corporate announcement, and then evolves into extended discussions, pages for sharing resources, and self-organized action teams, all working as "the organization."

When employees have an up-to-date understanding of the organization and its business, they can make timely, informed, and more effective contributions because they can put their work into the larger context of the organization's purpose. In preparation for the 2010 G20 Summit, government employees from 20 different countries used a digital, community-based collaboration tool to propose agendas, develop policy statements, and coordinate logistics. As a group, they were able to align their activities and expectations so that they arrived at the fiscal planning summit fully prepared to negotiate and establish policy. They could work more effectively because the software helped every participant contribute to the shared goal of maximizing the two days that the delegates would work together in person.

Enterprise social media links employees and their work tasks to larger important projects, and links employees' individual work to the work of others, giving them a sense of personal connection to the organization's purpose. With tools that display how an individual's discrete work actions contribute to and accumulate with the actions of others, employees can see how their individual efforts move the whole forward. Their small actions incrementally and perceptibly help the group reach larger goals. Small actions can snowball, and they can trigger related actions that shoot energy in other directions. Accounting for and acknowledging these small moves as they happen not only makes larger goals look more achievable, but also maximizes the sense of progress that employees can experience by providing regular, small kicks of motivation.

Seeing progress caused by other employees' actions can sustain an individual's engagement even when the employee herself is inactive. Seeing others' activity demonstrates momentum and also shows the employee that other employees are contributing to the same larger purpose. No one is working alone. Enterprise social media accumulates, organizes, synthesizes, and amplifies in a tangible way the employees' individual and collective efforts toward purpose, which in turn motivates employees to continue to engage.

From Enterprise Social Media to "Systems of Engagement"

By offering employees the opportunity to fulfill their social need for identity, voice, agency, community, and purpose, enterprise social media is designed to invite employees to put more of their selves into their activity at work. This potential for increasing engagement has led some technology advocates to start calling these tools "systems of engagement." (These technology advocates want to distinguish social communications tools from the enterprise-wide, interactive databases of numbers, activities, and texts collectively known as "systems of record.")

The idea of "systems of engagement" is a compelling one. What manager wouldn't want a system of unobtrusive, ubiquitous, useful, interactive communication tools that could engage employees in their work, with each other, and with the organization itself? But, it's jumping the gun to presume that enterprise social media will create systems of engagement just by being adopted by the organization.

While enterprise social media has the potential to support more engagement, these tools are merely tools for communication unless they are employed with a specific engagement agenda. Otherwise, enterprise social media will be deployed in ways that have no effect on engagement or that thwart engagement. It takes leadership to turn enterprise social media from communication systems into systems that generate employee engagement. Much depends on how the tools themselves are configured within each organization, and even more depends on how these systems are adopted, used, and adapted by the organization's leaders—managers like you.

Can You, as a Manager, Turn Enterprise Social Media Into Systems of Engagement?

To be sure, most managers don't get to design or select the technology systems in their organization. Many organizations have IT specialists who make those decisions, and so managers are usually on the receiving end of someone else's technology choices. That said, savvy managers can take a proactive approach to adapting and implementing these tools. If you personally make engagement the explicit focus of how you use these tools and how you teach others to use them, you can help to transform social media systems into systems of engagement. Here's how to begin.

First, ask how you and your colleagues could deploy and manage each social media tool so that it supports each of our five social needs. Get creative—your goal is to be able to demonstrate and explain how each tool might help employees enable their full identity, engage their distinctive voice, activate their agency, cohere into a community, and catalyze their individual and collective sense of purpose. Lead the way by asking these five questions:

- How can we use this tool to help employees express who they are?
- How can we use this tool to help employees say what they need to say, and be heard where they need to be heard?

- How can we use this tool to help employees take on new authority and new responsibility, while finding new situations and new ways to choose, decide, and act?
- How can we use this tool to help employees find, affirm, share, inspire, and collaborate with other people, directly and indirectly?
- How can we use this tool to help employees clarify and pursue a contribution here at work that is both individually and collectively meaningful?

You need to make a deliberate effort to use enterprise social media tools differently, or you and your organization run the risk of implementing the tools to reinforce the status quo rather than to build engagement.

Keep in mind that some employees will presume that adopting enterprise social media will be simple and obvious. After all, personal social media tools like LinkedIn are pretty straightforward. But using these tools to engage others and ourselves isn't automatic, since being engaged at work is not that common. We actually need to (re)learn how to engage ourselves and others, now that our digital tools make that easier.

Choose just one tool being offered in your organization, and host a conversation with your colleagues about how to use this tool to encourage employees to share more about who they are, to take a position on an issue, to contribute an idea or complete a task, to connect with like-minded others, and to discuss the big picture that your work contributes to. Get them to join you on a blog, a wiki, or a collaboration space, or even by filling out your online employee profiles in ways that are fun and self-expressive. Ask your IT department (if you have one) for guidelines and training sessions. Go online and search for examples, instructions, and best practices.

Second, you can experiment with and model how to use these tools in ways that increase your own engagement. Take each of the five questions, above, and restate it to ask, "How can *I* use this tool to help myself and my employees ... ?" Take your answers to these questions, and try them out. For example, create a blog where you post regular updates about a current project, and invite colleagues to share their comments. Keep it small as you experiment, and then share your successes.

Third, you can teach others how to use these tools to evoke their own engagement and to support the engagement of other employees. As you get more comfortable, take advantage of the public visibility of your own social media participation by recognizing that your experiments, your "mistakes," and your learning can be seen by others. Your role modeling will be more powerful, because your participation can influence more than just your direct reports and nearby colleagues. People throughout your organization, many of whom you've never influenced before, will be looking for ideas about how to use these tools. They may not have thought about using social media to foster engagement, but they will follow your lead when they see how it works.

Use these tools not only to invite yourself into more engaged participation, but also to call out and affirm the increased engagement of folks with whom you interact. Send them personal invitations to join you in using a particular tool. Help people out as they get started. Assume the role of the host, and make it part of your job to foster your co-workers' participation. You can create a welcoming committee of enthusiastic co-workers to work with you to reach out to other employees. You might even offer your own training sessions.

In the same way that touch-typing is not writing, using a tool is not the same as using it well. When Penn State Outreach launched its integrated social media platform, it invited everyone to a professional development series to learn how to use the tools. And, as it taught the nuts and bolts of each technology, it used examples that simultaneously demonstrated both how to get work done and how to reinforce collegial relationships as work gets done. It's not so much knowing where to click as it is knowing how to craft an inviting message or post, to search effectively by putting yourself in another person's mind frame, and to respond with positive, affirmative energy.

Finally, be sympathetic to those who resist enterprise social media. Some managers and employees will be tempted to view enterprise social media as just another tool set that adds only incremental value. Or, they might see the social elements of these tools as big black holes that will distract employees from actual "work." These managers and employees may not realize that research by firms as venerable as McKinsey Consulting continue to document that enterprise social media makes organizations more productive, not less.

It will also take some time for people to understand that social media inside organizations is intended not for "socializing" but rather for supporting the social relationships necessary for employees to work well together. Some managers will resist using social media for engagement until they let go of old-fashioned ideas that work should be done without any "social" touches. They will need to appreciate that rich person-to-person relationships must be created, maintained, and nurtured for engagement to be possible.

Employee engagement is not a new idea, but employee engagement using social enterprise media is a new opportunity. It invites you as a manager, and as a leader, to see engagement as the side benefit of helping employees create deep, wide, strong, and authentic personal connections to the work they do and the people they work with. It will take managers like you to bring the benefits of employee engagement to your organization by using these tools to their full potential. When you deliberately use these tools to help employees enable their full identity, contribute their distinctive voice, activate their agency, cohere into a community, and catalyze their individual and collective sense of purpose, your employees will voluntarily, even enthusiastically, engage more of themselves in meaningful collective work.

About the Author

CV Harquail is an organizational strategist, consultant, change advocate, and identity/reputation scholar with a PhD in leadership and organizations. She researches, writes, teaches, consults with, and advises organizations about the relationships between organizational identity, actions, and purpose. Her blog is called Authentic Organizations, and you can find her website at www.authenticorganizations.com.

Chapter 35

How to Run a Great Web Meeting

Wayne Turmel

Editor's Note

I asked Wayne to share several pearls of wisdom (he throws in the humor at no extra charge) about how to run web meetings because I see managers struggle with this nearly every day. His suggestions will apply to any conversation you are having that has the aim of helping one or more person be clear and motivated to act in the service of shared goals (that covers all business meetings, hopefully, unless you meet to discuss topics of no importance with no expectation of follow-through). Great conversations help teams think better, and when they think better, they consider and take better actions and get better results. Read and apply this chapter, and you will see improved team results.

If you've ever sat in on a web conference or meeting and been bored silly, or thought "what a great chance to catch up on my email," you're not alone. Neither participants nor meeting leaders like them much. Here's how to run a web meeting or virtual conference (or whatever the heck you want to call it) that won't make anyone (yourself included) miserable.

The biggest problem with these events is that they are called web meetings, or webinars, or virtual something-or-others. This implies that their problems are tied up with the technology, which is only partially the issue. Think about the most common complaints people have about these meetings:

- They're boring.
- There's no interaction.
- They waste precious time.
- They don't accomplish what they're supposed to do.
- They're hard to facilitate.
- They take *way* longer than they need to.
- The technology is a pain.

With the exception of the last bullet, these have nothing to do with sitting in front of a computer—they're the same complaints people have about regular meetings in the conference room (and if you can't get the computer and the projector to speak to each other, they all apply).

Face it—most meetings stink. Working online only makes the things that are bad, worse, and you've added a layer of complexity with the technology. Trying to monitor the screen, advance the slides, listen to input, capture notes, and watch the clock just makes a difficult job that much more difficult. It's a little like trying to run a meeting while programming your TiVo.

What we'll try to do in this chapter is break down what you want to achieve, what tools you have at your disposal, and how to run the meeting so that both you and your participants feel like you've invested time in solving a problem or moving your project along, instead of wasting precious time.

What Are You Trying to Achieve?

Traditionally, meetings are called to inform, gain input, build teams, and get to know each other. This means that there are several things that have to happen:

- You need to share information in a variety of ways (visuals, audio, documents, and pictures).
- You need to get input and capture it in a number of ways (written as well as spoken).
- Everyone needs to see the same information at the same time.
- Everyone needs to be able to refer to what's happened both during the meeting and afterward for accountability and accuracy.

Any meeting, regardless of whether it's a one-on-one meeting, a team status update, or a town hall with hundreds of angry participants, needs to have both a purpose and an outcome. If you know what your goal is in holding the meeting, and what the outcome should be, you know how to run the meeting. You know what is relevant, what's pulling the meeting off track, what you need to get from participants, and how to facilitate the meeting to fit the realities of the situation (this means things like time and format).

First, let's think about purpose. There are actually only a few reasons to hold a meeting. Most meetings are some combination of these reasons. You want to:

- share information with participants and answer questions
- gather information and feedback from participants
- brainstorm or collaborate to generate ideas or solve problems
- engage in team building and enhancing working relationships.

That's it. There may be secondary reasons (an unnatural desire for bad coffee, or it's better than doing that task sitting on your calendar), but this is pretty much it.

Notice that you don't hold a meeting simply to give people information with no feedback. If all you want to do is give your audience data, you'd just email it to people and have them call if they have questions. The ability to answer any questions or concerns is why you get together, either online or in the conference room.

You'll also notice that when you understand the purpose of a meeting, something odd happens. You begin to realize that some of those awful web meetings you've been on were simply doomed to failure from the start.

What do all of the reasons to hold a meeting have in common?

- You need to have information to share that's relevant to the people in the meeting.
- They need to be prepared and able to participate.
- They need to speak up to the leader and each other when appropriate.
- You need a method of capturing information and sharing it with participants in real time as well as after the meeting.
- People need to work together. Ideally they should see each other, but we've been on enough conference calls to know that isn't always necessary.
- Someone needs to run the show—keeping things on track, watching process, and guiding the session to a successful conclusion.

Does any of this sound like the typical web meeting? If you were holding a meeting, and you said to participants, "OK, don't talk to me or each other. Hold all your questions until the end. Just sit there and listen and, oh, I'm not going to look at you either," how well would that session go?

But that's how too many web meetings are run—too little input, data dumps, with unprepared and unresponsive participants—you know the drill.

So if the way you plan to run your meeting doesn't allow you to achieve your purpose for holding it, why bother? It's like they always said about trying to teach a pig to sing—it is ultimately pointless and only annoys the pig.

Now, let's look at the desired objective or outcome for your meeting. What do you want to achieve at when it's over?

- You want to share information and make sure people understand the information you've shared by answering their questions and concerns. That requires real-time, two-way communication. In this case, verbal communication is better, so you probably want to be able to talk to each other.
- You want to brainstorm and capture ideas. You know how to do this in a meeting—you'd use a flipchart or whiteboard to capture ideas and lead the group through the collaboration and finding a solution.
- You want to make sure that action items are clearly understood and people are held accountable for completing them. This means everyone needs to see and hear the items, questions get asked, and people verbally commit to them.
- You want people to work together, forge working relationships that build trust, and focus on fixing the problem at hand.

What's different between these outcomes and those of a live, face-to-face meeting? Nothing. Not a darned thing.

The reasons you meet, and what you want to have happen, don't differ in the slightest. In fact, if you're honest, you haven't been to that many great face-to-face meetings lately either. They fail for the same reasons all meetings succeed or fail: poor planning, bad meeting leadership, unresponsive participants. None of these things can be blamed (entirely) on the fact that the meeting is held virtually. Odds are it would stink even if you were all together.

OK, Let's Talk Technology

Let's be clear. I'm not saying technology doesn't matter or that it has no real impact. It just isn't the blanket excuse we use so often. Using web platforms allows some very good things to happen, as well as very bad things. It's not the tool itself; it's how we use it.

Part of the problem is that those of us not really comfortable with technology look at these tools as making the best of a bad situation. *"They* won't let us get together." *"They* won't give us the budget to travel." *"They* claim they're too busy to participate." If it makes you feel any better, the problem isn't technology. It's *them.*

Actually, technology can affect your meetings negatively, but it's not because it's inherently evil. It's what that technology does to both the meeting leader and the participants.

For participants, there are several dynamics at work. First of all, if I don't want to be at that meeting in the first place, technology gives me all kinds of excuses not to participate. I can just put the phone on mute, answer my email, and say I was there. After all, one of the key drawbacks for meeting leaders is that you can't actually see the other people. It's not that people wouldn't tune you out and answer email during the meeting; they just don't want to get caught doing it. Of course with smartphones in everyone's hand that rudeness is not restricted to cyberspace anymore.

But instead of looking at the glass as half empty and bemoaning all the things virtual meetings can't do, let's look at what they can do if you have the right tool and use it creatively. The trick is to understand what you want to accomplish, and then take a look at your web platform and calmly, objectively look at what that tool can do for you. Then use the features in that tool to help you achieve those outcomes.

According to vendors like WebEx and GoToMeeting, most users actually use fewer than 25 percent of the features those tools come with. Now, the features available to you will vary depending on which platform you use, but here's what you need to know: They all do 90 percent of the same thing. If you understand how to run a good web meeting on one platform, you can figure it out. It's like renting a car: You might not know where the gas tank opening is on the car you just got from the counter, or how to adjust the radio, but I'll bet you'll figure it out soon enough, and after that it's just another car.

Forget specific platforms. Let's take a look at several key components of a successful meeting. For each we'll take a look at how it is often handled in a regular meeting, and how that can be done online with the kind of tools normally at your disposal.

- **You want to see people's faces:** Depending on the platform you use and the number of participants, there are, in fact, ways to see the people you're working with. On the low-tech end of the spectrum, there are always pictures of the participants. Some team leaders have a slide with the team members' names and pictures on it. Some platforms allow people to upload pictures so that their face appears beside their name. If bandwidth and technology allow, you can also use low-resolution webcams to allow people to see each other in real time. In very small groups, many platforms allow you to just leave the webcams running, although this can cause bandwidth problems and possible screen freezing. The point is, while this might not be as easy as it is in the conference room, it can be done to some extent. It's in your favor to do the best you can.

- **You want people to interact with the speaker and with each other in real time:** One of the big differences between a well-run web meeting and a boring one is the way they mimic the back-and-forth of real-time interaction. The biggest mistake most web meeting leaders make is in limiting interaction for their own convenience—it's a hassle to monitor chat. It's easier to just ask everyone to hold questions until the end. You also know that in a live meeting you'd never stand for that. In small groups, allow people to speak on the phone or using the computer and their headsets. In larger groups, people can mute their phones and use the "raise hand" button or other signals to ask for the floor. It's really no different than the conference calls you're already running. Chat has a couple of additional advantages:

  - Your introverts and those with English as a second language are often more comfortable writing out what they want to say.
  - People can contribute in real time; they don't have to wait for the previous blowhard to shut up.
  - They can have private conversations as well (with the meeting leader or with each other). This might sound like a bad thing, but you know in a live meeting there's real value in being able to whisper over to your neighbor for clarification, or to ask a question that you don't necessarily want to share with everyone else.

- **You want to capture ideas and input:** Think of what you'd do in a real-life brainstorming session. You'd grab a marker and go to the flipchart or whiteboard and write ideas down as they come in. You can do that easily online using a couple of different methods. Use the "whiteboard" feature that is standard on almost every platform out there. (*Tip*: Don't try to lead the meeting and play scribe. Have someone else do the input for you.) There are actually a couple of ways that capturing input online is in some ways superior to a less-than-perfect live meeting. First, sharing applications allows you to change documents in real time, allowing all participants to see the impact of their input ("If we change that budget number, here's what it means…"). They can't claim they weren't involved. Additionally, recording the meeting means that there is a permanent record of what happened, and people who missed the meeting can get an accurate picture of why they wound up with those action items.

So If It's Not (Just) the Technology, What Is It?

There's no doubt that technology makes leading meetings more difficult. We've also shown that it's not impossible either. That means that the ultimate success or failure is up to the person running, and the people participating in, the meeting. That's you.

What happens before, during, and after any individual meeting will have an impact on everything the team does from that point on. It will set a tone, define expectations, and determine how accountable people will be to their manager and each other. No pressure. Basically, let's take a look at what needs to happen before, during, and after a meeting to ensure it has value long past the time you spend online.

Before the Meeting

Any good meeting starts with preparation. The person leading the session needs to be prepared, and the participants need to know what's expected of them and have the information and determination to help reach that objective.

By planning for success and communicating that plan to the group, everyone can show up informed, motivated, and with his or her expectations in line. It all starts with a plan that turns into an agenda.

Remember that everything you do in this meeting needs to help you meet your objective and reach your desired outcome. Before creating your agenda, think about what you need to accomplish. What's the best way to achieve your goals? Do you need lots of input? How will you capture that information? Who should be in on the meeting? (Face it, how many meetings have you been in or on that you had no idea why you were there? Do everyone a favor, and if someone doesn't need to be there, don't require it.)

Figure out the appropriate technology for the purpose. If a simple conference call will do, don't bother setting up a web meeting. On the other hand, if sharing information in real time, capturing input so everyone can see and process it, is critical, don't skimp on the technology to help you do that.

So you've decided that you need to brainstorm and collect input. Great, now it's time to create an agenda. A good agenda is *not* four bullets and a time to meet.

The agenda should be the one place people know to reference for all the answers to their questions. Don't assume because you use the same information all the time that they'll automatically know it. You will want to include:

- **What time it's going to start (and finish).** If your system allows you to easily enter this into people's calendars, take advantage of that and reduce the possible excuses for arriving late and leaving early.
- **How will you meet?** If it's a web meeting, include *all* relevant information with live links (URL for the meeting, audio information). Again, eliminate any possible questions by providing the information up front. (Remember, in a template you can just leave the information that doesn't change and update what does, instead of reinventing the wheel every time.)
- **A notice to log on a few minutes early, with instructions on how to test their system for compatibility**. Most web platforms build this in to their invitations automatically. Insist people actually do it. Why waste precious meeting time and tick off those who are actually prepared?
- **The purpose of the meeting with desired outcome.** People can't be prepared to participate fully if they don't know what's going to be covered. They'll also be less paranoid, which can only be a good thing. If they are expected to make a decision they should know that so they're in the right frame of mind. If it's a brainstorming session, they need to know they'll be called on for input. Tell them what's on the table—and what's not on the agenda so don't bother bringing it up—if you want them to comply.
- **Attendees and their roles.** Who is going to be on the meeting? What will they be doing? Give people fair notice and then hold them accountable. Include email addresses, if it's appropriate, so that people can provide input or answer questions in advance of the session. This will save time spent on minor issues.
- **What they need to read, prepare, or do in advance and how to find and share that information.** This is an area where meeting leaders are guilty of laziness, and it bites them when it comes to getting meetings started well and wasting too much time. Don't wait until the meeting starts to email that spreadsheet—and don't baby people who email you 10 minutes before the meeting starts asking for it (because they either deleted it or saved it somewhere and can't remember where). Have live links to all documents on the shared file site or intranet and insist people get those documents for themselves. Check to make sure they have them before the meeting starts so you don't kill momentum by waiting while people look for them.

If this all seems too simple, ask yourself what the most common meeting problems are: people arriving late, not knowing (or caring) what the meeting is designed to achieve, not being prepared to get down to business, having the wrong people in the meeting to achieve your outcomes, and not being held accountable for meeting success.

During the Meeting

Getting the meeting off to a great start is critical. Start well, and people will know their time will be well spent. They'll be energized, be focused, and stay with you. If it starts badly, every reason for not paying attention or contributing will suddenly be compelling. Even their email will look good to them.

Start the meeting by sounding confident. Obviously each meeting is different, and a standing project status meeting will have a totally different feel and set of needs than a first-ever launch. Here are some of the things a good meeting might contain:

- **Introduce yourself and anyone else people need to know.** If they all know each other, great. If they don't, help them understand who is on the call, what their role is, and what they're expected to contribute to the meeting or the group.
- **Go over the agenda, complete with expectations**. You've told people what to expect, and now you're stating it in plain language. You can't hold people accountable if they don't know what's expected. If they do know, it's on them. It might not help for this meeting, but you can be sure it will impact future get-togethers.
- **Check that all attendees have the documentation they need right at the beginning.** This will give them time to access it from wherever it's stored (you don't want to stop what you're doing and have to email it to them. Make them go get it so next time they'll know where it is) or have an assistant take care of that for you.
- **If you want people to participate using tools like chat and raising hands, make sure they know how to do that.** Don't assume people know how to use the technology as well as you do. Have everyone chat a quick hello to everyone just so you know they don't have technology issues that will haunt you later.
- **Allow voice contact if it's feasible.** For small groups, it's advisable to keep the phone lines open just as you would on a regular conference call so people can chime in, contribute, and ask questions. Depending on your system and how your team usually works, people can mute their phones and raise a hand or just announce that they have something to say or ask.
- **Recap the agenda, and then get right to the good stuff.** Many leaders try to take care of the petty stuff first, so they can spend time on what's more critical, only to find that they run out of time. The big stuff is what's most important to the team and what will keep people interested.

◾ **Let people know you will expect their attention and participation.** Set expectations for their attention and input. Let them know that you expect to hear from them and in what way. Don't hold all questions until the end of the meeting.

Soliciting Feedback

One of the great fears of meeting leaders is calling for feedback and receiving silence in return. Online, there is less natural give and take than in a regular meeting. You can't make eye contact with people who look like they have a contribution to make. You can't see when someone's confused. More importantly, people don't know when to butt in and when that will interrupt everyone else. You need to build those opportunities into the session. You can do this a number of ways:

◾ Let people know it's OK.

◾ Have them raise a hand or announce that they have something to say before talking so they aren't speaking over each other and the other attendees can focus on what they say.

◾ Stop talking periodically. Seriously, give them time to jump in. Announce, "What questions do you have?"

◾ Use tools like the whiteboard, or an application like Microsoft Word, to capture ideas just as you'd use a flipchart or whiteboard in a meeting room. You can use this for brainstorming, to create a "parking lot" items that are off-topic but important, and almost anything you'd use these tools for in a regular meeting. Plus you can save them and email them to everyone when you're done, which you can't do in the conference room.

◾ Have a questioning strategy.

What's a Questioning Strategy?

Meeting facilitation is as much art as science. One thing that all meeting facilitators do is have a strategy for getting input. Online the same strategy is necessary, although it usually requires more planning beforehand because our natural tendency is to try and sprint for the end instead of taking breaks where they belong.

In essence, a questioning strategy entails knowing where and how you want input from the audience, getting the best from people, and making sure everyone gets an equal chance to contribute. Unless you want to hear from no one but that same person who monopolizes your conference calls, you need a plan.

- **When do you want input?** There are probably logical breaks in the flow of the conversation where it makes sense to check understanding or ask for audience input. If you have a three-step process, and you wait until step three to make sure people are following you, you're likely to lose a few folks along the way. Determine the logical places to have discussion or ask questions and build it into your notes or your timeline. If you don't write it down, you'll forget to do it. Trust me.

- **How do you want the input?** Do you want people to ask by voice? Do you want them to write their comments in chat? Maybe you want them to write their ideas on the whiteboard themselves. Set ground rules for how you'll get their input.

- **Control the flow of information and ideas.** If you're a meeting leader, you know you have to control the flow of information. You can't have everyone talking at once. Additionally, there is a tendency for the same people to get heard and others ignored. Web meetings actually allow you to control this if you take charge. Using multiple media is a good idea. For example, many people with English as a second language (ESL) feel that their written English is better than their spoken English and feel more confident contributing that way. Your group's introverts may not be comfortable interrupting to make a point. Often people will make a comment in chat, and you can then give them the floor and allow them to elaborate verbally. Allowing more than one way to get input from people increases the odds they'll contribute in a way that's comfortable for them.

- **Assume there are questions and go after them.** Asking, "What questions do you have?" or "What do you need more information on?" presumes there will be questions and makes some people feel better about asking for what they need. Additionally, it projects a positive attitude. Many meeting leaders ask for questions like they're about to get shot for it. Q&A is a good thing.

- **There are three types of questions.** Just as with a regular conference-room meeting, there are three ways of asking for input from the audience:
    - **"Can anyone tell me ... "** questions. These are general questions, and you're looking for someone to give you an answer. In a room, people would raise their hands, and you could pick a speaker. Online it's a little trickier, but you can use the "raise hand" feature, or just ask people to say their name, rather than blurt out the answer. Try not to go to the same person every time (and you know who they are ... they answer every darned question and monopolize the conversation). Give priority to people you haven't heard from yet.
    - **Directed questions** are aimed at a specific person. You might do this because you know someone has the answer, or maybe you want to show how smart that person is. Either way you want to ask that question by starting

485

with the person's name ("Ramona, what do you think?") for a very good reason. You want to wake people up, refocus them, and give them a chance to unmute their phone before they have to answer.

- **"Anyone else?" questions** are a last-resort way of telling people they're overcontributing and you want to hear from someone new.

Close the Meeting and Do Great Follow-Up

Now that you have run a great meeting, you want to ensure that all your hard work has not been wasted. When you close a meeting:

- Make sure everyone knows what you've accomplished.
- Specify what action items are assigned to whom.
- Get everyone's commitment to them.
- Eliminate any cause for confusion or misunderstanding.
- Record any vital information for accuracy and to hold people accountable (you want to eliminate the "Oh, was that for me?" response).

It's in the meeting closure and follow-up where online meetings actually have an advantage over traditional meetings. Really. That's because technology handles many of the little tasks that are time-consuming, are prone to error, and mostly get ignored.

Here are just some of the ways online meetings can help you close out your meeting effectively:

- You can save the whiteboard or other documents you've created during the meeting and give people access to them. This can be done by emailing them, or simply allowing people to download directly through your WebEx, LiveMeeting, or other platform. (I bet you didn't know you could do that, did you? Take the time to learn what your platform can do for you.)
- You can record the meeting as either a video file or just an audio file and save it on the network. This is a far better permanent record than someone hurriedly trying to capture "minutes" of the meeting. Also, when people hear themselves say, "I will have it by Thursday," it's easier to hold them accountable. Additionally, anyone who missed the meeting can catch up later. There are fewer excuses for missing deadlines or not being prepared for the next meeting.

Final Tips

Here are a few more tips for running great online meetings:

- **Nobody says you have to run them yourself.** Especially when you're just learning the tools, it's very difficult to facilitate effectively and take charge of the technology. Use a co-presenter. Even better, share meeting leadership so that you get a chance to see your people in action and they get to see how competent their peers are. Maybe the best reason to let others lead the meeting is that you get to sit back and really listen to the group dynamics. It's amazing what you see when you're not worried about when to advance your PowerPoint slides.
- **Digitize as much as you can.** The more you let the technology do the work, the easier your life will be. Once a meeting agenda is created, for example, save it as a template so that you can just update it and send it out again. Put links to documents in the email rather than send attachments that will get misfiled or never read. Tie meeting invitations to your calendar invitations so that information gets put directly into people's calendars and time zone adjustments are made automatically.
- **Create a central repository for team information.** A single place people can go is always easier than figuring out where something's hiding. If you have a single repository like a shared team site on SharePoint, Google Docs, or even a team Facebook page, people will always know where relevant documents, recordings of past meetings, and other critical information is kept. The more excuses you can eliminate, the easier it is to hold people accountable for future meetings.

Reading about meetings is easy. Understanding why these ideas are probably useful is too. What's hard is actually doing the things we've talked about because it requires practice, planning, and thought. I wish that weren't so rare in the workplace, but there you have it.

Practice these skills. They will make your next meeting better. More importantly, it will set the groundwork for things to constantly improve. You and your meetings will get better, which has a long-term benefit. After all, if people know the meetings will be well run, productive, and painless, they will show up more prepared, participate more, and take them seriously.

About the Author

Wayne Turmel is the president of GreatWebMeetings.com, the author of *10 Steps to Successful Virtual Presentations* (ASTD Press, 2011), and the host of the Cranky Middle Manager podcast show. You can find Wayne's website here: www.greatwebmeetings.com.

Chapter 36

Convening: The Ultimate Management App

Patricia Neal and Craig Neal

Editor's Note

Authenticity *and* community *are popular buzzwords—we all want to imbue our workplaces with some of the great qualities of strong online networks. Patricia and Craig take these popular concepts several layers deeper, getting beyond the mom and apple pie rhetoric to provide managers with specific distinctions and best practices for how to use convening as part of their regular managerial practices. I love their idea of creating a productive container for conversations and partnership.*

Why is the Art of Convening more relevant than ever? The challenges we currently face as individuals, and as a global community, are more complicated than at any other point in human history and therefore require more effective modes of communication.

Why do we so often perceive meetings as a waste of time or unable to reach effective outcomes? How do we bring wholeness to our gatherings?

Most of us want to be effective and truly engaged with our fellow humans. We go into meetings or gatherings with high expectations and the desire for great outcomes. We make a conscious decision to do something *together*. We want to make plans, come to real consensus, innovate, pool our energies, commit to sustainable action, and so on.

The key to generating the kind of meaning and outcomes most of us really yearn for is *authentic engagement.* Authentic engagement is not tiring or draining, one-sided, manipulating, persuading, or controlling. It is, quite simply, a genuine expression of what is true for us, and listening attentively to what is true for others. Why this simple human interaction often eludes us can be a matter of habit, distrust, faulty modeling, lack of attention, or fear.

Connection, engagement, authenticity, and *trust* are not just the latest management buzzwords. They are pointers to what is becoming an emerging field of leadership development: bringing *authentic engagement* to meetings, gatherings, and conversations. This is an essential skill that improves outcomes and creates connection and positive transformation in our teams, work groups, and organizations. It is the *ultimate* leader/manager app.

Welcome to the Art of Convening: the art of gathering and "holding" people for the sake of authentic engagement and miraculous outcomes.

Much of the focus of the Art of Convening (AoC) is about preparing ourselves internally for a gathering. Consciously shaping how we interact with the others and how we observe and shepherd interactions between groups of people is a core leadership practice and the foundation of convening.

The AoC offers a set of practices and principles that lead to authentic engagement and authentic leadership in our meetings, our gatherings, and our conversations (1:1 or more). These practices and principles are at the nexus of leadership development and personal development and will bring an integrated, whole-systems dimension to those who use them.

> *"One way to encapsulate the leadership required to create an alternative future is to consider the leader as primarily a convener—not leader as special person, but leader as a citizen, sometimes with legitimate power, willing to do those things that can initiate something new in the world. In this way, 'leader' belongs right up there with cook, carpenter, artist, and landscape designer. All of us can develop this ability with a small amount of teaching, and an agreement to practice— the ultimate do-it-yourself movement."*
>
> —Peter Block, *Community: The Structure of Belonging*

When authentically engaged, people tend to feel energized and connected, leading to better outcomes. This shift in energy generates meaningful conversation, an emergence of something new, and an alignment that leads to true commitment from those who participate.

There are many methodologies and theories about best practices in meetings or gatherings. The Art of Convening is unique in that it can be used independently, but can also be used in conjunction with other models, methods, skills, and proficiencies we already utilize.

Over the past 17 years our company, Heartland, has created and developed national conferences and meetings and convened hundreds of Thought Leader Gatherings, a 13-year-old membership-based community of engagement for leaders, all based on the principles and practices of convening. We realized that we needed to write the "recipe" for how to convene and developed a suite of the Art of Convening trainings offering the principles, practices, and applications of convening.

The Technology of Relationships

If you hold as true that each interaction with another human being is an opportunity for authentic engagement or relationship, a shift occurs in that interaction. The Art of Convening is a "technology of relationships" that helps us integrate our personal values into positive relationships and generate the best possible outcomes for our interactions.

The AoC can produce breakthrough outcomes that are satisfying and extraordinary for the participants, as well as their organizations and communities. Convening guidelines and principles are for those of us seriously engaged and committed to making a life-changing difference in our own lives and the lives of those we gather.

To illustrate the concepts of the Art of Convening, we developed the Convening Wheel Model (see Figure 36-1) that begins by considering what is "At the Heart of the Matter," leading all the way to a "Commitment to Action," featuring the practices and principles needed for authentic engagement together as a whole—with a natural order and sequence that can be followed as needed.

The Convening Wheel Model explores the convergence of the inner and outer worlds of Conveners—those who engage others in meaningful meetings, discourse, and conversations. The integration of the personal practices of the Convener with the practical concerns of convening meetings and gatherings is the unique realm of the Art of Convening.

The structure of the Convening Wheel illustrates the various aspects of convening as a whole. As we progress through the aspects around the wheel (whether tentatively, fitfully, or gracefully), we cycle through the steps and considerations using this circular form to guide our way of "being" and "doing," creating a cycle of wholeness in our relationships and engagements.

Figure 36-1. The Convening Wheel Model

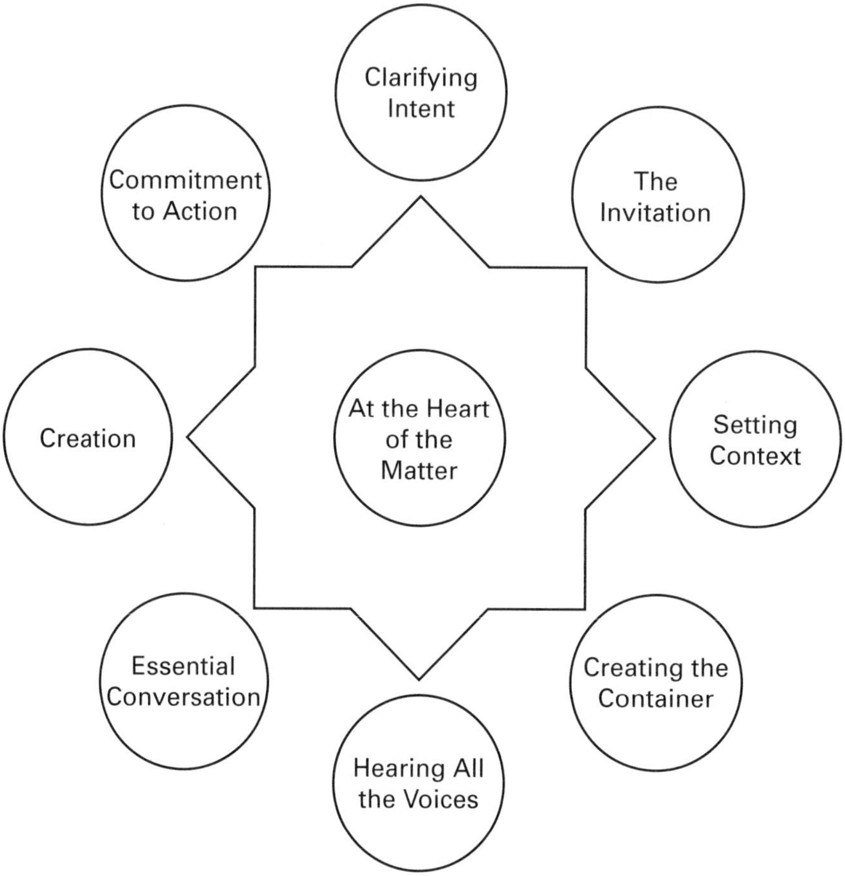

You may ask, "Do I really have to do all of these steps?" The short answer is: to get the best result, yes; to see an improvement, no. Begin where it makes the most sense, with a commitment to try following the wheel as your understanding and practice grow.

The Convening Wheel is flexible. Rather than being limited to a sequential progression, we are able to correct our course at any juncture along the path. As in our individual lives, we at times need to hit the "reset button" to refocus or step back a few paces to a place of balance and equilibrium. This is also true in our relational lives as leaders and Conveners. The path of the Convening Wheel isn't rigid or static any more than are our relationships.

There are nine aspects of the Convening Wheel:

At the Heart of the Matter: *Who we are in relationship with others.* Knowing who we are allows us to be in authentic engagement. The idea of knowing oneself is the foundational premise of countless leadership books and trainings as well as other self-improvement, motivational, and spiritual literature. There is a reason for that. It is important. Approaching the principles and practices of the Art of Convening without getting at this core aspect, one way or another, would be like trying to make a wheel without a hub; it can be done, but, well, that's one wobbly wheel. This central aspect serves as a stabilizer and calibrator for our convening practice; we return to it again and again.

Clarifying Intent: *The alignment of our intention with the purpose of our engagement.* It is generally accepted that 75 percent of our communications are nonverbal. Like a musical note that is not quite in tune, others may not be able to put their finger on the discord when purpose is not aligned with our intent and action, yet that still small voice inside each of us perceives this imbalance when it occurs. It has been the killer of countless meeting agendas in the early stages of development. Once we engage in a practice of examining our intentions and fearlessly identifying them, we have the conscious choice to move forward or not.

The Invitation: *A sincere offering to engage that integrates purpose and intent.* As a strong attractor for full presence, our invitation does not just ask for a body to show up at a date and time. It is designed for authentic engagement—to create the opportunity for those invited to bring themselves *fully present,* both when they arrive and continually throughout the gathering. We invite that presence through the sincere tone and warmth of our invitation. When participants have received this kind of invitation, there is a better chance that they will show up physically, and a much better chance they will arrive with *presence,* ready to participate fully in the gathering.

Setting Context: *Communicating the form, function, and purpose of our engagement and intent.* The clear articulation of purpose and intent allows the highest potential for the actualization of that purpose. We've all arrived at a meeting or conversation with someone only to realize early into the session that we didn't get "the memo" or the communication we did get was not clear. Once things get started, we find ourselves having to guess, reframe, or give up. Blank stares and deafening silence may be the telltale signs. No matter how important, or minor, the topic of the meeting, the assumption that the purpose, meaning, and needed framing have been fully absorbed and understood in advance is an all-too-often time-wasting assumption.

Creating the Container: *Creating the physical and energetic field within which we meet.* When the participants of our gathering feel honored as human beings and encircled in safety, authentic engagement can emerge. To achieve this, we pay attention to the space, both energetic and physical, in which we will be "held" during the duration of the meeting. The energetic field or inner container for our gathering refers to the energy or chemistry created and sensed within the people attending. This field is created with the "rules of engagement," or the agreements and protocols we hold for our gathering. Protocols and agreements serve as the social norms of our container, allowing people to feel safe enough to share their gifts at a meaningful level. Feeling safe is imperative if we are to bring authentic engagement to the group. The outer, or physical, container reminds us of our humanity and aliveness, and encourages connection.

The physical container is the location or place in which we meet. When the environment is alive and has beauty, the space itself feels inviting and welcoming. An office space or conference room with windows, a charming restaurant, a sidewalk café, or a public space with exposure to a pretty view, art, living plants, and beauty can be perfect for some types of gatherings. Sometimes, though, we don't have the luxury of choosing where we will meet or gather. As Conveners, we still ask ourselves how best to enliven the environment we will be in to honor the participants as living human beings.

Hearing All the Voices: *Each person speaks, is heard, and is present and accounted for.* If I think my voice, or my opinion, is needed, I engage at a level of meaning and purpose, knowing I have something essential to contribute. Hearing all the voices is when we begin to experience the emergence of wholeness in the gathering. With the coalescence of *intent within a safe container* and *hearing from each person*, a more whole picture begins to emerge. As each person speaks and is heard, people become more "present and accounted for" to the group. This is the beginning of what we call "listening ourselves into being."[1] A core principle is, if you haven't heard all the voices, you haven't heard all the wisdom that is needed for a complete and whole outcome or path forward.

> *"Deep listening is miraculous for both listener and speaker. When someone receives us with openhearted, non-judging, intensely interested listening, our spirits expand."*
>
> —Sue Patton Thoele

Essential Conversation: *Meaningful exchange within an atmosphere of trust.* Essential conversation is, in many ways, the meat of authentic engagement. To get there, we follow the aspects of the Convening Wheel that come before so that we may gracefully enter essential conversation with planning and respect. The presence of trust and safety plays an

---

[1] Barbara Waugh, *The Soul in the Computer* (Inner Ocean Publishing, 2001).

important role in the quality of the conversation and the ability to maintain authenticity. When we're authentic and engaged, we're more able and willing to work together to imagine, and be responsible for, the best possible future. When creativity and wisdom become activated, whatever outcomes the group is working toward can be enhanced or accelerated.

Creation: *Something new that emerges from engagements of shared purpose and trust.* The emergence of something new that did not exist before is the root of innovation and meaningful contribution. Depending on the purpose of our gathering, the creation could be a new product idea, a new marketing concept, or a way for the family to be together more meaningfully. It could also be a thought, a revelation about our relationship with others, or a modification of something old (which makes it new!). When we authentically engage, we are not recycling old dialogue or behavior; we're tapping what is true for us now, at this moment. Our authenticity allows us to bring a presence to the engagement that is unique to this moment in time. This unique presence means that what is occurring in our gathering has never happened before. If we have followed the aspects of the Convening Wheel and have entered essential conversation, every participant in our gathering is bringing this unique presence. Therefore, something new must emerge.

Commitment to Action: *An individual and/or collective agreement to be responsible and accountable for the way forward.* For the harvest of our creation to be of value we are compelled to take committed action. Without commitment, the creation that has emerged from our time together may be lost or greatly diminished.

This final aspect of the Convening Wheel generates new circumstances and situations that may well offer opportunities for further relationships. Since we are working with a wheel rather than a linear model, finding ourselves at the last aspect does not bring us to the end. In fact, we may find ourselves returning again and again to the Convening Wheel as a resource as we navigate the meetings, gatherings, and conversations of our lives. Like the wheel, the human experience is more a continuing journey than a destination.

> *"Commitment unlocks the doors of imagination, allows vision, and gives us the 'right stuff' to turn our dreams into reality."*
>
> —James Womack

Commitment to action may take many forms. It can be a decision to do something or a decision to do nothing. It can be one person agreeing to be accountable, or many people agreeing to be accountable—individually or as a collective whole. It can be shared, or it can be private. In a world where to-do lists may be jammed with action items, the commitment to action could be a question we commit to asking ourselves or a determined "stake in the ground."

As Conveners, we guide ourselves and the group through an internal and external journey so that we are all prepared for authentic engagement, where crucial connection and trust can be achieved. We then tend and nurture the creation of something new that emerges from the group, leading to the possibility and promise of commitment to action. Learning how to have committed action that develops through alignment is the gift of our authentic engagement, is effective, and is deeply satisfying. True buy-in, true understanding, and focused energy are the by-products of our time together, and committed action will bring this energy into the future.

The creative process for the Convener can be a time of "letting go and letting come" as well as a time to move things along. In its most elegant form, moving from creativity to commitment can be an effortless natural flow that seems logical and apparent to all participants based on the seamless unfolding of the convening process. We may also encounter resistance, pushback, and conflict.

During this phase we may very well experience the greatest expression of movement and energy. As the close of the meeting is upon us, there is a natural tendency to want to come to a conclusion or wrap things up in a tidy bow. We've spent our time together for a purpose, and the desire for action may be the driving force now.

Our encouragement and support for the creative process is crucial. We, as the Conveners, keep our eyes and ears open for dissent and inertia while allowing for chaos as well as order. Engagement and a sense of discovery within the community must be held as a necessary component to completion.

Our Invitation

There is always an inner game and an outer game to authentic leadership. We discovered while developing the Convening Wheel that the outer, physical, design-oriented delivery considerations in convening always seem to follow the same path as the inner life of the Convener. That is why the inner considerations are so prominent in our convening model. We believe that the Convener is a leader whose power and effectiveness are rooted in personal development, integrity, and coherence. By tapping into the generosity inherent in most people, the wealth of knowledge and wisdom in any gathering is revealed.

It takes courage to lead, try something new, and build new ways of being together, but the payoff is big. Through the principles and practices of the Art of Convening, anyone can learn that meaningful connection and engagement are not only possible but also imperative for obtaining sustainable, satisfying results in our businesses, organizations, communities, families, and personal relationships.

We invite you to join us in the creation of a new time lived in the fullness of each authentic engagement.

Heartland and the Art of Convening are integrally connected to a worldwide web of individuals and organizations actively creating a global renaissance of thought and behavior, based on restoring wholeness to ourselves, our communities, our organizations, and the world.

This notion of *restoring wholeness* is recognizable by an absence of fear and a generosity of spirit. When we, as Conveners, tap into the generosity inherent in people, the wealth of knowledge and wisdom in any gathering is revealed. That wisdom is felt as a connection to being whole, both individually and collectively.

When we feel and experience wholeness, our connection to one another and the world around us becomes less hostile and more inviting.

This is an invitation for you to open to the possibility that all those who walk through your door are whole and perfect just as they are, that each interaction with another human being is an opportunity for authentic relationship, and that a transformation occurs in that interaction.

This is a good time to be alive. Stay in touch.

Following are several stories from our book *The Art of Convening: Authentic Engagement in Meetings, Gatherings, and Conversations* and our work.

Stories From the Book and Our Work

From Patricia Neal

It was a remarkable meeting of senior-level women executives, gathering to explore the notion of convening as a leadership competency. I was the Convener, but it was clear from the onset that these women were used to running their own show. Many grew into their leadership in results-dominated environments driving definable goals and outcomes where listening skills and vulnerability were not often appreciated or wanted.

As the Convener I had done a considerable amount of preparation, internal and external—but I must admit, I was nervous. Most of those present were not familiar with Heartland's work and had never experienced the Art of Convening—and many were cutting-edge leaders in their own right, with very defined ways of doing things. I knew I would be challenged in this practice.

Following introductions and context setting we gathered in a large circle. I reminded myself that my intention here was to bring authentic engagement to the gathering, and to set aside any other motives that could interfere with that intention. Then I asked that each woman in turn speak to an important question they are dealing with as a leader. As each spoke, their responses deepening with each voice, I was reminded of why I love to do this work.

A few common themes emerged: "How do *I* have to change to bring about the change I want to see in my organization?" "How do I create authentic connections with my people when I rush from meeting to meeting?" "I'm tired of doing things the same old way, but don't know what else there is."

Once everyone had spoken, the majority welcomed the opportunity to take a deeper dive into their challenges. The room had become electric with energy. A window had been opened to a conversation of meaning and personal consequence. There were also those whose discomfort was palpable.

There were many competing agendas in the room and midway through the afternoon, I lost my internal focus and lost my way, getting off-track from the agenda. At this point a key leader left the room without comment, obviously disturbed. A flash of anxiety swept over me as my stomach tightened. Would the group be able to hold together? Would we be able to complete the day?

After years of witnessing the phenomenon of group breakdown, I knew that I had to stay present. I focused again on my intention to bring authentic engagement and suspended my judgment of others in the room and, more importantly, of myself. I was back on track to complete the day's agenda. The comfort level of the group gradually increased, and "ahas" and nuggets of wisdom emerged. There seemed to be an understanding and appreciation for being together in authentic conversation.

At the end of the day we closed as we had opened, hearing each voice. Although there were still voices of discord and disbelief, most of us appreciated the experience we had together.

Comments ranged from:

"This would never fly at my office—they'd think I was nuts."

"What does this really have to do with business?"

to:

"I have the courage to think differently and act on it."

"Hearing all the voices is a game-changer for me."

"My intention is to create purposeful meetings with mindfulness and presence."

What many of us began to see was the idea of leadership that is enhanced by the capacity to slow down for authentic engagement, to create authentic relationship, which is at the core of why convening with intention matters.

From Anne Griswold, Organizational Effectiveness, LifeScan, Inc.

As a group of cautious but willing learners, we stumbled through a new way of being together at work. The process provided an increasing recognition that convening and having a language and a process to generate solutions to our issues brought empowerment and built trust. We did not set out to "create" anything in particular, but one of the most powerful impacts was learning that having a place where you can have meaningful conversations creates power.

Most compelling was where we arrived after six months. We had, through this process become a "community." The principles and practices set us up to demonstrate care, create true understanding, and share thoughts and ideas in a productive manner. We made commitments to bring forward what we valued and what we saw as needed in our organization. We shared what we were learning with our peers and our clients, we told stories of our success and re-committed to our next series of applications and actions.

In terms of building capability, the skills, tools and application of the Art of Convening principles and practices are still being used. The business benefits are both tangible and intangible as the HR organization continues to meet with greater efficiency and effectiveness. I find it interesting that in business we typically shy away from getting to the heart of the matter, yet what we learned through this experience was being with the heart of the matter is where true performance contributions manifest and become significant business impacts.

The Retreat

There had been a history of tension between the doctors and administrators at the annual four-day retreat for the leadership of a large healthcare organization. The doctors often viewed administrators as uncaring "pencil pushers." The administrators often viewed the doctors as "only in it for the money," ignorant of what it took to operate as a viable business. This tension was not openly acknowledged, but would often show up as resistance when it was time to make a decision or get something done.

Carol, a Convener, was a senior director in the organization. She convinced the planning team to start the retreat that year with a large circle where everyone could "check in" (her culturally accepted term for "hearing all the voices"). Many of the participants were skeptical. Carol had earned enough respect for her competence and expertise in leading meetings that they were willing to go along with what she wanted, but most doubted that it would make a difference.

Carol had prepared for the retreat by doing her own internal work. She was confident in her purpose for being there at that time. She knew her intention to bring authenticity and cohesion to these leaders, and she had sincerely and warmly invited and welcomed each as they arrived that first day. She also thought deeply about a question that would tap the commonality of the group and require some thoughtful reflection.

When all were seated in a circle and it was time to "check in," Carol asked that each person, in turn, say their name, their title, and a couple of sentences about why they chose to be in the healthcare field. She asked that they keep their remarks short, from the heart, and that they listen attentively to each other. The responses were all very passionate.

- "I think of it as an honor to heal the sick."
- "I want to be part of preserving and improving human life."
- "Medicine is fascinating, but really I want to serve as a healer."
- "I wanted to choose a business that made a real difference in people's lives."
- "I have a passion for caring for the ill."

Those in the circle, both doctors and administrators, were all saying the same things. Judgment seemed to melt. There was an arc of recognition that happened, from each to the others, that brought the group together as a whole.

Later in the retreat, Carol reported that several "breakthroughs" had been made. Participants were able to say things to each other that they hadn't before. Many of the participants later told her that the circle "check-in" had made the difference in enabling all of the factions to see each other as human beings, similar to themselves—and that is what enabled them to dig deeper, reveal themselves authentically, and accomplish more.

A Joyful Hearing

Laurence headed the new product division at a manufacturing company. He reported that his greatest revelation of the utility of the Convening Wheel came with hearing all the voices.

When extra help was needed for a particular project, they often hired temporary consultants or contractors. It was Laurence's experience that for some of these projects, weeks of gnashing teeth, one-upping, resistance and getting past pre-judgment had to happen before useful collaboration could begin.

For a new project launch meeting that would include everyone involved, Laurence decided to try the Art of Convening.

He prepared himself as best he could in the time he had. When it was time to think about hearing all the voices, he considered the different personalities that would be in the room that day. There would be the usual engineers, but also support people, designers, programmers and project managers. A lot of information would be disseminated with many people to hear from just to "download" everyone's area of expertise and hear a short "bio" designed to let everyone know who would be doing what. He considered skipping hearing all the voices because of the time it would take and the discomfort it might cause some of the introverts in the room.

When the time came, however, he decided to include a "hearing." After welcoming everyone, "setting context" and "creating the container" by laying out the protocols for the meeting, he said, "Well, we're all going to be working together for awhile and, I don't know about you, but I'd like to know each of you a little better as we begin. So, right now, I'd like to go around the room and hear from each of you, one thing that brought joy to you today. It could be something that happens every day, or something unique. If nothing comes to you about today, just tell us something that has brought joy in the past. Take about 30 seconds or less. No more, since we have a lot to do today. I'll start."

Out of the corner of his eye, Laurence saw a couple of people look at each other with eyes rolling, but he didn't let that rattle him. He told of his drive to work that morning. He told them that as he crested a hill, the scene he saw of the sun coming up, creating a pink, otherworldly glow in the valley below brought him a sense of joy and awe. That was all he said.

Each person spoke in turn, going around the room clockwise. One man told of his autistic son who greeted him with a huge, heartfelt smile each morning. One woman told of her husband bringing her coffee to the bathroom because he knew she was in a hurry. Another told of the smell of lilacs in her driveway and another of lighthearted banter with the counter person at McDonald's that morning.

When everyone had spoken, Laurence looked around the room. There were lots of big smiles. People were looking at each other differently. They were "seeing" each other. There were no consultants, contractors, engineers, designers, or managers in the room at that moment, there were human beings.

As the meeting progressed, Laurence thought that some headway had already been made in the level of collaboration possible in this group. His courage in hearing all the voices had made a difference.

About the Authors

Craig and Patricia Neal are co-founders of Heartland Inc., and co-authors of *The Art of Convening: Authentic Engagement in Meetings, Gatherings, and Conversations* (2011, Berrett-Koehler Publishers, San Francisco.)

"Convening: The Ultimate Management App" has been adapted from *The Art of Convening: Authentic Engagement in Meetings, Gatherings, and Conversations* published by Berrett-Koehler.

Chapter 37

The Multicultural and Multigenerational Workplace: What Are the Future Challenges to Leaders?

Alfredo Castro

Editor's Note

It used to be that global management skills were rare, special, and not required for most jobs. Today, all managers can benefit from being—and many more need to be—globally savvy. The world is shrinking and nearly every organization has international connections, geographically dispersed teams, and highly diverse workforces. Alfredo Castro is a Brazilian management and leadership expert and consultant who has done work all over the world. In this chapter he offers us his perspective on what it means to build a multicultural and multigenerational workplace that works for everyone.

After experiencing dramatic changes in their workplaces, many organizations are recognizing that their leaders need more competence in cross-cultural communication and team building. Additionally, social media, informal learning, and generational differences are influencing the impact of multiculturalism in global organizations and providing new challenges and opportunities for leaders. The growth of global economies and the increasing diversification of workforces support the ongoing need for development in this area. Competent multicultural leaders are essential to an organization's success in the global market.

After designing and delivering leadership development programs for global organizations in five continents, I have developed a few ideas I hope you find helpful. The process and practices I will suggest here are meant to be applied flexibly, as you will each need to balance the needs of your organization with the needs of employees, and ensure all employees, customers, colleagues, and stakeholders in the organization are treated with respect and dignity regarding their individual, group, and cultural dimensions.

An Introductory View of the Future Workplace

Considering the changes in social and economic aspects of our societies, we must determine how to develop and prepare the leaders to lead us into the future. One of the key questions we have to answer is, What are the main trends that will influence and impact leadership development, especially regarding new cultural and multigenerational workplace trends? Multiculturalism in the workplace is stimulating changes in the scopes and the missions upon which leaders will focus. After developing many global leadership programs, I believe that leaders are beginning to understand that diversity is becoming more and more important, but some key questions remain. Are leaders prepared to leverage four generations in the workplace? Are we designing programs that will develop multicultural leadership skills? It is important to engage today's, and more importantly tomorrow's, leaders in addressing these questions.

To ensure that our development programs address current and emerging needs, my team interviewed and surveyed 200 future leaders from 100 major companies around the world. We learned that many organizations are beginning to adopt a broader concept and definition of the word *diversity,* including individual characteristics that affect the way employees think and perform. We asked these leaders about the skills that will be most needed today and in the future. As we would predict, some of the fundamental leadership skills, like creating a vision, acting with integrity, and focusing on results, will still be very important. In addition to these, however, we found that the following 10 leadership skills will increase in importance:

1. **Soft and hard skills:** having a balance of behavioral and technical knowledge and skills
2. **Self-awareness:** being self-aware of your behaviors and impact on others

3. **Global mindset:** the capacity to think and act globally, and an understanding of emerging economic and social changes

4. **Diversity:** understanding the broad concept of diversity and how it will affect the future

5. **Observant:** noticing what others do with some objectivity and low judgment

6. **Integrity:** being a good ethical role model—keeping promises and living your values

7. **Tech savvy:** using social media and collaboration tools

8. **Partnership:** building relationships and influencing others without authority

9. **Service oriented:** understanding and supporting employee needs

10. **Adaptable:** ability to change your leadership style; knowing when and how to vary from an authority to a coaching leadership style.

If we design programs for leaders that build these skills, we will be providing a good platform for the future. And how should we "do" this training? We must create developmental experiences that engage all learners. I like to suggest that instead of e-learning, we should practice "we learning." Instead of thinking only about the tools we use to foster learning and performance, we will benefit if we place interaction of diverse learners at the center of our concerns.

Rethinking the Meaning of "Diversity"

Let's redefine the term *diversity* and build its understanding into our leadership development programs. Traditionally, multiculturalism is a core topic discussed during diversity training programs. Multiculturalism includes characteristics such as race, ethnicity, gender, age, religion, and disability. Today, our concept of diversity includes these characteristics plus others including cultural background, sexual orientation, class, marital status, generations, and more. Diversity includes those characteristics and experiences that describe each of us as individuals. Communication style, work style, organizational role or level, economic status, and geographic origin (all of these affected by globalization, technology, and different generations) are also part of what makes a workplace diverse.

A company that embraces and values diversity as an integral part of its goals can have a positive impact on individual productivity, organizational effectiveness, and sustained competitiveness. Today and in the future, it is imperative to go beyond defining diversity based on numerical representations of certain groups. To maximize human capital capabilities, companies should adopt a systematic approach to learning about, utilizing, and valuing our broader view of diversity.

Traveling around the world to deliver training to global leaders has helped me consolidate my vision about the emerging demands for all leaders. A leader's primary responsibility is to ensure that everyone in the organization understands that working together is not negotiable. To build great teams we need to create a respectful, open, and inclusive environment where workers of all ages and cultural backgrounds can share who they are without fear of being judged, "fixed," or changed. Leaders must also remain open to new ideas and provide constant feedback, working with managers and staff to shape the company's strategic vision. They must avoid projecting their own expectations about work onto others and remain open to different perspectives.

Unfortunately, many leaders do not seem to value the competencies I have discussed in this chapter. Great managers get it, but we have a long way to go to ensure that valuing diversity—and all that is included in this concept—is a core competency for people managers. And in regard to these skills and capabilities, the newer managers might have the edge over more experienced managers. Historically, experienced leaders were expected to help mentor and develop future leaders. While this will still be true in the future, we need to add a twist to the process—newer leaders may be recruited to help mentor and develop experienced leaders.

Multiculturalism and Cross-Generational Leadership

The explosion of technology tools, the offer of virtual environments, and the new media portfolio are important factors that characterize recent organizational shifts. The opportunity to connect with whomever, wherever, whenever, has shaped our idea of a workplace and makes global thinking a fundamental skill required for managers. With the use of new technology it is feasible to expand the concept of exporting offices and work around the world. Organizational structures are using new models of reporting, management, and teamwork. Many managers are leading employees in different geographic locations who they have never met in person. Building great teams and managing performance under these conditions is a relatively new challenge for managers and will grow in prevalence. New technologies—and the willingness to use these tools to build relationships and collaboration—can help managers break down barriers to great global teaming. Managers who can make this shift will have a huge competitive advantage. Diversity is broader than nationality; it encompasses:

- new generations in the workplace creating new cultural demands
- new technology creating new pathways to interaction
- new patterns for the life cycle creating new possibilities in terms of careers and ways of living.

A leader must be developed to explore the benefits of a learning environment that includes all employees and concentrates on developing the necessary skills to eliminate barriers to learning opportunities. As the importance of globalization increases, future leaders will need to appreciate and create a work environment that values diversity. They will have to understand not only economic and legal differences, but also the social and behavioral differences that are part of working around the world (or with a worldly local team). The high-potential leaders I encounter believe that developing an understanding of other cultures and individual differences is not just an obligation; it is an opportunity.

We interviewed 200 multinational companies regarding their use of modern techniques and social media to improve the leadership style to build global leadership. We found that only 9 percent of these organizations currently address global management practices as part of their development and another 30 percent said they plan to add this training in the future. Over a third of those we interviewed did not know what we were even talking about. These numbers were disappointing but not a surprise. We also asked these companies to what extent social media affected the predominant leadership style, and over 60 percent said it had a high impact. More than 75 percent reported that generational issues influenced their leadership style. The key takeaway? While most companies are not addressing global management in their training programs, several key shifts (social media and generational trends, in this case) are affecting their managers. It is time to address the broader concept of diversity more fully to build prepared and capable managers.

When we interviewed the 200 companies we also asked whether their managers could use coaching principles as part of their leadership. Over 60 percent said that their leaders did not or could not. This is interesting and important because we believe that coaching practices are excellent for supporting and serving diverse employees.

Are we ready to support these new demands? Are your managers being prepared to value and maximize the benefits of a diverse team? New solutions in learning and performance can help address these issues.

Designing Global Leadership Development Programs

Designing programs for this new workplace will demand new and creative formats of learning, with new communication strategies. The learning environment should support a variety of styles and learning preferences; and more so, the learning environment should be an open invitation to integrate the many approaches. Here are a few specific recommendations:

- Talk about generational differences and help each generation better understand the points of view of its younger and older co-workers. Conduct generational information awareness and sharing sessions. These are a great way to get people to work together across the generations and to provide them with an opportunity to educate each other about each generation's own history, characteristics, milestone events, culture, language, and norms. This will help reduce communication clashes. Rather than implementing formal complex programs, try to have representatives from each age-based generation put together actions, initiatives, and programs to educate people (using their own vision about this multiculturalism and diversity).

- Help people find opportunities to build relationships and coach each other.
- Integrate the topic of multiculturalism into training programs. Make the topic of diversity a common point of discussion and apply it to all aspect of business management.
- Broaden diversity training programs to address many types of differences and how each strengthens the team when appreciated and cultivated. Identify the business implications of valuing diversity and examine the effects that personal attitudes and stereotypes have on behavior.
- Develop and use a communication model that emphasizes cultural diversity; and develop personal as well as professional strategies to help cultivate a climate that values diversity.
- Build coaching skills so that managers can better support each individual's needs. Focusing on coaching will also help you identify high-potentials and refine your core competencies. One of my favorite coaching models comes from Bianco-Mathis, Nabors, and Roman, and it's known as "The COACH Model." COACH stands for Current situation, Objectives, Alternatives, and CHoices, and it is a simple but powerful way to approach coaching opportunities.
- Make learning and development a fundamental part of daily work. Use projects and assignments (including international assignments were possible) to develop more worldly leaders. Use temporary projects and longer-term role changes.
- Develop talent in a global perspective and beware reinforcing separateness. Of course we all need symbols, flags, countries, and nations—I am not against them. But, consider the fact that, sometimes, those elements make us gravitate to those who are like us, searching for people who belong to our same group.

Each of these learning practices will strengthen your ability to build global management skills and reinforce your value for diversity.

Wrapping Up: What Should We Do Now?

The future will challenge all managers to cultivate diversity and value their multicultural and multigenerational workplace—there will be no doubt about it! They will have to demonstrate competencies to value both technological and personal knowledge. Let's make sure that our development programs are preparing our talented and hardworking managers for success.

Create new possibilities! Think of ways to improve your understanding and admiration for people who are different from you. This is a core skill for the global leader. As we build elements that foster diversity and value differences into our programs and practice, we create opportunities for transforming our workplace environment for the better.

The changing role of various stakeholders—customers, suppliers, and partners—has deep implications for leaders. In the past it was clear who were your friends and enemies. These roles are becoming more blurred. In fields as diverse as automotive, chemicals, energy, telecommunications, and pharmaceuticals, the same organization may be a customer, supplier, partner, and competitor. Building positive, long-term, win-win relationships is critical. Defeating an adversary who may turn out to be a potential customer can prove to be a short-term victory.

Managers need to change because their employees are and will continue to change. The old paradigm of telling people what to do and how to do it seems ridiculous, and great managers will ask for input and share information—use a coaching model—to bring out the best in everyone.

References and Resources

Bianco-Mathis, V., L. Nabors, and C. Roman. (2008). *Organizational Coaching: Building Relationships and Programs That Drive Results.* Alexandria, VA: ASTD Press.

About the Author

Alfredo Castro is a global leadership development consultant and expert who has worked in more than 25 countries. He is a certified coaching trainer and is the president of a global learning and development firm called MOT, Mudanças Organizacionais e Trein-amento Ltda. He has written several management books (in his native language of Portuguese) and is called upon to speak at many international conferences and events. He conducts projects for multicultural organizations such as Clariant, Ford, Sony, Schenker, Storaenso, and others. You can find Alfredo's website at www.motvirtual.com.br.

☙ **Conclusion**

Management Is a Craft

Imagine riding a roller coaster while holding a triple-dip ice cream cone in the middle of summer. Whee! Yum! Yikes! Being a manager is a bit like this, isn't it? You are pulled in a lot of directions and feel like you are moving a million miles an hour to chip away at your to-do lists. You love working with people but feel like the inertia of your crazy day often keeps you from spending quality time with your team. This is the nature of our situation as managers, and I don't think things will get any simpler.

But before you start running the other way or contemplate switching careers, let me make the case for why this chaotic job can and should be the best you have ever had—even if things gets nuttier instead of easier. There has never been a better time to make a contribution to the way people feel about their work and the quality of the work they perform. As managers, many of us live for these frantic but wonderful moments. It is why we signed up for this gig and what gives us the greatest source of satisfaction.

But we need help, right? And we need to take care of ourselves. And we need new ideas for how to get things done and how to focus on the most important work. We need coaches and mentors and sounding boards and supporters and friends. We need our team—the people we know and those we look to for guidance—to be there when our zigging and zagging brings us to unfamiliar or difficult terrain. Consider adding the contributing authors of this book to your team. Many of them are bloggers and speakers and active writers, and you can stay in touch and use them as part of your support network. If you are particularly interested in one author's work, I would encourage you to reach out to him or her. You will find information that should help you track the authors down in the Reference Section. I hope you will consider me a member of your support team, too.

Conclusion

I hope that you have found the *ASTD Management Development Handbook* helpful. Time is precious, and it is important to me that you believe that the time you spent exploring this book was beneficial. The contributing authors are amazing thinkers and practitioners who inspire and fascinate me. I trust that their work can do the same for you.

Enjoy the ride and savor the experience of management.

For Further Exploration!

Our contributing authors are amazing people who are active in their fields. Here are the various ways you can learn more about their works.

The Bloggers

Wendy Axelrod and Jeannie Coyle: http://talentsavvymanager.com/blog
Wally Bock: http://blog.threestarleadership.com
Jodee Bock: www.bocksoffice.com/you-already-know-blog
Randy Boek: www.route2results.com/category/management
Kevin Eikenberry: http://blog.KevinEikenberry.com
www.budtobosscommunity.com/blog/
Steve Farber and Steve Dealph: www.stevefarber.com
Tom Foster: http://managementblog.org
Lisa Gansky: www.facebook.com/pages/The-Mesh-Directory/139581839396226
Chris Grams: www.darkmattermatters.com
www.managementexchange.com
CV Harquail, PhD: http://authenticorganizations.com
Sally Hogshead: www.HowToFascinate.com
Karen Hough: www.improvedge.com/our-blog
Derek Irvine and Eric Mosley: www.recognizethisblog.com
Michael Kroth, PhD: www.michaelkroth.wordpress.com
www.transformationalirreverence.wordpress.com
www.managingthemobileworkforce.com/blog
Sharlyn Lauby: www.hrbartender.com
http://mashable.com/author/sharlyn-lauby
www.workshifting.com/author/sharlyn-lauby
www.weknownext.com/author/119
http://smartblogs.com/leadership/author/slauby

Patricia Neal and Craig Neal: http://theaocbook.com
Steve Roesler: www.allthingsworkplace.com
Todd Sattersten: www.toddsattersten.com
Tony Schwartz: www.theenergyproject.com/blog/author/tony-schwartz
Rajesh Setty: www.rajeshsetty.com/blog
Bret Simmons, PhD: www.bretlsimmons.com
Terry "Starbucker" St. Marie: www.terrystarbucker.com
Michael Lee Stallard: www.michaelleestallard.com
Wayne Turmel: The Cranky Middle Manager show (http://cmm.thepodcastnetwork.com)
The Connecectd Manager Blog (www.theconnectedmanager.com)
Tanmay Vora: http://qaspire.com/
Ellen Weber, PhD: www.Brainleadersandlearners.com
David Weinberger, PhD: www.hyperorg.com/blogger
David Zinger: www.davidzinger.com

Video Clips

Wendy Axelrod and Jeannie Coyle: http://talentsavvymanager.com/resources/make-talent-your-business
Alfredo Castro: www.youtube.com/watch?v=mbGjUT30sJE
www.youtube.com/watch?v=_ShXNQgY0Lk&feature=related
Kevin Eikenberry: www.youtube.com/user/KevinEikenberryGroup
www.youtube.com/user/BudtoBoss
Chris Grams: www.youtube.com/watch?feature=player_embedded&v=BLY80evYjE0
www.youtube.com/watch?v=DEb0M8PtOeA&feature=player_embedded
www.youtube.com/watch?feature=player_embedded&v=uOyaDj-Th28
www.youtube.com/watch?v=WzyqcbF3AWs&feature=player_embedded
Sally Hogshead: http://bit.ly/pyRlc5
http://bit.ly/pyqNd2
http://youtu.be/R4ClpNHu3oU
http://youtu.be/Vhn_97vhcLg
Derek Irvine and Eric Mosley: www.youtube.com/user/GloboforceInc#p/u/8/cDC2ZT-kfHCI
www.youtube.com/user/GloboforceInc#p/u/1/gt_CheC-FIs0
Sharlyn Lauby: The LPK Design Team:
www.lpk.com/2011/05/creators-thinkers-provocateurs-owners
www.lpk.com/2011/02/lpk-asks-what-is-design

Tony Schwartz: www.theenergyproject.com/about/videos/myth-1-productivity-about-
managing-your-time-better
www.theenergyproject.com/about/videos/myth-10-we-should-only-rely-
our-existing-strength
www.theenergyproject.com/about/videos/way-were-working-isnt-working
www.theenergyproject.com/about/videos/breathe
www.youtube.com/watch?v=6pm9R1d-7Us (Leading@Google)

Michael Lee Stallard: www.youtube.com/watch?v=Fw7H7tHnwtE

Tanmay Vora: www.QAspire.com/Videos

Margaret Wheatley, EdD: www.margaretwheatley.com/video.html

David Zinger: http://employeeengagement.ning.com/video

Books

Axelrod, Wendy, and Jeannie Coyle. (2011). *Make Talent Your Business: How Exceptional Managers Develop People While Getting Results.* San Francisco, CA: Berrett-Koehler Publishers, Inc.

Bock, Jodee. (2006). *The 100% Factor: Living Your Capacity.* Fargo, ND: Bock's Office Publishing.

Chermack, Thomas. (2011). *Scenario Planning in Organizations: How to Create, Use, and Assess Scenarios.* San Francisco, CA: Berrett-Koehler Publishers, Inc.

Eikenberry, Kevin. (2007). *Remarkable Leadership: Unleashing Potential One Skill at a Time.* San Francisco, CA: Jossey-Bass.

Eikenberry, Kevin. (2011). *From Bud to Boss: Secretes to a Successful Transition to Remarkable Leadership.* San Francisco, CA: Jossey-Bass.

Farber, Steve. (2009). *Greater Than Yourself: The Ultimate Lesson of True Leadership.* New York: Doubleday.

Farber, Steve. (2008). *The Radical Edge: Stoke Your Business, Amp Your Life, and Change the World.* New York: Kaplan Publishing.

Farber, Steve. (2009). *The Radical Leap: A Personal Lesson in Extreme Leadership.* New York: Kaplan Publishing.

Gansky, Lisa. (2010). *The Mesh: Why the Future of Business Is Sharing.* New York: Penguin Group.

Grams, Chris. (2011). *The Ad-Free Brand: Secrets to Building Successful Brands in a Digital World.* Indianapolis, IN: Que Publishing (an imprint of Pearson).

Hall, Thomas, and Wally Bock. (2010). *Ruthless Focus.* Indianapolis, IN: Dog Ear Publishing.

Hogshead, Sally. (2010). *Fascinate: Your 7 Triggers of Persuasion and Captivation.* New York: HarperCollins Publishers.

Hough, Karen. (2011). How to Handle Tough Conversations in Three Simple Steps. *Business Insider*, February 17. Retrieved from http://articles.businessinsider .com/2011-02-17/strategy/30070201_1_conversations-project-managers-coaching.

Hough, Karen. (2011). *The Improvisation Edge: Secrets to Building Trust and Radical Collaboration at Work.* San Francisco, CA: Berrett-Koehler Publishers, Inc.

Hough, Karen. (2009). *The Yes! Deck* (Cards).

Irvine, Derek. (2011). *Increase Employee Retention and Loyalty With Strategic Employee Recognition.* Southborough, MA: Globoforce Limited.

Irvine, Derek. (2011). *Transform Performance Management With Strategic Recognition.* Southborough, MA: Globoforce Limited.

Kroth, Michael, and McKay Christensen (2009). *Career Development Basics.* Alexandria, VA: ASTD Press.

Kroth, Michael, and David Clemons. (2011). *Managing the Mobile Workforce: Leading, Building, and Sustaining Virtual Teams.* New York: McGraw-Hill.

Kroth, Michael. (2006). *The Manager as Motivator.* Santa Barbara, CA: Praeger (an imprint of ABC-CLIO).

Kroth, Michael, and Patricia Boverie. (2001). *Transforming Work: The Five Keys to Achieving Trust, Commitment, and Passion in the Workplace.* Cambridge, MA: Perseus Publishing.

Lauby, Sharlyn. (2005). "Motivating Employees." *Infoline.* Issue No. 0510. Alexandria, VA: ASTD Press.

Martin, Steve. (2011). *Co-Create: How to Make Big Changes With Small Groups One Project at a Time.* Cincinnati, OH: Self-published book.

Mosley, Eric, and Derek Irvine. (2010). *Winning With a Culture of Recognition.* Southborough, MA: Globoforce Limited.

Murphy, Mark. (2010). *Hard Goals: The Secret to Getting From Where You Are to Where You Want to Be.* New York: McGraw-Hill.

Murphy, Mark. (2009). *Hundred Percenters: Challenge Your Employees to Give It Their All, and They'll Give You Even More.* New York: McGraw-Hill.

Neal, Craig, and Patricia Neal. (2011). *The Art of Convening: Authentic Engagement in Meetings, Gatherings, and Conversations.* San Francisco, CA: Berrett-Koehler Publishers, Inc.

Pfeffer, Jeffrey, and Robert I. Sutton. (2006). *Hard Facts, Dangerous Half-Truths, and Total Nonsense: Profiting From Evidence-Based Management.* Boston, MA: Harvard Business Review Press.

Pfeffer, Jeffrey, and Charles A. O'Reilly III. (2000). *Hidden Value: How Great Companies Achieve Extraordinary Results With Ordinary People.* Boston, MA: Harvard Business Review Press.

Pfeffer, Jeffrey. (1993). *Managing With Power: Politics and Influence in Organizations.* Boston, MA: Harvard Business Review Press.

Pfeffer, Jeffrey. (2010). *Power: Why Some People Have It—And Others Don't.* New York: HarperBusiness.

Pfeffer, Jeffrey. (1998). *The Human Equation: Building Profits by Putting People First.* Boston, MA: Harvard Business Review Press.

Pfeffer, Jeffrey. (2000). *The Knowing-Doing Gap: How Smart Companies Turn Knowledge Into Action.* Boston, MA: Harvard Business Review Press.

Pfeffer, Jeffrey. (2007). *What Were They Thinking? Unconventional Wisdom About Management.* Boston, MA: Harvard Business Review Press.

Sattersten, Todd, and Jack Covert. (2009). *The 100 Best Business Books of All Time.* New York: Penguin Group.

Sattersten, Todd. (2010). *Fixed to Flexible: Four Simple Lessons About Cost, Price, Margin and the Options Available to The 21st Century Business.* Self-published e-book can be found at http://toddsattersten.com/fixed-to-flexible-the-ebook.

Schwartz, Tony, Jean Gomes, and Catherine McCarthy. (2011). *Be Excellent at Anything: The Four Keys to Transforming the Way We Work and Live.* New York: Free Press.

Schwartz, Tony, and Jim Loehr. (2004). *The Power of Full Engagement: Managing Energy, Not Time, Is the Key to High Performance and Personal Renewal.* New York: Free Press.

Setty, Rajesh. (2011). *Beyond Code: Learn to Distinguish Yourself in 9 Simple Steps!* New York: Select Books.

Setty, Rajesh. (2009). *#THINKtweet Book01: Bite-Sized Lessons for a Fast Paced World!* Silicon Valley, CA: THINKaha.

Setty, Rajesh. (2009). *Upbeat: Cultivating the Right Attitude to Thrive in Tough Times.* Weston, CT: Prospecta Press.

St. Marie, Terry "Starbucker." (2010). *Leadership From a Glass Half Full: Five Lessons You Need To Learn Before You Jump Into The Pool.* Self-published e-book can be found at www.terrystarbucker.com/2010/04/29/my-free-e-book-leadership-from-a-glass-half-full.

Stallard, Michael. (2007). *Fired Up or Burned Out: How to Reignite Your Team's Passion, Creativity, and Productivity.* Nashville, TN: Thomas Nelson.

Turmel, Wayne. (2008). *6 Weeks to a Great Webinar.* Glen Ellyn, IL: Achis Marketing Services.

Turmel, Wayne. (2011). *10 Steps to Successful Virtual Presentations.* Alexandria, VA: ASTD Press.

Turmel, Wayne. (2008). *125 Quotes for Whacking Weasels: Centuries of Wisdom, Motivation and Snappy Comebacks From the Cranky Middle Manager Show.* Glen Ellyn, IL: Achis Marketing Services.

Turmel, Wayne. (2011). *#PresentationTweet Book01: 140 Ways to Present With Impact.* Silicon Valley, CA: THINKaha.

Vora, Tanmay. (2009). *#QUALITYtweet Book01: 140 Bite-Sized Ideas to Deliver Quality in Every Project.* Silicon Valley, CA: THINKaha.

Weber, Ellen. (2005). *MI Strategies in the Classroom and Beyond.* Boston, MA: Pearson Education.

Weinberger, David, Christopher Locke, Rick Levin, and Doc Searls. (2000). *The Cluetrain Manifesto: The End of Business as Usual.* New York: Perseus Books.

Weinberger, David. (2007). *Everything Is Miscellaneous: The Power of the New Digital Disorder.* New York: Henry Holt and Company, LLC.

Weinberger, David. (2002). *Small Pieces Loosely Joined: A Unified Theory of the Web.* New York: Perseus Books.

Wheatley, Margaret. (1998). *A Simpler Way.* San Francisco, CA: Berrett-Koehler Publishers, Inc.

Wheatley, Margaret. (2007). *Finding Our Way: Leadership for an Uncertain Time.* San Francisco, CA: Berrett-Koehler Publishers, Inc.

Wheatley, Margaret. (2006). *Leadership and the New Science: Discovering Order in a Chaotic World.* San Francisco, CA: Berrett-Koehler Publishers, Inc.

Wheatley, Margaret. (2010). *Perseverance.* San Francisco, CA: Berrett-Koehler Publishers, Inc.

Wheatley, Margaret. (2009). *Turning to One Another: Simple Questions to Restore Hope to the Future.* San Francisco, CA: Berrett-Koehler Publishers, Inc.

Wheatley, Margaret, and Deborah Frieze. (2011). *Walk Out Walk On: A Learning Journey Into Communities Daring to Live the Future Now.* San Francisco, CA: Berrett-Koehler Publishers, Inc.

Zinger, David. (2010). *Zengage: How to Get More Into Your Work to Get More Out of Your Work.* Self-published book.

Zinger, David. (2011). *Assorted Zingers: Poems and Cartoons to Take a Bite Out of Work.* Self-published book.

Twitter

Wally Bock: @wallybock

Jodee Bock: @jodeebock

Randy Boek: @randyboek

Alfredo Castro: @alfredomot

Thomas Chermack: @tjcher

Kevin Eikenberry: @kevineikenberry

Steve Farber and Steve Dealph: @stevefarber
Tom Foster: @fosterlearning
Lisa Gansky: @instigating, @sharethemesh
Chris Grams: @cdgrams
CV Harquail: @cvharquail
Sally Hogshead: @HowToFascinate, @SallyHogshead
Karen Hough: @karenhough
Michael Kroth, PhD: @michaelkroth
Sharlyn Lauby: @sharlyn_lauby, @hrnartender, @itmgroup
The LPK Design Team: @lpkdesign
Eric Mosley and Derek Irvine: @Globoforce @DerekIrvine
Mark Murphy: @leadershipiq
Craig and Patricia Neal: @artofconvening
Jeffrey Pfeffer: @jeffreypfeffer
Steve Roesler: @steveroesler
Todd Sattersten: @toddsattersten
Tony Schwartz: @tonyschwartz @energy_project
Rajesh Setty: @rajsetty
Bret Simmons, PhD: @drbret
Terry "Starbucker" St. Marie: @starbucker
Michael Lee Stallard: @michaelstallard
Wayne Turmel: @greatwebmeeting
Tanmay Vora: @tnvora
Ellen Weber, PhD: @ellenfweber
David Weinberger, PhD: @dweinberger
David Zinger: @davidzinger

Websites

Wendy Axelrod and Jeannie Coyle: http://talentsavvymanager.com
Vikram Bector: http://live.nelsoncohen.com/2009/12/19/weather-the-storm-prepare-for
the-next/
www.thehindubusinessline.in/2010/06/11/stories/2010061151741900.htm
www.thehindubusinessline.com/industry-and-economy/economy/
article2023701.ece
http://indiatoday.intoday.in/story/Art+of+living+for+stressed+
Satyam+sta
ff/1/27575.html
Wally Bock: http://blog.threestarleadership.com
Jodee Bock: http://www.bocksoffice.com

Randy Boek: http://www.route2results.com

Alfredo Castro: www.motvirtual.com.br

Thomas Chermack: www.thomaschermack.com
www.scenarioplanning.colostate.edu

Kevin Eikenberry: www.kevineikenberry.com

Steve Farber and Steve Dealph: www.stevefarber.com

Tom Foster: http://managementblog.org

Lisa Gansky: www.meshing.it

Chris Grams: www.newkind.com

CV Harquail: http://authenticorganizations.com

Sally Hogshead: www.HowToFascinate.com
www.SallyHogshead.com

Karen Hough: http://www.improvedge.com/

Michael Kroth, PhD: www.michaelkroth.com

Sharlyn Lauby: http://www.itmgroupinc.com

The LPK Design Team: www.lpk.com

Eric Mosley and Derek Irvine: www.recognizethisblog.com

Mark Murphy: www.leadershipiq.com

Craig and Patricia Neal: www.heartlandcircle.com

Jeffrey Pfeffer: www.jeffreypfeffer.com

Steve Roesler: www.steveroesler.com

Todd Sattersten: www.toddsattersten.com

Tony Schwartz: www.theenergyproject.com
www.tonyschwartz.com

Rajesh Setty: www.rajeshsetty.com

Bret Simmons, PhD: http://www.linkedin.com/in/bretsimmons

Terry "Starbucker" St. Marie: www.sobevent.com
www.inside-outthinking.com

Michael Lee Stallard: www.epluribuspartners.com
www.fireduporburnedout.com

Wayne Turmel: www.GreatWebMeetings.com

Tanmay Vora: www.QAspire.com

Ellen Weber, PhD: www.mitaleadership.com

David Weinberger, PhD: www.hyperorg.com/blogger

Margaret Wheatley, EdD: www.margaretwheatley.com

David Zinger: www.davidzinger.com
www.zinghive.com
www.employeeengagement.ning.com

❧ About the Editor

Lisa Haneberg, Vice President of Development, MPI Consulting, is a leadership and management author, speaker, researcher, and consultant. She has more than 25 years of experience providing executive and management development and training and coaching solutions for large and small organizations (including healthcare, manufacturing, services, nonprofits, and government organizations). She has particular expertise in the areas of senior team development, performance management, executive coaching, talent management, succession planning, organizational agility and alignment, and middle management effectiveness.

Lisa has published books about her models, processes, and approaches to coaching, management, and leadership. Her book titles include:

- *Organization Development Basics* (ASTD Press, 2005)
- *Coaching Basics* (ASTD Press, 2006)
- *Focus Like a Laser Beam: 10 Ways to Do What Matters Most* (Jossey-Bass, 2006)
- *Two Weeks to a Breakthrough: How to Zoom Toward Your Goal in 14 Days or Less* (Jossey-Bass, 2007)
- *10 Steps to Be a Successful Manager* (ASTD Press, 2007)
- *Developing Great Managers: 20 Power Hours* (ASTD Press, 2008)
- *Hip and Sage: Staying Smart, Cool and Competitive in the Workplace* (Davies Black, 2009)
- *The High Impact Middle Manager: Powerful Strategies to Thrive in the Middle* (ASTD Press, 2010)
- *High Impact Middle Management: Solutions for Today's Busy Public-Sector Managers* (ASTD Press, 2010)
- *Coaching Up and Down the Generations* (ASTD Press, 2010)
- *Connecting Top Managers* (Financial Times Press, 2011)

In addition, her work has been highlighted in publications such as *Leader to Leader, Washington CEO, Capital,* and *Leadership Excellence*. Lisa is a nationally recognized thought leader in the areas of management and leadership; she is called on to speak at private company events and national and regional professional organization conferences. Prior to joining MPI, Lisa ran a successful consulting practice and held internal leadership positions in several Fortune 500 companies. She has worked with organizations such as MedCentral, Black & Decker, Mead Paper, Intel, Amazon.com, Corbis, Promedica, MTD Products, Perfetti vanMelle, TUI Travel International, Aultman Health Care, Royal Thai Government, the FAA, the EPA, Microsoft, Premera Blue Cross Oregon, and the City of Seattle. She holds a bachelor of science in behavioral sciences from the University of Maryland and a master's degree in fine arts from Goddard College, and will soon receive her PhD in management from Walden University.

To learn more about Lisa's work, visit:
MPI Consulting: www.managementperformance.com
Lisa Haneberg's site: www.lisahaneberg.com
Blog: www.managementcraft.com

✣ **Index**

Note: *f* represents a figure; *t* represents a table